Building Successful Online Communities

Building Successful Online Communities

Evidence-Based Social Design

Robert E. Kraut and Paul Resnick

with Sara Kiesler, Moira Burke, Yan Chen, Niki Kittur, Joseph Konstan, Yuqing Ren, and John Riedl

The MIT Press
Cambridge, Massachusetts
London, England

For information about special quantity discounts, please email special_sales@mitpress.mit.edu

This book was set in Stone Sans and Stone Serif by Toppan Best-set Premedia Limited. Printed and bound in the United States of America.

Library of Congress Cataloging-in-Publication Data

Kraut, Robert E.
Building successful online communities : Evidence-Based Social Design / Robert E. Kraut and Paul Resnick with Sara Kiesler ... [et al.].
    p.   cm.
Includes bibliographical references and index.
ISBN 978-0-262-01657-5 (hardcover : alk. paper)
1. Online social networks—Planning.   2. Computer networks—Social aspects—Planning.
3. Internet—Social aspects.   4. Social psychology.   I. Resnick, Paul.   II. Kiesler, Sara, 1940–
III. Title.

HM742.K73   2012
302.30285—dc22

2011010842

10   9   8   7   6   5   4   3

"There is nothing so practical as a good theory."
"If you want truly to understand something, try to change it."
—Kurt Lewin

Contents

Acknowledgments   ix

1   **Introduction**   1
Paul Resnick and Robert E. Kraut

2   **Encouraging Contribution to Online Communities**   21
Robert E. Kraut and Paul Resnick

3   **Encouraging Commitment in Online Communities**   77
Yuqing Ren, Robert E. Kraut, Sara Kiesler, and Paul Resnick

4   **Regulating Behavior in Online Communities**   125
Sara Kiesler, Robert E. Kraut, Paul Resnick, and Aniket Kittur

5   **The Challenges of Dealing with Newcomers**   179
Robert E. Kraut, Moira Burke, John Riedl, and Paul Resnick

6   **Starting New Online Communities**   231
Paul Resnick, Joseph Konstan, Yan Chen, and Robert E. Kraut

Contributors   281
Index   283

Acknowledgments

This book grew out of the CommunityLab research project, a five-year grant from the National Science Foundation, involving seven professors and myriad graduate students from Carnegie-Mellon University, the University of Michigan, and the University of Minnesota. We conducted experiments testing alternative ways to elicit participation in online communities, and we published those results, replete with careful statistical analyses, in journals and conference proceedings. More broadly, we spoke at research-oriented venues, arguing that insights from social science theories could directly inform online community design and management, if only we took seriously the task of mining that theory.

By 2006, we thought that message should reach a broader audience, including practitioners and students. There was an emerging cadre of practitioners whose primary professional identity was as online community designers and managers. They worked as consultants or ran big online communities like ePinions or the Microsoft Developer Network. In addition, many more people were becoming "accidental community managers," managing the installation of enterprise social-computing platforms within their companies or creating communities of practice curating knowledge on particular topics or launching health-support communities. And professors were starting to teach courses at both undergraduate and graduate levels that devoted all or part of a semester to questions of how best to organize online interactions.

Two consultants, Amy Jo Kim and Derek Powazek, had written excellent books filled with examples and guidelines of what to do and what not to do. Jenny Preece, one of the pioneers of research on online communities, had written a nice textbook that summarized much of the research relevant to online communities, organized around the themes of usability and sociability. However, these texts were showing their age in a fast-moving field (they were all written well before the rise of Wikipedia or Facebook), and none of the existing books articulated our vision of generating specific design guidance from fundamental theories in the social sciences about individual and collective behavior.

Thus, the idea for this book was born. Everyone in the CommunityLab project thought it was a good idea, but no one wanted to take it on as sole author. So we parceled out the task of writing to subgroups. Eventually, two of us stepped forward to rewrite all the chapters, to give the book a consistent voice and structure.

This book would not have been possible without our collaborators Moira Burke, Yan Chen, Sara Kiesler, Aniket Kittur, Joseph Konstan, Yuqing Ren, and John Riedl. Not only are they coauthors on many of the book's chapters, but discussion with them as we planned individual research projects and the book itself improved our thinking and shaped every facet of the book. Loren Terveen was also an important contributor to the CommunityLab project and to the conceptualization of this book. The advisory board for the project, including Lee Sproull, Jenny Preece, and Jack Carroll also provided valuable input during that phase. In addition, we have been blessed with a wonderful group of doctoral and master's degree students. Working with them has been both intellectually exciting and fun. We acknowledge especially the contributions of Turadg Aleahmad, Kira Alexander, Gerard Beenen, Bo Reum Choi, Dan Cosley, Sara Drenner, Dan Frankowski, Derek Hansen, Franklin M. Harper, Youn-ah Kang, Shyong K. "Tony" Lam, Cliff Lampe, Sherry Li, John Lin, Kim Ling, Pam Ludford, Kathryn McCurdy, Sean Munson, Nathan Oostendorp, Bryan Pendleton, Al Mamunur Rashid, Shilad Sen, Xiaoqing Wang, and Haiyi Zhu. David Sánchez Bote from Mondragon University kept the flame alive and gathered many examples of reward mechanisms in use in online communities during his sabbatical stay at the University of Michigan.

We thank Mark Ackerman, Brian Butler, Jim Cashel, Joe Cothrel, Judith Donath, Randy Farmer, Lisa Joyce, Karrie Karahalios, John Levine, Andrew Monk, and Sean O'Driscoll for useful comments and suggestions at various stages. The book also benefits from feedback we received from students in our courses and participants in the presentations we have offered at Northwestern University, Cornell University, Microsoft, University of Canterbury, the Communities and Technologies conference, the Academy of Management conference, ForumOne's Online Communities Summit, and the International Conference on Weblogs and Social Media, and from feedback we have received, via their instructors, from students in courses at the University of Maryland and the University of Illinois.

Our work has been supported by several grants from the National Science Foundation, including IIS-0325049/Designing On-Line Communities to Enhance Participation, IIS-0729286/Solving Critical Problems in Online Groups, and

IIS-0808711/Designing Online Volunteer Communities. One goal of this book is to repay this research largess by making what we have learned available to a wider audience.

We also thank Douglas Sery and Mel Goldsipe at the MIT Press for editing and shepherding this book through the publication process.

We especially thank Brandy Renduels for her help in copyediting the manuscript draft and general wrangling.

Robert E. Kraut, Pittsbugh, PA
Paul Resnick, Ann Arbor, MI
March 2011

1 Introduction

Paul Resnick and Robert E. Kraut

What does social science tell us about how to make thriving online communities? Quite a lot, it turns out—but only if we listen very closely and, at times, employ a translator. Economics and various branches of psychology offer theories of individual motivation and of human behavior in social situations. The theories generalize from observations of naturally occurring behavior, from controlled experiments, and from abstract mathematical models. Properly interpreted, they can inform choices about how to get a community started, integrate newcomers, encourage commitment, regulate behavior when there are conflicts, motivate contributions, and coordinate those contributions to maximize benefits for the community. This book makes it easier for us to hear what social science has to tell us. It amplifies relevant theories and experimental evidence and then translates them into specific claims about the likely impact of particular design choices for online communities.

1 The Promise of Online Communities

By "online communities" we mean any virtual space where people come together with others to converse, exchange information or other resources, learn, play, or just be with each other. The term applies to many social configurations, from small close-knit groups to sites with millions of participants. Online communities may be supported by a wide variety of technology platforms, from email lists to forums, blogs, wikis, and networking sites. The common feature is ongoing interactions among people over time, with some of the interactions being technology mediated.

Online communities are among the most popular destinations on the Internet. The venerable Usenet had more than 160,000 active newsgroups in 2006 and Yahoo! (http://www.yahoo.com) alone claims to host more than a million online groups. Ravelry (http://www.ravelry.com), a hobby community for people who knit and crochet, claimed more than 1.2 million members as of March 2011. The product support community for Linksys, a division of Cisco that provides consumer and small-office networking technologies, handles more than 100,000 user sessions per day (Lithium Technologies 2009). More than 35,000 people made five or more edits on Wikipedia (http://en.wikipedia.org), an open source encyclopedia, during the month of February 2011 (Wikimedia 2011b). Facebook (http://www.facebook.com), an online social networking site, celebrated 500 million members in July 2010 (Zuckerberg 2010).

Online communities serve the same range of purposes that offline groups, networks, and communities serve. They provide their members with opportunities for information sharing and learning, for companionship and social support, and for entertainment. Online communities can also produce benefits for nonmembers—either public goods that benefit society as a whole, such as open source software, product reviews, and encyclopedia pages; or private goods, such as suggestions for product improvements or new product designs that benefit the organization that convened the community.

The promise of online communities is that they break the barriers of time, space, and scale that limit offline interactions. People with unusual medical conditions can get social support from others who share their condition but live far away, and they can do so whenever they need it rather than only at a weekly or monthly scheduled meeting. On Ravelry, knitters can share patterns with thousands more people than they could stitch with in person.

2 Critical Design Challenges

Although as a class these online communities are very successful, the success of particular communities varies widely. Some communities struggle to become successful, and others fail. For every Facebook, with its millions of current users, there is a Friendster (http://www.friendster.com) that was once successful but can no longer compete and scores of smaller social networking sites that never got enough members to be viable. Of 2,872 Usenet groups with "support" in their name, some—like alt.support.diet.low-carb, alt.support.depression, and alt.support.diabetes—are successful, with more than 5,000 people posting per year, but half had fewer than thirty posters during 2004 and a quarter had fewer than six (Kraut, 2011a). Smokefree.gov (http://www.smokefree.gov), an online tobacco-cessation program, attempted to add an online community for some of its users but was unable to garner enough activity in the community during the trial period to assess whether such a community, if it were active, would help members to quit smoking (Stoddard, Augustson, and Moser 2008). Although the English-language version of Wikipedia had more than 3.6 million articles in February 2011, the Korean version had fewer than 160,000 articles (Wikimedia 2011a). Across the more than 9,000 public information-sharing wikis, using the same Mediawiki software that Wikipedia uses, the median number of editors who have ever contributed is only seven (Kittur and Kraut 2011).

To become and remain successful, online communities must meet a number of challenges that are common to many groups and organizations, offline as well as online. The book is organized around these challenges, as described in the rest of this introduction.

Starting a New Community

Many online communities are successful because they have a rich inventory of content that attracts new members. In a conversational community, hosted at a cancer support group, the content might be the messages exchanged by cancer survivors and their caregivers. In an open source software (OSS) development community hosted at SourceForge (http://sourceforge.net), it might be a working base of computer code that provides raw material for developers to improve. On the popular entertainment site YouTube (http://youtube.com), the content consists of video clips that participants post. When creating an online community from scratch, designers and managers are faced with a critical mass problem: the fledgling site doesn't yet have enough content to attract users and there are thus too few users to create the content that might attract others.

Attracting and Socializing New Members

Even established online communities must attract a stream of new members to replace others who leave. For some online communities, a major component of this challenge is to identify and encourage potential members who have the characteristics, skills, and motivation to contribute. Thus, open-source development projects are looking for potential members who can build software. In contrast, many Facebook groups or email-based groups hosted by Yahoo! and Google (http://www.google.com) are more open and willing to accept almost anyone. Even while seeking and welcoming members, many communities also try to screen out inappropriate members. Thus, for example, health-support groups often restrict membership to people who have a particular illness or care for someone who does. Regardless of their selectivity, online groups have special problems because newcomers, who are potentially choosing from among other similar communities to join, frequently have insufficient information to make their choices and almost always have less commitment to a community than more established members have. These factors mean that their initial observations and interactions are likely to strongly influence whether they stick around long enough to learn whether the site provides a good match to their needs. In addition, because they have not yet learned the appropriate ways to behave in the community, their actions may disrupt the activity of existing members.

Encouraging Commitment

Commitment represents members' feelings of attachment or connection to the group, organization, or community. Commitment underlies members' willingness to stay in the community and contribute to it. Both offline and online, people who are more committed to an organization tend to be more satisfied, are less likely to look for alternatives, are less likely to leave, and tend to perform better and contribute more (Mathieu and Zajac 1990). All organizations must manage the challenge of creating commitment, but because the forces keeping someone in an online group are weaker than those operating in a conventional organization, challenges of commitment are more difficult. For example, in most conventional software companies, employees have an employment contract. If they decide to leave, they lose salary, seniority, and job status. In contrast, most developers in open-source software projects participate voluntarily, with no employment contract encouraging them to stay and contribute. The physical location of a conventional organization also places constraints on members' willingness to go elsewhere. If someone wants to leave a job, church, or club, for example, only a relatively small number of alternatives are nearby and convenient to join. In contrast, if someone wants to leave a particular online community, he or she could join any other comparable community online with no constraints imposed by geographic proximity.

Encouraging Contribution

To be successful, online communities need the people who participate in them to contribute the resources on which the group's existence is built. The types of resource contributions needed differ widely across different types of groups, from the conversations in many online health- and technical-support groups to the code in open-source development projects and the music and video in media-sharing sites. Typically, online communities exhibit a power-law distribution of contribution, with a small minority contributing most of the content. For example, in the Freenet development project, only 30 people of the 369 who participated in the discussion lists ever wrote any code. Although inequality of contribution is not necessarily a problem, undercontribution is. For example, most Usenet support groups, as mentioned earlier, were relatively inactive. Even apparently highly successful online communities suffer from problems of undercontribution. Roughly two-thirds of the articles in the English version of Wikipedia have been classified during quality-assessment drives as "stubs," articles with only a few sentences of content that are too short to provide encyclopedic coverage of a topic (Wikipedia 2010).

Regulating Behavior

The people who participate in online groups often have different and sometimes competing interests. Most large online discussion groups—especially those that deal with controversial topics—attract trolls, people who post controversial, inflammatory, irrelevant, or off-topic messages to provoke other users into an emotional response (Schwartz 2008). Commercial spammers would like to drive traffic to their external websites. In more mundane conflicts of interest, some participants in a hobby site may prefer that the discussion stay focused on the hobby, but others may want to engage in more personal conversation with other members they have become friends with. When there are conflicting interests in a group, there must be mechanisms to help participants regulate behavior. The challenges here are to deter inappropriate behavior by group members, prevent trolls and other outside attackers, and limit the damage that is caused when inappropriate behavior occurs.

   Although these challenges confront almost all groups and organizations, online communities may have more difficulty overcoming them than conventional groups and organizations because of three characteristics that are typical of online communities but unusual in conventional groups and organizations. The first is anonymity. Old-timers may be less able to vet anonymous newcomers, and newcomers may feel less inhibited by social accountability. The second is ease of entry and exit, which can lead to high turnover and thus inhibit interpersonal ties or commitment to the group and affect how sanctions and other deterrence strategies work in regulating behavior. The third is textual communication, which may be prone to misinterpretation because it lacks some of the fluidity and nonverbal cues of face-to-face interaction.

   On the other hand, online communities have resources for meeting these challenges that are not available to offline groups. First, the communications—and indeed almost all of the behavior exhibited by participants in an online community—are in digital form and can be archived. Second, online communities can benefit from computation. For example, computers can summarize traces of past behavior as quantifiable and viewable reputations, as eBay (http://www.ebay.com) does with its feedback profiles. Computers can execute search and matching algorithms to introduce people and content to each other and can notify people when events of interest occur. And computers can enforce access controls so that different people are permitted to see or do different things.

3 Levers of Change: Sociotechnical Systems Design

Students in our classes sometimes challenge the notion that online communities can be designed. A product designer can specify functional and aesthetic features in order to create a desired user experience, but an online community is not so easily controlled. Even if a designer wants an online community to be larger, or more active, or more friendly in tone, he or she may not be able to make that happen. People are the key actors in online communities, and they cannot be shaped or programmed in the way physical materials or software can.

The first central argument of this book is that despite the limited direct control of individual people's actions, online communities can be designed and managed to achieve the goals that their owners, managers, or members desire. Designers are far from powerless. Throughout this book, we identify a wide variety of levers of change, features of online communities that can be deliberately and strategically chosen. Some of these levers involve technical configuration, such as whether a chat feature is enabled or whether special privileges are required to start new conversation threads. Other levers involve social configurations, such as how much externally provided content to include and whether leaders and administrators ignore, cajole, or ban people who disrupt the community.

We classify the levers of change into eight broad categories, described as follows. We will often call these levers of change "design alternatives" or "design options" to highlight the idea that their configurations can result from deliberate choices that managers, designers, or members make.

The first category of design alternatives involves the community structure. The size of the community can make a difference, as can the degree of homogeneity of member interests, whether there is a subgroup structure, and whether membership is recruited through existing social ties.

The second category of design alternatives involves the content, tasks, and activities in the community. There can be opportunities for self-disclosure (e.g., in user profiles). Content can be imported from outside or professionally generated, in addition to that which is generated by members. Welcoming activities and safe spaces for exploration can be offered to newcomers. Tasks can be independent or interdependent and can be embedded in immersive or social experiences.

Table 1.1
Types of design alternatives and the chapters in which their implications are analyzed

Type	Chapter 2: Contribution	Chapter 3: Commitment	Chapter 4: Regulation	Chapter 5: Newcomers	Chapter 6: Startup
Community structure	x	x	x		x
Content, tasks, and activities	x	x		x	x
Selection, sorting, highlighting	x	x	x		x
External communication				x	x
Feedback and rewards	x		x		x
Roles, rules, policies, and procedures			x	x	
Access controls		x	x	x	
Presentation and framing	x	x	x	x	x

Communities often have more content and opportunities than any one person will want to take advantage of. The third category of design alternatives deals with ways to select, sort, and highlight things so that people can find the ones that are best for them. These alternatives include dividing the community into separate spaces, highlighting good content, removing inappropriate content, and friend feeds or even full-blown recommendation systems that show different slices of the content to different people.

The fourth category of design levers involves external communication. Content can be imported from or exported to other communities. Identities and profiles can be shared or hidden. Facilities can be provided to allow people to invite friends or forward content to them.

The fifth category involves feedback, rewards, and sanctions. Feedback tells people how others have reacted to their participation in the community. Such feedback can be informal or structured in the form of ratings or a button to click to indicate the liking of something. Rewards and sanctions give or remove something that people value in response to the actions they take. They can be intangible, in the form of approval or disapproval or status in the community. But they can also take the more tangible form of additional privileges in the community or even money or prizes.

Sixth, communities can articulate different roles, such as welcomers for newcomers or dispute handlers. They can also have rules and guidelines about how people should behave, which can have a big impact on the nature of interactions in the community. Finally, they can establish procedures for decision making and conflict resolution.

Seventh, there are access controls, which place limits on who can join the community and what actions they can take. For example, credentials may be checked to allow only qualified people to join, or completion of a CAPTCHA (Completely Automated Public Turing test to tell Computers and Humans Apart) such as transcribing distorted text may be required to prevent computer programs from creating accounts. Moderation privileges may be extended only to members in designated roles. Alternatively, people may need to pay, using some internal currency, to perform certain actions.

Finally, in every chapter, we find that simple communication choices—ways of framing what the community is and what happens there[1]—can have a big impact on how the community functions. For example, a community can highlight bad behavior and how it is punished or can try to hide that it ever happens. A community can present itself as similar to others or highlight characteristics that distinguish it from others. It can prime norms of reciprocity. It can choose a tagline that emphasizes different aspects of the community. These and many other communication and framing choices can affect all five of the challenges, from getting a new community started through regulating behavior in an established community.

Note that with a few exceptions, we consider only design alternatives that vary how people perceive a community and what they give to or get from it. There are a variety of other alternatives in the realm of interaction design that are beyond the scope of this book. For example, though we discuss the impact of including photos of people and associating the photos with the content they contribute, this book is silent about the size, placement, or other aesthetics of the photos. And though we discuss the time cost for people of browsing through a collection of mostly irrelevant items, we do not analyze the various techniques that could be used to reduce those browsing costs, such as showing collapsed summaries with the full contents prefetched so that they can be displayed without delay if a user hovers or clicks on an item summary. Interaction design choices can have a profound effect on the user experience of an online community and can nudge people toward certain behaviors just as well as the design levers we focus on. The subtleties of interaction design, however, are beyond the scope of our expertise and beyond the scope of this book.

4   The Morality of Design

Even if convinced of the feasibility of designing online communities, some of our students question its morality. The terms "social engineering" and "paternalism" have acquired negative connotations in American political discourse. Generally, people dislike the idea of being manipulated, even if it's for their own good. Viewed in that light, designing the interaction environment of an online community in order to elicit individual behavior that benefits the community as a whole seems morally repugnant.

Weighed against this value of freedom from manipulation, however, there is also a moral imperative to create online communities that work well. People gain immense value from the education, social support, and entertainment that online communities provide to their members and from the information products that they produce for society. If different design alternatives can make the communities more attractive for their members or more productive, then forgoing those benefits may be a significant cost.

Moreover, decisions will be made anyway—through inaction if not through action—about all the design alternatives considered in this book. Any such choices, no matter how they are made, will inevitably influence members and prospective members to behave in certain ways. There is no default, morally neutral online-community design that has no manipulative effect on members.[2]

We argue that the primary moral arguments are thus not about whether to make explicit design choices in order to achieve community goals but about which community goals are the right ones. Making an online community function better may not always be a worthy goal. In some cases, an online community that functions well may produce negative effects for its members (for example, a community that encourages and supports its members to continue their bulimia) or for society as a whole (for example, a terrorist cell). In other cases, it is not so clear what it means for an online community to function better. Most goals, if achieved, involve improving the community in the eyes of some people and making it worse in the eyes of some others. For example, trolls gain enjoyment from disrupting some communities. A design that effectively deters trolling benefits most of the community members but makes things worse for the trolls.

In the remainder of this book, we leave moral judgments—about which goals are worth designing for—to our readers. Our focus is on identifying the likely effects of particular design alternatives in meeting the fundamental design challenges of online communities. We sometimes adopt shorthand like "good behavior" and "bad behavior," but these should be taken as good or bad relative to the goals of the designer, whomever that may be.

5 The Promise of Mining Social Science

How can an online-community designer build up intuitions about the likely impacts of alternative design choices? Previous practitioner-authors have offered many helpful insights based on design decisions that were made when building online communities that they advised or observed (e.g., Kim 2000; Powazek 2002; O'Keefe 2008). Wenger, White, and Smith (2009) provide several useful frameworks for thinking about online-community design decisions, based on conceptualizing them as communities of practice. Preece (2000) summarized terminology and findings of research related to interpersonal communication and networks and groups that may provide useful background knowledge for a designer.

The second central argument of this book is that social science findings can and should inform more directly the choices that online community designers make. There is a rich research literature in psychology, economics, and the other social sciences about the individual motivations and conditions under which individuals, groups, and organizations are successful. Although most of this research has developed in the context of offline interactions, some has now been replicated in online social settings.

Social science research can inform design in several interrelated ways. First, it can be used to identify problems or challenges that will be faced by most online communities. For example, the theory of network externalities in economics, which we discuss in chapter 6, and the empirical research from which it grew, explore the impact of how the attraction of many groups for potential members grows with the number of people who already participate. This relationship between the attractiveness of a community and its size raises problems for new communities because during their start-up phases, they do not have enough members to provide the resources that will attract other members and allow growth. As another example, the theories of public goods from economics and of social loafing from psychology predict that when individual contributions are needed to produce outcomes that benefit everyone equally, voluntary contributions will be at suboptimal levels. The information contributions that people make to online communities often have this public goods character, and encouraging contributions is thus an important challenge for many online communities.

Second, social science theories provide ideas for solutions to the problems. Thus, if, as theories of network externalities predict, new online communities struggle because they initially have too few members and too little content to attract and retain members, creating compatibility between communities can overcome this problem (Shapiro and Varian 1999). This is the solution adopted by the makers of Scrabulous, who introduced their game in Facebook, which already had a large number of members available as potential players. As another example, theories of collective effort identify several potential solutions to communities facing problems of undercontribution. Because feeling that one's contribution will be redundant is one reason that people undercontribute, a solution is to make potential contributors believe that their contributions are important. Designers have a number of ways to make potential contributors feel that a contribution will matter, such as partitioning the group so that each contributor is a member of a smaller subgroup or reminding potential contributors about the uniqueness of their contributions.

Finally, and perhaps most important, the social science research base provides predictions about likely consequences of various design decisions. For example, theories about interpersonal bond formation yield a prediction that target members will become more committed to a community to the extent that they have repeated interactions with other members and to the extent that those other members are similar to them. As another example, theories about goal setting and monitoring yield a prediction that contribution goals will be more effective at eliciting member contributions the more challenging they are. We refer to predictions of this sort as "design claims" and describe the structure and limits of such claims in more detail in the next section.

One strand of theory we draw on starts from a premise of individuals making choices that increase their own utility, that is, the difference between their benefits and costs. Thus, many design choices are geared to reducing costs, increasing benefits, or changing individuals' ability to assess the costs and benefits. Game theoretic models enable analysis of interdependent choices and predictions about equilibrium outcomes. For example, in a situation in which many people would want to join an online community only if others also joined, there are two equilibrium outcomes: one in which everyone joins and one in which none do. In such situations, one task of the designer is to shape people's expectations about what others are likely to do. Models of incomplete information permit reasoning about situations in which there is uncertainty. For example, such models can help to understand whether a seller's previous feedback on eBay can be expected to serve as a reliable signal about his or her trustworthiness.

We also draw on a variety of other theories from the fields of social psychology and organizational behavior that predict individual behavior in group and organizational settings. We use the plural "theories" advisedly: there is no unified theory in modern social psychology with pretensions of explaining all of social behavior. Rather, the intellectual style has been to build and test a large number of midlevel theories, each attempting to account for an interesting social phenomenon in a limited domain. For example, we draw on theories of goal setting, social comparison, persuasion, conformity, and interpersonal bond and group identity formation. Despite the lack of a single overarching theoretical framework analogous to that of evolution in biology or utility maximization in microeconomics, these midlevel theories provide a rich and empirically verified understanding of some of the central phenomena of behavior in social settings.

Although social science theory is helpful in identifying problems that online communities face, suggesting potential solutions to them, and articulating claims about the likely impacts of design choices, it has its limits. First, the theories are incomplete; they offer no guidance on some important design choices. Second, they may be incorrect; like all scientific theories, they are subject to revision based on new data from new experiments. Third, creativity and care are required to map general theories to the particular context of online communities; here, we hope that this book makes a contribution by translating social science findings into useful design claims.

6   Design Claims

We use the device of design claims to translate theory to design alternatives that achieve community goals. Design claims follow a positivist scientific paradigm, seeking to state general claims—that under certain observable conditions certain outcomes can be expected. In our case, the conditions that are of particular interest are design alternatives and the outcomes are desirable features of an online community, which we refer to as "design goals." For example, we state the following design claim in the chapter on motivating contributions: *Small tangible rewards are likely to reduce contributions for intrinsically interesting tasks.* Here, the design alternative is promising small tangible rewards and the design goal is maximizing the efforts that members contribute to tasks that benefit the community. We restrict the scope of applicability of design claims by specifying a restricted set of context conditions for their applicability. Thus, the claim applies only to intrinsically interesting tasks, not to boring tasks. The context conditions will specify properties of the community (e.g., size, purpose), properties of members (e.g., newcomer or long-time member, gender or other demographic characteristics), or properties of tasks (e.g., challenging, interesting).

Table 1.2
The logical structure of design claims

Type	Logical structure
Noncomparative	Alternative X helps/hinders achievement of goal Y under conditions Z
Comparative	Alternative X1 is more effective than X2 at achieving goal Y under conditions Z

Many of our design claims are comparative. For example, the chapter on contributions also includes this design claim: *Nontransparent eligibility criteria and unpredictable schedules lead to less "gaming of the system" than do predictable rewards.* Here there are two design alternatives: predictable rewards versus rewards with nontransparent eligibility criteria and unpredictable schedules. The claim is that one is better than the other at achieving the goal of people not doing useless or destructive actions just to get the rewards (gaming the system).

Thus, we have two logical structures for design claims (see table 1.2).

Whenever we state design claims, we offer evidence in support of them. In some cases, the evidence comes from social science theories or findings that have been articulated for more general settings beyond online communities. Usually, these theories have been tested abstractly in laboratory settings. In other cases, the evidence comes from experiments specific to the online community setting. Evidence may also come from observational studies of particular online communities. Observational data may be quantitative (e.g., counts of how many posts were made) or qualitative (e.g., analysis of their content, or subjective reports from interviewing participants). In some cases, observational studies will be used merely to offer an example consistent with the design claim (i.e., here is a site that used alternative X and it achieved goal Y). This, of course, is relatively weak evidence, as the only information it provides about whether X had anything to do with the achievement of Y comes from the subjective reports of the designers or participants.

Our project of collecting and organizing design claims is akin to efforts to codify what are called "pattern languages" (Alexander, Ishikawa, and Silverstein 1977; Rising 2001). Crumlish and Malone (2009) nicely present a collection of useful design patterns that have been used in online communities. There are a couple of differences in our approach, however, from most work on design patterns. First, although we are sometimes inspired by a bottom-up approach of noticing commonly occurring features of online communities, more often we start from a design goal and some relevant theories and try to systematically explore the space of possible design choices that could help achieve the goal. In some cases, we identify choices that *should* help achieve the goal, but have not yet, to our knowledge, been tried in existing communities. Second, although approaches to pattern languages vary, usually the design alternative itself is the central element, presented with ancillary information about when it might be best to use it, what it can be expected to accomplish, and hints and cautions about implementing it. By contrast, as we discuss shortly, we have organized our exposition around goals and challenges, presenting together all the design alternatives that have an impact on that goal. Third, we have chosen the term "claim" rather than "pattern" to emphasize that we are laying out causal claims in which design X leads to outcome Y rather than merely observing that X occurs frequently in practice. The preface to *A Pattern Language: Towns, Buildings, and Construction* indicates that Alexander (1977) intended patterns to convey causal claims—indeed, that they should convey necessary as well as sufficient conditions (if you want to achieve an outcome Y, then X is necessary). Not all of the actual design patterns, however, in Alexander's work or among others adopting the pattern language approach, seem to make such causal claims.

It is worth noting that both design alternatives and design goals can be expressed at varying levels of abstraction. For example, a design alternative at a high level of abstraction might be to provide tangible rewards for activity. At a much more specific level of abstraction, two design alternatives might be to provide a user with a $5 gift certificate or to make a $5 donation to a charity that the user chooses. Throughout the book, our design claims are made at whatever level of abstraction is most appropriate. It is also worth noting that what is expressed as a design alternative at a high level of abstraction may be expressed as a goal at a more specific layer of abstraction. For example, at a high level, we might say that the design alternative of making people feel unique helps achieve the goal of motivating effort. A more specific design claim might state that reminding people of unusual actions they have taken helps achieve the goal of making people feel unique.

It is also worth noting that a design alternative X may be compound, combining simpler alternatives. For example, a design claim might state that having a forum and a separate email list will make it harder for either of them to get to a critical mass of usage. Or a design claim might state that for technical support communities, an email list and wiki used together are more effective than either one on its own (Hansen 2007).

The design claims are not prescriptive rules that a designer can or should follow blindly, for two reasons. First, the predictive claims state only that a design alternative X helps or hinders achievement of a goal Y, not that it will always achieve or prevent the achievement of the goal. A claim that *small tangible rewards are likely to reduce contributions for intrinsically interesting tasks* is a claim about the effect on average. In a particular situation, a designer will need to judge how intrinsically interesting a task is, whether a reward is likely to be perceived as small or large, and whether there are any extenuating circumstances.

Second, multiple design claims may suggest implications of a single design choice for more than one design goal, and the designer may have to trade off achieving one goal against interfering with another. For example, in an open source project, the design alternative of giving lots of people commit privileges (so they can easily add their contributions to the group's code base) would be likely to increase the number of contributors but decrease the amount of effort by each person and may also increase the number of bugs in the code. A designer will need to judge whether that trade-off is worthwhile in the particular situation.

Third, the theories from which our design claims derive, and thus our design claims as well, usually state the effects of manipulations holding everything else constant. On the other hand, whether designing from scratch or changing an existing system, designers typically make a number of choices at the same time. For example, at the same time that a community introduces a point system to track and acknowledge member contributions, it may also change its tagline and frequently asked questions (FAQ) section to suggest a more collaborative, less competitive atmosphere. Design claims offer guidance on the likely impact of either of these changes separately, not their joint impact. A designer will need to rely on intuition to judge whether a set of design choices are complementary or whether they interfere with each other.

7 Organization of the Book

We have organized the book around the high-level design challenges described in section 3. Thus, design claims related to a particular goal are presented together, even though they may involve quite different design elements. This organizational scheme serves several purposes. First, for a student or practitioner new to online community design, it highlights the challenges that typically arise in online communities so that some thought can be given to them before they arise. Second, it offers a systematic way to consider and compare alternative approaches to handling those challenges. For example, a designer who begins with a particular design element—perhaps because a boss has encountered the feature in another community and asks him or her to investigate its use—will naturally be led also to consider alternative ways to achieve the goals that design element normally promotes because they are presented near each other in the book.

We try to salvage some of the benefits that could be gained from alternative organizational schemes through cross-indexing. Design claims related to achieving the same design goal appear linearly near each other in the same chapter. When a particular design element or theory used in one design claim also appears in other sections or other chapters, we indicate that. Each chapter concludes with a summary of all the design levers considered in the chapter, grouped by the eight categories, to provide an alternative index into the contents of the chapter.

Chapters 2 through 6 discuss the high-level design challenges:

- Chapter 2: Encouraging contributions to online communities
- Chapter 3: Encouraging commitment to online communities
- Chapter 4: Regulating behavior in online communities
- Chapter 5: Dealing with newcomers
- Chapter 6: Starting a community

The chapter ordering reflects our pedagogical experience of presenting this material in workshops and courses. While community startup clearly precedes the other issues chronologically for any community, the material in that chapter focuses on the special problems of the startup phase, beyond those that face communities on an ongoing basis. It is hard to separate out and focus on those special problems before developing a clear idea about how the community might operate on a steady-state basis. Similarly, while people must first be newcomers before they can be long-time members of a community, we have found that it is easier for audiences to set aside the challenges of how new people will be recruited and initiated until after thinking through how veterans will interact. Readers are, of course, free to sample the chapters in any order. Although there are many cross-references, the chapter can be read independently, in any order.

No book is ever complete. There are always more topics at the periphery that could be included. Our book says much about beginnings—new communities and the entry of new members to existing communities. By contrast, it says little about endings. A future book could usefully examine when and how to gracefully handle individual departures and how to gracefully close a community that no longer serves a clear purpose. The book also says little about the challenge of keeping an online community fresh over time. As with other organizational forms, if they last a long time, there is a danger that the world will pass them by. Designers and managers can make choices that enhance a community's ability to monitor changes in the larger environment and to innovate in its practices in response to those changes. A future edition of this book could usefully include a chapter on organizing online communities in a way that encourages innovation. Finally, while this book discusses how to motivate effort-ful contributions, it says little about how to coordinate those efforts, a topic that is beginning to get a lot of research attention, including by some of the coauthors of chapters in this book. A future edition could include a chapter on coordinating effort.

Despite these limitations, we think that this book will provide useful guidance to practitioners as well as an introduction to online communities suitable for advanced undergraduates and professional master's degree students. Through specific design claims, backed up with supporting examples, the book provides a wealth of design guidance. By organizing the exposition around fundamental design challenges, however, we encourage practitioners to consider alternative solutions to challenges they face, rather than simply adopting a feature that they have seen in other sites. Moreover, by grounding the design claims in theory as well as empirical examples, readers will be better able to reason about whether a particular technique is likely to work in particular online communities.

We hope to evolve the set of design claims and their justifications over time. Please send us your examples, both those that support our design claims and those that do not. Or post a public comment on our website, SuccessfulOnlineCommunities.com: join the online community of online community students, practitioners, and researchers!

Notes

1. In the field of behavioral economics, "decision frame" refers to the decision maker's concep-tion of the acts, outcomes, and contingencies associated with a particular choice. Tversky and Kahneman (1981) use the term more broadly, beyond the context of specific choices or decisions.

2. We are indebted to Thaler and Sunstein (2008), who nicely articulated a similar argument in the context of choice environments, such as the selection of healthy or unhealthy foods from a cafeteria or whether to set aside money from each paycheck to invest for retirement. They argued that any choice environment will predictably nudge people toward making one choice or another and that there is no way to pick a default, morally neutral choice environment. Either the apples or the chocolate bars can be at eye level in the cafeteria checkout line, and whichever one is there will be consumed more often than it otherwise would.

References

Alexander, C., S. Ishikawa, and M. Silverstein. 1977. *A Pattern Language: Towns, Buildings, Construc-tion.* New York: Oxford University Press.

Crumlish, Christian, and Erin Malone. 2009. *Designing Social Interfaces*. Sebastopol, CA: O'Reilly.

Hansen, Derek L. 2007. *Knowledge Sharing, Maintenance, and Use in Online Support Communities*. PhD diss., University of Michigan.

Kim, Amy Jo. 2000. *Community Building on the Web: Secret Strategies for Successful Online Communities*. Berkeley: Peachpit Press.

Kittur, A., and R. E. Kraut. 2011. Unpublished data.

Kraut, R. E. 2011. Unpublished data.

Lithium Technologies. 2009. The Linksys ROI Story: Support Community Delivers Significant Savings from Call Deflection. http://www.lithium.com/pdfs/casestudies/Linksys-ROI-Case-Study.pdf.

Mathieu, J. E., and D. M. Zajac. 1990. A Review and Meta-Analysis of the Antecedents, Correlates, and Consequences of Organizational Commitment. *Psychological Bulletin* 108 (2): 171–194.

O'Keefe, Patrick. 2008. *Managing Online Forums: Everything You Need to Know to Create and Run Successful Community Discussion Boards*. New York: AMACOM Books.

Powazek, D. M. 2002. *Design for Community: The Art of Connecting Real People in Virtual Places*. Indianapolis: Pearson Technology.

Preece, Jenny. 2000. *Online Communities: Designing Usability and Supporting Sociability*. New York: John Wiley & Sons.

Rising, Linda. 2001. *Design Patterns in Communications Software*. Cambridge: Cambride University Press.

Schwartz, M. 2008. The Trolls among Us. *New York Times*. http://www.nytimes.com/2008/08/03/magazine/03trolls-t.html?_r=2&oref=slo.

Shapiro, Carl, and Hal R. Varian. 1999. *Information Rules: A Strategic Guide to the Network Economy*. Cambridge, MA: Harvard Business School Press.

Stoddard, J. L., E. M. Augustson, and R. P. Moser. 2008. Effect of Adding a Virtual Community (Bulletin Board) to Smokefree.gov: Randomized Controlled Trial. *Journal of Medical Internet Research* 10 (5): e53.

Thaler, Richard H., and Cass R. Sunstein. 2008. *Nudge: Improving Decisions about Health, Wealth, and Happiness*. New Haven, NH: Yale University Press.

Tversky, Amos, and Daniel Kahneman. 1981. The Framing of Decisions and the Psychology of Choice. *Science* 211 (4481):453–458.

Wenger, Etienne, Nancy White, and John D. Smith. 2009. *Digital Habitats: Stewarding Technology for Communities*. Portland, OR: CPSquare.

Wikimedia. 2011a. Wikipedia Statistics: Article Count (Official). http://stats.wikimedia.org/EN/ TablesArticlesTotal.htm.

Wikimedia. 2011b. Wikipedia Statistics: Active Wikipedians. http://stats.wikimedia.org/EN/ TablesWikipediansEditsGt5.htm.

Wikipedia. 2010. Wikipedia: Version 1.0 Editorial Team/Index. http://en.wikipedia.org/wiki/ Wikipedia:Version_1.0_Editorial_Team/Index.

Zuckerberg, Mark. 2010. 500 Million Stories. http://blog.facebook.com/blog.php?post =409753352130.

-

2 Encouraging Contribution to Online Communities

Robert E. Kraut and Paul Resnick

1 Problems of Contribution

Many hands make light work, according to the proverb. But only if all those hands actually do some work. To be successful, online communities need the people who participate in them to contribute the resources on which the group's existence is built. The types of resource contributions needed differ widely across different types of groups. Volunteers in NASA's Clickworker community (http://beamartian.jpl.nasa.gov), for example, help space scientists analyze data by clicking on Mars photographs to trace the outline of craters. In social media communities, like YouTube, where users upload videos, or Gnutella, where participants share their music collections, the contributed resources are the digital artifacts that users share with each other. In communities such as Wikipedia or the Apache OSS project, which produce a product for external consumption, contributions consist of the direct production work that creates the artifacts (e.g., editing articles or source code), the coordination work done behind the scenes to plan the artifacts and the production process, and the managerial and administrative work that sustains the community as a whole. In many discussion communities, it is the conversations that participants exchange with each other that provide benefits to others in the community. In a technical support group, for example, participants provide answers to others' questions; in health support groups, they also provide emotional support and tell personal stories that engage the interests of others.

In almost every online community, even successful ones, important contributions are not being made. The introductory chapter mentioned that about two-thirds of articles on Wikipedia are marked as stubs, which have "very little meaningful content" and "may be little more than a dictionary definition" (Wikipedia 2011c). Even among articles marked by editors as relevant to a popular topic like aviation, there are more than 17,000 marked as stubs and 12,000 labeled as start, described as providing "some

Table 2.1
Open GNOME bugs (as of December 6, 2010)

Top 15 GNOME Modules

Product	Open bugs	Opened in last 7 days	Closed in last 7 days
gtk+	2,395	22	−14
Evolution	2,193	25	−45
nautilus	1,286	22	−30
doxygen	943	6	−1
rhythmbox	796	15	−11
glib	703	24	−12
gnome-panel	687	10	−3
banshee	664	26	−30
GStreamer	659	31	−53
epiphany	568	7	−4
GnuCash	511	9	−18
metacity	460	0	0
gnome-shell	426	30	−39
f-spot	409	2	0
gvfs	367	2	−1

meaningful content, but the majority of readers will need more," with less than 5,000 articles total in the five higher-quality levels (Wikipedia 2010).

Similarly, consider GNOME, the open-source graphical user interface for Unix-like operating systems. As of December 2010, the 15 most important modules in this open source desktop project had a total of 13,067 open bugs (see table 2.1). Of these, the developers working on the project classified 9.4 percent of them as either critical or major.

Sometimes the contribution gap occurs because there is simply too much work to do with the number of hands available. This seems to be the case with the backlog for fixing bug requests in the GNOME project and with stubs in Wikipedia. Sometimes, however, hands are available but idle. One reason is that people don't know what to do. It may be possible to increase contributions just by directing people to useful tasks. Because not everyone can do the same things, section 2 of this chapter explores the coordination effects of requests that ask people to do specific tasks.

Sometimes the needs are clear but volunteers don't find the tasks appealing. For example, most writers of software code don't have the same enthusiasm for writing documentation or translating it into a wide range of languages. Similarly, the core developers may not want to create drivers for specialized peripherals unless they

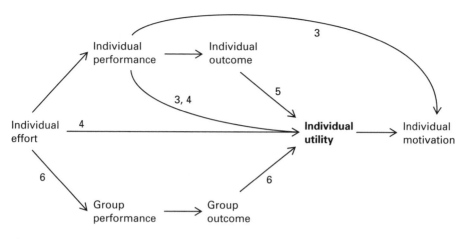

Figure 2.1
Motivators of individual effort and the sections of the chapter where they are explored.

happen to be using those devices. In addition, volunteer developers often find providing user support less attractive than creating new software or even fixing bugs. One of the reasons that high-technology companies like IBM, Sun, Nokia, and Red Hat have paid employees working on volunteer-initiated, open source software development projects is that the volunteer workforce didn't spontaneously do some of the work needed to make the software successful or to adapt it to commercial uses.

The remainder of the chapter explores ways to increase people's motivation. We use theories from psychology and economics to identify techniques that can increase resource contributions from members and to identify common ways to go wrong. Figure 2.1 summarizes the causal pathways that theory and empirical evidence suggest lead to increased motivation to contribute, labeled by the sections in this chapter where they are discussed. Many of the pathways derive from an expected utility framework that is common in both economics and psychology. For example, classic expectancy-value models in organizational behavior hold that people will work hard if they think that doing so will lead to outcomes they value (Vroom 1995; Vroom, Porter, and Lawler 2005). Motivation is a multiplicative function of *expectancy* (i.e., their beliefs about the probability that their action will lead to the outcome) and *value* (i.e., the value of the outcome or satisfaction they will receive if they achieve the outcome). Where utility is derived from outcomes of the actions, psychological theories often posit a two-stage process in which individual effort has some impact on performance, and performance has some impact on outcomes. For example, in a running race, increased effort in the form of training might lead to completing the race faster (performance), which might lead to winning the race and collecting a trophy (outcome). In the online community setting, exerting effort may lead to the creation of a new video (performance) that, upon upload, may lead to positive comments or status in the community (outcomes).

Satisfaction or utility need not come only from external outcomes such as comments from other people. It may also come directly from the actions that people pursue or the performance level they achieve. Since at least the time of Aristotle (Aristotle 330 BCE), philosophers and psychologists have distinguished between intrinsic motives, in which the performance of some activity is an end in its own right, and extrinsic motives, in which the activity is a means to achieve some other outcome. For example, some people may slay monsters in the multiplayer online game World of Warcraft for intrinsic motives (i.e., because they enjoy the task itself or the camaraderie that develops among players who work together to fight difficult monsters), and others may do so for extrinsic motives (i.e., because they enjoy the status that comes from achieving a high level in the game). Some people edit many articles in Wikipedia because of the intrinsic pleasure they derive from writing about topics they care about (Burke and Kraut 2008). Sections 3 and 4 in this chapter explore intrinsic motivations that are tied to effort or performance rather than extrinsic motivations tied to outcomes.

Section 3 continues the exploration of requests, begun in section 2 with a focus on their coordination effects, but focuses on a variety of persuasive techniques that may motivate people to comply with the requests. For example, people may be more motivated to complete tasks when asked by friends or people with high status. Because people seem to respond to many persuasive techniques by following heuristics rather than carefully assessing the utility they might gain, we can think of these techniques as creating direct links from individual performance (task completion) to motivation. People are also motivated to achieve challenging goals because it enhances self-efficacy. Thus, we can think of persuasive techniques that establish goals and provide feedback as enhancing a direct link between task performance and utility and as not requiring the mediation of externally visible outcomes.

Section 4 describes other ways to enhance intrinsic motivators, in particular, things that make tasks fun or interesting irrespective of the outcomes of that effort. For example, effort on the task may be more rewarding if it is undertaken as part of a social experience, if it is immersive, or if it affords a sense of control and mastery. Providing feedback about performance is one of the central design levers explored in this section.

Section 5 explores the design space of external rewards that can be offered for individual performance as a way to increase the expected utility of individual effort and thus enhance extrinsic motivations. Performance can lead to status rewards, privileges within the community, or more tangible rewards such as money or prizes. For example, building up a public reputation is not the primary motivator for most contributors to open source projects, but it is one of the factors that makes a difference for many (Roberts, Hann, and Slaughter 2006). Similarly, some Wikipedia participants are motivated to edit in part because they hope to get promoted to an administrator role (Burke and Kraut 2008).

Section 6 addresses ways to increase the expectancy value from group effort and outcomes. In online communities, many of the benefits created by a member's contributions are realized by other members, or even by the general public, and coordinated contributions of many people may be required to produce an outcome that is valued by all of them. We draw heavily from Karau and Williams's *collective effort model* (Karau and Williams 1993). The group context may affect *expectancies*, beliefs about the marginal impact of the user's behavior on group performance. Thus, for example, professors may decline to correct errors in Wikipedia articles on which they have expertise because they believe that many other contributors could easily do the work (i.e., they have a low expectation that their edits would improve the article over what it would be without their contribution). The group context may also influence the value an individual will receive from the outcome of the effort, should the effort succeed in producing the group outcome. First, people may vary in how much they value the group outcome. For example, members of WikiProjects (groups of people who curate collections of articles on defined topics) may vary in how much they like the group and thus in the degree that they gain satisfaction when the group achieves some goal such as increasing the number of high quality articles in its domain. This liking of the group affects participants' willingness to contribute effort to group goals. Second, people may not value group success because they may not get a fair share of credit for it. Thus, for example, professors may decline to correct errors in Wikipedia articles on which they have expertise because they get fewer reputation benefits from editing Wikipedia articles than from writing short notes in a professional journal.

2 Ask and Ye Shall Receive

It is axiomatic that people won't be able to contribute what a community needs unless they are aware of those needs and have the skills and resources to contribute them. For this reason, many production-oriented online communities publicize lists of needed contributions. As discussed previously, the GNOME open source development project has many open bugs. To let the developers know what work the project needs, the project maintains reports like the one in table 2.1 that count the bugs in each of the modules and classify them by severity and priority. Interested developers can drill down to access prioritized lists of specific bug reports.

Similarly, the community portal in Wikipedia contains numerous lists of actions that people can take to improve the encyclopedia (Wikipedia 2011b). These provide links to specific pages requiring specific kinds of attention, such as fact checking, providing citations for quotes, contributing photographs or drawings, filling in useful content on stubs, "wikifying" (i.e., improving the formatting), and giving feedback to editors explicitly seeking feedback about their editing.

Broadcasting a description of the work may by itself elicit contributions from the volunteers who frequent an online community, assuming that appropriate community members who have the motivation, knowledge, or skill and available time notice and respond to the request. In many discussion sites, for example, community members see requests for information or other support as a part of monitoring the message boards for other purposes. In the Apache server community, system administrators who run Apache servers often monitor discussion posts because the posts can provide background information about problems and solutions relevant to the administrators' paid jobs. If they see requests that they can handle without much effort while monitoring the sites, they answer them because the costs of monitoring and responding are low (Lakhani and von Hippel, 2003).

Design Claim 1   Making the list of needed contributions easily visible increases the likelihood that the community will provide them.

Some communities provide tools that reduce the burden on volunteers for monitoring the tasks that they are both motivated and competent to do. The "watchlist" in Wikipedia is such a monitoring tool; it allows a registered editor to be alerted whenever anyone changes or comments on a set of pages that the editor has designated. In other online communities, it is often possible for a community member to monitor certain types of content using a combination of simple filters and email, RSS feeds, or similar alerting mechanisms. The Bugzilla software, used as a bug tracking system for many open source development projects, offers advanced search and alerting features that allow developers to "get an email about any change made in Bugzilla, and which notifications you get on . . . bugs is fully controlled by your personal user preferences" (Bugzilla 2011). Similarly, Facebook provides awareness features that show members changes in information generated by other people in their social networks and allows them to be notified of these changes by electronic mail, if they are not frequent visitors. These awareness features in turn lead to increased communication among Facebook friends. A number of products exist to make programming an RSS filter easier by helping people match changed content with keywords they care about , such as Feed Rinse (http://www.feedrinse.com) and FilterMyRSS (http://filtermyrss.com). However, even with these tools, programming filters is effortful and may require skill and foresight, which deters most community members from using these features. The more automatic these tools are, and the easier to use, the more effective they will be.

Design Claim 2   Providing easy-to-use tools for finding and tracking work that needs to be done increases the amount that gets done.

If designers have information about community participants' interests and behavior, this information can be used to direct them to appropriate tasks in the site. Research on offline volunteerism shows that when potential volunteers are recruited through appeals that match their motivations, the appeals are more persuasive and lead to stronger intentions to volunteer. For example, appeals that focus on the career benefits of volunteering are most persuasive to those who volunteer for careerist reasons (Clary et al. 1998). This principle of creating requests that match the interests of potential contributors works in online settings as well. For example, consider the case of a designer trying to increase conversation on a movie discussion forum. Asking people to respond to posts mentioning movies they had rated in the movie review portion of the site increased their likelihood of reading and responding to those posts, compared to asking them to reply to random posts (Harper et al. 2007). Cosley and colleagues developed such an application, called SuggestBot, for Wikipedia (Cosley, Frankowski, Terveen, and Riedl 2007). Wikipedia editors were four times more likely to complete a backlogged task if SuggestBot directed them toward work that matched their interests and competence as determined from their prior editing in Wikipedia, instead of directing them to a random page. Although Cosley was able to direct Wikipedians to particular articles, it might be possible to use similar techniques to identify roles for which members of the community are well suited. For example, machine learning techniques can identify people who are suited to be administrators in Wikipedia (Collier et al. 2008), and one could use these techniques to recruit volunteers to become administrators.

Design Claim 3   Compared to asking people at random, asking people to perform tasks that interest them and that they are able to perform increases contributions.

3 Structuring Requests to Enhance Motivation

How one asks for contributions makes a difference. When trying to elicit information or some other contribution in an online community, for example, asking a specific question rather than making a statement or asking an open-ended question increases the likelihood of getting a response by 50 percent (Burke, Kraut, and Joyce 2010). More than half a century of research on attitude change and persuasion provides some guidance about how to make requests work. Although we do not review all the conclusions from that literature here, we identify some important lessons. Cialdini and Goldstein provide useful reviews of the literature (Cialdini 2001; Cialdini and Goldstein 2004).

In many cases, it is better to identify particular people and personally ask them to contribute. For example, as shown in figure 2.2, in an online chat room requests for help are answered up to 50 percent faster when a recipient is addressed by name than when the request is broadcast to everyone present in the chat room, and the speedup increases with the number of people present (Markey 2000). The recommendation to ask a particular person is consistent with decades of research on conformity (Milgram 1963), "get out the vote" campaigns (Green and Gerber 2008), and helping in emergencies (Darley and Latané 1968). For example, research on get-out-the-vote

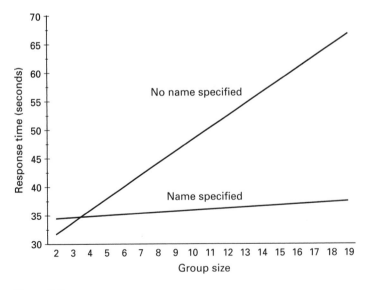

Figure 2.2
Group size and directing the request to a particular person (Markey 2000).

campaigns shows that door-to-door canvassing and phone calls in which the canvasser makes a request to a particular voter are much more cost effective in increasing the total vote than are campaigns using email or paper leafleting, even though email and leafleting can target a wide audience at low cost. Research on bystander interventions in emergencies shows that bystanders are much more likely to help if they are singled out and given a specific request than if the help request is broadcast to a group as a whole. More generally, Latané's social impact model of persuasion (1981) holds that the power of a persuasive attempt increases with the number and immediacy of the people making the attempt and decreases with the number of people whom the persuaders are attempting to influence simultaneously.

Design Claim 4   Compared to broadcasting requirements for contribution to all community members, asking specific people to make contributions increases the likelihood that they will do so.

Researchers who have examined persuasive communication note two separate processes in responding to a persuasion attempt (Chaiken, Liberman, and Eagly 1989). People sometimes systematically process messages that concern issues that they care strongly about, evaluating the evidence mostly in a rational way. Such deep processing is likely to occur, for example, when people are making an expensive purchase, such as a car, or deciding on a potentially dangerous medical procedure. For these types of decisions, they might run though an informal cost-benefit analysis, comparing the cost of performing an action against the benefits they will receive. In processing messages about these types of decisions, they will be strongly influenced by the quality of evidence and the reasoning presented. For example, they might analyze how a purchase or medical decision will influence outcomes they value. However, for persuasion attempts surrounding many routine decisions that people do not care strongly about, they use more superficial or heuristic processing. When deciding whether to jaywalk at the intersection, what to eat for lunch, or whether to answer a question in an online group, they are less likely to do a rational analysis of the decision and the information presented to them, and are more likely to be influenced by superficial cues and to use rules of thumb to help them make their decisions. For example, when choosing what to order in a fast-food restaurant, they are unlikely to conduct an analysis of salt and fat contained in an entrée, even though this information is available to them (Krukowski et al. 2006). On the other hand, they are likely be influenced by irrelevant factors such as the choice they made in this type of restaurant in the past, the order made by the person ahead of them in line, the combinations that the chain has preorganized for them, or advertising showing the choices made by good-looking consumers. These cues play into heuristics that often lead to a satisfactory decision while minimizing decision costs. It is as if the consumer is reasoning, "If I liked it in the past, I will probably like it now" or "If others like it, it is probably good for me, too."

Many of the requests members receive in online communities involve actions and decisions that they don't care strongly about and are therefore unlikely to evoke deep processing. This will be especially true for newcomers in an online community who haven't yet become committed to it and don't necessarily yet care about its welfare. Therefore, when asking for small contributions, requests without elaborate justification may be successful for the casual visitor to a site. Wikipedia, for example, asks for financial contributions with the simple phrase "You can support Wikipedia by making a tax-deductible donation" on its home page without elaborate rationale for why the donation is needed or how the money would be used to benefit either Wikipedia or the reader.

Elaborating these simple requests with messages that emphasize the benefits that people will receive is unlikely to help much. Prior experimental research shows that although a short rationale may help increase compliance with the request, the quality of the rationale doesn't matter for small requests, because they are likely to evoke heuristic processing, but that the quality does matter for large contributions, which are likely to evoke deep processing (Langer, Blank, and Chanowitz 1978). Providing a rationale may even hurt. For example, an experiment by Ling and colleagues showed that sending an email message emphasizing the benefits to the recipient or the community of making contributions in the MovieLens movie recommendation site actually decreased contributions (Ling et al. 2005). Participants may have seen these messages as manipulative and acted opposite to their recommendations simply to preserve their autonomy.

Design Claim 5   Simple requests lead to more compliance than do lengthy and complex ones for decisions about which members do not care strongly.

The depth of processing theory indicates that the more people care about the decision domain, the more they will be willing to go through an informal cost-benefit analysis when making a decision. Managers of online communities can use preexisting differences among visitors to their site to differentiate more involved people from less involved ones and develop different appeals for those with high and low involvement. For example, they can use participation logs to provide some estimate of involvement and then display different requests to those who are long-term, actively involved members versus those who are first-time or casual visitors.

Design Claim 6   Messages stressing the benefits of contribution have a larger effect on people who care about the domain of the contribution.

Alternatively, managers can use the nature of the request itself to increase people's involvement in decision making. In general, messages with strong fear appeal are compelling (Witte and Allen 2000). In addition, because such messages cause people to take the decision process more seriously, they cause them to be especially sensitive to the evidence and rationale for the decision. Public broadcasting stations routinely resort to these types of fear appeals, warning that the station might be shut down without sufficient member support. One public radio station in Pittsburgh had its most successful fund raising campaign in history, raising more than half a million dollars in ten days when it announced that its license was for sale, raising fears of its commercialization. One can imagine that an appeal that emphasized that Wikipedia would need to shut down if it did not raise additional money would be effective at increasing contributions among committed Wikipedians, for whom the message conveys a strong threat against an institution they value, even though the same message might have no effect or even turn off casual visitors to the site.

Design Claim 7   Fear campaigns lead members to increase contributions in response to persuasive appeals.

Design Claim 8   Fear campaigns cause people to evaluate the quality of persuasive appeals.

When creating persuasive messages to appeal to casual visitors, it makes sense to rely on heuristics that influence people who will not think deeply about the decision or the persuasive appeal. Among the heuristics that Cialdini and Goldstein identify, we concentrate here on authority, liking, social proof, commitment, and reciprocity as ones that are especially applicable to online communities (Cialdini 2001; Cialdini and Goldstein 2004).

People are persuaded by others with status and authority. As Milgram (1963) showed in his famous obedience experiment, people will agree to requests from an authority figure even if they think they are killing someone by doing so. These authority and status effects occur even if the source of the status and authority is irrelevant to the persuasion attempt. Although expertise—a legitimate source of authority—increases persuasion and compliance with requests (Wilson and Sherrell 1993), non-relevant sources of authority do so as well. For example, pedestrians are more than three times more likely to jaywalk behind a man dressed in a business suit than one dressed in workers' clothes (Lefkowitz, Blake, and Mouton 1955). Online, when students were asked to comply with a request to fill out a questionnaire, they were 50 percent more likely to do so if the request came from a professor than from another student, even if the requester was not from their university (Guadagno and Cialdini 2005). In Wikipedia, pronouncements and recommendations from Jimmy Wales, one of the cofounders, have much more weight than those from other editors. For example, his quote that becoming a system operator or administrator in Wikipedia is "not a big deal" is still quoted as part of the rationale in elections to administratorship or in policies, seven years after he made it (Wikipedia 2011a). Although not all requests in online communities need to come from the founder, contribution requests that come from others with formal roles (e.g., administrators in Wikipedia) or from frequent posters are more likely to be acted upon than unidentified requests or requests from people with little visibility in the site.

Design Claim 9   Requests from high-status people in the community lead to more contribution than anonymous requests or requests from low-status members.

As Dale Carnegie argued in his self-help classic *How to Win Friends and Influence People* (1936), getting people to like you increases your ability to persuade them, sell to them, and get them to comply with your requests. This principle works online. In a phishing attack, perpetrators try to get victims to reveal confidential information by sending them email as if it came from a legitimate site. People are 4.5 times more likely to fall for a phishing attack when the email appears to come from one of their friends (whose name was extracted from the victim's online social network) than when it comes from a stranger (Jagatic et al. 2007).

Design Claim 10   People are more likely to comply with requests the more they like the requester.

Psychologists have long studied the factors that lead to liking (Berscheid and Reis 1998) and have shown that most of the factors that lead one person to like another also increase their ability to persuade each other. For example, we tend to like others if they are more similar to us on any number of dimensions, from social class

subject   "George Bush"   60:40 Blend

Figure 2.3
Facial similarity leads to political influence (Bailenson et al., 2009).

to attitudes, behavioral mimicry, and physical appearance (Byrne 1997), and these factors all influence persuasion as well. In some clever experiments, Bailenson and colleagues morphed photographs of research participants with those of political candidates, as illustrated in figure 2.3. Voters are more willing to vote for candidates the more they liked the subject with whom the politician's photo was morphed (Bailenson et al. 2009). The effect was stronger for less partisan participants and for unfamiliar candidates. In another experiment, research participants conversed with a digital avatar delivering a persuasive message that college students must always carry their identity cards as a security measure (Bailenson et al. 2009). Participants were more persuaded by the avatar when it mimicked their head movements. The online retailer Threadless (http://www.threadless.com) uses this similarity effect when it posts pictures of customers, not professional models, wearing its customer-designed T-shirts (see figure 2.4).

We also like others who are more physically attractive or have other desirable traits (Eagly et al. 1991). The physical attractiveness increases persuasion and compliance (Eagly and Chaiken 1975). It is for this reason that so many advertisements in print, television, and the web use images of attractive people to sell their products (Baker and Churchill 1977). There are many other sources of appeal besides physical attractiveness and similarity. For example, we also tend to like people we have often seen in the past. All of these sources of liking could be used to increase compliance to requests in online communities.

Design Claim 11   People will be more likely to comply with requests if they come from others who are familiar to them, similar to them, are attractive, are of high status, or have other noticeable socially desirable characteristics.

Figure 2.4
Customers as models in Threadless (http://www.threadless.com).

Designers can also use the group context to directly increase peoples' perceptions of the value of an activity through various conformity and compliance techniques (Cialdini 2001). One of the most powerful techniques to change attitudes is what Cialdini terms "social proof," whereby people come to believe that an action or outcome is valuable when they are led to believe that other people are performing the actions or espousing a belief. For example, hotel patrons are more likely to reuse their towels when their hotel bathroom includes a sign saying "Join your fellow guests in helping to save the environment. Almost 75 percent of guests . . . [use] their towels more than once" than when the sign used the standard environmental pitch "Help save the environment . . . show your respect for nature," and the effect was even stronger when guests were told that 75 percent of *those who had previously stayed in their room* had reused a towel.

Indeed, social proof partially accounts for the preferential attachment that characterizes so much of the online world (Barabási and Albert 1999), where more people connect to sites, objects, and other people who already have many people connected to them. Salganik, Dodds, and Watts (2006) demonstrated this effect experimentally when they created several different markets for music downloads, each with the same music but different consumers. Versions of the market that showed the numbers of people who previously downloaded each song exhibited much more inequality in music popularity than did versions where the previous downloads were hidden, and this social influence effect was strongest when the songs were displayed in a list with the most popular songs on top. In addition, the experiment showed that this social influence led to unpredictability about popularity, with the songs that were downloaded first getting a boost, even holding constant their overall quality. Social proof is one reason that a small number of the articles in Wikipedia have a disproportionate number of people editing them (Capocci et al. 2006) and why a small number of people have very large social networks on social networking sites (Backstrom et al. 2006).

Although social proof and preferential attachment often lead to an oversupply of some contributions and an undersupply of others, these principles can be leveraged to convince people to contribute in cases where they otherwise would not. For example, the homepage of Games with a Purpose (http://gwap.com) shows the top 10 for the day's point scorers. A precursor site for one of the games announced "10 million labels collected" and showed the number of people currently logged in (von Ahn et al. 2004). In either case, evidence of others' participation is used as social proof to convince latecomers to play the games.

Design Claim 12   People are more likely to comply with a request when they see that other people have also complied.

Decades of research in psychology and organizational behavior indicate that goals and goal setting strongly motivate people. Goals are objects or conditions that one seeks to obtain (Locke and Kristof 1996). They can be long-term (e.g., create the world's best web server) or short-term (e.g., fix all bugs by the February software release), vague (e.g., "work on the article today") or specific (e.g., "write 500 words"), and easy (e.g., "fix ten typos") or challenging (e.g., "restructure the argument"). Hundreds of studies have shown that people work harder when they adopt concrete goals as an objective than when they have no goal or only vague goals. Specific, challenging, and immediate goals stimulate higher achievement than do easy goals, vague "do your best" goals, or long-term goals with few milestones.

High-challenge goals energize performance in four ways. First, these external goals lead people to set higher personal goals, in turn increasing their effort. Second, goals cause people to persist at tasks longer than they would otherwise. Third, goals cause people to pay attention to and expend their effort toward thoughts and behavior that are relevant to the achievement of the goals and away from irrelevant or distracting ones. Fourth, achieving an assigned goal leads to task satisfaction, which enhances both self-efficacy (i.e., belief in one's own ability to complete a task; Bandura 1993) and commitment to future goals, resulting in an upward performance spiral. Both personal goals (e.g., to run an eight-minute mile) and organizational goals (e.g., President Kennedy's goal for NASA to send people to the moon) can increase motivation and performance.

Goal setting can be used strategically to increase contributions. For example, the membership campaigns conducted by public radio and television stations effectively create concrete and challenging goals. Not only do these stations identify major goals for their listeners ("We need $250,000 during the fall pledge campaign to keep this station on the air"), but they also create a cascade of subgoals, such as meeting a challenge grant of raising $500 in the next hour, to motivate listeners. Fund raisers are explicit when describing to potential sponsors their goal-setting strategies: "Challenge grants are a great way to support [the station]. When you designate your [gift] . . . to be used as an on-air challenge, then other listeners are inspired to help us make the goal of the challenge" (KJZZ 2011).

Beenen and colleagues (2004) demonstrated experimentally the power of goals in the MovieLens community (http://www.movielens.org). MovieLens is a movie recommendation site whose members evaluate movies; on the basis of their evaluations, they and other members receive recommendations. Members rated more movies when they were sent an email asking them to rate a specific number of movies in the next week than when the message asked them to "do your best" (DYB) to rate more movies.

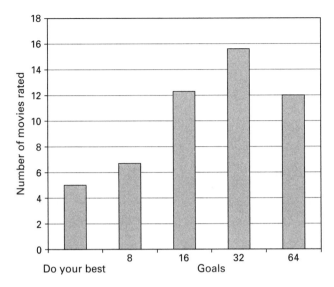

Figure 2.5
Ratings per person in the week following a request to rate as many movies as possible or to rate a specific quantity (Beenen et al. 2004).

For example, when asked to rate sixteen, thirty-two, or sixty-four movies, they provided more than thirteen on average; when asked to rate as many as they could, they provided only five (see figure 2.5). Both theory and experiments suggest that—within reason—the more challenging goals are, the more effort they motivate. However, when goals are so challenging as to be obviously out of reach, they undermine commitment to the goal and may even be demotivating (Locke, Latham, and Erez 1988). Although it's possible that asking members to rate a thousand movies in the next week would have yielded fewer ratings, a request for sixty-four did not produce a statistically significant drop-off in contributions as compared to a request for thirty-two.

Although many people use self-imposed goals as a source of self-regulation, research has shown that the goals people develop for themselves are not necessarily more powerful than goals assigned to them by an outside agent (Locke and Latham 1991). As long as people think the goals are important and have committed themselves to the goals, whether the goals were self-generated or imposed by an outsider has little impact on the effectiveness at shaping behavior.

Design Claim 13 Providing members with specific and highly challenging goals, whether self-set or system-suggested, increases contribution.

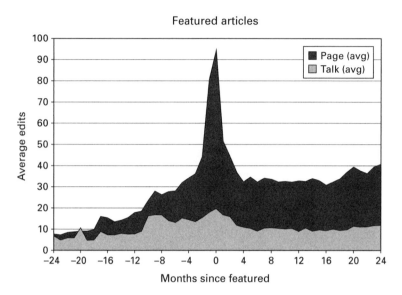

Figure 2.6
Wikipedia edits before and after reaching featured status (Kittur 2011).

Some online communities routinely make effective use of group goal setting. For example, editors in Wikipedia use the challenge of applying for Featured Article status, under which the article they are tending is eligible to appear on Wikipedia's front page, as a self-management technique, thus motivating themselves to do the necessary work to improve their article enough to clear this hurdle. Figure 2.6 shows the number of edits on article pages and the talk pages associated with articles in the months surrounding their move to Featured Article status. On average, the amount of work the editors contribute in the month prior to the featured article decision is two to four times as much as they were doing in prior months and over three times as much as they do after the status shift (Kittur 2011).

WikiProjects, where groups of editors in Wikipedia organize to improve articles in a defined domain area, use goals organized into what they call "Collaborations of the Week." These encourage project members to work on specific high-priority articles. The project chooses one or two articles under its purview and advertises that editors should improve them during a defined time period (typically a week). These collaborations of the week are highly successful. They cause project members in particular to triple the work they do on the designated articles during the collaboration period (see figure 2.7). The motivational effects of these goals also spill over, causing project members to do more project-related work generally, editing articles beyond those listed

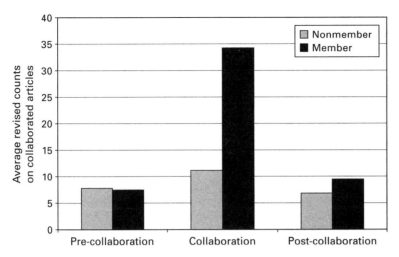

Figure 2.7
Revisions made to articles by project members and nonmembers before, during, and after a Collaboration of the Week (Zhu, Kraut, and Kittur In press).

in the collaboration of the week. In particular, people who have participated in collaborations of the week then go on to engage in what organizational scholars call "organizational citizenship behavior," those behaviors vital to group functioning that aren't explicit parts of people's job descriptions. For example, in Wikipedia, in contrast with tasks like editing the main body of the articles, citizenship behaviors include fighting vandalism, maintenance work, and clean-up work. (Wilson, Straus, and McEvily 2006).

GNOME uses six-month release cycles to coordinate work (The GNOME Project 2011). Each date is fixed, and the release planning document lists a set of new features and bug fixes. Besides coordinating the work, the release schedule helps to motivate developers. As in the case of Wikipedia, a large fraction of all work is done in the month before release or the code freeze preceding the release.

As Ducheneaut and colleagues (2007) note, World of Warcraft has an interesting twist on the imposition of goals. As players "level up" in the game (i.e., gain more experience points by completing game-specific tasks), they are given more talents, skills, and resources that allow them to complete increasingly more difficult tasks. The goal structure is arranged so that players gain substantial new talents and skills every tenth level. The amount of time players commit to the game is partially driven by the goals represented by these periodic increments in talents and skills. As shown in figure 2.8, the time players spend in the game increases with their level; high-level

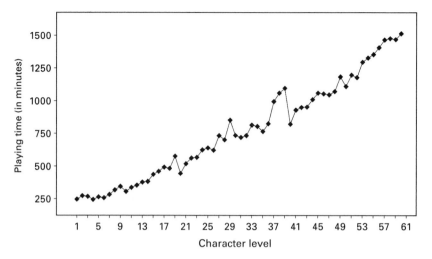

Figure 2.8
Weekly minutes playing World of Warcraft, by level (Ducheneaut et al. 2007).

players spend more time than lower-level ones. However, the opportunity to receive qualitative increases in talents, skills, and resources at each tenth level serves as a goal for players, and they increase their playing just before every tenth level to achieve the goal and then decrease their time in the game afterward. We return to this discussion of instituting goals through the use of incentives and reinforcements in section 5.

Design Claim 14   Coupling goals with specific deadlines leads to increases in contribution as the deadlines approach.

Goals are more effective when accompanied by frequent feedback about progress. The feedback helps to remind people about the goals and evokes a "high performance cycle" in which success enhances self-efficacy (belief in one's ability to accomplish goals), which in turn enhances commitment to goals (Locke and Latham 2002). Thus, for example, fund-raising campaigns commonly display a thermometer to show progress toward a collective goal. Some online communities display progress toward assigned goals, such as completing all elements of their user profiles. Performance feedback, which is not necessarily tied to goal completion, is considered more generally in section 4, and public display of feedback is considered as a reward in section 5.

Design Claim 15   Goals have greater effects when people receive frequent feedback about their performance with respect to the goals.

4   Enhancing Intrinsic Motivations

Many members of online communities are motivated because either effort toward the task or successful completion of the task is intrinsically rewarding, independent of other downstream consequences of performing the task. It is intrinsically rewarding to communicate with others in a health support group, solve programming challenges in an open source community, or kill monsters in an online game.

Intrinsically motivated actions are ones that directly fulfill some basic desire. For example, White (1959) identified a basic motivation for competence or mastery that he claimed to be at the root of the intrinsic motivation for curiosity, autonomy, and play. Others emphasize hedonic pleasure as the primary motive (e.g., Kahneman, Diener, and Schwartz 1999).

Others, such as Reiss (2004), see the basic drives as more diverse. He identified sixteen of them (as shown in table 2.2). Thus, satisfying a drive for social contact brings fun, for curiosity brings wonder, and for status brings self-confidence. He holds that people behave as if they are trying to maximize these sixteen types of joys.

Table 2.2
Reiss's sixteen motives (2004)

Motive name	Motive	Intrinsic feeling
Power	Desire to influence (including leadership; related to mastery)	Efficacy
Curiosity	Desire for knowledge	Wonder
Independence	Desire to be autonomous	Freedom
Status	Desire for social standing (including attention)	Self-importance
Social contact	Desire for peer companionship (including play)	Fun
Vengeance	Desire to get even (competition and wining)	Vindication
Honor	Desire to obey a traditional moral code	Loyalty
Idealism	Desire to improve society (including altruism, justice)	Compassion
Physical exercise	Desire to exercise muscles	Vitality
Romance	Desire for sex (including courting)	Lust
Family	Desire to raise own children	Love
Order	Desire to organize (including ritual)	Stability
Eating	Desire to eat	Satiation (lack of hunger)
Acceptance	Desire for approval	Self-confidence
Tranquility	Desire to avoid anxiety, fear	Safe, relaxed
Saving	Desire to collect, value of frugality	Ownership

Although he holds that these basic motives are universal, different people value the different joys at different levels. For example, intellectuals may especially value the joy of wonder derived from curiosity, athletes may especially value the vitality that comes from physical exercise, and extroverts especially value the fun that comes from social contact.

Regardless of whether one believes that there are very few primary motives such as mastery or pleasure or a more diverse set, designers should create the tasks they ask people to do in a way that engages these motives and thereby heightens potential contributors' intrinsic motivation. Here we focus on the ways in which one can design tasks to fulfill four types of motivations: social contact, optimal challenge, mastery, and competition. However, designers should be able to link tasks to other important motivations as well, including romance, idealism, and family, for example.

Social contact is a powerful motivator. Studies that correlate the tasks people are engaged in with their moods show that for most people, being engaged socially is associated with positive moods. For example, a national sample shows that the most positive moods of the day occur when teens are talking and doing activities with their best friends, and the lowest moods of the day occur when they are alone (Csikszent-mihalyi and Hunter 2003). Studies of the general public find similar results, with the greatest happiness occurring when people are interacting with others (Kubey and Csikszentmihalyi 1990). It is the intrinsic interest that so many people have in social interaction that makes discussion in many online forums so appealing and that augments the game play in multiplayer games.

It is possible to make otherwise-tedious tasks more engaging by combining them with social interaction. Traditional American quilting bees, husking bees (see figure 2.9), and barn raisings rely on this principle. In online question-answering sites—whether implemented as question-answering services such as Yahoo! Answers (http://answers.yahoo.com), or as Internet forums such as those devoted to health problems or technical support—questions are frequently posted to instigate personal conversations that extend well beyond factual information exchange (Harper, Moy, and Konstan 2009). These social components increase people's willingness to contribute.

Many open-source software development projects surround their development activities with various types of social interaction. Consider GNOME: in addition to mailing lists and developer and user forums for the subprojects encompassed by the GNOME umbrella, GNOME also has local developer/user groups because, as their website says, "These groups provide a forum for people with an interest in GNOME and opportunities to network, learn GNOME, get more involved with the GNOME project and community, help each other, *and socialize*" (emphasis added). The GNOME foundation also supports several conferences a year—to bring developers together. The confer-

Figure 2.9
Cozard, Nebraska: corn husking bee, 1943.
Source: http://news.webshots.com/photo/1035397830001186366wNqISF. Photo courtesy of Richard V. Smith.

ences combine technical talks about GNOME subprojects—intense coding sessions, very similar to husking bees, at which developers work simultaneously on the software— and after-hours dining, conversation, and drinks sessions. One conference announced a slogan of "Meet, Plan, Party," highlighting the interplay between the work-oriented and social features of these conferences (GUADEC 2007).

Design Claim 16   Combining contribution with social contact with other contributors causes members to contribute more.

Academics who study human play and other positive experiences, as well as game and other interactions designers who build positive interactive experiences, have developed theories and principles to describe some of the features that make activities fun (Blythe, Overbeeke, and Monk 2003). One of the best known is Csikszentmihalyi's theory of *flow*. Flow is "the holistic sensation that people feel when they act with total involvement" (Csikszentmihalyi 1997, 36). It is akin to Reiss vitality motive mentioned earlier (2004). Csikszentmihalyi identifies the following characteristics of situations that are likely to lead to the flow state (Csikszentmihalyi and Rathunde 1993). First, the challenges raised by the activities that players are engaged in should match or slightly exceed their skills. As a consequence, the enjoyment they receive from a situation depends not only on situational characteristics but also on their current skill level. In solving a crossword puzzle, for example, ones that are too easy will be boring and ones that are too hard will be frustrating, but some puzzles will be enjoyably challenging. The most enjoyable situations are ones in which people feel barely in control. Of course, what is challenging is likely to change as players' skill increases. A second feature of flow-inducing situations is that they have clear goals and feedback. Competition with an appropriate competitor is a simple way of ensuring that an activity has the appropriate challenges, complexity, and feedback to be enjoyable, but it is not the only way. People are happier, more satisfied, more creative, more attentive, and more satisfied when performing tasks in which the challenges match their skills than when engaged in similar activities in which the challenges and skills aren't well matched.

Game designers have created a similar set of principles for making computer games enjoyable. Table 2.3 is an analysis mapping the principles of flow to the heuristics game designers use to make games engaging (Sweetser and Wyeth 2005). Although these principles were developed to describe the design of online games, similar principles could be used in the process of making important contributions to online communities more enjoyable and game-like. Consider, for example, the techniques that von Ahn and Dabbish (2008) used to design the website Games with a Purpose. On the site, in the ESP Game a player collaborates with a partner, under a time limit, to guess the partner's names for pictures (see figure 2.10). As with many games, each round has a clear goal—naming the picture—and a player gets immediate feedback when a partner picks the same name for a picture. Pictures differ in difficulty, and "easy names" (i.e., one that others pairs have picked multiple times) are placed on a list of taboo words. Although players are randomly matched with other players and are given a random sample of pictures from the inventory, they have some degree of control, because they can cancel a trial and request a new picture at any time. The game is quite engaging, as evidenced by the amount of voluntary play it has received, but perhaps the game could have been made even more engaging if it had followed more of the design principles in table 2.3. For example, as the game accumulated information about a player's skill level, it could have given him or her progressively more challenging pictures to name, for example, by selecting from among pictures with more words on the taboo list. Although opportunities for more extensive social

Table 2.3
Mapping flow to principles of game design (adapted from Sweetser and Wyeth 2005)

Flow criteria	Principles of game design
Concentration Games should require concentration, and the player should be able to concentrate on the game	Provide a lot of stimuli from different sources that are worth attending to Quickly grab the players' attention and maintain their focus throughout the game Do not burden players with unimportant tasks Have a high workload, while still being appropriate for the players' perceptual, cognitive, and memory limits Do not distract players from tasks that they want or need to concentrate on
Challenge Games should be sufficiently challenging and match the player's skill level	Increase level of challenge as players increase their skill levels Provide new challenges at an appropriate pace
Skills Games must support player skill development and mastery	Allow players to start playing the game without reading the manual Make learning the game be part of the fun Include online help so players don't need to exit the game Teach the game through tutorials or initial levels that feel like playing the game Increase players' skills at an appropriate pace as they progress through the game Reward players appropriately for effort and skill development Have interfaces and mechanics that are easy to learn and use
Control Players should feel a sense of control over their actions in the game	Support players' sense of control over their characters or units and their movements and interactions in the game world Support players' sense of control over the game interface and input devices Support players' sense of control over the game shell (starting, stopping, saving, etc.) Prevent players' from making errors that are detrimental to the game and support recovering from errors Support players' sense of control and impact onto the game world (their actions matter and they are shaping the game world) Support players' sense of control over the actions that they take and the strategies that they use, and that they are free to play the game the way that they want (not simply discovering actions and strategies planned by the game developers)

Table 2.3
(continued)

Flow criteria	Principles of game design
Clear Goals Games should provide the player with clear goals at appropriate times	Present overriding goals early and clearly Present intermediate goals clearly and at appropriate times
Feedback Players must receive appropriate feedback at appropriate times	Provide players feedback on progress toward goals Provide players immediate feedback on their actions Provide players with ability to always know their status or score
Immersion Players should experience deep but effortless involvement in the game	Make players less aware of their surroundings Make players less self-aware and less worried about everyday life or self Make players experience an altered sense of time Make players feel emotionally involved in the game Make players feel viscerally involved in the game
Social Interaction Games should support and create opportunities for social interaction	Support competition and cooperation between players Support social interaction between players (chat, etc.) Support social communities inside and outside the game

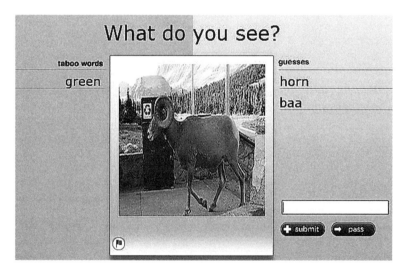

Figure 2.10
ESP Game (http://web.archive.org/web/20050120023005/http://www.espgame.org).

interaction would make the game more fun, this richer social interaction would defeat the purpose of this game by allowing players to collude on naming pictures.

Design Claim 17 Immersive experiences with clear goals, feedback, and challenges that exercise people's skills to their limits but still leave them in control are intrinsically motivating.

Feedback about one's performance—especially positive feedback—can be quite motivating. Performance feedback—whether positive or negative—can be motivating because of people's desire for self-improvement, that is, to learn and gain competence. Positive feedback may be especially motivating because of people's desire for self-enhancement, in other words, to feel good about themselves and maintain positive self-esteem.

Such feedback can be verbal, in the form of comments from other people. This feedback may be part of the explanation for why people are more likely to continue participating in discussion groups when their initial posts get responses from others, which we discuss in chapter 5. Feedback can also be nonverbal, in the form of quantitative performance measures. For example, at the site 43Things (http://www .43things.com), where members post personal goals that they are trying to achieve, other users can click on a "cheer" button to praise someone else's goal. In systems like Slashdot (http://slashdot.org, a technical news and discussion site), where members moderate others' comments, achieving a score of 5 on a comment is a form of positive feedback. As shown in figure 2.11, the site ccMixter (http://ccmixter.org) provides several forms of positive feedback to authors who post audio clips, including a tally of how many people have recommended it or added it to a playlist and links to reviews. Sites with mechanisms for participants to give each other systematic, quantitative feedback also generate more ad hoc verbal feedback. The systematic feedback also seems to reduce turnover in these sites, at least for people who ask questions (Moon and Sproull 2008). In the online community context, performance feedback is often given publicly: the praise or gratitude is displayed not only to the recipient, but to everyone, and is sometimes used as the basis for awarding privileges in the site. In that case, it can create a more external reward, which is discussed in section 5.

Design Claim 18 Performance feedback—especially positive feedback—can enhance motivation to perform tasks.

Design Claim 19 Site designs that encourage systematic, quantitative feedback generate more verbal feedback as well.

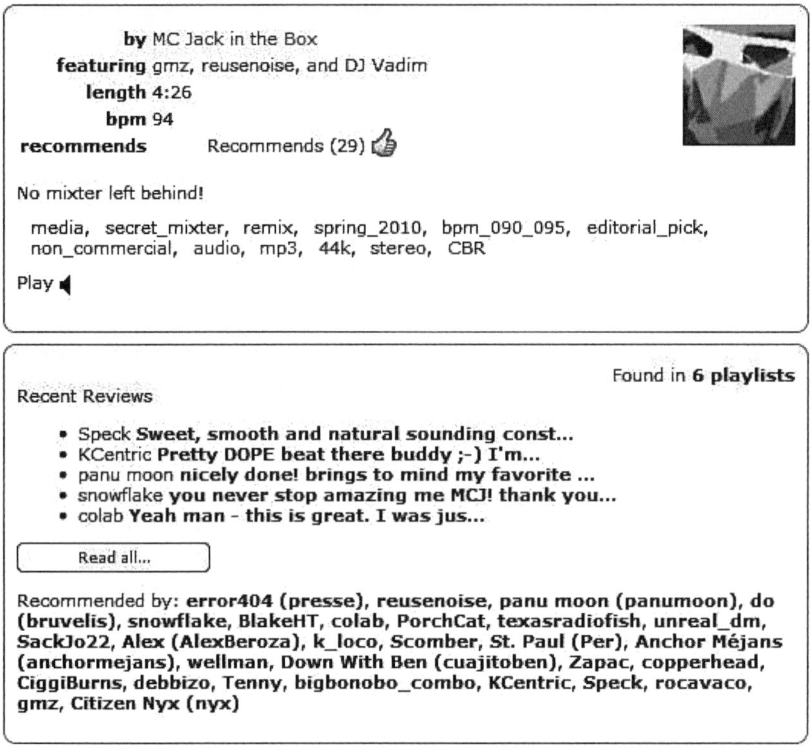

by MC Jack in the Box
featuring gmz, reusenoise, and DJ Vadim
length 4:26
bpm 94
recommends   Recommends (29) 👍

No mixter left behind!

media, secret_mixter, remix, spring_2010, bpm_090_095, editorial_pick, non_commercial, audio, mp3, 44k, stereo, CBR

Play ◀

Found in **6 playlists**

Recent Reviews

- Speck **Sweet, smooth and natural sounding const...**
- KCentric **Pretty DOPE beat there buddy ;-) I'm...**
- panu moon **nicely done! brings to mind my favorite ...**
- snowflake **you never stop amazing me MCJ! thank you...**
- colab **Yeah man - this is great. I was jus...**

> Read all...

Recommended by: **error404 (presse), reusenoise, panu moon (panumoon), do (bruvelis), snowflake, BlakeHT, colab, PorchCat, texasradiofish, unreal_dm, SackJo22, Alex (AlexBeroza), k_loco, Scomber, St. Paul (Per), Anchor Méjans (anchormejans), wellman, Down With Ben (cuajitoben), Zapac, copperhead, CiggiBurns, debbizo, Tenny, bigbonobo_combo, KCentric, Speck, rocavaco, gmz, Citizen Nyx (nyx)**

Figure 2.11
Information displayed on the site ccMixter (http://www.ccmixter.org) about an audio clip posted by a member. Feedback about who has recommended the clip and the first lines of recent reviews commenting on the clip are prominently displayed.

However, as Henderlong and Lepper note in their review of the effects of praise on children's intrinsic motivation (2002), praise enhances intrinsic motivation when it enhances children's sense of competence and autonomy. If the conditions for enhancing competence and autonomy are not right, praise may have no effects on intrinsic motivation or may even undermine it. First, the receivers must think the praise or other feedback is sincere. If not, they will not interpret it as a reliable signal about competence and may perceive it as controlling.

False praise is frequent enough in real-world settings, where, for example, teachers might praise to manipulate, motivate, or protect a particular student. In online settings, praise might be judged as insincere or not credible if it is automatically given by a bot (a computer program) or calculated based on an unrealistic or inaccurate formula. Praise or other feedback is likely to be seen as most credible if it is specific and transparent and reflects the judgment of the entire community. Thus, receiving a score of 5 on a comment posted to Slashdot should be credible because it is based on the assessments of many independent readers; receiving a barnstar in Wikipedia is less credible because it is based on the judgment of only a single editor. In Wikipedia, barnstars received for well-defined activities, such as the Graphic Designer's Barnstar awarded to those who work tirelessly to provide Wikipedia with free graphic files, are more likely to be seen as credible than those that reward a diffuse pattern of behavior, such as the Random Acts of Kindness Barnstar, awarded for "going the extra mile to be nice, without being asked" or even the Original Barnstar for "particularly fine contributions to Wikipedia."

Design Claim 20   Performance feedback enhances motivation only when it is considered to be sincere.

Performance feedback that is comparative in nature can be especially motivating. Some people enjoy the thrill of competition and the feeling of beating a competitor. Even those who are not naturally competitive may gain a sense of competence from knowing that their performance was better than that of other people, especially if the other people are known to have tried hard. Many online communities maintain scores or levels for members, based on their cumulative activity, and display the scores prominently enough that members are naturally drawn to compare their own scores or levels with others. World of Warcraft provides a good example because players are always exposed to their current level, as well as to the levels of other players, as labels attached to their avatars. Sometimes explicit comparisons are made, especially in the form of "leaderboards" or top-ten lists. For example, the Hall of Fame at Slashdot shows the ten most active authors and submitters; Threadless shows the ten who have earned most points for submitting designs, referring customers, submitting photos, or performing other actions that the site owners value.

Comparative performance feedback, however, can also decrease motivation, for several reasons. First, if people feel ambivalent about their participation in the community or about the desirability of performing the tasks, comparisons showing that they have done more than others may demotivate them. For example, some users of an online gaming site might play less if reminded about how many hours they had "wasted" on the site. Second, people who are informed that their contributions are unusually high may feel that they have "done enough." For example, in a field experiment, users of the MovieLens site were told how the number of movies they had rated compared to the median of all users. Those who were below or near the median rated more movies in the subsequent time period than a control group did. However, those who were well above the median did not increase their contributions (Chen et al. 2010).

Third, if others' performance is seen as unattainably high, people may be discouraged from even trying. This is especially problematic when leaderboards elevate the top ten or twenty-five participants in populations of tens of thousands. Although the leaderboards may be motivating for the participants already on the list or within striking distance, they may be demotivating for the vast majority of members who perceive that they have no chance of making the list. One solution to this problem is to make comparisons based only on recent activity, such as the previous week. Another possibility is to tailor them to the individual, identifying some dimension on which the individual stands at the most motivating level. Amateur sports competitions use this technique when they have separate categories for seniors, for example. An extreme example comes from a location-based game for iPhone: outWord. It provides feedback that a user has the highest score within a certain area (see figure 12). The user is always the best, but the size of the area increases as the user plays more.

Design Claim 21   Comparative performance feedback can enhance motivation, as long as high performance is viewed as desirable and potentially obtainable.

Finally, publicly displayed performance feedback—especially leaderboards—can create a competitive, game-like atmosphere, which may demotivate participation and contribution, especially for noncompetitive participants and especially in communities in which a supportive atmosphere is desirable. For example, when teaching a course on online communities, one of the authors frequently requires students to engage in online discussion of course materials and provides students with the ability to "vote up" the comments of their peers that they like. In the initial design of the course, those votes were accumulated into a leaderboard showing the top vote getters for the previous week and cumulatively. However, after a few weeks, a competitive atmosphere emerged that led some students to stop participating. In later versions of the course, the leaderboard was turned on for only a week or two, just to let students experience its impacts.

Design Claim 22 Performance feedback—especially comparative performance feedback—can create a game-like atmosphere that may have undesirable consequences in some communities.

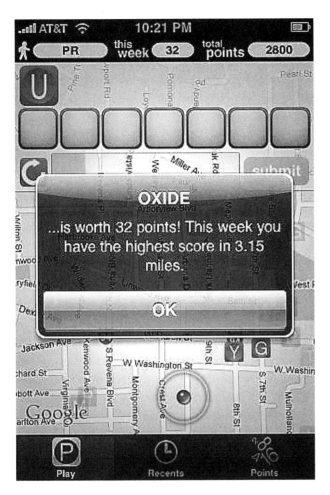

Figure 2.12
outWord is an outdoor spelling game that compares a player's scores with other players within a variable radius that grows as scores do.

5   Enhancing Extrinsic Motivations

In contrast to intrinsic motivations, rewards are extrinsic motivators. There are plenty of reward programs in online communities that appear to have the desired effects. For example, Sermo (http://www.sermo.com), an online community for doctors, introduced a reward of an iPod for any member who brought in at least ten new members. In the first few months of the program, although eleven members referred exactly ten

new members, only four referred exactly nine, and three referred exactly eight, suggesting that the iPod had a motivating effect—at least for those who were close to
achieving the reward. But reward programs don't always work, and sometimes they
have undesirable side effects, so even if a community can afford to give out expensive
rewards, that may not always be the most effective strategy. To guide choices, we start
by examining the types of rewards and why they work.

Recipients may value reputation or status markers because these rewards can change
how other people interact with them. Many online communities maintain reputation
information based on the history of someone's participation in a community and
display it next to the person's username wherever it appears in the online community's
content or in the user's profile page. For example, at Cisco's tech support forums
(http://homecommunity.cisco.com), poster IDs are shown with labels like "newbie,"
"regular visitor," "senior contributor," or "expert." Presumably, experts are treated with
more respect and deference.

Privileges can also act as rewards. In many online communities, not all the activities in the community are open to everyone. Initially, newcomers may be allowed to
read but not to post, or their posts may have to be moderated before becoming publicly
visible. Eventually, they may earn the privilege of posting without moderation. On
Slashdot, users can earn the privilege of moderating others' comments and of posting
comments that start with a score of 2 rather than 1. Other online communities require
members to earn the privilege of uploading a personal photo to their profile. Members
may see privileges as desirable either because they directly value the activity granted
to them or because they value it indirectly, for what it symbolizes. For example, privileges can serve as status symbol or a validation of a recipient's competence or sense
of belonging.

Last but not least, online communities can provide tangible rewards. Money is the
purest form of tangible reward—it can be spent on anything that the recipient chooses.
Amazon's Mechanical Turk (https://www.mturk.com), where people are paid small
amounts of money to complete small tasks, uses financial rewards to motivate contribution. It is a marketplace for work, where those with tasks to be done list them to
be completed by Turkers (as members of the Mechanical Turk community are known).
Each task has a piece rate wage associated with it. For example, Turkers might be asked
to fill out a short survey for ten cents or describe an image for eight cents. On May
20, 2010, Amazon had more than a hundred thousand tasks posted on Mechanical
Turk. Often, however, rather than cash, tangible rewards are given in the form of
specific prizes, such as an iPod, or points that can be redeemed for a limited set of
prizes, or charitable donations to causes that the recipients support.

Design Claim 23   Rewards—whether in the form of status, privileges, or material benefits—motivate contributions.

Rewards may be contingent on the quality of the contributions that are made (*performance-contingent rewards*) or may be contingent solely on effort (*task-contingent rewards*). In many online community settings, once people choose to engage in small, discrete tasks, they will perform them to the best of their ability, regardless of the reward level, even if the reward is not performance-contingent. For example, two separate field experiments conducted by different authors on the now-defunct question-answering site Google Answers found that questions accompanied by larger payments were more likely to be answered, but among questions that were answered under either payment system there was no difference in answer quality (Jeon, Kim, and Chen 2010). Similarly, on Amazon Mechanical Turk, higher prices for tasks increased the quantity of tasks completed but not the quality of work that people did (Mason and Watts 2009).

Design Claim 24   With task-contingent rewards for small, discrete tasks, larger rewards motivate people to take on tasks but do not produce higher effort on accepted tasks.

Perverse Incentives: Gaming the System

Although external rewards can encourage contributions, two caveats are in order. The first caveat is that rewards sometimes create the wrong incentives. When the rewarded activities are imperfect proxies for the behaviors that the community really wants to encourage, rewards may induce "gaming the system," in which members take actions that are rewarded but are not actually valuable. If the action to be rewarded is inviting new members, an attacker may invite new members who have no interest in the community or even invent fictitious entities to invite and then collect the reward for inviting them. If the action to be rewarded is posting comments or reviews, the attacker can post blank messages, nonsense messages, or copies of text provided by other people. If the action to be rewarded is to rate or vote, an attacker can choose randomly rather than providing a considered opinion. What's worse, bots can be written to carry out these unhelpful but rewarded actions on a large scale. If that happens, the net effect of the rewards may be detrimental to the online community even if the rewards motivate useful contributions from most members.

Design Claim 25   Rewards cause some people to "game the system," undertaking counterfeit actions that will be rewarded but that do not actually contribute to the community.

Rewards that are contingent solely on task completion, rather than on quality, are especially vulnerable to the counterfeit action of low effort. On Amazon's Mechanical Turk, researchers have found it necessary to include some validation that checks whether tasks are being completed too quickly and compares results among several people doing the same task to avoid getting contaminated results from people trying to collect the money without seriously attempting the tasks (Kittur, Chi, and Suh 2008).

Another example comes from Sermo, the online community for doctors. The primary interaction is sharing case consults, each with a mini-poll asking what other physicians thought of the case as well as an opportunity for free-response comments. The business model for the site, however, is to provide information from doctors to other interested parties such as insurance companies and hedge funds. In order to encourage physicians to respond to polls on the site, some of which come from outside parties, physicians were offered monetary payments for responding to those polls. The rewards seemed to influence a few doctors to game the system in the first few months that it was in operation. For example, a few doctors voted on nearly every item in the system, spending only a couple of seconds on each item, and voting disproportionately for the first option in each poll. The site has since reduced its emphasis on monetary rewards and taken countermeasures to discourage such gaming.

Rewards for engaging in internal site moderation can create the same perverse incentives. For example, Slashdot awards "karma points" to members for various activities, including voting on the quality of others' comments. A similar "experience points" system exists at the Everything2 site (http://everything2.com), an edited web publication where members write essays about almost anything, with experience points gained for using one's available votes. This system naturally leads to "vote dumping," wherein people vote without thinking very deeply about what they're voting on or whether they're voting up or down. Although such behavior was a negative contribution to the community it still gains points. On Everything2, there's even a post—lovingly updated for several years—with suggestions of ideas for where to dump one's votes (Footprints 2005).

Similar problems can occur in online communities that provide privileges, status cues, or other rewards based on the number of posts made. In an effort to increase post counts, some users contribute many short and not very informative posts. If only status is at stake, the danger may be small because people may gain official status from having a high post count but members who regularly interact with them will remember them as making low-quality contributions. When the stakes are higher, however, this effect can be a problem. For example, the product review site Epinions (http://www.epinions.com) paid royalties to people who post reviews. Initially, this was paid based on the number of readers of each review, which was affected more by the popularity of the product than the quality of the review.

Design Claim 26   Rewards that are task-contingent but not performance-contingent lead to members gaming the system by performing the tasks with low effort.

If counterfeits can be detected, rewards for counterfeit actions can be withheld. The reward for a real action can then be set sufficiently high to counteract the difference in cost between the high-effort real action and the low-effort counterfeit action. Thus, for example, rather than rewarding people for any post they make, rewards may be offered only for posts that others read, made many replies to, or rated highly. Over time, ePinions shifted to a reward based on the extent to which the information was used by consumers as part of buying decisions, a reward that is arguably more performance-contingent. Rewards for bringing in new members can be contingent on the new people sticking around for some time or making contributions themselves. Slashdot introduced a system called "meta-moderation" that eliminates the incentive for vote dumping: each moderation vote is examined by five other users, selected at random, who opine on whether the moderation was fair. Members whose votes are often marked as unfair lose karma points and may even lose the privilege of moderating. (Of course, if meta-moderation gains karma, then the same problem of vote dumping may occur there.)

Unfortunately, because many genuine contributions involve providing information in the form of messages, ratings, tags, and so on, it is often not possible to tell with certainty whether a contribution is genuine or counterfeit, even in hindsight. For example, a movie rating that disagrees with everyone else's may be a counterfeit, i.e., may be selected at random in order to receive a reward merely for rating, or may reflect a genuine—though unpopular—opinion about the movie. Thus, a rating that disagrees with the consensus may be a good candidate to be a counterfeit, but refusing to reward all such ratings reduces the rewards that are made to genuine ratings as well.

As long as there is a performance metric that tends to be higher, on average, when people exert higher effort on the task, scores can be assigned in a way that eliminates incentives for gaming. Consider, for example, a simplified situation in which there are only two possible performance outcomes: Good and Bad. Suppose that exerting high effort leads to a Good performance measurement 80 percent of the time and that low effort leads to a Good performance measurement only 10 percent of the time. If a reward of 10 is given for a Good and 0 for a Bad evaluation, the expected reward for high effort is 8, and the expected reward for a counterfeit, low-effort action is 1. Thus, even though there is some reward for a low effort, there is additional expected reward from effort. If the cost of effort is more than 7, the reward can be scaled in order to make the additional expected reward large enough to create an incentive for high effort. Thus, even though there may be benefits from low-effort contributions, the benefits from high-effort contributions are enough better to make that preferable. If we wish to make the expected reward for the counterfeit action 0, we can simply subtract an appropriate amount from everyone's reward. Doing so creates the risk, however, that a genuine action will get a negative reward 20 percent of the time, which may not be desirable or feasible. This technique can, in principle, be extended to situations in which there is no objective way to evaluate task performance but performance can be compared among a set of contributors (Miller, Resnick, and Zeckhauser 2005).

Design Claim 27 Performance-contingent rewards can be set in a way that prevents gaming; this is true even if performance evaluation is imperfect, as long as it is somewhat informative.

Although performance-contingent payments may be designed to prevent gaming in principle, in practice it may be difficult to calibrate rewards to produce the precise expected payoffs and to convince the participants that gaming is not in their interest. Thus, other simpler approaches to rewarding while discouraging gaming are often appropriate.

People are unlikely to experience positive utility from privately delivered praise and thank-yous for counterfeit actions. For example, if someone enters a rating selected at random or a comment with no new information in it, even if praise or thanks are received, the recipient is unlikely to gain utility from it, knowing that the contribution was really a counterfeit. Knowing that praise and gratitude are undeserved destroys their utility. The key insight here is that the same verbal feedback may have different utility to people depending on whether they undertook genuine or counterfeit actions.

The same logic can be applied to differentiate between status and privileges on one hand and tangible rewards on the other. Status and privileges within the community may induce less gaming than rewards that are valuable outside the community because status and privileges within the community may not be very valuable to people who do not make genuine contributions to the community. In some communities, however, such as Slashdot, even status and privileges within the community were sufficient rewards to engage many people in gaming the system.

Design Claim 28   Status and privileges are less likely to lead people who are not invested in a community to game the system than are tangible rewards.

An alternative approach tries to limit gaming by making it harder for the attacker to find counterfeit actions, rather than by eliminating incentives for an attacker to choose the counterfeit actions. Imagine that an attacker is trying to get rewards by performing low-cost actions that do not actually contribute to the community. If the eligibility criteria are transparent, it will be easy for the attacker to find actions that will be eligible. Moreover, if the schedule is predictable, the attacker will get immediate feedback about whether a particular action was successful in meeting the eligibility criteria and can thus learn quickly which actions to keep doing. By contrast, if the criteria are not transparent and the schedule is unpredictable, it will be harder for an attacker to find a set of rewarded actions that he or she can undertake at low cost. Moreover, in a dynamic cat-and-mouse game in which the attackers keep finding new attacks and the system designers keep adjusting the eligibility criteria in an attempt to disrupt the attacks, it will take attackers longer to adjust to the countermeasures. Nontransparency and unpredictability do not eliminate the possibility of gaming. But they do make gaming harder, and that difficulty may be sufficient in many practical situations, especially if the rewards are of only moderate value.

One online community that has adopted this approach is Slashdot. We have already discussed the problem of vote dumping, which Slashdot tried to counteract by evaluating the quality of votes through meta-moderation. Karma points are also awarded for a variety of other actions, including posting comments that are voted up by other people. Though this might seem to be a performance-contingent reward, there are well-known tricks for posting comments that will be well-received, even though they contribute little to the conversation, such as reposting popular comments from previous conversations or reciting inside jokes. Such activities earned their own colloquial name "karma whoring." The site administrators then made the criteria less transparent. Although most of the source code that runs the Slashdot site is made freely available, some key elements that determined point allocations were kept hidden so that karma whores would not be able to inspect the exact rules or know about changes to them. Finally, they made the feedback about karma scores imprecise: instead of displaying an exact numeric score, each user's karma level is now displayed using very coarse-grained categories ("none," "positive," "good," or "excellent"), so that it is very difficult to track the effect on one's numeric score of a particular action.

Google has adopted a similar strategy of nontransparency with its algorithm for ranking web pages. Google assigns a numeric score to every web page that it indexes.

Pages with higher scores are shown higher in search results. The initial algorithm, PageRank, was published as an academic publication. Generally, pages get higher scores (or PageRanks) if they are linked to by other sites with high scores. Because many sites would like to appear higher in search results, there is a large incentive to game the system: indeed, the whole field of search engine optimization (SEO) marketing emerged to help website operators increase their PageRank. Academic researchers have demonstrated that it is impossible to make any algorithm like PageRank completely immune to gaming and still have some other desirable properties in assigning scores to naturally occurring pages (Altman and Tennenholtz 2008). It is possible, however, to make it quite difficult. Google has made revisions to the initial PageRank algorithm but has not publicly revealed what they are. Moreover, the exact PageRank for a web page is not publicly available—only an integer score in the range 1–10. Together, these elements of nontransparency make it difficult to develop and test strategies for gaming PageRank. Most SEO marketing firms now focus on helping their clients make pages that will legitimately earn high PageRanks (e.g., by posting content that is of genuine interest) rather than on gaming the Google algorithm.

Design Claim 29   Nontransparent eligibility criteria and unpredictable reward schedules lead to less gaming of the system than do predictable rewards.

Trade-offs between Intrinsic and Extrinsic Motivation

The second caveat concerning external rewards is that although they can increase extrinsic motivation, they may not leave all other costs and benefits unchanged. Both psychologists and economists have argued that one should be careful about providing rewards and other extrinsic motivators for activities that people find intrinsically interesting, because doing so undermines their intrinsic interest in the task. Conceptually, intrinsically motivated activities are ones people are willing to do for their own sake, without an external incentive. Psychologists use the term "intrinsically motivated activities" narrowly to refer to activities that commonsense or empirical data show are fun, interesting, or challenging. Economists use a broader definition (Frey and Jegen 2001) referring to activities that people perform without external incentives, regardless of whether they are fun. For example, economists include as intrinsic motivations an altruistic concern for others' welfare, such as parents' personal bonds with daycare teachers that cause them to retrieve their children on time, a desire to comply with social norms, or the "civic virtue" that causes some people to pay their taxes without compulsion or fear that their tax evasion will be uncovered (Gneezy and Rustichini 2000a; Meyerson, Weick, and Kramer 1996, 2006).

Several meta-analytic reviews (i.e., quantitative reviews) of the experimental literature show that providing rewards for performing behaviors can have a small but reliable and substantively significant effect of undermining the performers' intrinsic motivation (Cameron, Banko, and Pierce 2001; Deci, Koestner, and Ryan 1999). In laboratory experiments, for example, children are less likely to play with art materials that they enjoy if they were first rewarded for playing with them and then the rewards were removed (Lepper and Greene 1975).

Although the theory is still incomplete, tangible incentives seem to undermine intrinsic motivation in part because they undercut people's feelings of autonomy and competence (Deci, Koestner, and Ryan 1999). In particular, cognitive evaluation theory (Deci and Ryan 1985) and the larger self-determination theory (SDT) of which it is a part hold that people will be more intrinsically interested in tasks under environmental conditions that cause them to feel competent and autonomous when acting. When people perceive rewards as controllers of their behavior, rewards typically decrease their intrinsic motivation in the task. This principle is consistent with the empirical findings that task-contingent tangible rewards depress intrinsic motivation. These are exactly the types of rewards that people will perceive as likely to control their behaviors. On the other hand, when people see the rewards as positive feedback that they are competent, then the rewards should enhance intrinsic motivation rather than undermine it. This principle is consistent with empirical findings that both verbal rewards (e.g., "You are doing fine") and tangible rewards received for exceeding others' performance enhance intrinsic motivation, because both give people feedback about how well they are doing.

Figure 2.13 from Cameron et al.'s (2001) meta-analysis provides a summary of the experimental evidence from many studies; the findings are largely consistent with the CET theory (Cameron, et al. 2001). First, rewards undermine motivation only when the activities were intrinsically motivating to start with. In contrast, when the activities are initially dull, uninteresting, or aversive, extrinsic rewards seem to enhance intrinsic motivation.

The form of tangible rewards may also affect whether they crowd out intrinsic motivations. Monetary rewards frame an interaction as purely a transaction, inviting recipients to assess whether the payment is sufficient compensation for the action. On the other hand, prizes may be viewed as bonus thank-you gifts acknowledging the work and thus supplement rather than supplant any intrinsic motivations recipients might have had. For example, participants in lab experiments work harder for a 50-cent candy bar, which they perceive as a gift, than for 50 cents in cash, which they perceive as insufficient payment for the work they are doing (Martins, Gilson, and Maynard 2004). Similarly, rewards in the form of donations to the recipients' chosen charity

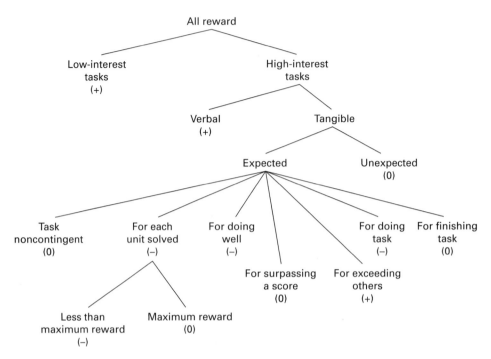

Figure 2.13
Summary of the meta-analysis showing when rewards undermine free-choice intrinsic motivation. 0 = no reliable effect; – = statistically significant negative effect of reward; + = statistically significant positive effect of reward.
Source: From Cameron et al. 2001.

may also avoid framing the interaction as a transaction. In a field experiment, women were less likely to donate blood when offered a small payment for their contribution, but allowing the subjects to redirect the payment to a charity eliminated the crowding out effect (Mellström and Johannesson 2008). Prizes and status rewards may also have an added benefit if they serve as a public signal of a recipient's affiliation or generosity. For example, a mug with an NPR logo may be worth more to an NPR contributor than the cost of providing that mug: a Wikipedia T-shirt may be more valuable as a prize for Wikipedia editors than would a cash prize equal to the cost of the T-shirt.

Design Claim 30 Adding a task-contingent reward (for doing or finishing a task, regardless of performance) to an already interesting task causes people to be less interested in the task. The effect is larger for monetary rewards than for prizes, status rewards, and charitable donations.

Psychologists who have studied the trade-offs between rewards and intrinsic motivation believe that the preservation of intrinsic motivation for learning is an important goal in its own right. Because many of them are concerned with educational applications of rewards, they want to know whether students will read, write stories, draw, track down information on the Internet, or do other fun, educational activities in settings in which they are no longer rewarded for them.

However, designers and managers of online communities are less likely to care about intrinsic motivations per se and more likely to care about the combined effect on an ongoing basis of rewards and intrinsic motivation on community members' contributions. They want to know, for example, whether people will write and comment more on Slashdot when doing so earns them karma points. Will they contribute more T-shirt designs to Threadless if they are paid for good designs? Will they edit more articles in Wikipedia if doing so earns them barnstars or a promotion to administrator status? The designers and managers don't care if the contributions are the result of intrinsic or extrinsic motivations.

Because both extrinsic and intrinsic motivations can lead people to perform activities, the effects of a reward are likely to depend on how it simultaneously influences extrinsic and intrinsic motivations. In particular, rewards that reduce intrinsic motivation more than they increase extrinsic motivation are likely to have the overall effect of reducing the probability that people will perform the activity. However, even if a reward decreases intrinsic motivation, if it increases extrinsic motivation more, it will have its desired design effect of increasing the probability that people will perform the action. The net effects of a reward will depend upon how it simultaneously influences these two types of motivations. If designers offer a tangible incentive for a contribution, like the money that Threadless contributors can earn for their T-shirt designs, the incentive is likely to increase their extrinsic motivations. It will also invoke the perception that people contribute *in order to* earn prizes and thus reduce people's intrinsic motivation to draw and submit design. If the incentive is too small, then the increase in extrinsic motivation will not compensate for the reduction in intrinsic motivation.

This reasoning is consistent with a series of observations and experiments among economists that show that small rewards reduce the probability of people performing an activity compared to either no reward or a large reward. For example, in Switzerland, about 20 percent of political volunteers reported receiving some financial rewards for their work (Frey and Goette 1999). Those who received monthly fees less than US\$35 worked for fewer hours (12 hours per month) compared to people who received no fees (14 hours per month) and to those who received fees greater than US\$50 (21 hours per month), even when controlling for hours worked per week in regular jobs and for gender. Two experiments by Gneezy and Rustichini (2000b) show similar results using more controlled methods. College students who were given 60 New Israeli Shekels (NIS) to participate in an experiment answering IQ test–type questions answered fewer of them when they were given an additional 0.1 NIS for each answer than when they were given no additional money or either 1 or 3 NIS per answer (Gneezy and Rustichini 2000b). In a related experiment, schoolchildren collected one-third less money for a charity when they were told that the experimenters would pay them a fee of 1 percent of the money they collected than when they were not told they would receive fees (36 percent reduction) or were told that they would get a fee of 10 percent of the collection (30 percent reduction).

How small must the incentive be before it fails to compensate for a reduction in intrinsic motivation? As Gneezy and Rustichini state, "the exact determination of this quantity in experimental or real-life situations is likely to be difficult and subtle" (Gneezy and Rustichini 2000b, 806). The incentives that Threadless offers its members as a challenge to submit winning T-shirt designs on a theme is probably sufficient: travel, accommodations, and three-day tickets for two to a music festival, along with a $500 gift certificate, $2,000 in cash, and a "commemorative swag bag" for the loot. Had it offered only the swag bag without the free trip, the incentive might have invoked the work-for-reward schema while providing insufficient reward. In other settings, the trade-offs are less clear. If the barnstars in Wikipedia evoke the work-for-reward schema, it is not clear without deep immersion in Wikipedia culture how the relative value of one type of barnstar compares to other types of barnstars and to the fun of editing.

Design Claim 31   Small tangible rewards are likely to reduce contributions for intrinsically interesting tasks; larger rewards are likely to increase contributions.

6   Enhancing the Expectancy Value of Group Outcomes

The previous two sections considered ways to increase the intrinsic and extrinsic benefits that accrue directly to the individual; in this section, we consider the indirect benefits that accrue to an individual through the impact of individual effort on a collective outcome. The collective effort model, described in the introduction to this chapter and illustrated in figure 2.1, predicts that people will contribute more in a group setting when they value group outcomes more and when they expect their own effort to have a greater influence on the group's performance and hence on outcomes.

We consider design alternatives that can influence both expectations about impact on group outcomes and valuations of group outcomes.

Empirical research shows less social loafing in group settings when people like the group more (Karau and Williams 1993). Chapter 3 explores in detail how to enhance individual liking for and commitment to an online community, both by building bonds with particular members and by increasing their attachment to the group as whole. Here we simply note that any design alternatives that increase liking of or commitment to the group should also increase willingness to contribute.

Design Claim 32   Commitment to an online community group increases willingness to contribute to it.

According to the collective effort model, people will contribute more to a group if they think their contributions make a difference to the group's performance. One way to influence beliefs about the efficacy of individual effort on group performance is to reduce or cap the size of the group (Latane and Nida 1981). Markey and colleagues, for example, showed that people participating in online chat groups were less likely to answer questions posed by newcomers when more people were present (Markey, Wells, and Markey 2002). Clearly, there are trade-offs in online communities between having large numbers of participants, each of whom can provide content or make some other type of contribution, and capping their size, so that each participant contributes more and likes the communities better (see chapter 3). As Kim (2000, chapter 9) suggests, creating subcommunities by partitioning a larger one into interest groups or separate forums addresses this dilemma. Thus, both Facebook and LinkedIn get the best of both worlds by exploiting a huge membership base subdivided into subcommunities based on the college from which members graduated, their prior employers, issues around which they rally, or their personal social networks.

Design Claim 33   People will be more willing to contribute in an online group when the group is small rather than large.

In addition to capping the size of online groups, one can also enhance the expectancy link in the collective effort model by directly informing people about the uniqueness of their contributions. According to the collective effort model, if people believe that their contributions are redundant with those that others in the group can provide, then there is little reason to contribute because their contributions have little likelihood of influencing group outcomes. Conversely, if they think they are unique, they should be more motivated to contribute because their contributions are likely to influence the group. Ling and colleagues (2005) have shown experimentally that this is the case in online communities. For example, in one experiment using the MovieLens movie-recommendation site as a testbed, they showed that people who had seen art-cinema movies—which few MovieLens members rate—and who were reminded of their unique movie tastes rated 40 percent more of such movies than a matched sample who had seen similar movies but were reminded of their common movie tastes. That is, they were more likely to contribute ratings when reminded that they had previously rated *Das Boot*, a 1981 Oscar nominee but not currently popular, than if they were reminded that they had rated *Titanic*, the 1997 Hollywood blockbuster. In a related experiment, Ludford and colleagues (2004) showed that members posted almost twice the number of messages to a movie discussion group and rated more than twice the number of movies when they were reminded of how their movie ratings differed from others in a discussion group vis-à-vis a discussion topic as compared with participants who did not receive this comparison.

The uniqueness principle could have broad utility in improving contributions to online communities. In many online communities, some tasks have many people contributing; a much larger number have very few people contributing. For example, in Wikipedia, both the number of edits and number of editors contributing to an article represent an inverse power law: 5 percent of articles in Wikipedia have more than fifty different editors involved over a three-month period, and more than 50 percent of the articles have fewer than ten (Kittur et al. 2008). Similarly, there are many more copies available of pop songs in peer-to-peer file sharing sites than of jazz or emerging artists (Asvanund et al. 2004). Therefore, according to the collective effort model, one can increase people's likelihood of editing in Wikipedia or contributing a song in a music sharing site by pointing them to the articles that few others have edited or the songs that few others have contributed, assuming that one can identify people who can indeed make those contributions. Another way to operationalize the uniqueness principle is to constitute teams in task-based communities, such as open-source-software development communities, so that each member of a work team has unique skills.

Design Claim 34   People will be more willing to contribute in an online group when they think that they are unique and that others in the group cannot make contributions similar to theirs.

Previously, we claimed that people will be more likely to comply with a request when they see that others have also complied. One reason is that seeing others' behavior activates the social proof heuristic (Cialdini 2001). There are other reasons, however, why showing that others are contributing can increase contributions, beyond the social proof that contributing is appropriate. One is that people do not want to contribute to a lost cause; evidence that others are also contributing increases potential contributors' perception that valuable group outcomes will be achieved. For example, many fund-raising campaigns are announced to the public only after half of the funds have already been collected in a quiet period. This way, people who are asked to contribute later will think that the fundraising goal is likely to be reached. Similarly, people do not want to be taken advantage of by contributing while others shirk. Also, people's sense of fairness sometimes creates an obligation to contribute when they see that others have done so, as described in chapter 3. Finally, seeing that others have contributed may establish a descriptive norm that people naturally conform to, as will be discussed in greater detail in chapter 4.

In many cases, there is a tension between showing that other people are contributing and creating a sense that each individual is needed. One way to resolve that tension is to show complementary contributions rather than substitutes. Thus, in an open source community, the software developers could be shown demonstrations of how much effort the documentation writers have expended and vice versa. Another way to resolve the tension is by informing people of others' commitments to contribute that are contingent on their own contributions. For example, challenge grants are commitments by large donors that are contingent on other donors also contributing. They provide social proof of the value of contributing while increasing the importance of the additional contributions rather than substituting for them. Similarly, the site PledgeBank (http://www.pledgebank.com) relies extensively on pledges of contingent contributions, as illustrated in figure 2.14.

Figure 2.14
Sample contingent commitments on PledgeBank (http://www.pledgebank.com).

Design claim 35   People will be more willing to contribute in an online community if they see that others are making complementary or contingent contributions than if they see others making substitute contributions.

7   Conclusion and Implications for Contest Design

Online community designers and managers should consider many options for encouraging needed contributions of effort and other resources to their communities. One approach is to make requests. Another is to increase individuals' expected utility of contributing by enhancing the intrinsic interest of the tasks, by providing extrinsic rewards, or by increasing the expected benefits that will accrue through the individual's contribution to group outcomes. A third approach, taken up in chapter 4, is based on establishing social norms of contributing effort and other resources; it is more often used as a way to limit bad behavior than as a way to encourage valuable contributions. For each of our approaches, we have mined prior research in economics and psychology to formulate design claims, and each of the design claims was illustrated with one or more examples from online community settings.

Often, seemingly simple high-level design decisions require a large number of more detailed design decisions, and these may have a variety of impacts on the community's ability to elicit needed work contributions from members. To illustrate, consider contests, whose configurations have implications for many of the motivational pathways discussed in this chapter.

Contests have attracted a lot of attention recently in the online world. For example, online movie-rental company Netflix (http://www.netflix.com) offered (and eventually awarded) a $1,000,000 prize for any team that could improve the accuracy of predictions about how much consumers would enjoy particular movies based on their prior movie ratings. Statistical software development company MathWorks (http://www.mathworks.com) holds contests to solve difficult programming challenges (MathWorks 2010). The Defense Advanced Research Projects Agency (DARPA) held a $40,000 online contest to spot ten red balloons it had positioned across the United States (Markoff 2009).

Online communities also often conduct contests. For example, Threadless is organized around a continuous contest to have submitted T-shirt designs selected for printing and sale. Winners are selected in part based on votes and reviews from other members. InnoCentive (http://www.innocentive.com) is a company that connects Seekers—companies, academic institutions, and government and nonprofit organizations—with Solvers—engineers, scientists, and business people—to solve

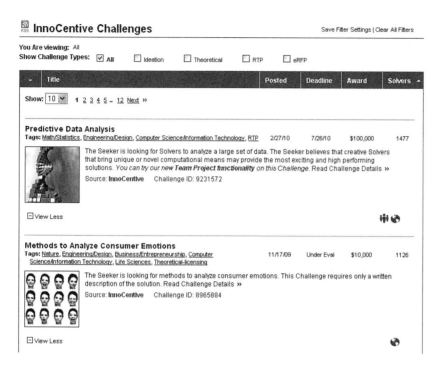

Figure 2.15
Sample of InnoCentive challenges (http://www.innocentive.com).

tough problems posed by the Seekers. Seeker organizations post their challenges on the InnoCentive website and offer registered Solvers significant financial awards for the best solutions. Figure 2.15 shows a sample of some challenge contests.

A contest is a request for a particular kind of contribution. Thus, the first requirement for contest designers is that they think carefully about what tasks they wish to base contests on. Contests that are specific and challenging and that provide intermediate feedback on performance will engage goal-setting motivations well. For example, the Netflix prize had a clear performance target (10 percent improvement in predictions) and clear feedback (an automated site that graded one submission per day). Contests that involve public commentary about work in progress can add the social interaction motivator. A contest also provides comparative feedback: there are winners and losers, so care needs to be taken to avoid demotivating all of the losers. Moreover, contests should be avoided in settings in which a competitive atmosphere would poison the community. The rewards of the contest are likely to induce people to "game the contest." For example, if community votes determine winners, there may be efforts to "stuff the ballot box" with shill votes. Countermeasures may be needed to prevent such gaming. A contest may undermine intrinsic motivations to perform tasks: some people may be more attracted to tasks that they or others will attribute to purer motives rather than trying to win the contest. Finally, contests with entries by groups rather than individuals, thus involving group outcomes, will involve choices about how to make people feel like their contributions are essential to the group outcome.

8 Summary of Design Alternatives

Thus far, we have explored the challenge of encouraging contributions largely through the lens of different motivators, identifying design alternatives that might activate each motivator. We conclude by inverting that focus. We reflect on the design space of alternatives and the ways to make an impact through different regions of that space, as summarized in table 2.4.

The first thing we note is the power of the tools that select, sort, and filter the content in the online community. These tools can help draw people's attention to tasks that are important and that the people are capable of doing. The selective presentation of tasks can create implicit requests for action, and the better targeted those implicit requests are, the more effective they will be.

Next, there are many ways that designers can set the frame through which people will view both implicit and explicit requests, following principles of persuasion. The requests can appear to come from high-status people or people that the recipient likes or is similar to. They can be lengthy and appeal to reasoned cost-benefit analysis, such as dangers to the community, the inability of anyone else to substitute for the individual's unique contributions, or the presence of others' complementary contributions. The requests can also be brief and rely on a context that conveys social proof that contributing to the community is something that everyone does. Deadlines create a frame of urgency and difficult tasks may challenge people to meet goals in order to maintain self-efficacy.

Third, feedback on and record keeping of contributions that people make can be a powerful motivator. Individual feedback, even if provided privately, can act as an informational reward, especially when combined with some kind of goal-setting process. Comparative feedback can evoke social comparisons and a competitive drive for self-enhancement. Making the contribution records public can turn them into a status reward. Performance tracking can also be the basis for privileges or more tangible rewards.

There are two design levers involving the user experience of contributory tasks. Designers can motivate contributions by embedding the contributory acts in a social

Table 2.4
Summary of design alternatives relevant to contribution, ordered by type

Type	Design alternative	Design claim
Selection, sorting, highlighting	Easily visible list of needed contributions	1
	Easy-to-use tools for finding and tracking work that needs to be done	2
	Target requests to people's interests and capabilities	3
Framing	Broadcast requests versus requests to specific people	4
	Simple requests versus lengthy, complex requests	5
	Requests that stress the benefits of contribution	6
	Requests that make fear appeals	7, 8
	Requests issued by high-status people	9
	Requests from people who are attractive, have high status, or the requestor likes, is familiar with, or is similar to	10, 11
	Showing that other people are contributing	12
	Specific and highly challenging requests	13
	Requests with deadlines	14
	Showing the uniqueness of potential contributions	34
	Showing that others have made complementary or contingent contributions	35
Feedback and rewards	Performance feedback	15, 17, 18, 19, 20
	Status, privileges, and tangible rewards	23, 25, 28, 30, 31
	Comparative performance feedback	21, 22
	Task-contingent rewards	24, 26, 30
	Performance-contingent rewards	27
	Nontransparent eligibility criteria	29
Content, tasks, and activities	Combining contribution with social contact with other contributors	16
	Immersive experiences	17
Community structure	Group/community size	33

experience. They can also make the individual experience more immersive. Either lever will make the tasks more intrinsically rewarding.

The community size is a final design lever. On one hand, a larger community reduces the marginal impact of any one member's actions and thus reduces motivations to contribute. On the other hand, larger groups may be able to accomplish more and thus generate more commitment and motivation to contribute.

There are thus many ways to elicit contributions. A few involve changes in the composition or activity of the group. Many involve the addition of record-keeping systems that reflect the contributions of members back to themselves or others. Such record-keeping systems can also be the basis for awarding privileges or more tangible rewards. It is easy to overlook the simplest methods, however. Just asking—either implicitly through selective presentation of tasks or explicitly through requests that are designed around principles of persuasion—may be one of the most effective ways to get things done.

References

Altman, A., and M. Tennenholtz. 2008. Axiomatic Foundations for Ranking Systems. *Journal of Artificial Intelligence Research* 31 (1): 473–495.

Aristotle. [330 BCE] 1953. *The Nicomachean Ethics*. New York: Penguin.

Asvanund, A., K. Clay, R. Krishnan, and M. D. Smith. 2004. An Empirical Analysis of Network Externalities in Peer-to-Peer Music-Sharing Networks. *Information Systems Research* 15 (2): 155–174.

Backstrom, L., D. Huttenlocher, J. Kleinberg, and X. Lan. 2006. Group Formation in Large Social Networks: Membership, Growth, and Evolution. *Proceedings of the 12th ACM SIGKDD International Conference on Knowledge Discovery and Data Mining*, 44–54. Philadelphia: ACM Press.

Bailenson, J. N., S. Iyengar, N. Yee, and N. A. Collins. 2008. Facial Similarity between Voters and Candidates Causes Influence. *Public Opinion Quarterly* 72 (5): 935–961.

Baker, M. J., and G. A. Churchill. 1977. The Impact of Physically Attractive Models on Advertising Evaluations. *Journal of Marketing Research* 14 (4): 538–555.

Bandura, A. 1993. Perceived Self-Efficacy in Cognitive Development and Functioning. *Educational Psychologist* 28 (2): 117–148.

Barabási, A. L., and R. Albert. 1999. Emergence of Scaling in Random Networks. *Science* 286 (5439): 509.

Beenen, Gerard, Kimberly Ling, Xiaoqing Wang, Klarissa Chang, Dan Frankowski, Paul Resnick, and Robert E. Kraut. 2004. Using Social Psychology to Motivate Contributions to Online Communities. In *CSCW '04: Proceedings of the ACM Conference on Computer-Supported Cooperative Work*, 212–221. New York: ACM Press.

Berscheid, Ellen, and Harry T. Reis. 1998. Attraction and Close Relationships. In *The Handbook of Social Psychology*, vol. 2, ed. Daniel T. Gilbert, Susan T. Fiske, and Gardner Lindzey, 193–281. New York: McGraw-Hill.

Blythe, M. A., K. Overbeeke, and A. F. Monk. 2003. *Funology: From Usability to Enjoyment*. Kluwer Academic Pub.

Bugzilla. 2011. Features. http://www.bugzilla.org/features/#searchpage.

Burke, Moira, and Robert E. Kraut. 2008. "Mopping Up: Modeling Wikipedia Promotion Processes." In *CSCW 2008: Proceedings of the ACM Conference on Computer-Supported Cooperative Work*. New York: ACM Press.

Burke, Moira, Robert E. Kraut, and E. Joyce. 2010. Membership Claims and Requests: Some Newcomer Socialization Strategies in Online Communities. *Small Group Research* 4 (1): 4–40.

Byrne, Donn. 1997. An Overview (and Underview) of Research and Theory within the Attraction Paradigm. *Journal of Social and Personal Relationships* 14 (3): 417–431.

Cameron, J., K. M. Banko, and W. D. Pierce. 2001. Pervasive Negative Effects of Rewards on Intrinsic Motivation: The Myth Continues. *Behavior Analyst* 24 (1): 1–44.

Capocci, A., V. D. P. Servedio, F. Colaiori, L. S. Buriol, D. Donato, S. Leonardi, and G. Caldarelli. 2006. Preferential Attachment in the Growth of Social Networks: The Internet Encyclopedia Wikipedia. *Physical Review E: Statistical, Nonlinear, and Soft Matter Physics* 74 (3): 36116.

Carnegie, D. 1936. *How to Win Friends and Influence People*. New York: Simon and Schuster.

Chaiken, S., A. Liberman, and A. H. Eagly. 1989. Heuristic and Systematic Information Processing within and Beyond the Persuasion Context. In *Unintended Thought*, ed. James S. Uleman and John A. Bargh, 212–252. New York: Guilford Press.

Chen, Y., F. M. Harper, J. Konstan, and S. X. Li. 2010. Social Comparisons and Contributions to Online Communities: A Field Experiment on Movielens. *American Economic Review* 100 (4): 1358–1398.

Cialdini, R. B., and N. J. Goldstein. 2004. Social Influence: Compliance and Conformity. *Annual Review of Psychology* 55 (1): 591–621.

Cialdini, Robert B. 2001. *Influence: Science and Practice*. 4th ed. New York: Allyn and Bacon.

Clary, E. G., M. Snyder, R. D. Ridge, J. Copeland, A. A. Stukas, J. Haugen, and P. Miene. 1998. Understanding and Assessing the Motivations of Volunteers: A Functional Approach. *Journal of Personality and Social Psychology* 74:1516–1530.

Collier, Ben, Moira Burke, Niki Kittur, and Robert E. Kraut. 2008. Retrospective Versus Prospective Evidence for Promotion: The Case of Wikipedia. Paper presented at the 2008 Annual Meeting of the Academy of Management, Anaheim, California.

Cosley, Dan, Dan Frankowski, Loren Terveen, and John Riedl. 2007. SuggestBot: Using Intelligent Task Routing to Help People Find Work in Wikipedia." In *Proceedings of the 12th ACM International Conference on Intelligent User Interfaces*. New York: ACM Press.

Csikszentmihalyi, Mihaly. 1997. *Finding Flow: The Psychology of Engagement with Everyday Life.* The Masterminds Series. New York: Basic Books.

Csikszentmihalyi, M., and J. Hunter. 2003. Happiness in Everyday Life: The Uses of Experience Sampling. *Journal of Happiness Studies* 4 (2): 185–199.

Csikszentmihalyi, Mihaly, and Kevin Rathunde. 1993. The Measurement of Flow in Everyday Life: Toward a Theory of Emergent Motivation. In *Nebraska Symposium on Motivation, 1992: Developmental Perspectives on Motivation*, ed. Janis E. Jacobs, 57–97. Lincoln, NE: University of Nebraska Press.

Darley, John M., and Bibb Latané. 1968. Bystander Intervention in Emergencies: Diffusion of Responsibility. *Journal of Personality & Social Psychology* 8 (4): 377–383.

Deci, Edward L., Richard Koestner, and Richard M. Ryan. 1999. A Meta-Analytic Review of Experiments Examining the Effects of Extrinsic Rewards on Intrinsic Motivation. *Psychological Bulletin* 125 (6): 627–668.

Deci, E. L., and R. M. Ryan. 1985. *Intrinsic Motivation and Self-Determination in Human Behavior.* New York: Plenum Press.

Ducheneaut, Nicolas, Nicholas Yee, Eric Nickell, and Robert J. Moore. 2007. The Life and Death of Online Gaming Communities: A Look at Guilds in World of Warcraft. In *CHI '07: Proceedings of the ACM Conference on Human Factors in Computing Systems*, San Jose, California.

Eagly, A. H., R. D. Ashmore, M. G. Makhijni, and L. C. Longo. 1991. What Is Beautiful Is Good, But . . . : A Meta-Analytic Review of Research on the Physical Attractiveness Stereotype. *Psychological Bulletin* 110 (1): 109–128.

Eagly, A. H., and S. Chaiken. 1975. An Attribution Analysis of the Effect of Communicator Characteristics on Opinion Change: The Case of Communicator Attractiveness. *Journal of Personality and Social Psychology* 32 (1): 136–144.

Footprints. 2005. What to Do If You've Got Too Many Votes on Your Hands. Everything2. http://everything2.com/title/What+to+do+if+you%2527ve+got+too+many+votes+on+your+hands.

Frey, B. S., and L. Goette. 1999. *Does Pay Motivate Volunteers?* Working paper. Institute for Empirical Research in Economics, University of Zurich.

Frey, B. S., and R. Jegen. 2001. Motivation Crowding Theory. *Journal of Economic Surveys* 15 (5): 589–611.

Gneezy, U., and A. Rustichini. 2000a. A Fine Is a Price. *Journal of Legal Studies* 29:1–18.

Gneezy, U., and A. Rustichini. 2000b. Pay Enough or Don't Pay at All. *Quarterly Journal of Economics* 115 (3): 791–810.

GNOME Project. 2011. Release Planning. GNOME.org. http://live.gnome.org/ReleasePlanning.

Green, D. P., and A. S. Gerber. 2008. *Get out the Vote: How to Increase Voter Turnout.* Washington, DC: Brookings Institute Press.

Guadagno, R., and R. Cialdini. 2005. Online Persuasion and Compliance: Social Influence on the Internet and Beyond. In *The Social Net: Understanding Human Behavior in Cyberspace*, ed. Yair Maichai-Hamburger, 91–114. New York: Oxford University Press.

Harper, Franklin, Dan Frankowski, Sara Drenner, Yuqing Ren, Sara Kiesler, Loren Terveen, Robert E. Kraut, et al. 2007. Talk amongst Yourselves: Inviting Users to Participate in Online Conversations. In *IUI 2007: Proceedings of the ACM Conference on Intelligent User Interfaces*, 62–71. New York: ACM Press.

Harper, F. M., D. Moy, and J. A. Konstan. 2009. Facts or Friends?: Distinguishing Informational and Conversational Questions in Social Q&A Sites. In *CHI '09: Proceedings of ACM Conference on Human Factors in Computing Systems*. New York: ACM Press.

Henderlong, J., and M. R. Lepper. 2002. The Effects of Praise on Children's Intrinsic Motivation: A Review and Synthesis. *Psychological Bulletin* 128 (5): 774–795.

Jagatic, T. N., N. A. Johnson, M. Jakobsson, and F. Menczer. 2007. Social Phishing. *Communications of the ACM* 50 (10): 94–100.

Jeon, G. Y. J., Y. M. Kim, and Y. Chen. 2010. Re-Examining Price as a Predictor of Answer Quality in an Online Q&A Site. In *CHI 2010: Proceedings of the ACM Conference on Human Factors in Computing Systems*, 325–328. New York: ACM Press.

Kahneman, Daniel, Ed Diener, and Norbert Schwarz, eds. 1999. *Well-Being: The Foundations of Hedonic Psychology*. New York: Russell Sage Foundation.

Karau, S., and K. Williams. 1993. Social Loafing: A Meta-Analytic Review and Theoretical Integration. *Journal of Personality and Social Psychology* 65 (4): 681–706.

Kim, Amy Jo. 2000. *Community Building on the Web: Secret Strategies for Successful Online Communities*. Berkeley, CA: Peachpit Press.

Kittur, A. 2011. Unpublished data.

Kittur, A., E. Chi, B. A. Pendleton, B. Suh, and T. Mytkowicz. 2008. Power of the Few vs. Wisdom of the Crowd: Wikipedia and the Rise of the Bourgeoisie. In *CHI '08: Proceeding of the ACM Conference on Human Factors in Computing Systems*. New York: ACM Press.

Kittur, A., E. H. Chi, and B. Suh. 2008. Crowdsourcing User Studies with Mechanical Turk. In *CHI '08: Proceeding of ACM Conference on Human Factors in Computing Systems*, 453–456. New York: ACM Press.

KJZZ. 2011. Challenge Grants. http://kjzz.org/support/challengegrants.

Krukowski, R. A., J. Harvey-Berino, J. Kolodinsky, R. T. Narsana, and T. P. DeSisto. 2006. Consumers May Not Use or Understand Calorie Labeling in Restaurants. *Journal of the American Dietetic Association* 106 (6): 917–920.

Kubey, Robert, and Mihaly Csikszentmihalyi. 1990. *Television and the Quality of Life: How Viewing Shapes Everyday Experience, Communication*. Hillsdale, NJ: Lawrence Erlbaum Associates.

Lakhani, Karim R., and Eric von Hippel. 2003. How Open Source Software Works: "Free" User-to-User Assistance. *Research Policy* 32 (6): 923–943.

Langer, Ellen J., Arthur Blank, and Benzion Chanowitz. 1978. "The Mindlessness of Ostensibly Thoughtful Action: The Role of "Placebic" Information in Interpersonal Interaction. *Journal of Personality and Social Psychology* 36 (6): 635–642.

Latane, B. 1981. The Psychology of Social Impact. *American Psychologist* 36: 343–356.

Latane, Bibb, and Steve Nida. 1981. Ten Years of Research on Group Size and Helping. *Psychological Bulletin* 89 (2): 308–324.

Lefkowitz, M., R. R. Blake, and J. S. Mouton. 1955. Status Factors in Pedestrian Violation of Traffic Signals. *Journal of Abnormal Psychology* 51 (3): 704–706.

Lepper, M. R., and D. Greene. 1975. Turning Play into Work: Effects of Adult Surveillance and Extrinsic Rewards on Children's Intrinsic Motivation. *Journal of Personality and Social Psychology* 31 (3): 479–486.

Ling, Kimberly, Gerard Beenen, Pamela J. Ludford, Xiaoqing Wang, Klarissa Chang, Xin Li, Dan Cosley, et al. 2005. Using Social Psychology to Motivate Contributions to Online Communities. *Journal of Computer Mediated Communication* 10 (4).

Latham, G. P., and E. A. Locke. 1991. Self-Regulation through Goal Setting. *Organizational Behavior and Human Decision Processes* 50 (2): 212–247.

Locke, E. A., and G. P. Latham. 2002. Building a Practically Useful Theory of Goal Setting and Task Motivation: A 35-Year Odyssey. *American Psychologist* 57 (9): 705–717.

Locke, E. A., G. P. Latham, and M. Erez. 1988. The Determinants of Goal Commitment. *Academy of Management Review* 13 (1): 23–39.

Locke, Edwin A., and Amy L. Kristof. 1996. Volitional Choices in the Goal Achievement Process. In *The Psychology of Action: Linking Cognition and Motivation to Behavior*, ed. Peter M. Gollwitzer and John A. Bargh, 365–384. New York: Guilford Press.

Ludford, P. J., D. Cosley, D. Frankowski, and L. Terveen. 2004. Think Different: Increasing Online Community Participation Using Uniqueness and Group Dissimilarity. In *CHI '04: Proceedings of Human Factors in Computing Systems*, 631–638. New York: ACM Press.

Markey, P. M. 2000. Bystander Intervention in Computer Mediated Communication. *Computers in Human Behavior* 16 (2): 183–188.

Markey, Patrick M., Shannon M. Wells, and Charlotte N. Markey. 2002. Social and Personality Psychology in the Culture of Cyberspace. In *Advances in Psychology Research*, vol. 9, ed. Serge P. Shohov, 94–113. Hauppauge, NY: USishers, Inc.

Markoff, John. 2009. Looking for Balloons and Insights to Online Behavior. *New York Times*, December 1, D2.

Martins, L. L., L. L. Gilson, and M. T. Maynard. 2004. Virtual Teams: What Do We Know and Where Do We Go from Here? *Journal of Management* 30 (6): 805–835.

Mason, W., and D. J. Watts. 2009. Financial Incentives and the Performance of Crowds. In *KDD-HCOMP '09: Human Computation Workshop*, ed. Paul Bennett, Raman Chandrasekar, Max Chickering, Panos Ipeirotis, Edith Law, Anton Mityagin, Foster Provost and Luis von Ahn, 77–85. New York: ACM Press.

MathWorks. 2010. MathWorks Announces Winner of MATLAB Central Online Programming Contest. MathWorks. http://www.mathworks.com/company/pressroom/articles/article42050.html.

Mellström, C., and M. Johannesson. 2008. Crowding Out in Blood Donation: Was Titmuss Right? *Journal of the European Economic Association* 6:845–863.

Meyerson, D., K. E. Weick, and R. M. Kramer. 1996. Swift Trust and Temporary Teams. In *Trust in Organizations: Frontiers of Theory and Research*, eds. Roderick M. Kramer and Tom R. Tyler, 166–195. Thousand Oaks, CA: Sage.

Meyerson, D., K. E. Weick, and R. M. Kramer. 2006. Swift Trust and Temporary Groups. In *Organizational Trust: A Reader*, ed. Roderick M. Kramer, 415–444. Oxford: Oxford University Press.

Milgram, S. 1963. Behavioral Study of Obedience. *Journal of Abnormal and Social Psychology* 67 (4): 371–378.

Miller, N., P. Resnick, and R. Zeckhauser. 2005. Eliciting Honest Feedback: The Peer Prediction Method. *Management Science* 51 (9): 1359–1373.

Moon, J. Y., and L. S. Sproull. 2008. The Role of Feedback in Managing the Internet-Based Volunteer Work Force. *Information Systems Research* 19 (4): 494–515.

Reiss, S. 2004. Multifaceted Nature of Intrinsic Motivation: The Theory of 16 Basic Desires. *Review of General Psychology* 8:179–193.

Resnick, P., R. Zeckhauser, J. Swanson, and K. Lockwood. 2006. The Value of Reputation on eBay: A Controlled Experiment. *Experimental Economics* 9 (2): 79–101.

Roberts, Jeffrey A., Il-Horn Hann, and Sandra A. Slaughter. 2006. Understanding the Motivations, Participation, and Performance of Open Source Software Developers: A Longitudinal Study of the Apache Projects. *Management Science* 52 (7): 984–999.

Salganik, M. J., P. S. Dodds, and D. J. Watts. 2006. Experimental Study of Inequality and Unpredictability in an Artificial Cultural Market. *Science* 311 (5762): 854–856.

Sweetser, P., and P. Wyeth. 2005. Gameflow: A Model for Evaluating Player Enjoyment in Games. *Computers in Entertainment* 3 (3): 1–24.

von Ahn, Luis et al. 2004. ESP Game. http://web.archive.org/web/20050120023005/http://www.espgame.org.

von Ahn, Luis and Laura Dabbish. 2008. Designing Games with a Purpose. *Communications of the ACM* 51 (8): 58–67.

Vroom, V., L. Porter, and E. Lawler. 2005. Expectancy Theories. In *Organizational Behavior 1: Essential Theories of Motivation and Leadership*, ed. John B. Miner, 94–113. Armonk, NY: ME Sharpe.

Vroom, V. H. 1995. *Work and Motivation*. San Francisco: Jossey-Bass.

White, Robert W. 1959. Motivation Reconsidered: The Concept of Competence. *Psychological Review* 66 (5): 297–333.

Wikipedia. 2010. Category: Aviation articles by quality. http://en.wikipedia.org/wiki/Category:Aviation_articles_by_quality.

Wikipedia. 2011a. Wikipedia: Administrators. http://en.wikipedia.org/wiki/Wikipedia:Administrators.

Wikipedia. 2011b. Wikipedia: Community portal. http://en.wikipedia.org/wiki/Wikipedia:Community_portal#Todo.

Wikipedia. 2011c. Wikipedia: Version 1.0 Editorial Team/Assessment. http://en.wikipedia.org/wiki/Wikipedia:Version_1.0_Editorial_Team/Assessment#Grades.

Wilson, E. J., and D. L. Sherrell. 1993. Source Effects in Communication and Persuasion Research: A Meta-Analysis of Effect Size. *Journal of the Academy of Marketing Science* 21 (2): 101–112.

Wilson, J. M., S. G. Straus, and B. McEvily. 2006. All in Due Time: The Development of Trust in Computer-Mediated and Face-to-Face Teams. *Organizational Behavior and Human Decision Processes* 99 (1): 16–33.

Witte, K., and M. Allen. 2000. A Meta-Analysis of Fear Appeals: Implications for Effective Public Health Campaigns. *Health Education & Behavior* 27 (5): 591.

Zhu, H., R. E. Kraut, and A. Kittur. In press. Organizing without Formal Organization: Group Identification, Goal Setting, and Social Modeling in Directing Online Production. In *CSCW 2012: Proceedings of the ACM Conference on Computer-Supported Cooperative Work*. New York: ACM Press.

3 Encouraging Commitment in Online Communities

Yuqing Ren, Robert E. Kraut, Sara Kiesler, and Paul Resnick

Community designers can draw from theories of commitment to make design decisions that influence whether and how people will become committed to a community. Commitment is harder to achieve than a flow (or trickle) of visitors, but for most online communities, commitment is crucial. Committed members work harder, say more, do more, and stick with a community after it becomes established. They care enough to help with community activities and to sustain the group through problems. Committed members are those most likely to provide the content that others value, such as answers to people's questions in technical and health support groups (Blanchard and Markus 2004; Fisher et al. 2006; Rodgers and Chen 2005), code in open source projects (Mockus et al. 2002), and edits in Wikipedia (Kittur et al. 2007). They are more likely to exercise voice, demanding change and improvement when dissatisfied, than to exit (Hirschman 1970).

Indeed, commitment is a building block for solving challenges described in the remaining chapters of this book. Commitment to the community makes people care enough to respond to and to enforce norms of appropriate behavior (Smith, McLaughlin, and Osborne 1997); thus, commitment is a building block for regulation, as discussed in chapter 4. Commitment to the community makes people motivated to exert effort behind the scenes to keep the online community going (Butler et al. 2007), and commitment is thus a building block for motivating contributions, as discussed in chapter 2. And commitment to a new community leads people to overlook growing pains or outside alternatives during a community startup phase, as discussed in chapter 6.

Social scientists have devoted years of research to discovering the difference between commitment and flight. Commitment to a group, organization, or community can be based on feelings of closeness to other individuals in the group, feelings of strong identification with the group or its main interest, feelings of obligation to the community, or even the costs or risks of leaving the community (Festinger, Schachter, and Back 1950; Allen and Meyer 1990; Prentice, Miller, and Lightdale 1994). Our knowledge about why and how people become committed to communities has its roots in a post–World War II theory of groups, *field theory*. Field theory was invented by Kurt Lewin, a psychologist who emigrated to the United States when the Nazis took over Germany. Lewin was fascinated by group dynamics. He wondered what caused people to follow a leader, form cohesive units, and develop loyalty as members of a group. Lewin rejected the idea that people's loyalty to a group is based only in their individual personality or personal history. He observed that in the right environment, a group could attract very strong group feelings from all sorts of people. Field theory looked to the forces in people's environment (or *field*) that attracted them to a group and kept them loyal (Lewin 1951).

Lewin and his graduate students—including Leon Festinger, Bernice Lott, and Roger Barker—devised ingenious laboratory experiments on group dynamics as well as methods for measuring people's behavior in naturally formed groups. They discovered many patterns that occurred over and over again, such as the *principle of proximity*, that is, the way in which simply living or working near people initiates a sense of identity and group feelings with those nearby. They discovered various ways that a group's autocratic or democratic management changed the group's dynamics. Lewin's passion for empiricism and insights into how people experienced the group environment were major influences on the science of commitment that exists today.

Hundreds of studies later, theories of group psychology distinguish among three types of commitment that we can apply to online communities: (1) affective commitment, based on feelings of closeness and attachment to a group or members of the group, (2) normative commitment, based on feelings of rightness or felt obligation to the group, and (3) need-based or continuance commitment, based on an incentive structure in the group and alternatives available to members from outside that increase the net costs of leaving the group (Allen and Meyer 1996; Meyer and Allen 1991; Meyer, Stanley, Herscovitch, and Topolnytsky 2002). These forces combine to determine an individual's decision to continue membership in a group. According to this perspective, a committed person has one or more of three subjective experiences in the group: wanting to continue as a member of the group (*affective commitment*), feeling he or she ought to continue (*normative commitment*), and feeling that he or she must continue—or at least is better off in the group than out of it (*need-based commitment*). The rest of this chapter discusses how online community design influences each of these experiences.

1 Affective Commitment: Wanting to Stay

Social psychologists who study groups distinguish between two bases for the affective commitment that people have toward groups. Identity-based affective commitment is a feeling of being part of the community and helping to fulfill its mission. In contrast, bond-based affective commitment is feeling close to individual members of the group. The person who feels attached to the community as a whole will want to be part of the community and to further its purpose. The person who feels attached to specific people in the group may be more committed to these close individuals than to the group as a whole. Of course, people can feel both types of attachment in the same community, but these feelings stem from different causes, so for purposes of design, we need to distinguish between identity-based commitment and bonds-based commitment. Even though both identity-based commitment and bond-based commitment lead people to feel loyalty to their community, stay with it longer, and contribute more to it, we highlight the distinction between the two commitments here because these types of commitment have some distinct causes and consequences and implications for how designers can encourage and exploit the two types of commitment (Ren, Kraut, and Kiesler 2007).

The distinction between identity-based commitment and bonds-based commitment can be traced to Festinger, Schachter, and Back's (1950) theory of group cohesiveness. They identified two ways in which commitment to a group is formed: through the attractiveness of the group or through the attractiveness of individual group members. Commitment because of the attractiveness of the group as a whole became the focus of social identity theory (Hogg and Abrams 1988). This theory emphasizes how sharing a common social category with others—such as gender, race, geographic location, nationality, hobby, or political party—causes people to categorize themselves as a rightful member of a group and to identify with it. Thus, a woman in the information technology industry in Pittsburgh might feel connected to an online community for women in computer science such as Systers (http://anitaborg.org/initiatives/systers), the Pittsburgh Steelers football team (http://www.steelersfever.com), or the Facebook (http://www.facebook.com) alumni group for her alma mater. Having members with identity-based commitment has many interesting effects on an online community. For example, when members feel strong identity-based commitment, they may stick with the group even if their friends leave.

Interpersonal-based commitment is the type that forms when members of a community become psychologically close to some others in the community and feel bonds of mutual liking. This form of commitment is based upon idiosyncratic preferences and is firmly dependent on close personal interaction (Lott and Lott 1965). Friendship groups are vulnerable to member turnover because friends can leave as a clique (e.g., Krackhardt and Porter 1986).

The differences in attitudes of those who feel identity-based commitment versus bonds-based commitment have been demonstrated in empirical studies. Prentice, Miller, and Lightdale (1994) classified topic-based university student groups such as art groups, school newspapers, and sports teams as common identity groups. These are groups to which students belong more because of the activities they do than because of individual friendship. The researchers differentiated these groups from friendship-based, common bond groups such as fraternities and eating clubs. Members of the common identity groups reported feeling more attached to their group as a whole than to their fellow group members, whereas members of the common bond groups reported feeling attached both to the group as a whole and to group members. The authors argued that "the two perspectives might . . . be viewed as describing two separable processes in the development and maintenance of groups, either of which might dominate under a given set of circumstances" (Prentice, Miller, and Lightdale 1994, 490).

The distinction between identity-based and bonds-based attachment also has been made in studies of online communities (e.g., Postmes, Spears, and Lea 2000; Sassenberg and Postmes 2002; Utz 2003; Utz and Sassenberg 2002). In general, common identity in the online context implies that members feel a commitment to the online community's purpose or topic. The following message sent to a new member of the email list colon@listserv.acor.org, a cancer support group, illustrates this identity-based attachment: "Welcome to the list nobody wants to join. While it really stinks to have to be here, you'll find a wealth of experience. You'll find many excellent suggestions and tips prior to surgery in the archives" (Jan. 11, 2003). A common bond in the online context, in contrast, implies that members feel socially or emotionally attached to particular members of the online community. The following quote from a thank-you note from one member of the cancer support group to another illustrates the closeness of the bond developed between the two: "Thanks for your kind words – YOU are an inspiration to me . . . ! I still remember that you were the first to respond to my first post on this list, more than 4+ years ago."

Encouraging Identity-Based Commitment

Social identity theory states that identification with a social group or category is a very powerful force that can keep people in a group. Identity-based commitment occurs when people feel connected to the group as a whole or its purposes, incorporating aspects of the group into their personal sense of identity or the way they think about themselves. For instance, people can become strongly committed to the Sierra Club, the National Rifle Association, a movie discussion group, a software development project, or a blog community without knowing others in these organizations.

When people identify with a community or group as a whole, they tend to perceive other members in the group as interchangeable (Turner 1985). One consequence is that their commitment to the group is stable in the face of turnover in membership, at least in comparison to bond-based attachment (Abrams, Ando, and Hinkle 1998).

Design Claim 1   Instilling identity-based attachment leads people to continue their participation in the group in the face of membership turnover.

Postmes, Spears, and Lea (2002) compared the influence of group norms in common-identity versus common-bond online groups. They found that attitudes were more similar in common-identity groups than in common-bond groups. Sassenberg (2002) found similar results using a behavioral measure of compliance to group norms. Research so far indicates that online community members who feel identity-based attachment to the community will be more likely to conform with group norms than those who feel bonds-based attachment to the community. As discussed in chapter 4, group norms are especially valuable in regulating misbehavior.

Design Claim 2   Identity-based commitment makes people more compliant with norms than does bonds-based commitment.

Similarity can create identity-based attachment. (It can also lead to bonds-based attachment, as described in the next section.) Similar member background such as profession, school, locality, race, ethnicity, occupation, and age—especially when these attributes are shared among people who are otherwise strangers—may lead to common category membership. Further, people tend to dislike groups whose members are heterogeneous, and these groups experience high turnover, especially when conflict arises (Williams and O'Reily 1998). Similarity of background or expertise leads to common identity most when the similarity is relevant to the group's context and functioning (Cartwright 1968). Recruiting similar people into a community or clustering existing members so that similar people can form subgroups will increase identity-based commitment to a community. ACOR, the Association of Cancer Online Resources (http://www.acor.org), a support community for patients with cancer and their caregivers, offers support through more than 150 distinct mailing lists for people suffering with different types of cancer. In contrast, the support groups at the Cancer Support Community are heterogeneous in terms of diagnosis (Cancer Support Community 2010). The research literature indicates that because of its specificity, the ACOR approach will be more successful in developing identity-based commitment. Communities can let individuals select into homogeneous subgroups, as ACOR does, or can use statistical techniques to assign people with similar attributes together. For example, Harper and his colleagues developed efficient algorithms to subdivide a larger community into approximately equally sized clusters of participants who are similar to each other (Harper, Sen, and Frankowski 2007).

Design Claim 3   Recruiting or clustering those who are similar to each other into homogeneous groups fosters identity-based commitment to a community.

Community designers can encourage people to identify with an online community or with subgroups within it by highlighting members' common social characteristics and by drawing boundaries around this category. In traditional groups, people categorize themselves on criteria such as gender, home town, religion, job, academic major, leisure interests, organizational membership, or political values that they care about deeply. However, a social category does not have to be meaningful in the larger population or even important to the individual to induce identification with a group. Tajfel et al. (1971) demonstrated that randomly labeling a group with an arbitrary label ("overestimators" or "underestimators") could activate common identity in research groups, even if people did not know others in their group. This phenomenon has been replicated many times in laboratory experiments and online. One can induce social identity by categorizing people with fictional personality traits (Amichai-Hamburger 2005), team uniforms (Dabbish and Kraut 2008; Worchel et al. 1998), or arbitrary group names (Michinov, Michinov, and Toczek-Capelle 2004; Ren et al. Under review).

Design Claim 4   Providing a collection of individuals with a name or other indicator that they are members of a common group increases their identity-based commitment to the community.

In most online communities, people have come to the group based on their shared interests in a particular domain (e.g., Perl programming), topic (e.g., autism, greyhound rescue, the Steelers), or common cause (e.g., building a free online encyclopedia). People are attracted to the community to the extent that they identify with the domain, topics, or causes on which the community is based and find them meaningful. They value their membership because affiliation with the community enables them to affiliate with the topic or cause, access and share useful information, or contribute toward a meaningful cause.

In chapter 6, we argue for the importance of a clearly articulated scope with a clever name and tagline because it helps to define a community's niche and differentiate it from competitors. In chapter 5, we argue that a clearly articulated scope helps potential new members assess whether they fit well. Here, we point out a third benefit of a clear scope, especially one that is articulated through a distinctive name: it induces identity-based attachment. Good examples are Wikipedia (http://www.wikipedia.org), "the free encyclopedia that anyone can edit"; Dogster (http://www.dogster.com), "for the love of dog"; or Hattrick (http://www.hattrick.org), a multiplayer fantasy European football (i.e., soccer) site whose motto is "Everybody deserves their own football team."

Design Claim 5   A name and tagline that articulate the shared interests of a community's members increases the members' identity-based commitment to the community.

However, as the community grows, members may start to cluster into natural subgroups. Subgroup identity can be as powerful as whole-community identity in eliciting commitment in its own right and can enhance commitment to the whole community (Zaccaro and Dobbins 1989). To further this process, designers can actively promote or create subgroups. Kittur and Kraut (2008) found that when Wikipedia editors joined a named subproject within the larger encyclopedia, they increased their overall editing in the encyclopedia and directed more of their editing to work that was within the scope of the project they joined. In an experiment in an online setting, Beenen and colleagues (2004) increased contributions to an online movie site by telling people that they were members of the fictitious "Explorers' group" and then assigning the Explorers a group goal. In actuality, the Explorers were a group in name only: "members" never found out who the other members were or communicated with them. Yet people assigned to the Explorers and given a group goal logged in 10 percent more and contributed 65 percent more movie ratings than those who were given a commensurate individual goal but not assigned to a group.

Design Claim 6   Creating named groups within a larger online community increases members' commitment to the subgroups.

In most cases, identity-based attachment to subgroups complements rather than supplants commitment to the community as a whole. Ren and colleagues (Under review) created subgroups among people with similar movie tastes within a movie community, giving them arbitrary names like the Eagles or Gorillas. Creating these subgroups increased members' self-reported commitment to the overall community and increased their frequency of visiting the site over a six-month period by 44 percent compared to other participants who were not assigned to subgroups.

Sometimes, however, the subgroup identity can be stronger than the group identity, and when there is a conflict between the two, the subgroup identity may prevail. Guilds are the named and persistent teams that players in many massively multiplayer online role-playing games join to accomplish difficult tasks and to engage in social interaction. Amy Jo Kim chronicles the "Group That Got Away," a guild in Meridian 59 (http://www.meridian59.com) that left en mass to play another game (2000, 319).

Design Claim 7   Creating named groups within a larger online community increases members' commitment to the community as a whole, as long as the subgroup identity is not in conflict with the larger community identity.

A common fate, goal, purpose, or task can enhance identity-based commitment (Sherif et al. 1961). Common fate is the perception that all community members either benefit from the same reward or suffer the same costs (Michinov, Michinov, and Toczek-Capelle 2004; Worchel, et al. 1998). For example, if a community is in danger of closing because its servers cost too much to run or it is in danger of being overwhelmed by spam messages, everyone will be affected. A common goal in a community is a goal that the group as a whole can attain, such as a high score, ratings, or some tangible outcome. When a guild in a multiplayer game goes on a quest, the players will either all succeed or all fail together. Guilds in online game environments often identify their group goals in their profiles. The guild Lords of Eternity in World of Warcraft declares, "Our goal is to defeat current raid content and work towards the heroic hard modes and meta-achievements as efficiently as quickly as possible. We strive for five-night progress on a three-night schedule." Like many guilds, Lords of Eternity tallies its achievements and progress toward its goals on the guild website. Another example of common goals can be seen in political subgroups on Facebook, whose members share the mission of getting their candidate elected. During the 2008 presidential campaign, the John McCain Facebook Challenge group expressed a mission was to "Get every Republican on Facebook to go to John McCain's Facebook page . . . and become a supporter," and the largest Facebook group for Barack Obama put a goal right into its title: "One Million Strong for Barack."

Advocacy communities and production-oriented communities such as open source software or open content repositories often articulate a common purpose that generates identity-based commitment, even when the purpose is not translated into quantifiable goals against which progress can be tracked. Bryant, Forte, and Bruckman (2005) describe how the common goal of developing the world's best encyclopedia led readers of Wikipedia to become "Wikipedians," active contributors committed to the community. As three Wikipedia participants remarked:

"I really got inspired by the idea [of the Wikipedia]. I'd say a lot of what hooked me was the community aspect and knowing that I was contributing something that was going to be around for a while."

"I believe in the integrity of the project. I want to see it succeed, especially the articles people will look up."

"It has a dedicated task and it's producing a product . . . at least with the Wikipedia [versus Usenet and the like] you can convince yourself you're doing something to benefit mankind."

Design Claim 8 Making community fate, goals, or purpose explicit increases members' identity-based commitment to the community.

A joint task is one that involves inputs from all members. Groups whose members are cooperatively interdependent because they have a joint task tend to be more cohesive and committed to the group (Gaertner et al. 2000; Worchel et al. 1998). Indeed, assigning people a difficult, interdependent task is a powerful way to overcome even strongly felt animosity among subgroups within a community (Sherif et al. 1961). Interdependence through a joint task fosters not only identification with the community as a whole, but also normative commitment. Members come to feel that the group depends on them and will actually use and benefit from their work. Many online communities try to foster the perception of task interdependence. Guilds in massively multiplayer games that take on difficult tasks, like receiving good loot from killing powerful monsters, are creating identity-based commitment. WikiProjects do the same thing when they attempt to improve one of their articles to "featured" class so that it appears on the Wikipedia home page.

Design Claim 9 Providing community members with interdependent tasks increases their identity-based commitment to the community and reduces conflict among subgroups.

Ingroups imply outgroups. By definition, being in a group means that there are one or more contrasting groups that one is not in. People who define and categorize themselves as members of a group often compare themselves with those in other groups (Hogg and Terry 2000). Making these contrasts explicit can intensify people's identification and commitment. In experiments, researchers have divided participants into two or more groups to highlight group boundaries, which intensified participants' identification with their own group (Postmes et al. 2001; Rogers and Lea 2005; Worchel et al. 1998). The outgroup did not have to be physically or even virtually present to elicit intergroup comparisons and ingroup commitment (Utz 2003; Yuki et al. 2005).

In online communities, designers can encourage members to attend to group boundaries and their identification with the group by increasing members' awareness of a different outgroup. Blizzard, the developer and operator of World of Warcraft, built comparisons at the core of their game by requiring that each player become a member of one of two opposing factions, the Alliance or the Horde (see figure 3.1). Also, guild-level rankings in World of Warcraft and other group-oriented online games increase identification by highlighting the presence and threat of an outgroup. More informally, posters on the Apache FAQ page (http://www.apache.org) compare the speed, performance, and market share of the Apache server with those of other commercial servers, fostering the common identity of those who work on Apache software. The Wikipedia project site uses a similar technique by highlighting competition with other encyclopedias. The Wikipedia entry on Wikipedia itself contains may references to the *Encyclopedia Britannica*, and a 2006 version of the article noted that Jimmy Wales, the founder of the project, "intends for Wikipedia ultimately to achieve a 'Britannica or better' level of quality and be published in print" (Wikipedia 2006).

Figure 3.1
The Horde and the Alliance in World of Warcraft.

Design Claim 10   Highlighting an outgroup (and competing with it) increases members' identity-based commitment.

The power of an outgroup to intensify group commitment is enhanced when people already feel connected to the group and perceive their group to be threatened (Hutchison et al. 2006). The surge of American patriotism after the September 11, 2001, terrorist attacks on the World Trade Center and Pentagon illustrate this point. Some citizens reacted with anger, and some with sadness, but both groups increased their commitment to the United States. Research suggests that failure or threat is especially likely to strengthen commitment to a community when it comes from external sources or can be overcome with collective effort from group members (Lott and Lott 1965), which is why many political leaders prefer to blame other countries for problems in their own.

Community designers must be careful when highlighting a threat to a group because the effects of threat can backfire. In general, research shows that people prefer to stay with a group that is successful or has high status (Hinds et al. 2000). Moreover, core and peripheral members may respond to failure and threats differently—core members may strengthen their attachment to justify the additional effort they exert to overcome the difficulty, whereas peripheral members are more likely to leave the group when it is an option (Festinger et al. 1956). When leaving is not an option, in the face of threat, both core and peripheral members identify more strongly with the group (Ouwerkerk, de Gilder, and de Vries 2000; Ethier and Deaux 1994).

Design Claim 11   Emphasizing a threat to the group, especially from an external source, increases the identity-based commitment among core members but may undermine the commitment of more peripheral members.

Generally, anonymity of individual group members fosters community identity and strong group norms because it deemphasizes individual distinctions. By contrast, making personal identity salient or individual members identifiable decreases identity-based attachment, although it may increase bond-based attachment (Postmes et al. 2005; Postmes et al. 2001; Sassenberg 2002; Sassenberg et al. 2003; Sassenberg and Postmes 2002).

Design Claim 12   Making group members anonymous will foster identity-based commitment.

Bonds-Based Commitment

People also become committed to a group by developing connections to the people who constitute it. In this case, their commitment is not necessarily to the group as a whole but to the other members they know and like. Gross and Martin (1952, 553–554), in their discussion of bonds-based commitment, talked about group cohesiveness as "the resistance of a group to disruptive forces" and stated that such cohesiveness is associated with the strength of the relational bonds among group members (see also Lott and Lott 1965).

In order to build bonds-based commitment, online community designers can either try to recruit members who are already friends, or build new friendships. Backstrom and colleagues (2006) showed that the likelihood that a person would join a group in the social networking and blogging site LiveJournal (http://www.livejournal.com) increased with the number of current members of that group they were linked to (see figure 3.2). Leskovec and colleagues (2010) showed empirical support for this prediction in both Epinions (http://www.epinions.com) and Wikipedia. People who like the same things tend to form direct links between each other, although balance theory is not the only explanation for this result (Leskovec, Huttenlocher, and Kleinberg 2010).

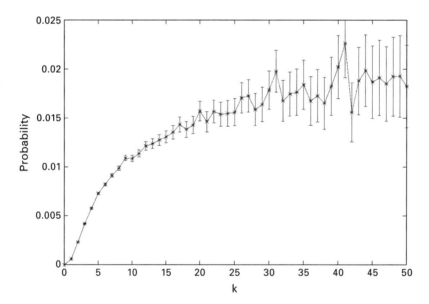

Figure 3.2

The probability p of joining a LiveJournal (http://www.livejournal.com) community as a function of the number of friends k already in the community.

Source: From Backstrom et al. 2006.

Many online communities recruit among friends, for example, by mining current members' email lists. Facebook suggests "friending" people with common network ties. Doing so not only increases the likelihood that a newcomer will join a community because it is frequented by friends, but it also increases the mutual bonds among community members.

Design Claim 13   Recruiting participants who have existing social ties to be members of the community increases their bonds-based commitment to the community.

The next best thing to building a site with people who have existing friendships may be to encourage friends of friends to join. Research on psychological balance demonstrates that people who are both friends of a friend are likely to know and like each other and their friendship to a common partner is likely to lead to their becoming friends as well (Curry and Emerson 1970; Heider 1958). The logic behind these findings guides many social network sites. For example, LinkedIn (http://www.linkedin.com) provides tools for people to see friends of their friends (see figure 3.3); Facebook also encourages peoples to connect with friends' friends.

Design Claim 14   Facilitating interaction with "friends of friends" can enhance bonds-based commitment.

Network Statistics

Here you see statistics about your network, including how many users you can reach through your connections. Your network grows every time you add a connection — **invite connections now.**

Your Network of Trusted Professionals

You are at the center of your network. Your connections can introduce you to 131,400+ professionals — here's how your network breaks down:

1 **Your Connections** Your trusted friends and colleagues		**18**
2 **Two degrees away** Friends of friends; each connected to one of your connections		**1,600+**
3 **Three degrees away** Reach these users through a friend and one of their friends		**129,700+**
Total users you can contact through an Introduction		**131,400+**

2,756 new people in your network since September 23

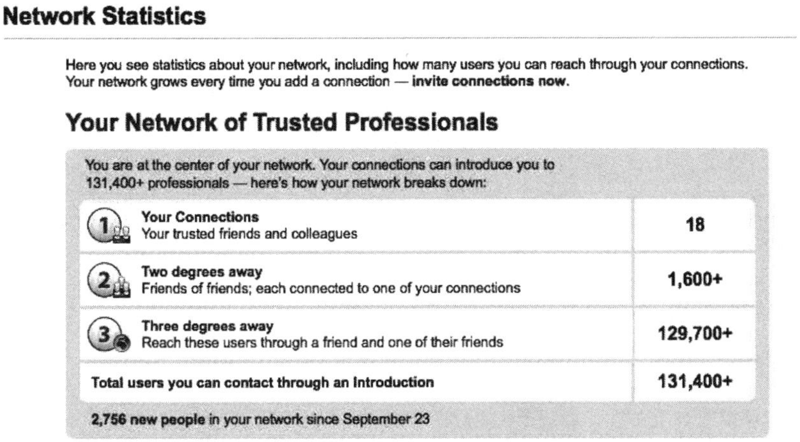

Figure 3.3
LinkedIn's tools for seeing friends of friends (http://www.linkedin.com).

Another technique to foster bond-based attachment is to build features into the community that build and maintain new friendships among participants. Although psychologists have extensive theories about the factors that lead to interpersonal attachment (see Berscheid and Reis 1998 for a review), here we concentrate on factors that can be influenced by community designers and that have robust effects on interpersonal attraction: repeated exposure, similarity, social interaction, and self-disclosure.

Milgram's discussion of the familiar stranger (1977) suggests that merely seeing other people in an online group repeatedly, even without communicating with them, may be a precursor to forming a personal attachment to them. When applied to the challenge of increasing bond-based attachment to an online group, the implication is that designers should make the identity and behavior of the participants in the group known to each other. Seeing pictures of other people or even their avatars increases attraction, especially when people are just getting to know each other (Walther, Slovacek, and Tidwell 2001; Yee, Bailenson, and Rickertsen 2007)). Providing a stream of fresh information about the others enhances this familiarity effect.

Facebook does an excellent job of leveraging these principles. The home pages of many groups feature photos of a selected set of members, recent discussion posts, and photos, videos, and links shared by members. Even applications on social networking sites are often surrounded by pictures of users and fans. These images increase the likelihood that people will form an attachment to another member, even if they originally joined just to play a single-person game. (See figure 3.4, showing the use of pictures of people to build attachment to the single-player game Bejeweled.)

Figure 3.4
Use of friends' pictures to increase commitment to the Bejeweled game.
Source: From http://www.popcap.com.

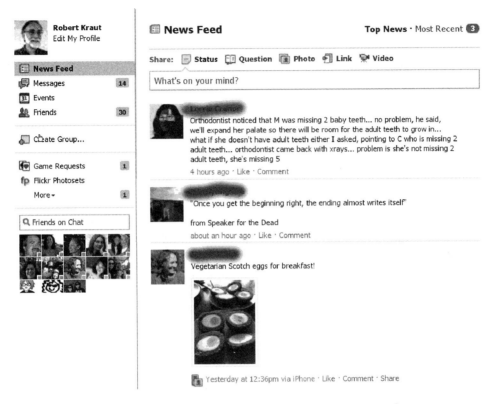

Figure 3.5
Facebook news feed (http://www.facebook.com).

Facebook incorporates the familiarity principle into its core features, such as its "what's on your mind" newsfeed features (see figure 3.5). The typical homepage on Facebook shows frequently updated information and a constant stream of comments, videos, and activities of friends, continually reminding users of their friends' existence. Through these techniques, Facebook helps to build and maintain the bonds among friends and through this route keeps users attached to Facebook itself.

Design Claim 15   Displaying photos and information about individual members and their recent activities promotes bonds-based commitment

Social interaction is the primary basis for building and maintaining social bonds. The experience and familiarity we gain through social interaction with others increases our liking for them (Homans 1958). Conversing with people and doing things with them provides opportunities for people to get better acquainted and to build trust. As the frequency of interaction increases, their liking for one another also increases (Festinger, Schachter, and Back 1950; Newcomb 1961). Some studies have discovered an approximately linear relationship between liking of group members in small groups and frequency of interaction with them (Lott and Lott 1965).

In online communities, members' frequency of interaction with others is a major determinant of the extent to which they build relationships with one another (McKenna, Green, and Gleason 2002). More exchanges among community members— through private messages, for example—provide opportunities for members to create liking and trust. Utz's (2003) study of MUD (Multi-User Dungeon game) players showed that the longer their involvement in the MUD and the more real-world contact they had with other members, the more of a bond they felt with other players. Interpersonal connections become even stronger if members have a sense of virtual copresence or a subjective feeling of being together with others (Slater et al. 2000).

Design Claim 16 Providing opportunities for members to engage in personal conversation increases bonds-based commitment in online communities.

In offline environments, physical proximity causes clustering of interpersonal interactions. That is, people nearby are likely to interact often. For example, students tend to form closer friendships with those they sit next to in class (Back, Schmukle, and Egloff 2008; Sykes, Larntz, and Fox 1976) and are more likely to marry people who live in the same neighborhood or go to the same school (Bossard 1932). Proximity is a reliable predictor of interaction, interpersonal attraction, and close bonds in many natural settings, such as boarding schools, college classes, large corporations, and housing projects (Newcomb 1961).

Online, there is no physical proximity to enforce clustering. Thus, it would be possible, in principle, for interaction pairings to be generated uniformly. Without sufficient repeat exposure, people would be less likely to form interpersonal bonds. Thus, designers need to create other mechanisms that generate clustering of interpersonal interactions.

One way to create clustering is to create within the larger online community *neighborhoods*, in which a subset of the population can congregate. Online role-playing games such as World of Warcraft use the consistency of the server on which an individual subscriber plays the game as a device to ensure that the subscriber repeatedly runs into others assigned to the same server. In addition, these games typically have special communication features that alert players when other members

asbruckman

Amy Bruckman
@peggyorenstein my dad the orthopedist says no
trampolines, no bunk beds, no motorcycles
1:43 PM Jan 15th

grammarnerd

Moira Burke | Pittsburgh
RT @ipeirotis: @grammarnerd This version is much
better: http://archive.nyu.edu/handle/2451/29799
12:36 PM Jan 14th

jrgalegher

Jolene Galegher
@feedly Don't see how to make new mini toolbar
appear. Have downloaded new version and checked
yes in preferences. What else should I do?
4:10 AM Nov 9th, 2010

Figure 3.6
Following people on Twitter (http://twitter.com).

of their guilds are online and that allow them to broadcast communication exclusively to guildmates wherever they are in the sprawling virtual words they inhabit. The "rooms" in a traditional MUD serve a similar function to increase repeated interaction among a subset of users. So, too, do separate topical threads or rooms in forum-based communities and tag-based groups in the photo-sharing site Flickr (http://www.flicker.com).

Content feeds based on already articulated relationships also serve to generate repeated exposure and thus bonds-based attachment. For example, following people on Twitter (http://www.twitter.com; see figure 3.6), friending them on Facebook, or subscribing to RSS feeds of their blogs leads to repeated exposure to their posts. Content feeds, however, can strengthen only ties that are already strong enough to have been explicitly articulated.

More sophisticated technical mechanisms are also possible that need not rely on spatial metaphors, bounded groups, or previously articulated links. For example, software could automatically monitor which people someone has interacted with previously and highlight or sort new content in a way that makes people more aware of content from those with whom they had previous interacted. Although such mechanisms have been proposed (Resnick et al. 2005) and implemented in research prototype systems (Ren et al. In press), we are not aware of any commercial online communities that have deployed them.

Design Claim 17   Places, spaces, groups, friend feeds, and other mechanisms that increase the likelihood that people will encounter the same people they have previously encountered increase bonds-based commitment.

Self-disclosure—the exchange of personally revealing information—is both a cause and a consequence of interpersonal attraction. People not only like others about whom they know more, but also like others to whom they reveal more (Collins and Miller 1994). Accordingly, members of online communities are more likely to form relationships if they have opportunities to self-disclose and learn personal details about each other. Opportunities for self-disclosure shift attention from the group as a whole to individual members (Postmes, Spears, and Lea 2002; Sassenberg and Postmes 2002).

Personal information not only increases people's liking for each other, but also their likelihood of interacting. It increases their ability to choose people they will trust and like. Knowing information about potential communication partners opens up topics of conversation. Knowing others' home towns and current residences enables members to identify those who live in the same region. They can then become real-life contacts. Likewise, the inclusion of contact information such as phone numbers, email addresses, and instant messaging (IM) accounts enable members to connect and interact through other channels.

In online communities, any communication channel permits self-disclosure, but more structured technical and social features can encourage it. The most common feature is a user profile with personal information such as photos, background, experience, and interests, which helps members know more about the people in the group. Many discussion-based communities include a forum or thread dedicated to self-introductions.

In a field experiment with a movie discussion community, we found that members with access to individual profiles with information about others' history, location, and movie preferences visited the site more frequently than those that did not have access to individual profiles (Ren et al. Under review). For individual profiles to lead to commitment, however, designers need to be thoughtful about what fields to include and what information to encourage. For example, at professional social networking sites like LinkedIn, it is more meaningful to include fields related to people's professional experiences such as education and work experiences, whereas at a movie discussion site, it is more meaningful to include fields related to people's movie tastes. The health support group Breastcancer.org (http://www.breastcancer.org) encourages participants to enter information about their diagnosis and medication in their profiles, and this information is revealed in automatically generated signature lines added to their discussion posts.

There is evidence that personal information such as pictures promotes interpersonal bonds among people who have not yet interacted (Walther, Slovacek, and Tidwell 2001). Compared to strangers, people who were able to see another's online Facebook profile before conversing caused the conversation partners to like them more by engaging in more effective small talk and self-presentation (Hancock, Toma, and Fenner 2008).

Design Claim 18   Providing user profile pages and flexibility in personalizing them increases self-disclosure and interpersonal liking and thus bonds-based commitment.

Somewhat paradoxically, revelation of personal information may actually increase if the most personal information—one's true identity—is hidden. For example, in the fitness and weight-loss community SparkPeople (http://www.sparkpeople.com), many people use pseudonyms rather than their real names, but reveal quite detailed information, including daily weigh-ins. In their blogs, they also reveal their struggles and difficulties as well as triumphs. In interviews, people who used Facebook and SparkPeople said that they felt much more comfortable revealing detailed personal information on SparkPeople, where that information could not be associated with real-life identities or easily found by their real-life friends (Newman et al. 2011).

Design Claim 19   Allowing participation under a pseudonym will increase self-disclosure and interpersonal liking and thus bond-based commitment in communities where sensitive information is shared.

One surprising finding from the psychological research is that people like others to whom they disclose personal information (Collins and Miller 1994). In offline conversation, people can identify people in the conversation with them and therefore know to whom they have revealed information about themselves. This awareness of the audience isn't necessarily the case online, especially when people are posting their communication publicly in blogs, discussion forums, and the like. Because the effect of disclosure may be stronger when people know whom they have disclosed to, an automatic report about who has read one's profile or a social convention of leaving a "guest book" entry or comment could enhance feelings of closeness from self-disclosures.

Although personal profiles permit people to learn about others, they do not facilitate self-disclosure as a communicative act—a decision to reveal particular information to particular others in particular circumstances. It is likely that the decision to reveal oneself to others is what makes one like them and not just their possession of the information. Moreover, the act of sharing generates a reciprocal obligation to self-disclose that may not be triggered by simply seeing information in someone's user profile.

Some online community moderators have a deft touch for asking questions that lead members to self-disclosure. For example, in a forum for people participating in a pedometer-based walking program, a moderator posted a question about fitting in exercise during a sister's graduation weekend. Perhaps because it was self-revelatory, it led to self-revelatory responses from other group members (Resnick, Janney, Buis, and Richardson 2010). Other, more structured ice-breaker activities and games are possible. For example, in our research group, we once added an ice-breaker game to our online profile pages. Each person posted three interesting personal stories, only two of which were true, and everyone had to vote on which was the tall tale (see figure 3.7). People revealed personal stories that had not come up in our usual interactions. One intriguing option that we have not yet seen would be to have people interactively choose profile fields to reveal to particular others. This approach might be especially effective in an online dating site, for which each act of disclosure would signal a continuing interest based on the interactions up to that point.

Design Claim 20   Active self-disclosure with visible responses leads to more bonds-based commitment than does passive disclosure.

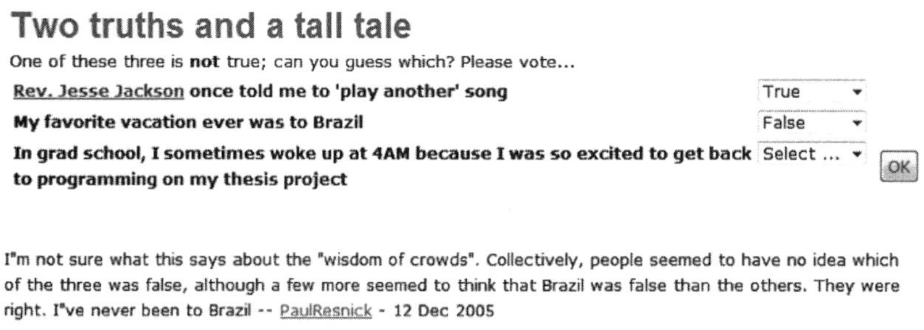

Two truths and a tall tale

One of these three is **not** true; can you guess which? Please vote...

<u>Rev. Jesse Jackson</u> once told me to 'play another' song	True ▾
My favorite vacation ever was to Brazil	False ▾
In grad school, I sometimes woke up at 4AM because I was so excited to get back to programming on my thesis project	Select ... ▾ OK

I"m not sure what this says about the "wisdom of crowds". Collectively, people seemed to have no idea which of the three was false, although a few more seemed to think that Brazil was false than the others. They were right. I"ve never been to Brazil -- <u>PaulResnick</u> - 12 Dec 2005

Figure 3.7
An online ice breaker.
Source: Paul Resnick.

Just as people like groups whose focus seems similar to their own interests and goals, they also like other people who are similar to them in preferences, attitudes, and values, and they are likely to work or interact with similar others. In his pioneering longitudinal study of college students, Newcomb (1961) found that high interpersonal attraction developed among those who initially had attitudes in common. Experimenters frequently manipulate similarity in dyads to increase their liking of each other (e.g., Byrne 1997). Typically, participants completed a personality and friendship questionnaire and were told that they were assigned to a group whose members probably would become close friends (Hogg and Turner 1985; Postmes et al. 2001). When similarity was presented as the sharing of unique personal attributes between the self and other members (e.g., unique movie tastes or personal preferences for celebrities), it triggered bonds-based attachment with other group members who could not necessarily be replaced with any other group member (Hogg 1992, 100). Figure 3.8 shows a "compatibility" report comparing the movie tastes of two members of the MovieLens site (http://movielens .umn.edu).

Design Claim 21   Highlighting interpersonal similarity fosters closeness among individual members and bonds-based commitment.

Reducing Repelling Forces that Undercut Personal Commitment

People feel more committed to smaller groups than to larger ones (Carron and Spink 1995). One reason is that interpersonal bonds are difficult to maintain with a larger number of individuals. When people relate to others, they devote time and attention to them. Thus, people are able to maintain only a limited number of strong ties with others. The anthropologist Robin Dunbar (1993) proposed that humans evolved having a cognitive limit on the number of individuals with whom they could maintain close, stable relationships. According to Dunbar, this limit is approximately 150 people. (Of course, this number varies across different people. Extraverts know more people than do introverts, and they spend more time communicating with others, seeking out relationships, and engaging in social events.) Even though social networking sites have greatly expanded social circles and reduced the cost of maintaining weak ties (Granovetter 1973), these sites do not necessarily increase the number of close ties people have. As of March 2011 the average active Facebook user maintained ties to 130 friends on the site (Facebook 2011).

Another reason for the preference for smaller groups is that when many people are communicating, each pair may not have enough repeated interactions for bonds to

Movie Compatibility Report

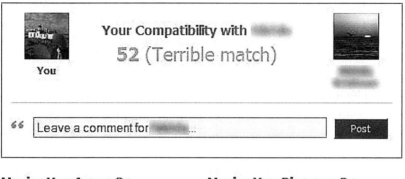

Movies You Agree On

Love Actually
You: ☆☆☆☆☆
▓▓▓: ☆☆☆☆☆
Match: Exact

The Chronicles of Narnia: The Lion, The Witch and The Wardrobe
You: ☆☆☆☆☆
▓▓▓: ☆☆☆☆☆
Match: Exact

Movies You Disagree On

Spider-Man
You: ☆☆☆☆☆
▓▓▓: ☆☆☆☆☆
Match: Very Bad

Charlie and the Chocolate Factory
You: ☆☆☆☆☆
▓▓▓: ☆☆☆☆☆
Match: Bad

Figure 3.8
Compatibility report for MovieLens (http://movielens.umn.edu).
Source: Ren et al. In press.

form unless, as indicated previously, some mechanism is in place to cluster people. For example, the Internet Movie Database site (http://www.imdb.com) hosts messages from thousands of people. Posts arrive in such quantity that a new post remains on the front page for less than twenty minutes. Under these conditions, it will be difficult for pairs of people to come across each other frequently enough to form bonds. In one analysis of a large sample of Usenet newsgroups, the more messages posted in a group during a month, the smaller the proportion was of posters who returned in the subsequent month (Jones, Ravid, and Rafaeli 2002). Similar phenomena occurred in synchronous communication channels, such as Internet Relay Chat (Raban, Moldovan and Jones 2010). Although email-based LISTSERV communities attracted more new members per month if they were larger, those with more traffic had higher turnover rates (Butler 2001).

Larger community size and communication volume do not limit identity-based commitment in the same way. Identity-based commitment does not depend on repeated communication or on personal ties with specific other members. In principle, with identity-based commitment, other individual members are interchangeable representatives of the community. This reasoning is consistent with a field experiment in a movie discussion community in which the use of algorithms to repeatedly expose individuals to movie groups led to a significant increase in member commitment to these groups, whereas the same algorithm to repeatedly expose individuals to familiar others did not have such an effect (Ren et al. Under review).

Design Claim 22 Large communities with a large volume of communication reduce bonds-based commitment unless some means of clustering communications is used.

Most people feel psychologically safer when a community's membership is more homogeneous than when there is a diversity of member backgrounds and views. Membership diversity can lead people to feel that there is less coherence of community purpose than they would like and a fracturing of community communications. The growth of a community can lead to more diversity of membership than the community had in the past, if only because new cohorts are younger and have different concerns than older members have. Such diversity of membership attributes can threaten people's sense of common social identity and lead to turnover in groups (Williams and O'Reilly 1998). New cohorts are likely to differ from old-timers not just in their personal attributes, but also in attitude and motivation. For example, when Systers—a LISTSERV for mostly university-based female computer scientists—started recruiting many younger women, the newcomers were more likely to be employed by industry and to be interested in success in that nonacademic domain. Many older Systers left, and a new effort had to be mounted to keep the community going (Jeffries, Kiesler, Goetz, and Sproull 2000; Spertus, Jeffries, and Sie 2001).

Design Claim 23 Diversity of members' interest in an online community can drive away members, especially those with identity-based commitment.

A special problem of diversity among member interests is the management of off-topic conversations, that is, conversations that are irrelevant to the main purpose of a community, such as political comments or revelations about personal experiences in a movie discussion group.

Community designers must decide whether to try to keep discussion on topic or to let it stray. (Chapter 4, on regulating behavior, discusses ways to keep discussion on topic, if that is desired.) Many topical discussion communities discourage off-topic communication. For example, the introductory message to the JoBlo Movie Network (http://www.joblo.com) emphatically states, "Our board is for MOVIE TALK only. If you bring personal issues up on our board, you will be banned. If you discuss your ex-girlfriend, you will be banned. If you announce your comings and goings or gossip about so-and-so, you will be banned. . . . This is . . . not a place for you to discuss your personal life or boo-hoo about how your lover just broke up with you" (JoBlo Movie Network 2005). On the other hand, on the AOL message board X-Fileaholics, whose nominal topic was discussion of the TV show *The X-Files*, it was normal for members to discuss everything but the show, including favorite music, other television shows or movies, humorous polls, unpleasant events, and recent achievements. Newcomers, in an official welcome message posted within the joining thread, are encouraged to "act demented [because] it runs in the family" (Honeycutt 2005). One study found that 36 percent of Q&A threads on Yahoo! Answers were "conversational" rather than "informational" (Harper, Moy, and Konstan 2009).

A community's policy to either constrain or open up content has trade-offs that designers need to address. Off-topic conversation, by distracting from the unifying feature around which people identify, reduces identity-based commitment. But it can help a subset of individuals discover additional common interests beyond those defining the community and allows them to share personal information, thus enhancing interpersonal bonds. The kind of self-disclosing conversation that we previously argued builds bonds is off-topic. An empirical investigation confirmed that restricting conversation to specific domains makes a site less appealing to people who want to know individuals better, whereas a policy of encouraging off-topic conversation can undercut identity-based attachment (Postmes, Spears, and Lea 2002).

Design Claim 24   Off-topic communication reduces identity-based commitment and increases bonds-based commitment to an online community.

Sometimes a community that forms for one purpose will temporarily shift its focus due to special circumstances. For example, following the Pacific Tsunami in December 2004, a knitting hobbyist who went by the screen name of Yarn Harlot started publicizing a Knitters Without Borders challenge in knitting groups she participated in. She has tracked more than $1 million in donations to the organization Doctors Without Borders (Yarn Harlot 2010). Around the time of an election, some groups that normally do not discuss politics take up this topic.

We have coined the phrase "going off-topic together" to describe situations where something that would normally be considered off-topic (such as fundraising or politics) becomes on-topic—at least temporarily. Going off-topic together can build both bonds-based and identity-based attachment. Bonds can form because people see another side of each other that was not revealed in previous interactions. Whereas previously identification with the group was primarily through identification with the topic, going off-topic together creates an opportunity to identify with the group of people separately from the topic. Although we use the term "online community" broadly in this book, in classes we find that some students prefer to reserve that term for groups with affective ties and multiplex relationships that are akin to close-knit geographic neighborhoods. Given that distinction, going off-topic together is one marker for when a group has truly become a community.

Design Claim 25   Going off-topic together can increase both bonds-based commitment and identity-based commitment.

A flexible approach to off-topic conversation could serve both needs for identity and bonds-based commitment. A computer simulation model by Ren and Kraut (Under review) suggests that personalized filtering, in which people in a community are exposed only to communications that match their interests, will lead to greater commitment than regimes that do not moderate communications at all or moderate it so that off-topic messages are removed for all community members. According to the simulation, these positive effects of personalization seem to be strongest in larger groups or groups encompassing a diversity of topics and support both identity-based and bond-based attachment.

A number of approaches can be used to personalize the content of a site. The simplest is to provide separate areas for on-topic and off-topic conversation. Many topic-based communities, such as the movie web forum Rotten Tomatoes (http://www.rottentomatoes.com/vine) and the CNET site for equipment reviews (http://reviews.cnet.com), provide separate off-topic discussion boards. The Off Topic Discussion forum on the Rotten Tomatoes site and the off-topic Speakeasy forum on the CNET site are highly popular. Having separate areas for off-topic conversation has the drawback of segregating it, so that it is seen only by those who explicitly decide to view it. People may need to already have bonds-based connections with others in order to want to visit the place where bonds can form.

Online communities can also identify off-topic content without segregating it by, for example, using tags. When traffic expanded in the online soap opera newsgroup rec.arts.tv.soap, people started complaining about messages that were unrelated to soap operas. Some members proposed marking messages that were not directly related to soap operas by "TAN" (for tangent) in the subject line so that members who were not interested could easily ignore them while preserving them in the group for those who were interested (Baym 1999). Information retrieval techniques (Foltz and Dumais 1992; Landauer, Foltz, and Laham 1998) can be used to estimate how similar a focal message is to other messages recently posted on a forum, and readers can decide to view messages of varying relevance. An administrator of an identity-based site could set a threshold to visually differentiate the off-topic content or make it more difficult for newcomers to see.

Design Claim 26   Personalized filters, which differentially expose members to communications that match their personal interests, reduce the negative effects that off-topic communication has on identity-based commitment.

2   Normative Commitment

Normative commitment is a feeling that one has obligations to the community, to be loyal and act on its behalf. Many factors can contribute to creating normative commitment to a community. Here we consider three: commitment to the cause, others' normative commitment, and reciprocity.

One reason people feel a normative commitment to an online community is because they have a preexisting commitment to the purpose that the community serves. This feeling may be a stronger resource for generating commitment in advocacy communities and production communities than in hobbyist communities. In open source software (OSS) development projects, having common values about the importance of sharing and helping each other predicts group members' commitment to the group, which in turn predicts the effort they contribute (Stewart and Gosain 2006). But even in hobbyist and support-oriented communities, people may feel a strong commitment to advancing the hobby or helping people suffering from a particular health condition or life circumstance. To translate normative commitment to a community's purpose into commitment to the community itself, the community will need to keep its purpose salient throughout its activities and show that it is having some success in achieving its purpose. For example, open source communities would want to highlight statistics and stories about the usefulness of the software and the importance of the next version's planned improvements.

Design Claim 27 Highlighting a community's purpose and successes at achieving that purpose can translate members' commitment to the purpose into normative commitment to the community.

Another reason people accept a normative obligation is if there is a shared norm about that obligation. For people who are unsure whether something is a shared norm, social proof that others believe it is can help resolve the uncertainty. In other chapters, we point out the power of social proof about the value of joining a community and about norms of good behavior. Here, we argue that demonstrations that others feel a normative obligation to the community are a powerful way to spread that feeling of obligation. Narrative testimonials are powerful ways for a community to indicate the obligations that members have toward the group. Raymond points out the moral obligation of participants in OSS development projects to help each other: "To behave like a hacker, you have to believe that the thinking time of other hackers is precious— so much so that it's almost a moral duty for you to share information, solve problems and then give the solutions away just so other hackers can solve new problems instead of having to perpetually re-address old ones" (Raymond 2003). These types of testimonials, whether offered by community leaders or regular members during the regular course of conversation, are likely to make explicit obligations towards the community.

Design Claim 28 Testimonials about people's normative commitment to the community increase others' normative commitment.

A third generator of normative commitment is the widely shared norm of reciprocity. Reciprocity is one of the strongest and most universal of human norms (Gouldner 1960). People think that those who have given should get something back and that those who have received should give something back. Researchers have distinguished between direct reciprocity, in which people feel obliged to help particular others who have helped them, and indirect or generalized reciprocity, in which people feel obliged to "pay it forward" to somebody, even if it's not the specific person who helped them (e.g., Nowak and Sigmund 2005; Yamagishi and Kiyonari 2000). These feelings of obligation are one reason that cancer survivors or caregivers in online support groups continue to participate, offering advice to others, even after their own cancer is in remission or after the person they had cared for has died. Researchers have argued that this indirect reciprocity is critical to the development of human groups and society more generally and that people will forego their own economically rational self-interest to punish those who don't reciprocate (Fehr and Gächter 2000).

Designers can prime the norm itself, making it more salient, by using language such as "reciprocity," "obligation," "giving back," "paying it forward," or terms that otherwise activate altruistic motivations. Psychologists have found that priming— even unrelated to the specific context of action—can have surprisingly strong effects on people's actions in laboratory settings. For example, compared with subjects in a word recognition experiment who saw neutral words, those who saw words with a positive religious tone (e.g., heaven, faith) were willing to distribute twice as many pamphlets to help a charity (Pichon, Boccato, and Saroglou 2007).

Design Claim 29   Priming norms of reciprocity by highlighting concepts that get people to think of their normative obligations increases normative commitment to an online community.

More directly, designers can highlight what individual members have received from a community. An experiment on MovieLens movie recommendation site gave people feedback about their "net benefit" score, estimated from their previous activity. Subjects told that they had above-average net benefit scores were more likely to select additional activities that benefited the community rather than benefiting themselves (Chen, Harper, Konstan, and Li 2010). Similarly, rather than providing a strict accounting, designers can highlight more general benefits that members receive. For example, when soliciting support for Wikipedia in 2010, Wikipedia founder Jimmy Wales emphasized generalized reciprocity when he said that "It stopped being just a website a long time ago. For many of us, most of us, Wikipedia has become an indispensable part of our daily lives" (Wikimedia Foundation 2010).

Design Claim 30   Showing people what they have received from the community increases their normative commitment to it.

Perhaps even more powerfully, designers can also invoke a direct reciprocity norm. For example, the open source project Drupal has a bottleneck on incorporating new code contributions: members are contributing code faster than it is getting reviewed. This bottleneck is frustrating to the coders whose patches are left in limbo, and it is inefficient for the project. We are working with the community to design a feature that will highlight code patches awaiting review that were written by people who have previously reviewed your code. We expect that people will feel an obligation to help others who have helped them and will thus spend more time reviewing their code.

Design Claim 31 Highlighting opportunities to return favors to specific others increases normative commitment to the community.

3 Needs-Based Commitment

Needs-based (or *continuance*) *commitment* refers to attachment to an online community that depends on the net benefits that people experience from the community. According to needs-based models of social cohesion, people stay in a group only as long as they perceive the group and other members as being attractive and instrumental in fulfilling their personal goals (Homans 1961). When net benefits are positive, members predict that they get sufficient rewards to warrant the time, effort, and frustration they spend on the community. When benefits are low and the costs of leaving the community are low, commitment will also be low. Although most research suggests that the direct benefits people personally receive from the community are not the only source of commitment, most members do care about these benefits. These benefits include information, social support, companionship, and reputation, among others (Ridings and Gefen 2004). The importance of these benefits vary across both different types of communities and different individuals. For example, Ridings and Gefen (2004) asked almost four hundred participants in twenty-seven online discussion groups why they joined. As seen in figure 3.9, members of most types of communities valued getting information. However, health and wellness groups were relatively less interested in information and more interested in social support, and those in many hobby groups were disproportionately interested in companionship. In a discussion group for legal professionals, many members' commitment levels derived from perceptions that participation in the group would lead to enhanced reputation (Wasko and Faraj 2005). In many gaming communities, such as World of Warcraft, members' commitment derives from the challenge and fun the game provides as well as the opportunities to hang out online with friends (Ducheneaut and Moore 2004; Ducheneaut et al. 2006a, 2006b). Owners and moderators of voluntary discussion groups tend to be less motivated by getting information and more by interest in friendships and other social benefits (Butler et al. 2007). As we discuss in more detail in chapter 5,

Community type	Motivational category			
	Info. exchange	Companionship	Social support	Fun
Professional	53%	11%	22%	10%
Health	38%	17%	38%	4%
Hobby	52%	29%	2%	9%
Sports	58%	18%	4%	11%
Pets	48%	36%	3%	9%
Other interests	53%	26%	0%	9%
Overall percentage	50%	24%	11%	9%
Total N (reasons)	257	124	56	45

Figure 3.9
Reasons for joining different types of discussion groups.
Source: From Ridings and Gefen 2004.

participants who do not perceive the community as providing the benefits they desire are especially likely to leave.

Designing experiences that meet members' needs requires knowing what these needs are. If you don't know what members want, then it is hard to satisfy them. Sometimes the members' motivations are not obvious, even to insiders. For example, even though most developers who participate in OSS development projects do so for instrumental reasons (e.g., to get better code or a better job) or for identity-based ones (e.g., to feel part of a social movement that they consider ideologically important), some also want to develop friendship with other developers they meet online. To satisfy this need, some open source development projects host "code fests" at which developers can meet each other and form relationships. For example, the GNOME software project—a graphic desktop for the Linux operating system—hosts the GNOME Users' and Developers' European Conference, whose motto is "Meet, Plan, Party!" (see figure 3.10).

Some research has developed validated survey instruments and other techniques to assess the motivations of volunteers in conventional organizations, such as altruism, career, or social contact (Clary et al. 1998). Matching recruiting materials and experiences with the reasons that particular people volunteer increases their willingness to join, their satisfaction, and their willingness to continue in the organization (e.g., Crain, Omoto, and Snyder 1998; Williamson, Snyder, and Omoto 2000). These general survey instruments can be adapted to use in assessing motivations in online

MEET PLAN PARTY!

The GNOME Conference 2008

Figure 3.10
Logo for the GNOME Users' and Developers' European Conference (http://guadec
.expectnation.com).

communities. In addition, others have developed survey instruments to assess motivations for participating in online communities, such as open source development
projects (Ghosh 2005) and Wikipedia (Nov 2007). By understanding the profile of
motivations of participants in an online community, designers are better able to craft
experiences that match these motivations.

Design Claim 32   Providing participants with experiences that meet their motivations
for participating in the community increases their needs-based commitment to the
community.

As with interpersonal relationships, the net benefit that people need to achieve to
decide to stay in a community depends upon the alternatives that are available
(Thibaut and Kelley 1986). Simply put, people will be satisfied with fewer benefits and
will tolerate more some of the unpleasantness associated with any group membership
when they have fewer alternatives available. For example, employees are less likely to
quit their company when there are fewer equivalent jobs available (e.g., Hulin,
Roznowski, and Hachiya 1985). In the online world, people stay in Usenet groups
longer if there are fewer Usenet groups in the same ecological niche or serving similar
content (Wang 2007). The implication is that to build needs-based commitment, an
online community must meet the needs of its members more when it has many competitors than when it has few. Although community designers cannot control the

Figure 3.11
Showing links to competitors reduces needs-based commitment.
Source: From http://www.advancedbreastcancercommunity.org.

competition, they can raise or lower the visibility of these alternatives when members are actually participating in the community. For example, including links to competing communities increases the ease with which a member can defect by clicking competitors' sites. Wang (2007) found that the more cross-posted messages (i.e., messages that also were posted to competitor groups) that were displayed in a Usenet group during a month, the more quickly members defected from the group. Some online communities do post links to competitors. For example, the Advanced Breast Cancer Community (http://advancedbreastcancercommunity.org) posts links to its main competitors, including CancerCare and the Cancer Support Group, but those other groups do not (see figure 3.11).

Design Claim 33   Showing information about other communities in the same ecological niche reduces needs-based commitment.

Some online communities try to supplement the psychological benefits members derive from being in the community with specific benefits for those who participate and contribute. For example, Epinions offers profit sharing, Slashdot (http://slashdot.org) offers recognition, and the crowdfunding site 8-Bit Funding (http://8bitfunding.com) offers T-shirts and other swag that symbolize that the wearer has made a meaningful contribution (Tedjamulia et al. 2005). Many sites offer ratings, status, or points to reward contributions. According to some researchers, these direct rewards for contributions can rob people of the intangible pleasure they get from contributing and their sense of identity with the community (Deci, Koestner, and Ryan 1999), but other researchers believe that direct rewards can usefully supplement psychological incentives (Cameron, Banko, and Pierce 2001; Eisenberger, Pierce, and Cameron 1999). We consider the trade-offs of offering direct rewards in chapter 2 on contributions.

A variant of needs-based commitment, sometimes referred to as *lock-in* (Shapiro and Varian 1999), occurs when members accumulate community-specific assets that retain their value only through continued participation in the community. These assets can include resources in the community, both people and content. For example, the friends one is connected to on Facebook are an asset, in that they produce value when one continues to use Facebook. The status and privileges that one has accumulated are also community-specific assets. For example, in World of Warcraft, players can buy a mount to transport them rapidly across the landscape only after they have completed enough quests to reach level 20 or 40 in the game and have accumulated the price of the mount in in-game gold. Once acquired, the steed is a community-specific asset. One's historical data with a site can also be an asset. For example, the ratings one has entered in a recommender site, like Netflix (http://www.netflix.com) or MovieLens, or the financial information that one has posted in financial sites like Vanguard (http://vanguard.com) or Intuit (http://www.intuit.com), are also community-specific assets that improve service quality. In a study of turnover in customers' use of online brokerage sites, Chen and Hitt (2003) showed that established customers were less likely to leave than were new customers when sites provided relationship services, which included personalizing data, reusing customer data to facilitate future transactions, using customer data to support business or personal needs such as filing taxes, and allowing a customer to customize the site. A controlled experiment on eBay showed that an established history or reputation was an asset worth about 8 percent in additional revenue for a seller (Resnick et al. 2006).

To generate needs-based commitment, an asset must be difficult for a member to transfer to a new community. Chapter 6 discusses the advantages of importing resources of various kinds from external sources. To keep members locked in, however, it can be helpful to limit exports. For example, Facebook makes it difficult to export friends lists or accumulated personal information such as profiles. Netflix does not provide a history of one's ratings in a format that is easily exported to other movie recommendation sites. Similarly, because Amazon does not allow a customer to export his or her own purchase and shopping history, only Amazon can provide useful customization based on that history. Similarly, eBay has not participated in open reputation systems that would allow reputations built on eBay to be used (and put at risk) on other sites.

Skills are an interesting special case of a community-specific asset. Members learn technical skills at operating a community's software, as well as social skills of effective participation. To the extent that the software, modes of interaction, and social etiquette are unique, learning them creates a community-specific asset. Indeed, Chen and Hitt's study (2003) showed more turnover in sites that were easier to use, presumably because ease of use reduced customers' investments in learning how to use the site.

To generate needs-based commitment, an asset must also be difficult to transfer to another member. Otherwise, a member would be able to sell assets when leaving the community, and the assets would not create the same lock-in. Thus, developers of multiplayer games put policies in place to depreciate the value of these accumulated assets if players leave. Selling in-game currency, loot, or other virtual items for real money is against the terms of service for most multiplayer games. In 2006, Blizzard banned or suspended more than fifteen thousand World of Warcraft accounts for selling virtual property (Dobson 2006). The operators of some multiplayer games also persuaded eBay to delist auctions for virtual items (Slashdot 2007).

Design Claim 34   Making it difficult for members to export assets or transfer them to other members increases needs-based commitment.

Members' community-specific investments that cannot be recouped when they leave can generate commitment even when those investments are merely sunk costs that do not create any value going forward. For example, even if a member has not yet found the upper levels of a multiplayer game particularly enjoyable, the member may remain committed to the game because of the extraordinary efforts he or she has already invested to reach those levels.

From a purely rational cost-benefit analysis, such sunk costs, once incurred, should have no influence on members' choices. Yet they frequently do (Arkes and Blumer 1985). One reason is heuristic processing: when it is not clear how valuable an asset will be, a larger investment made to acquire it can be interpreted as an indicator of its value. A second reason is cognitive dissonance (Festinger 1957): people need to believe that their previous investment decisions were good ones, so they make further choices that could result in justifying the earlier ones. Arkes and Hutzel (2000) demonstrated in lab experiments that at least some of the reason that sunk costs influence future choices comes from the latter effect. Consistent with this explanation, experimental research demonstrated that people like groups more if they have to endure a severe initiation process to join them than if they undergo a milder initiation (Aronson and Mills 1959; Gerard and Mathewson 1966). According to Aronson, people come to like things for which they suffer because this is the only way in which they can reconcile their views of themselves as intelligent people with the actions they have performed (Aronson 1997).

In an online community context, Drenner, Sen, and Terveen (2008) introduced effortful barriers to MovieLens. All users of the site were asked to rate five movies in order to let the site know about their movie tastes. Some new registrants were in addition required to apply twenty-five descriptive text tags to movies before they were allowed to register (Tag 25), some had to apply five tags (Tag 5), some were simply shown the tagging interface but not required to tag any movies (Tag 0), and some were not even shown the tagging interface (Control). As expected, as the amount of work required in the registration process increased, the proportion of registrants who completed the full registration process declined, from 90 percent completion in the control condition to 85 percent in the Tag 0 condition, 80 percent in the Tag 5 condition, and 69 percent in the Tag 25 condition. More interestingly, new users who were assigned to do more work as part of their registration process were four times more likely to provide tags once they become members and contributed more than ten times the number of tags as those in the control condition. The effects were only partly the result of the greater motivation of those who overcome the barriers. As the light-colored bars in figure 3.12 illustrate, the effects of the entry barriers were strong even

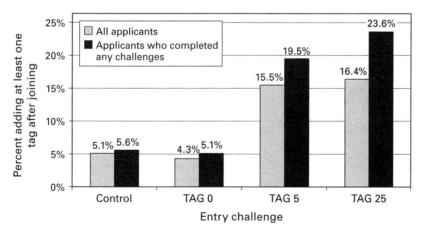

Figure 3.12

Effects of entry barriers on post-entry contributions to MovieLens (http://movielens.umn.edu). *Source*: From Drenner, Sen, and Terveen 2008.

when considering all potential members exposed to them, not just those who surmounted them.

In an open source community, requiring programmers to complete many bug fixes before earning full membership privileges has two effects. In chapter 5, we point out that such a requirement serves as a screening mechanism, weeding out potential members who are not a good fit for the open source project. But it may also act as an initiation rite, increasing the commitment of those who attain those privileges. Of course, any requirement of time investment is a double-edged sword: it increases commitment (and fit) among those who make the investment but may drive away some potentially valuable members who are unwilling to make the initial investment.

Design Claim 35 Entry barriers and other opportunities for members to make community-specific investments, even if they are merely sunk costs that do not create valuable assets, increase needs-based commitment.

4 Summary of Design Alternatives

As in other chapters, we conclude with a table of the design alternatives considered in this chapter and an index to the design claims that discuss their implications (table 3.1). The chapter examined the challenge of increasing commitment to online communities. Commitment enhances a community's ability to surmount other challenges—getting newcomers to stick around, getting members to contribute, and encouraging community members to behave appropriately. Scholars have identified several types of commitment to groups and organizations: affective commitment

Table 3.1
Summary of design alternatives relevant to commitment, ordered by type

Type	Design alternative	Design claim
Community structure	Recruiting or clustering those who are similar to each other into homogeneous groups	3
	Creating named groups within a larger online community	6, 7
	Recruiting participants who have existing social ties	13
	Large communities with a large volume of communication	22
	Diversity of members' interest in an online community	23
	Making group members anonymous	12
	Participation under a pseudonym	19

Table 3.1

(continued)

Type	Design alternative	Design claim
Content, tasks, and activities	Providing interdependent tasks	9
	Facilitating interaction with "friends of friends"	14
	Displaying photos and information about individual members and their recent activities	15
	Providing opportunities for members to engage in personal conversation	16
	Providing user profile pages and flexibility in personalizing them	18
	Active self-disclosure with visible response	20
	Off-topic communication	24, 25
	Making it difficult for members to export assets or transfer them to other members	34
	Creating opportunities for members to make community-specific investments	35
Selection, sorting, and filtering	Places, spaces, groups, friend feeds, and other mechanisms that increase the likelihood that people will encounter the same people they have previously encountered	17
	Personalized filters that differentially expose members to communications that match their personal interests	26
	Highlighting opportunities to return favors to specific others	31
Presentation and framing	Providing a collection of individuals with a name or other indicator that they are members of a common group	4
	A name and tagline that articulate the shared interests of a community's members	5
	Making community fate, goals, or purpose explicit	8
	Highlighting an outgroup (and competing with it)	10
	Emphasizing a threat to the group, especially from an external source	11
	Highlighting interpersonal similarity	21
	Highlighting a community's purpose and successes at achieving that purpose	27
	Testimonials about people's normative commitment to the community	28
	Priming norms of reciprocity by highlighting concepts that get people to think of their normative obligations	29
	Showing people what they have received from the community	30
	Showing information about other communities in the same ecological niche	33

based on common identity or interpersonal bonds, normative commitment based on feelings of obligation, and needs-based commitment based on perceived benefits of staying and the costs of leaving. We conclude by inverting that focus. We reflect on the design space of alternatives and the ways in which alternative designs affect the various types of commitment.

Some design alternatives affect the membership composition of the community or its substructure. For example, diversity of members' interests can reduce identity-based commitment; one way to combat this effect is to limit diversity, either in the group as a whole or in subgroups. Recruiting participants based on existing ties can also enhance bonds-based commitment. Larger communities with a large volume of communication limit bonds-based commitment; subdividing into smaller groups can help. Naming those subgroups can help generate identity-based commitment as well.

The next group of design levers changes the content or activities that are available in the online community. Interdependent tasks can enhance identity-based commitment. Interactions with "friends of friends" can enhance bonds-based commitment, as can displaying photos and profile pages and offering opportunities for personal conversation and personal information revelation. Off-topic conversation can enhance bonds-based commitment but interfere with identity-based commitment. Activities that generate community-specific assets that are difficult to export or transfer can build needs-based commitment.

Designers can also build commitment through clever selection, sorting, and filtering of the content that is displayed to people. Creating repeated exposure to the same people helps build bonds-based commitment, and limiting exposure to content not meeting individual topical interests enhances identity-based commitment. Selectively presenting opportunities to reciprocate favors to others induces normative commitment.

We identified one way in which controlling access to information can be used to affect commitment: Anonymity may actually increase identity-based commitment. Of course, it is also likely to interfere with bonds-based commitment. We suspect that only in very special cases will anonymity have a net positive impact on member commitment to a community.

Finally, there is a variety of ways in which designers can influence commitment without making changes to the structure or technological features of a community, just by changing the contextual information that provides a frame through which members understand what they are doing. To generate identity-based commitment, a name and tagline can help, as can articulating the community's goals or purpose or highlighting an outgroup to compete with or an external threat. Highlighting interpersonal similarities among members can build bonds-based commitment. Normative commitment can be enhanced through highlighting the importance of the community's purpose, testimonials about others' commitments, priming the norm of reciprocity, and showing people how they have benefited. Presenting another similar community as an outgroup to compete with is a double-edged sword. On the positive side, it may enhance identity-based commitment. On the negative side, it can reduce needs-based commitment as members become more aware of an alternative community that they could explore and possibly switch to.

As with many of the design alternatives presented in this book, the design claims do not imply definitive design guides. Some of the options discussed here, such as recruiting participants who have existing social ties, will—to the extent that they are feasible—enhance most online communities. But even those options will generally have exceptions; for example, some people may be more comfortable sharing information about addictions or health problems with strangers than with friends. Many other design alternatives—such as homogeneity, small size, anonymity, off-topic communication, and competition with a related community—have different effects on different desirable outcomes. The right choices for building commitment in each particular community will depend on a careful analysis of that community and a healthy dose of designer intuition.

References

Abrams, D., K. Ando, and S. Hinkle. 1998. Psychological Attachment to the Group: Cross-Cultural Differences in Organizational Identification and Subjective Norms as Predictors of Workers' Turnover Intentions. *Personality and Social Psychology Bulletin* 24 (10): 1027–1039.

Allen, N. J., and J. P. Meyer. 1990. The Measurement and Antecedents of Affective, Continuance, and Normative Commitment to the Organization. *Journal of Occupational Psychology* 63 (1):1–18.

Allen, N. J., and J. P. Meyer. 1996. Affective, Continuance, and Normative Commitment to the Organization: An Examination of Construct Validity. *Journal of Vocational Behavior* 49 (3): 252–276.

Amichai-Hamburger, Y. 2005. Internet Minimal Group Paradigm. *Cyberpsychology & Behavior* 8 (2): 140–142.

Arkes, H. R., and C. Blumer. 1985. The Psychology of Sunk Cost. *Organizational Behavior and Human Decision Processes* 35 (1): 124–140.

Arkes, H. R., and L. Hutzel. 2000. The Role of Probability of Success Estimates in the Sunk Cost Effect. *Journal of Behavioral Decision Making* 13 (3): 295–306.

Aronson, E. 1997. Back to the Future: Retrospective Review of Leon Festinger's "A Theory of Cognitive Dissonance." *American Journal of Psychology* 110 (1): 127–137.

Aronson, Elliot, and Judson Mills. 1959. The Effect of Severity of Initiation on Liking for a Group. *Journal of Abnormal and Social Psychology* 59:177–181.

Back, M. D., S. C. Schmukle, and B. Egloff. 2008. Becoming Friends by Chance. *Psychological Science* 19 (5): 439.

Backstrom, L., D. Huttenlocher, J. Kleinberg, and X. Lan. 2006. Group formation in large social networks: Membership, growth, and evolution. *Proceedings of the 12th ACM SIGKDD International Conference on Knowledge Discovery and Data Mining*, 44–54.

Baym, N. 1999. *Tune In, Log On: Soaps, Fandom, and On-Line Community*. Newbury Park, CA: Corwin.

Beenen, Gerard, Kimberly Ling, Xiaoqing Wang, Klarissa Chang, Dan Frankowski, Paul Resnick, and Robert E. Kraut. 2004. Using Social Psychology to Motivate Contributions to Online Communities. In *CSCW '04: Proceedings of the ACM Conference on Computer-Supported Cooperative Work*, 212–221. New York: ACM Press.

Berscheid, Ellen, and Harry T. Reis. 1998. Attraction and Close Relationships. In *The Handbook of Social Psychology*, Vol. 2, ed. Daniel T. Gilbert and Susan T. Fiske, et al., 193–281. New York: McGraw-Hill.

Blanchard, A. L., and M. L. Markus. 2004. The Experienced "Sense" of a Virtual Community: Characteristics and Processes. *ACM SIGMIS Database* 35 (1): 64–79.

Bossard, J. H. S. 1932. Residential Propinquity as a Factor in Marriage Selection. *American Journal of Sociology* 38 (2): 219–224.

Bryant, Susan L., Andrea Forte, and Amy Bruckman. 2005. Becoming a Wikipedian: Transformation of Participation in a Collaborative Online Encyclopedia. In *Proceedings of the 2005 International ACM SIGGROUP Conference on Supporting Group Work*, 1–10. New York: ACM Press.

Butler, Brian. 2001. Membership Size, Communication Activity, and Sustainability: A Resource-Based Model of Online Social Structures. *Information Systems Research* 12 (4): 346–362.

Butler, Brian, L. Sproull, S. Kiesler, and R. Kraut. 2007. Community Effort in Online Groups: Who Does the Work and Why? In *Leadership at a Distance*, ed. Suzanne Weisband, 171–194. Hillsdale, NJ: Lawrence Erlbaum Associates.

Byrne, Donn. 1997. An Overview (and Underview) of Research and Theory within the Attraction Paradigm. *Journal of Social and Personal Relationships* 14 (3): 417–431.

Cameron, J., K. M. Banko, and W. D. Pierce. 2001. Pervasive Negative Effects of Rewards on Intrinsic Motivation: The Myth Continues. *Behavior Analyst* 24 (1): 1–44.

Cancer Support Community. 2010. Cancer Support Community. http://online.cancersupportcommunity.org.

Carron, A. V., and K. S. Spink. 1995. The Group Size-Cohesion Relationship in Minimal Groups. *Small Group Research* 26 (1): 86.

Cartwright, D., and A. Zander. 1968. *Group Dynamics: Research and Theory.* Evanston, IL: Row Peterson.

Chen, P. Y., and L. M. Hitt. 2003. Measuring Switching Costs and the Determinants of Customer Retention in Internet-Enabled Businesses: A Study of the Online Brokerage Industry. *Information Systems Research* 13 (3): 255–274.

Chen, Y., F. M. Harper, J. Konstan, and S. X. Li. 2010. Social Comparisons and Contributions to Online Communities: A Field Experiment on MovieLens. *American Economic Review* 100 (4): 1358–1398.

Clary, E. G., M. Snyder, R. D. Ridge, J. Copeland, A. A. Stukas, J. Haugen, and P. Miene. 1998. Understanding and Assessing the Motivations of Volunteers: A Functional Approach. *Journal of Personality and Social Psychology* 74:1516–1530.

Collins, N., and L. Miller. 1994. Self-Disclosure and Liking: A Meta-Analytic Review. *Psychological Bulletin* 116 (3): 457–475.

Crain, A. L., A. M. Omoto, and M. Snyder. 1998. What If You Can't Always Get What You Want? Testing a Functional Approach to Volunteerism. Paper presented at the annual meetings of the Midwestern Psychological Association, Chicago.

Curry, T. J., and R. M. Emerson. 1970. Balance Theory: A Theory of Interpersonal Attraction? *Sociometry* 33 (2): 216–238.

Dabbish, Laura, and Robert E. Kraut. 2008. Awareness Displays and Social Motivation for Coordinating Communication. *Information Systems Research* 19 (2): 221–238.

Deci, Edward L., Richard Koestner, and Richard M. Ryan. 1999. A Meta-Analytic Review of Experiments Examining the Effects of Extrinsic Rewards on Intrinsic Motivation. *Psychological Bulletin* 125 (6): 627–668.

Dobson, Jason. 2006. Blizzard Bans, Suspends over 16,000 World of Warcraft Accounts. Gamasutra. http://www.gamasutra.com/php-bin/news_index.php?story=8907.

Drenner, S., S. Sen, and L. Terveen. 2008. Crafting the Initial User Experience to Achieve Community Goals. In *Proceedings of the 2008 ACM Conference on Recommender Systems*, 187–194. New York: ACM.

Ducheneaut, Nicolas, and Robert J. Moore. 2004. The Social Side of Gaming: A Study of Interaction Patterns in a Massively Multiplayer Online Game. In *CSCW '04: Proceedings of the ACM Conference on Computer-Supported Cooperative Work*, 360–369. New York: ACM Press.

Ducheneaut, Nicolas, Nicholas Yee, Eric Nickell, and Robert J. Moore. 2006a. Alone Together? Exploring the Social Dynamics of Massively Multiplayer Online Games. In *CHI 2006: Proceedings of the ACM Conference on Human-Factors in Computing Systems*. NY: ACM Press.

Ducheneaut, Nicolas, Nicholas Yee, Eric Nickell, and Robert J. Moore. 2006b. Building an MMO with Mass Appeal: A Look at Gameplay in World of Warcraft. *Games and Culture* 1 (4): 1–38.

Dunbar, R. I. M. 1993. Co-evolution of Neocortex Size, Group Size, and Language in Humans. *Behavioral and Brain Sciences* 16 (4): 681–735.

Eisenberger, R., W. D. Pierce, and J. Cameron. 1999. Effects of Reward on Intrinsic Motivation—Negative, Neutral and Positive: Comment on Deci, Koestner, and Ryan (1999). *Psychological Bulletin* 125 (6): 677–691.

Ethier, Kathleen A., and Kay Deaux. 1994. Negotiating Social Identity When Contexts Change: Maintaining Identification and Responding to Threat. *Journal of Personality and Social Psychology* 67 (2): 243–251.

Facebook. 2011. Statistics. http://www.facebook.com/home.php?#!/press/info.php?statistics.

Fehr, E., and S. Gächter. 2000. Fairness and Retaliation: The Economics of Reciprocity. *Journal of Economic Perspectives* 14 (3): 159–181.

Festinger, Leon. 1957. *A Theory of Cognitive Dissonance.* Stanford: Stanford University Press.

Festinger, L., H. W. Riecken, S. Schachter, and E. Aronson. 1956. *When Prophecy Fails.* Minneapolis: University of Minnesota Press.

Festinger, L., S. Schachter, and K. Back. 1950. *Social Pressures in Informal Groups: A Study of Human Factors in Housing.* Palo Alto, CA: Stanford University Press.

Fisher, D., M. Smith, et al. 2006. You Are Who You Talk To: Detecting Roles in Usenet Newsgroups. In *Proceedings of the 39th Hawaii International Conference on System Sciences*, Waikoloa, Big Island, Hawaii, IEEE.

Foltz, P. W., and S. T. Dumais. 1992. Personalized Information Delivery: An Analysis of Information Filtering Methods. *Communications of the ACM* 35 (12): 51–60.

Gaertner, Samuel L., John F. Dovidio, Brenda S. Banker, Missy Houlette, Kelly M. Johnson, and Elizabeth A. McGlynn. 2000. Reducing Intergroup Conflict: From Superordinate Goals to Decategorization, Recategorization, and Mutual Differentiation. *Group Dynamics* 4 (1): 98–114.

Gerard, Harold B., and Grover C. Mathewson. 1966. The Effect of Severity of Initiation on Liking for a Group: A Replication. *Journal of Experimental Social Psychology* 2 (3): 278–287.

Ghosh, R. A. 2005. Understanding Free Software Developers: Findings from the Floss Study. In *Perspectives on Free and Open Source Software*, ed. Joseph Feller, Brian Fitzgerald, Scott A. Hissam, and Karim R. Lakhani, 23–45. Cambridge, MA: MIT Press.

Gouldner, A. W. 1960. The Norm of Reciprocity: A Preliminary Statement. *American Sociological Review* 25 (2): 161–178.

Granovetter, M. S. 1973. The Strength of Weak Ties. *American Journal of Sociology* 78 (6): 1360–1380.

Gross, N., and W. E. Martin. 1952. On Group Cohesiveness. *American Journal of Sociology* 57 (6): 546–564.

Hancock, J. T., C. L. Toma, and K. Fenner. 2008. I Know Something You Don't: The Use of Asymmetric Personal Information for Interpersonal Advantage. In *CSCW '08: Proceedings of the 2008 ACM Conference on Computer Supported Cooperative Work*. New York: ACM.

Harper, F. M., D. Moy, and J. A. Konstan. 2009. Facts or Friends? Distinguishing Informational and Conversational Questions in Social Q&A Sites. In *CHI '09: ACM Conference on Human Factors in Computing Systems*, 759–768. New York: ACM.

Harper, F. M., S. Sen, and D. Frankowski. 2007. Supporting Social Recommendations with Activity-Balanced Clustering. In *Proceedings of the ACM Conference on Recommender Systems*, 165–168. New York: ACM.

Heider, F. 1958. *The Psychology of Interpersonal Relations*. New York: Wiley.

Hinds, P. J., K. M. Carley, D. Krackhardt, and D. Wholey. 2000. Choosing Work Group Members: Balancing Similarity, Competence, and Familiarity. *Organizational Behavior and Human Decision Processes* 81 (2): 226–251.

Hirschman, A. O. 1970. *Exit, Voice, and Loyalty: Responses to Decline in Firms, Organizations, and States*. Cambridge, MA: Harvard University Press.

Hogg, M. A. 1992. *The Social Psychology of Group Cohesiveness: From Attraction to Social Identity*. New York: NYU Press.

Hogg, M. A., and D. Abrams. 1988. *Social Identifications: A Social Psychology of Intergroup Relations and Group Processes*. New York: Routledge.

Hogg, M. A., and D. J. Terry. 2000. Social Identity and Self-Categorization Processes in Organizational Contexts. *Academy of Management Review* 25 (1): 121–140.

Hogg, M. A., and J. C. Turner. 1985. When Liking Begets Solidarity: An Experiment on the Role of Interpersonal Attraction in Psychological Group Formation. *British Journal of Social Psychology* 24 (4): 267–281.

Homans, George C. 1958. Social Behavior as Exchange. *American Journal of Sociology* 63 (6): 597–606.

Homans, George C. 1961. *Social Behavior: Its Elementary Forms*. New York: Harcourt, Brace & World.

Honeycutt, Courtenay. 2005. Hazing as a Process of Boundary Maintenance in an Online Community. *Journal of Computer-Mediated Communication* 10 (2).

Hulin, C. L., M. Roznowski, and D. Hachiya. 1985. Alternative Opportunities and Withdrawal Decisions: Empirical and Theoretical Discrepancies and an Integration. *Psychological Bulletin* 97 (2): 233–250.

Hutchison, P., J. Jetten, J. Christian, and E. Haycraft. 2006. Protecting Threatened Identity: Sticking with the Group by Emphasizing Ingroup Heterogeneity. *Personality and Social Psychology Bulletin* 32 (12): 1620.

Jeffries, Robin, Sara Kiesler, Jennifer Goetz, and Lee Sproull. 2000. Systers: Contradictions in Community. http://www.anitaborg.org/files/contradictionsincommunity.pdf.

JoBlo Movie Network. 2005. Basic Rules and Guidelines. http://www.joblo.com/forums/announcement.php?s=641f9cd5b47beab4ad423f0c861dba3c&forumid=21.

Jones, Quentin, Gilad Ravid, and Sheizaf Rafaeli. 2004. Information Overload and the Message Dynamics of Online Interaction Spaces: A Theoretical Model and Empirical Exploration. *Information Systems Research* 15 (2): 194–210.

Kim, Amy Jo. 2000. *Community Building on the Web: Secret Strategies for Successful Online Communities.* Berkeley, CA: Peachpit Press.

Kittur, A., B. Suh, B. A. Pendleton, and E. H. Chi. 2007. He Says, She Says: Conflict and Coordination in Wikipedia. In *CHI '07: Proceedings of the ACM Conference on Human Factors in Computing Systems.* New York: ACM Press.

Kittur, Aniket, and Robert E. Kraut. 2008. Harnessing the Wisdom of Crowds in Wikipedia: Quality through Coordination. In *CSCW '08: Proceedings of the ACM Conference on Computer-Supported Cooperative Work,* 37–46. New York: ACM Press.

Krackhardt, David, and Lyman W. Porter. 1986. The Snowball Effect: Turnover Embedded in Communication Networks. *Journal of Applied Psychology* 71: 50–55.

Landauer, T. K., P. W. Foltz, and D. Laham. 1998. Introduction to Latent Semantic Analysis. *Discourse Processes* 25:259–284.

Leskovec, J., D. Huttenlocher, and J. Kleinberg. 2010. Signed Networks in Social Media. In *CHI 2010: Proceedings of the ACM Conference on Human Factors in Computing Systems,* 1361–1370. New York: ACM.

Lewin, Kurt. 1951. *Field Theory in Social Science; Selected Theoretical Papers,* ed. D. Cartwright. New York: Harper & Row.

Lott, A. J., and B. E. Lott. 1965. Group Cohesiveness as Interpersonal Attraction: A Review of Relationships with Antecedent and Consequent Variables. *Psychological Bulletin* 64 (4): 259–309.

McKenna, Katelyn, Amie S. Green, and Marci Gleason. 2002. Relationship Formation on the Internet: What's the Big Attraction? *Journal of Social Issues* 58 (1): 9–31.

Meyer, J. P., and N. J. Allen. 1991. A Three-Component Conceptualization of Organizational Commitment. *Human Resource Management Review* 1 (1): 61–89.

Meyer, J. P., D. J. Stanley, L. Herscovitch, and L. Topolnytsky. 2002. Affective, Continuance, and Normative Commitment to the Organization: A Meta-Analysis of Antecedents, Correlates, and Consequences. *Journal of Vocational Behavior* 61 (1): 20–52.

Michinov, N., E. Michinov, and M. C. Toczek-Capelle. 2004. Social Identity, Group Processes, and Performance in Synchronous Computer-Mediated Communication. *Group Dynamics* 8 (1): 27–39.

Milgram, S. 1977. The Familiar Stranger: An Aspect of Urban Anonymity. In *The Individual in a Social World: Essays and Experiments*, ed. S. Milgram. Reading, MA: Addison-Wesley.

Mockus, A., R. T. Fielding, et al. 2002. Two Case Studies of Open Source Software Development: Apache and Mozilla. *ACM Transactions on Software Engineering and Methodology* 11 (3): 309–346.

Newcomb, T. 1961. *The Acquaintance Process*. New York: Holt, Rinehart, & Winston.

Newman, M. W., D. Lauterbach, S. A. Munson, P. Resnick, and M. E. Morris. 2011. It's Not That I Don't Have Problems, I'm Just Not Putting Them on Facebook: Challenges and Opportunities in Using Online Social Networks for Health. In *CSCW 2011: Proceedings of the ACM Conference on Computer-Supported Cooperative Work*, 341–350. ACM: New York.

Nov, O. 2007. What Motivates Wikipedians? *Communications of the ACM* 50 (11): 60–64.

Nowak, M. A., and K. Sigmund. 2005. Evolution of Indirect Reciprocity. *Nature* 437 (7063): 1291–1298.

Ouwerkerk, Jaap W., Dick de Gilder, and Nanne K. de Vries. 2000. When the Going Gets Tough, the Tough Get Going: Social Identification and Individual Effort in Intergroup Competition. *Personality and Social Psychology Bulletin* 26 (12): 1550–1559.

Pichon, I., G. Boccato, and V. Saroglou. 2007. Nonconscious Influences of Religion on Prosociality: A Priming Study. *European Journal of Social Psychology* 37 (5): 1032.

Postmes, Tom, Russell Spears, and Martin Lea. 2000. The Formation of Group Norms in Computer-Mediated Communication. *Human Communication Research* 26 (3): 341–371.

Postmes, Tom, Russell Spears, and Martin Lea. 2002. Intergroup Differentiation in Computer-Mediated Communication: Effects of Depersonalization. *Group Dynamics* 6 (1): 3–16.

Postmes, Tom, Russell Spears, Antonia T. Lee, and Rosemary J. Novak. 2005. Individuality and Social Influence in Groups: Inductive and Deductive Routes to Group Identity. *Journal of Personality and Social Psychology* 89 (5): 747–763.

Postmes, T., R. Spears, K. Sakhel, and D. de Groot. 2001. Social Influence in Computer-Mediated Communication: The Effects of Anonymity on Group Behavior. *Personality and Social Psychology Bulletin* 27 (10): 1243–1254.

Prentice, Deborah A., Dale T. Miller, and Jenifer R. Lightdale. 1994. Asymmetries in Attachments to Groups and to Their Members: Distinguishing between Common-Identity and Common-Bond Groups. *Personality & Social Psychology Bulletin* 20 (5): 484–493.

Raban, D. R., M. Moldovan, and Q. Jones. 2010. An empirical study of critical mass and online community survival. In *CSCW '10 Proceedings of the 2010 ACM conference on Computer supported cooperative work*. New York: ACM Press.

Raymond, Eric S. 2003. The Jargon File. http://www.catb.org/jargon.

Ren, Yuqing, F. Maxwell Harper, Sara Drenner, Loren Terveen, Sara Kiesler, John Riedl, and Robert E. Kraut. In press. Increasing Attachment to Online Communities: Designing from Theory. *Management Information Systems Quarterly.*

Ren, Yuqing, and Robert E. Kraut. Under review. A Simulation for Designing Online Community: Member Motivation, Contribution, and Discussion Moderation. *Information Systems Research.*

Ren, Yuqing, Robert E. Kraut, and Sara Kiesler. 2007. Applying Common Identity and Bond Theory to the Design of Online Communities. *Organization Studies* 28 (3): 379–410.

Resnick, P., D. Hansen, J. Riedl, L. Terveen, and M. Ackerman. 2005. Beyond Threaded Conversation. *Conference on Human Factors in Computing Systems*, 2138–2139.

Resnick, Paul, Adrienne Janney, R. Lorriane Buis, and Caroline R. Richardson. 2010. Adding an Online Community to an Internet-Mediated Walking Program. Part 2: Strategied for Encouraging Community Participation. *Journal of Medical Internet Research* 12 (4): e71.

Resnick, P., R. Zeckhauser, J. Swanson, and K. Lockwood. 2006. The Value of Reputation on eBay: A Controlled Experiment. *Experimental Economics* 9 (2): 79–101.

Ridings, Catherine M., and David Gefen. 2004. Virtual Community Attraction: Why People Hang out Online. *Journal of Computer Mediated Communication* 10 (1).

Rodgers, Shelly, and Qimei Chen. 2005. Internet Community Group Participation: Psychosocial Benefits for Women with Breast Cancer. *Journal of Computer Mediated Communication* 10 (4).

Rogers, P., and M. Lea. 2005. Social Presence in Distributed Group Environments: The Role of Social Identity. *Behaviour & Information Technology* 24 (2): 151–158.

Sassenberg, K. 2002. Common Bond and Common Identity Groups on the Internet: Attachment and Normative Behavior in On-Topic and Off-Topic Chats. *Group Dynamics: Theory and Practice* 6 (1): 27–37.

Sassenberg, Kai, Margerete Boos, Tom Postmes, and Ulf-Dietrich Reips. 2003. Studying the Internet: A Challenge for Modern Psychology. *Swiss Journal of Psychology* 62 (2): 75–77.

Sassenberg, Kai, and Tom Postmes. 2002. Cognitive and Strategic Processes in Small Groups: Effects of Anonymity of the Self and Anonymity of the Group on Social Influence. *British Journal of Social Psychology* 41 (3): 463–480.

Shapiro, Carl, and Hal Varian. 1999. *Information Rules: A Strategic Guide to the Network Economy.* Boston: Harvard Business School Press.

Sherif, M., L. J. Harvey, B. J. White, W. R. Hood, and C. W. Sherif. 1961 [1988]. *Intergroup Conflict and Cooperation: The Robbers Cave Experiment.* Middletown, CT: Wesleyan University Press.

Slashdot. 2007. eBay Delisting All Auctions for Virtual Property. http://games.slashdot.org/story/07/01/26/2026257/eBay-Delisting-All-Auctions-for-Virtual-Property.

Slater, M., A. Sadagic, M. Usoh, and R. Schroeder. 2000. Small-Group Behavior in a Virtual and Real Environment: A Comparative Study. *Presence* 9 (1): 37–51.

Smith, Christine B., Margaret L. McLaughlin, and Kerry K. Osborne. 1997. Conduct Control on Usenet. *Journal of Computer Mediated Communication* 2 (4).

Spertus, E., R. Jeffries, and K. Sie. 2001. Scaling Online Communities with Javamlm. Paper presented at the Fifteenth Systems Administration Conference (LISA), USENIX. San Diego.

Stewart, K. J., and S. Gosain. 2006. The Impact of Ideology on Effectiveness in Open Source Software Development Teams. *Management Information Systems Quarterly* 30 (2): 291–314.

Sykes, R., K. Larntz, and J. Fox. 1976. Proximity and Similarity Effects on Frequency of Interaction in a Class of Naval Recruits. *Sociometry* 39:263–269.

Tajfel, H., M. G. Billig, R. P. Bundy, and C. Flament. 1971. Social Categorization and Intergroup Behaviour. *European Journal of Social Psychology* 1 (2): 149–178.

Tedjamulia, S. J. J., D. L. Dean, D. R. Olsen, and C. C. Albrecht. 2005. Motivating Content Contributions to Online Communities: Toward a More Comprehensive Theory. In *Proceedings of the 38th Annual Hawaii International Conference on System Sciences (CD)*, 193b. Waikoloa, Big Island, Hawaii Computer Society Press.

Thibaut, J. W., and H. H. Kelley. 1986. *The Social Psychology of Groups*. New Brunswick, NJ: Transaction Publishers.

Turner, J. C. 1985. Social Categorization and the Self-Concept: A Social Cognitive Theory of Group. *Advances in Group Processes* 2:77–121.

Utz, S. 2003. Social Identification and Interpersonal Attraction in MUDs. *Swiss Journal of Psychology* 62 (2): 91–101.

Utz, S., and K. Sassenberg. 2002. Distributive Justice in Common-Bond and Common-Identity Groups. *Group Processes & Intergroup Relations* 5 (2): 151.

Walther, Joseph B., Celeste L. Slovacek, and Lisa C. Tidwell. 2001. Is a Picture Worth a Thousand Words? Photographic Images in Long-Term and Short-Term Computer-Mediated Communication. *Communication Research* 28 (1): 105–134.

Wang, Xiaoqing. 2007. An Ecological Perspective on Online Communities. Ph.D. thesis, University of Pittsburgh.

Wasko, Molly McLure, and Samer Faraj. 2005. Why Should I Share? Examining Social Capital and Knowledge Contribution in Electronic Networks of Practice. *Management Information Systems Quarterly* 29 (1): 35–57.

Wikimedia Foundation. 2010. Support Wikipedia. http://wikimediafoundation.org/wiki/2010 _Landing_6/en.

Wikipedia. 2006. Wikipedia. http://en.wikipedia.org/wiki/Wikipedia.

Williams, K., and C. O'Reilly. 1998. Demography and Diversity in Organizations: A Review of 40 Years of Research. *Research in Organizational Behavior* 20:77–140.

Williamson, I., M. Snyder, and A. M. Omoto. 2000, May. How Motivations and Re-Enlistment Frames Interact to Predict Volunteer Attitudes and Intentions: A Test of the Functional Matching Effect. Paper presented at the Annual Meeting of the Midwestern Psychological Association, Chicago.

Worchel, S., H. Rothgerber, E. A. Day, D. Hart, and J. Butemeyer. 1998. Social Identity and Individual Productivity within Groups. *British Journal of Social Psychology* 37:389–414.

Yamagishi, T., and T. Kiyonari. 2000. The Group as the Container of Generalized Reciprocity. *Social Psychology Quarterly* 63 (2): 116–132.

Yarn Harlot. 2011. Knitters without Borders. http://www.yarnharlot.ca/blog/tsffaq.html.

Yee, N., J. N. Bailenson, and K. Rickertsen. 2007. A Meta-Analysis of the Impact of the Inclusion and Realism of Human-Like Faces on User Experiences in Interfaces. In *CHI '07: Proceedings of the SIGCHI Conference on Human Factors in Computing Systems*. New York: ACM Press.

Zaccaro, S. J., and G. H. Dobbins. 1989. Contrasting Group and Organizational Commitment: Evidence for Differences among Multilevel Attachments. *Journal of Organizational Behavior* 10 (3): 267–273.

4   Regulating Behavior in Online Communities

Sara Kiesler, Robert E. Kraut, Paul Resnick, and Aniket Kittur

1   Introduction

"One bad apple spoils the barrel."

In thriving communities, a rough consensus eventually emerges about the range of behaviors the managers and most members consider acceptable, what we will call *normative behaviors*, and another range of behaviors that are beyond the pale. *A Rape in Cyberspace*, a newspaper report by Julian Dibbell (1993), describes a classic example of unacceptable behavior in LamdaMOO, an early virtual environment. Mr. Bungle, an avatar in the online community, wrote a program that forced two avatars controlled by other participants to have virtual sex with him and with each other, and to do brutal things to their own bodies. In describing the event online the next day, one of the victims begged, "I am requesting that Mr. Bungle be toaded for raping Starsinger and I [sic]"; "toad" is the command that would turn Bungle's avatar into a toad, annihilating the character's original description and attributes. Within twenty-four hours, fifty other characters also called for his toading. Three days later, the community had a real-time discussion of the issue. A system administrator who observed this discussion eventually ran the toad command to eliminate the Mr. Bungle character. Although LamdaMOO did not have a policy against cyberrape, when one occurred in its midst, the action instigated widespread discussion and crystallized a view among many inhabitants of what constituted correct and incorrect types of behavior in this community.

Communities differ on which behaviors are normative and which are not. Personal insults may be the primary way to interact in one community, but frowned upon in another. Wikipedia expects writers to adopt a neutral point of view when writing articles; the Huffington Post (http://www.huffingtonpost.com) expects guest bloggers to express a viewpoint. Psych Central (http://psychcentral.com), a site with 160 health support communities, forbids members or outsiders from conducting any type of research on the site for publication or educational purposes (Psych Central 2008); JoBlo's Movie Club (http://www.joblo.com) wants only on-topic posts on it forums; and while the image-based bulletin board 4Chan (http://www.4chan.org) encourages posts with pictures of naked women, cute guys, and erotic anomie, it prohibits this content from appearing in its forum designated as "work safe," which should contain only "content that is safe for viewing in the average working environment" (4chan 2011a). As we explore in this chapter, the normative behaviors may be codified and articulated or left implicit, and they may be contested by some members at some times, but most of the time, most people will agree about behaviors that are acceptable and those that are not.

Having a rough consensus about normative behaviors can help the community achieve its mission. In many technical and health support communities, it is expected that responses to questions will be supportive rather than antagonistic, aiding the mission of helping the members deal with problems they are having. Many open source software (OSS) development communities expect that discussion of plans, features, and bugs will occur in open discussion lists, rather than in private email conversations between developers. The Apache Web Server project notes, "Public forums, which include all developer and user mailing lists, wikis, and issue reporting systems, are essential to the Apache Software Foundation (ASF). We strive to do our work in public forums in a spirit of transparency and openness. They are our preferred means of communication" (Apache Software Foundation 2011). This norm is functional in groups where developers are not colocated and work is interdependent. It enables project members to maintain an awareness of the state of the project by making available information that can affect the work of others. The neutral-point-of-view norm in Wikipedia supports the community's goal to write a trustworthy encyclopedia (Wikipedia 2011b), and the norm that editors take particular care when adding information about living persons can reduce threats from lawsuit (Wikipedia 2011a).

Expectations about how to handle conflicts are especially important to keeping a community productive. Conflicts are inevitable in social interactions, but if they become personal and escalate, they can derail a community, drawing attention away from its mission. Extended "flame wars"—protracted hostile online interactions—can start between two people and grow to involve many. Before they end, some people may be sufficiently alienated to leave the community. The LinuxChix community (http://www.linuxchix.org), which encourages women's participation in Linux OSS development, prides itself on its nurturing atmosphere, unlike other Linux communities, which LinuxChix characterizes as "dominated by flame wars and ego battles, which tend to drive people away" (Vesperman and Henson 2004, 1). Many communities have behavioral norms governing conflicts, such as avoiding personal attacks, moving conflicts to special locations, or using special mediation processes. A common source of conflict in Wikipedia is differences among editors in beliefs about the content that should appear on a particular page. This conflict can lead to "edit wars" in which editors repeatedly undo each other's work in an attempt to make their own preferred version of the article visible (Kittur et al. 2007). These edit wars can even occur in seemingly nonpolarized topics. For example, Viegas, Wattenberg, and Dave (2004) demonstrated an edit war in the Wikipedia entry for chocolate over whether a kind of chocolate sculpture called "coulage" really existed and whether the paragraph describing it should appear on the article. The existence of edit wars resulted in the three-revert rule in Wikipedia. (A reversion in Wikipedia occurs when a document is restored to its previous version, negating someone's edits.) The three-revert rules holds that an editor may revert an article to a previous state a maximum of three times per day (Wikipedia 2011d).

Not everyone complies with the consensus standards of normative behavior all the time. The Internet is filled with *trolls* and *griefers*, people who derive satisfaction from disrupting communities. Trolls pose as legitimate members and post inflammatory comments designed to provoke other members. For example, the website Democratic Underground (http://www.democraticunderground.com) is a community for liberals to post and discuss news. Members of this community expressed concern with a troll "who professes complete faith in the progressive cause, who deliberately works to destroy it by claiming falsely that our displays of courage and strength are actually a weakness," such as when they post comments like, "I am a lifelong Democrat but I just feel the party is being damaged by association with Howard Dean/Russ Feingold/DailyKos" (bunkerbuster1 2006). Both essays by game designers (Bartle 1996) and empirical factor-analytic studies by social scientists (Seay and Kraut 2007; Smith 2007) indicate that some players in online games are motivated by causing problems for other players. For example, in World of Warcraft, a popular role playing game, a griefer might engage in what is known as "corpse camping," in which the griefer remains near the corpse of other players after killing them in game and repeatedly rekills them whenever they resurrect themselves.

Trolls can do a lot of damage. Consider, for example, the alt.hackers newsgroup. Ordinarily, to post to alt.hackers, newcomers must hack into the board. Once in, the poster is expected to include an ObHack—information about technology shared with others. Wysocki (2003) describes the regulatory breakdown in this community after a Usenet bulletin board in Italy started leaking messages into the alt.hackers site. A member of alt.hackers complained about these new posts, written in Italian, "why, oh, why do these RUDE BASTARDS *still* post here in a language only morons would speak?" Another member replied that this poster, besides being racist, had not included the obligatory ObHack. A spirited discussion and pursuit of the mysterious foreign messages ensued. Venom, an Italian hacker, bragged, "They can read any message you post, the complaints too, they simply don't care, and taunt you." Ultimately, the Italian hackers left, but at least one member of alt.hackers quit publicly in disgust because an alt.hackers member had violated the group's secret procedures: "Idiot. This whole situation was brought about by someone posting instructions on how to bypass the /one/ thing that prevented lusers."

Another threat comes from manipulators. They do not gain utility from disrupting the community but from getting the community to produce particular outcomes. For example, in communities like Yelp (http://www.yelp.com) or TripAdvisor (http://www.tripadvisor.com) that review and recommend commercial establishments, manipulators may want to pump up the ratings of a particular venue. Or on Wikipedia, they may want particular pages to reflect their point of view rather than a neutral one. Manipulators will make use of multiple "shill" accounts to carry out their manipulations. Wikipedia, for example, has a policy again using shill accounts, also known as "sock puppets" (Wikipedia 2011c).

Trolls and manipulators are outsiders who have no vested interest in the community functioning well. This problem is especially difficult to deal with because social sanctions (being disliked or publicly disparaged, or losing status in the community) may either have no effect, or, in the case of trolls, may actually increase their activity.

Insiders, however, may also violate behavioral norms. In discussing the socialization of newcomers, we note in chapter 5 that new members of a community may often act nonnormatively simply because they do not know the rules of the community. Failing to understand the norms of a community may also result from a number of causes besides members' lack of experience in the community. For example, some members may have cognitive or social impairments that make it difficult for them to infer rules from observations. As Burke and her colleagues notes, young adults with Asperger's syndrome or other disorders on the autism spectrum are socially awkward in part because of their difficulties in generalizing social norms from repeated exposure to examples of people following them (Burke, Kraut, and Williams 2010). These authors describe young men who were cut off by communication partners after sending them a few hundred text messages over a two-day period or because they revealed too much information about their childhood (i.e., a "creepy" amount) when trying to reconnect to grade-school friends on Facebook.

Even insiders who know the norms may not comply with them. Existing norms may be contested, and they may follow other expectations that they think *should* be the norms for the community. They may also fail to comply simply because it is in their own interest to do so in particular situations.

Social scientists use the term *social dilemma* to describe situations in which everyone is better off if everyone complies with the norms than if no one does, but each individual is even better off if he or she does not comply and the others do. One form of social dilemma is called a *public goods problem*, in which everyone is better off if everyone contributes some effort to the community but there is a temptation to free-ride on others' contributions. We consider ways to motivate public goods contributions in chapter 2. Another form of social dilemma is the *common pool resource* or *public bad problem*, in which individuals are tempted to take actions that use up or pollute a shared resource. In his famous paper "Tragedy of the Commons," Garrett Hardin explained the problem:

Picture a pasture open to all. It is to be expected that each herdsman will try to keep as many cattle as possible on the commons. . . . As a rational being, each herdsman seeks to maximize his gain. Explicitly or implicitly, more or less consciously, he asks, "What is the utility to me of adding one more animal to my herd?" This utility has one negative and one positive component. The positive component is a function of the increment of one animal. Since the herdsman receives all the proceeds from the sale of the additional animal, the positive utility is nearly +1. The negative component is a function of the additional overgrazing created by one more animal. Since, however, the effects of overgrazing are shared by all the herdsmen, the negative utility for any particular decision-making herdsman is only a fraction of –1.

Adding together the component partial utilities, the rational herdsman concludes that the only sensible course for him to pursue is to add another animal to his herd. And another; and another. . . . But this is the conclusion reached by each and every rational herdsman sharing a commons. Therein is the tragedy. Each man is locked into a system that compels him to increase his herd without limit—in a world that is limited. (Hardin 1968, 1244)

In economics and psychology, different versions of this fundamental conflict have been modeled as games and tested in experiments. Walker, Gardner, and Ostrom (1990) used this setup: Each subject begins with an endowment of tokens. Each token "invested" in the common pool resource market earns twenty-three tokens minus a quarter of the total tokens contributed by all the subjects. Investing in this market is analogous to grazing a sheep on the common pasture: it creates some value for the herdsman but reduces the value of every other sheep using the pasture. This situation sets up a social dilemma because it is in each subject's self-interest to put all their tokens into the market that uses the common pool resource. Collectively, however, this is a disaster, because they all earn less than they could have had they coordinated on a strategy of putting fewer tokens in (using less of the common pool resource).

In online communities, people's attention (or bandwidth, as Kollock and Smith [1996] describe it) is a limited resource. People may be motivated to participate in a community for many reasons: to amuse themselves, to help a favorite cause, to utilize their expertise, to get people to talk to them, to enhance their reputations, or because they expect that they will receive useful help or information in return (Constant, Sproull, and Kiesler 1996; Butler et al. 2007). These multiple motivations can lead many people to post messages and be actively involved, but if their contributions are trivial or silly, these contributions consume others' attention for little benefit. Many low-quality contributions create a social dilemma wherein these contributions drown out the worthy contributions and exhaust the available attention. Like the herdsmen using up the limited grassland for his own herd, members of the community may use up every-one's attention on messages that meet their own needs but not those of the recipients.

Similar reasoning applies to the cheats that occur in many multiplayer online games that allow one player to gain advantage over other players, while polluting the experi-ence for other players. For example, in online role playing games, *God-modding* is when players create a character that is virtually indestructible. As one commenter discussing this practice for the Marvel Heroes RPG (role playing game) notes, "This is frowned upon by other members of the RPG and is extremely annoying" (Orion 2010).

Ostrom studied a number of institutions that have successfully self-governed common pool resources over a long period of time (Ostrom 1990, 90). The resources included forest and grazing grounds, fisheries, and water for irrigation. She identified seven design principles that seemed to underlie their success. We will revisit several throughout the chapter, including the need for: community participation in rule making, monitoring, graduated sanctions, and conflict-resolution mechanisms. We adopt the term "regulation" to describe any efforts to decrease the frequency of non-normative behaviors or lessen their impacts on the community. Lessig (1999) identifies four elements that regulate behavior online: laws, norms, markets, and technology (or code, or architecture, as he called it). Laws are rules propagated and sometimes enforced by government and are external to the community itself. For example, most western countries have laws against the creation, possession, and distribution of child pornography, and these laws are often enforced when these images are distributed over the Internet (Akdeniz 2008). Lessig argued that laws are difficult to enforce on the Internet and urged policy makers to consider other means of regulation, especially technology. In any case, online community designers generally have little control over the laws governing their communities, though they can publicize them more or less. Thus, for example, the first of the 124 rules posted at the 4chan website to guide participants' behavior is "Do not upload, post, discuss, request, or link to, anything that violates local or United States law. This will be severely punished and strictly enforced" (4chan 2011b) Communities can proactively cooperate more or less with law enforcement.

This chapter considers means of regulation that fall into the other three categories. Some design alternatives, such as making norms more salient or shaming people who violate them, create psychological motivations for compliance. Some, such as reputation systems and internal currencies, create economic incentives. And some employ technical means such as moderation systems and reversion tools to prevent and recover from bad behavior. Often, means of different kinds complement each other. For example, as we shall explain, reputation systems function better in combination with technical mechanisms that limit the ability to create new accounts.

This chapter begins with an analysis of ways to limit the damage that bad behavior causes when it occurs. Next, we consider ways to limit the amount of bad behavior that a bad actor can do. Finally, in the third and longest section, we consider ways to encourage compliance with norms through psychological and economic incentives.

2 Limiting Effects of Bad Behavior

In asynchronous conversation communities, posts can be screened. In some email lists, for example, a moderator must approve each message before it is forwarded to all the members. In many forums, moderators can remove inappropriate messages after they are posted or move them to other forums where they may be more appropriate. Messages may also be degraded but left in place. For example, *disemvoweling* removes all the vowels from a message. Readers are quickly aware that the message has been degraded, but can still read it, with some effort. Alternatively, posts can be labeled or rated, and individual readers can sort or filter what they read. For example, at Slashdot (http://slashdot.org), where comments are scored from –1 to +5, the default reading settings hide comments with scores of 0 or –1, but individual readers can change their own settings.

All of these techniques limit the impact of inappropriate messages because they reduce the number of people who will read them. To the extent that people are psychologically vested in the community and its reaction to their posts, these techniques also act as sanctions against them. We analyze how to make sanctioning mechanisms effective later in the chapter.

Design claim 1   Moderation systems that prescreen, degrade, label, move, or remove inappropriate messages limit the damage those messages cause.

One of the problems with moderation systems is that people may not agree with the moderators' decisions. If they do not accept the legitimacy of the action, they may take further actions (e.g., posting additional inflammatory messages). The net damage may even be greater than that caused by the original message, had it gone unmoderated. Thus, moderation systems are more effective when the decisions are perceived as more legitimate. A similar logic applies to the use of reversion tools.

Moderation actions that do not silence the speaker will be met with less resistance. Many communities try to keep conversation limited to designated topics. When off-topic conversation arises, if it is redirected to another, more appropriate forum—either by directly moving it or posting a response suggesting where the conversation should be continued—people are less likely to insist on their right to talk about the topic in its original location. One common approach is to have a special space or spaces where the normal rules of behavior do not apply. For example, an off-topic forum can handle the messages that don't belong elsewhere. Online community organizer Caleb Clark, in an interview with Derek Powazek, reports that he has found it effective to create an "Outside" space for flames and fights:

Well, I thought, why not have an "Outside" in an online community? A place to go when what you are doing is bothering other people, but you still need to do it. Most people hate to be told what they can't do. But they don't seem to mind so much a little structure on what they can do. So it's worked great whenever I've tried it. When I encounter flames sparking up, I send an email saying, "Take it outside." It's a great re-director of bad energy in a community. Interestingly, it seems to take the gas out of flames very fast, since there are not a bunch of people "watching" the flame. (Powzek 2002, 113)

Design claim 2   Redirecting inappropriate posts to other places creates less resistance than removing them.

One source of legitimacy comes from the notion of procedural justice: that sanctions are given through a fair procedure. In fact, people would rather take a more severe punishment after they have had their "day in court" than a milder punishment without any hearing (Tyler 1990). In two-party conflicts, people prefer arbitration after both sides present information on their case over arbitrary top-down decision making (Ross and Conlon 2000). People's perceptions that they have been treated fairly are greater if procedures: (a) are applied consistently across people and time, (b) are free from bias, (c) collect and use accurate information in decision making, (d) have some mechanism to correct flawed or inaccurate decisions, (e) conform to personal or prevailing standards of ethics or morality, and (f) ensure that the opinions of various groups affected by the decision have been taken into account (Colquitt et al. 2001, 426; Leventhal 1976). In conventional organizations, perception of procedural justice is associated with such desirable outcomes as satisfaction with the outcome of decisions; positive evaluations of decision makers; organizational commitment; willingness to engage in voluntary, organizational citizenship behaviors; and good job performance (Colquitt et al. 2001, table 5).

This research on perceptions of fairness reviewed by Colquitt et al. (2001) suggests that online community members are more satisfied with moderation decisions if they are delivered through fair procedures. Thus, legitimacy is enhanced if criteria for moderation are clearly spelled out and consistently applied. It is also enhanced if people have a chance to argue their cases with the moderator and even appeal to a third party. Of course, those procedures may be costly, taking the time of moderators and other authorities, so they may not be practical in all situations.

Design claim 3   Consistently applied moderation criteria, a chance to argue one's case, and appeal procedures increase the legitimacy and thus the effectiveness of moderation decisions.

Procedural justice considerations also have implications regarding who is chosen to make moderation decisions. Community members often have mixed feelings about moderators' interventions. Members are more positive about these authorities if they feel this power is deserved (through past contributions to the community or demonstrated expertise) or if the community had a say in the selection of these persons. Authorities who "deserve" their posts or who are selected by the community are more likely to be perceived as less biased and more likely to reflect the prevailing standards of the community than those who are self-appointed or appointed by site owners. As they enact their roles impartially, they will be seen as more predictable and less biased.

For example, Slashdot instituted a moderation system in which community members rate the quality of contributions to recognize poor or good contributions (CmdrTaco 2003). The system was designed to "promote quality, discourage crap," that is, to encourage contributions that meet the community's norms of quality. The moderation system is also community-based to prevent a single moderator from exercising a "reign of terror." Moderators cannot assign points to their own posts, to "prevent abuses." Finally, "to address the issue of unfair moderators," Slashdot created a meta-moderation system, in which any logged-in community member can evaluate the quality of others' moderation. Whatever other virtues this moderation system possesses, it increases community members' perceptions that the moderation process is fair and is not subject to the capricious actions of just a few people.

Design claim 4   Moderation decided by people who are members of the community, who are impartial, and who have limited or rotating power is perceived as more legitimate and thus is more effective.

Production communities often employ quick-reversion tools that allow community members to repair damage done by vandals, newcomers, or people who harm the product by mistake. OSS repositories use version-control tools such as Subversion or Git for quick reversion, allowing administrators to easily roll back the code to a previous state when people offer buggy or inelegant code. Many wiki-based communities have tools to show differences between any two versions of a document and to revert a document instantly to a previous form. For example, the open-source content-management system Drupal and the open-source wiki software MediaWiki, upon which many online communities are built, provide built-in tools that allow users with a certain level of permission to revert any document (see figure 4.1).

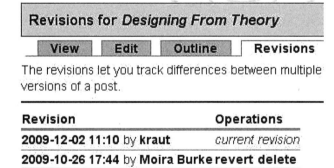

Figure 4.1
Reversion mechanism in Drupal (http://drupal.org).

Design claim 5 Reversion tools limit the damage that disrupters can inflict in production communities.

In recommendation systems such as TripAdvisor or MovieLens, where the threat is people trying to manipulate the recommendations that are made, the analog of moderation and reversion is to filter out or discount ratings suspected of coming from shills. Researchers have developed algorithms that look for suspicious patterns (e.g., too many in a short period of time or insufficient variability). For a survey, see Mobasher and colleagues (2007). Another approach, the *influence limiter*, does not throw out suspect ratings completely but instead partially discounts them: the discounting declines as the system gains confidence that the rater is honest rather than a shill for a manipulator (Resnick and Sami 2007). The problem with systems that partially discount or completely filter out ratings from suspect raters is that when they make mistakes, information from honest raters is not fully utilized. An analytic model showed that such mistakes are inevitable: any system that limits the damage of shills will have to throw away some information from honest raters as well (Resnick and Sami 2008).

Design claim 6 Filters or influence limits can reduce the damage of shill raters in recommender systems, but they do so at the cost of ignoring some useful information from honest raters.

One of the ways that trolls are able to disrupt is by eliciting reactions from community members that create strife within the community. For example, Herring and colleagues describe how a troll in a feminist forum was able to provoke not only angry responses to him, but also disagreements among other members about whether his behavior was acceptable and what to do about it (Herring, Job-Sluder, Scheckler, and Barab 2002). For a troll who is seeking to disrupt, sowing contention among other members is clearly a victory. Several group members argued that ignoring the troll would be more effective. However, doing so would have required everyone to recognize the troll and to follow a norm of ignoring him. As more people become experienced with participating in online communities, it may get easier for communities to follow a norm of ignoring trolls. Indeed, attempts to spread the norm have yielded the acronym DNFTT: Do Not Feed the Troll (see figures 4.2 and 4.3).

Design claim 7 A widely followed norm of ignoring trolls limits the damage they can do.

Do Not Feed The Troll

Message Board:

Guy #1:"I hate all you F***ers and your mothers - all of you should go
die in a hole!"
Guy #2:"Oh yeah, well F*** you, too, and I poop on your face because
you're such a F***er!"
Guy #3: "Hey Guy #2 - DNFTT."

by Troll Hunter Dec 3, 2004 share this

Figure 4.2
Definition for DNFTT from Urbandictionary (http://www.urbandictionary.com).

Figure 4.3
An ASCII-art image encouraging people to ignore a troll, culled from Usenet.
Source: Collected at http://jni.sdf-eu.org/trolls.html.

3   Coerced Compliance: Limits on Bad Behavior

Even if each individual action can cause only limited damage, the damage can accumulate with many actions. Next, we consider ways in which to limit the amount of bad behavior that a bad actor can do.

Throttles or *quota mechanisms* are one way to prevent large-scale damage by a disrupter, especially damage caused by repetitive actions. For example, chat rooms can automatically block participants from posting too many messages in too short a time or limit the number of links in those messages. The throttle prevents a person or program from barraging a community, whether intentionally, as in the case of a spammer, or unintentionally, as in the case of an overzealous newcomer unaware of community norms. Similarly, when Facebook detects unusual speed or frequency of a behavior, such as friending other users or posting on their walls, it sends a warning to the user (Facebook 2010). Though Facebook does not disclose its precise quotas, the warning message links users to relevant guidelines, such as how to promote a business or an event. Twitter lists spam-like activities that lead to an account being investigated, removed from search, or terminated, including "aggressive follower churn," updates composed primarily of links, or large numbers of duplicate @-prefixed replies to other users (Crystal 2009).

Design claim 8   Activity quotas allow people to participate in a community but prevent repetitive, spam-like activity.

Rather than responding to the quantity of activity, a member's activity may be limited based on a moderator's assessment of its quality. In PalTalk's chat rooms (http://www.paltalk.com), for example, a room's current owner can "gag" any of the participants. In other systems, a more severe gag or ban imposed on a member would apply across the community, not just within a particular space. Gags and bans may be temporary, imposing a cooling-off period of a few minutes, hours, or days, or they may be permanent.

As in moderating individual messages, gags and bans that are perceived as unfair may be resisted by the affected individual and his or her supporters in the community, which can cause significant disruption and damage as well. The considerations mentioned earlier regarding procedural justice and legitimacy of the moderators apply here as well, perhaps even more strongly. Gags and bans are often used as part of an escalating regime of sanctions intended to induce good behavior—a topic analyzed in more detail in the next section.

Beyond the resistance that they may cause, gags and bans may be ineffective if they are easy to circumvent by using a different account. For example, in a chat room where people choose a handle to use as they enter the room, it may be trivial for someone who has been gagged to exit and come back a few seconds later. More generally, a gag or ban stops misbehavior only as long as it takes to register for a new account.

When it is easy for people create new accounts, gags or bans may be more effective if the target is not immediately aware of the ban. There are several ways to disguise a gag or ban. For example, in a chat room, the gagged person may see an echo of everything he or she types, but his or her comments may not be displayed to others in the room. The gagged person may think that everyone is just ignoring her. Another possibility is to display a system error message suggesting that the site is temporarily out of service, but show it to only the gagged person.

Design claim 9   Gags and bans can limit the continuing damage of a bad actor, but only if it is hard for the bad actor to use a different account or if the ban is disguised.

As with moderation decisions, a perception of procedural justice makes people think that gags and bans are more legitimate, which makes people more willingly acquiesce to them. For example, in Wikipedia, editors can be banned from particular pages or from editing all pages. These actions are taken following a standardized procedure. Wikipedia's blocking policy lists types of behavior that warrants blocking an editor, evidence that someone needs to produce to request that an editor be blocked, and specifies review by impartial administrators and an appeals process (Wikipedia 2010a).

Design claim 10   Consistently applied criteria for gags and bans, a chance to argue one's case, and appeal procedures increase the legitimacy and thus the effectiveness of gags and bans.

Another approach for limiting damage is to require people to earn the privilege of taking actions that are potentially harmful. OSS projects have explicit ladders of access. Although most projects allow anyone to post a bug report to a public form, people who want to change code must go through a vetting process. Typically, they must send their patches or other small bug fixes to more senior developers, known as *committers*, before their code is integrated into the main software program. Only after participants have shown a substantial history of offering high-quality code and technical discussion are they granted committer status themselves (Ducheneaut 2005; Krogh, Spaeth, Lakhani, and Hippel 2003).

The Omidyar Network's community (http://www.omidyar.com), where people discussed issues related to philanthropy, used an internal currency that could be spent to create new groups or discussions. The currency was acquired through participation in discussions, but was capped at three times the person's feedback score. This approach limited the ability to accumulate currency for those who participated in ways that others disapproved of.

The influence limiter for recommendation systems, mentioned earlier, also instantiates this approach in the recommender system context (Resnick and Sami 2007). New raters begin with a very small amount of reputation currency. Influencing others' ratings requires placing a bet: those without sufficient currency are limited in their ability to influence recommendations for others. Normal users who report on their actual opinions about items will naturally accumulate reputation currency, and thus influence on predictions, for other people who share their tastes. An attacker who has no information about the items being rated, however, and who employs some automated strategy for generating ratings, not revealing any real information about those movies, will on average not accumulate any currency with those fake ratings. The only way to gain currency and thus influence is to provide genuine information, which is easy for normal participants to do but hard for attackers to do.

Design claim 11   Paying to take actions in the community with currency accumulated through normal participation reduces the ability for trolls and manipulators to act.

Even if someone can do only a little damage with one account before being detected and stopped, if it is possible to create new accounts automatically, the cumulative effect can be quite large. For example, the influence limiter described previously gives a little bit of reputation currency and thus influence to new raters so that they can place bets and prove themselves. An attacker who can create thousands or millions of new accounts is able to manipulate recommendations.

A CAPTCHA (Completely Automated Public Turing test to tell Computers and Humans Apart) is a test presented to a user that should be easy for a human to pass but very difficult for a computer. Figure 4.4, for example, illustrates a CAPTCHA in which the distorted words from old scanned text, which are already difficult to read, are then rendered more difficult by adding additional distortions. By requiring applicants to complete a CAPTCHA before subscribing, the community can eliminate automated spammers and other computer agents who are attempting to violate the community's norms.[1] Craigslist (http://www.craigslist.org) uses a related technique requiring someone who posts a classified ad to enter an email address and then respond to an invitation sent to that address before the ad goes public. Only bots that have access to a large number of distinct email addresses using a variety of different email-provider domain names are able to post large numbers of classified ads.

Rather than proving only that they are human, account registrants may need to prove their identity by providing a driver's license number or credit card number. Chapter 5 discusses methods for ensuring a good match between newcomers and the communities they join.

reCAPTCHA IS A FREE ANTI-BOT SERVICE THAT HELPS DIGITIZE BOOKS.

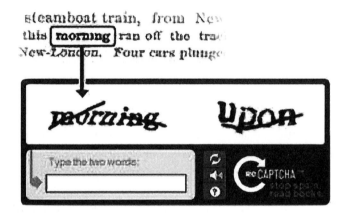

Figure 4.4
The reCAPTCHA service.

Design claim 12   Limiting fake accounts with CAPTCHAs or identity checks limits automated attacks.

4   Encouraging Voluntary Compliance

Compliance can be coerced (and damage limited) by behavior norms; in addition, people can be encouraged to comply voluntarily. Techniques for encouraging voluntary compliance tend to be more effective with insiders, who care about the community's health and their own standings within the community. To gain voluntary compliance with behavior norms, designers face two challenges. First, members of the community have to know the norms and be aware of them when making behavior choices. Second, members have to want to follow the norms, even when there are countervailing forces drawing them toward nonnormative behavior.

Making Norms Clear and Salient

People learn the norms of a community in three ways:

1. Observing other people and the consequences of their behavior

2. Seeing instructive generalizations or codes of conduct

3. Behaving and directly receiving feedback

Psychologists distinguish between *descriptive norms* and *injunctive norms*. Cialdini defines descriptive norms as beliefs about typical behavior (2003). Injunctive norms, on the other hand, define which behaviors people approve or disapprove of.

People tend to conform to descriptive norms even though they lack the moral force of injunctive norms. The behaviors that others engage in may become a focal point and the first option that people consider. In addition, people may want to fit in by doing what others do. And they may interpret the descriptive norm—what people tend to do—as social proof of what the underlying injunctive norms are; indeed, in some circumstances, what people do may be a stronger indicator of what they truly believe is acceptable than any explicit statements they make.

In 1936, Muzafer Sherif put people in a dark room and showed them a stationary pinpoint of light, which appeared to move anywhere from 1 to 10 inches. (This phenomenon is a perceptual illusion called the *autokinetic effect*.) After hearing other group members announce their estimates of how far the light moved, the group converged upon a norm, such as 3 inches, with individual group members' estimates varying in small amounts from this norm. Sherif's study was one of a long tradition of research into conformity—how people in groups learn what is acceptable behavior and adopt these norms without any external pressure. The power of observing others act in particular ways has been demonstrated repeatedly. The effect of the descriptive norms in the Sherif experiment can last over a year, even when individuals are tested individually (Rohrer et al. 1954).

People's behavior produces signals about acceptable and unacceptable behavior to others outside of experimental labs as well. Erving Goffman's influential ethnographic studies of face-to-face interaction in mental hospitals, elevators, dinner parties, stadiums, and even casinos (where he became a skilled blackjack pit boss) described how people negotiate their way around often-packed urban spaces, mark their territories while so doing, signal their relationships to others by various "tie-signs," and manage their appearances so as to appear normal or unremarkable (Goffman 1959, 1963). Using a theatrical metaphor, he described how people act in ways that convey how they can be trusted to act predictably within the range of acceptable behavior for their role. For instance, people eating alone in a restaurant often peruse a newspaper or paperback book to look occupied because staring into space looks abnormal. When people fail to look normal, their behavior signals moral failure, which can lead to their stigmatization.

It follows from this discussion that one way to encourage normative behavior is to make others' normative behavior visible to all members of the community. Highlighting descriptive norms can change behavior. Many colleges and universiti es use social norm marketing to attempt to reduce binge drinking among students by publishing accurate information about how much the typical student drinks. In these campaigns, the universities conduct surveys to identify the actual amount of drinking on campus and then advertise these rates via posters, direct mail, campus newspapers, and other means. Studies have shown that the actual rates are lower than many students think (Perkins et al. 1999). DeJong and his colleagues conducted a large randomized field experiment of the effectiveness of these social marketing programs at eighteen universities. Compared to universities that were not assigned to conduct a social norm marketing campaign, students in universities randomly assigned to participate in campaigns increased the accuracy of their estimates of the others' drinking behavior on campus and decreased their own drinking, and these effects were stronger the more intensely the university participated in the campaign (DeJong et al. 2006).

Online community designers have a number of options for highlighting the typical behavior in the group (i.e., the descriptive norms). At one extreme, they can simply make samples of individuals' actual behavior in the community visible to others. If the behavior is relatively homogeneous and the typical behavior is also the desirable behavior, this technique should lead others to act similarly, that is, in desirable ways. Buyers and sellers on the online auction community eBay can leave each other positive and negative comments. Both buyers and sellers overwhelmingly give positive feedback (about 99 percent positive approval ratings, according to Dellarocas and Wood 2008 and Resnick and Zeckhauser 2002). Thus, when members of the community browse the site, they are likely to see that others are typically responsible and to be motivated to be responsible themselves. Although the comments typically posted on news feeds on Facebook are more varied than the feedback sellers receive on eBay (figure 4.5), most are casual and benign (e.g., "has a cold and skinned knees. Totally reliving third grade"). Therefore, these examples of public user behavior provide descriptive norms for the prevalent behavior and should encourage similar casual and benign conversation.

Feedback earned for transactions on eBay

Positive feedback: **100%** | Feedback score: **145**

Figure 4.5
Typical seller feedback rating on eBay (http://www.ebay.com).

Rather than depending on random encounters, designers can also choose to highlight particular exemplars of desirable behavior. For example, in a forum-based community, a "post of the week" could be highlighted on the front page.

Design claim 13   Publicly displaying examples of appropriate behavior on the site shows members what is expected and increases their adherence to those expectations.

Showing members a small sample of norm violations can encourage appropriate, normative behavior if it contrasts with the clearly more prevalent descriptive norm. According to Cialdini's focus theory (Cialdini, Kallgren, and Reno 1991), people learn norms from salient behaviors—actions that stand out and point out to people what is appropriate to do in a situation. Abstractions and routine behavior can be hard to make salient, but negative behavior catches people's attention. Negative examples thus may highlight the background norm. Cialdini and his colleagues have shown that when people see a model littering in the context of an already littered environment, they litter more than if they hadn't seen the model. However, seeing the same littering behavior in the context of a clean environment causes people to litter less than they would otherwise (see figure 4.6; Cialdini, Kallgren, and Reno 1991, study 1). That is, a negative example that violates a descriptive norm makes the norm more salient and causes more people to act consistently with it.

In the context of online communities, one example of nonnormative behavior may bring into clearer focus a pattern of normative behavior. Many online communities such as discussion boards or wikis preserve records of misbehavior and make them salient. For example, when moderators flag or disemvowel a message, or respond to it with a suggestion that the conversations move elsewhere, there is still a visible trace that nonnormative behavior occurred. When a message is moved or removed without leaving a trace, others will no longer know that a violation occurred.

Wookieepedia, a wiki dedicated to *Star Wars* (http://starwars.wikia.com, Wookieepedia 2010), has a prominent page on being civil and respectful, which includes

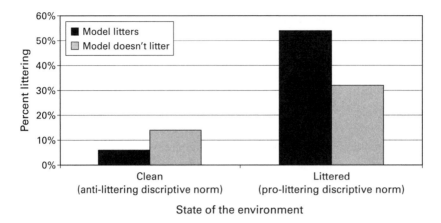

Figure 4.6
The effect of behavioral exemplars on highlighting descriptive norms.

examples of personal attacks that should be avoided. Sometimes conflict continues to escalate and mediators are brought in to help resolve it, in which case records of such conflicts are preserved for the community to potentially reference in the future.

Design claim 14   Publicly contrasting examples of inappropriate behavior in the context of a descriptive norm of appropriate behavior highlight the descriptive norm and increase people's adherence to it.

The tactic of highlighting nonnormative behavior can backfire if it leads to the impression that the behavior is engaged in by large numbers of people and thus is in fact a descriptive norm. In the experiment described previously, seeing someone litter in an already littered environment led even more subjects to litter than those who simply observed the littered environment. As another example, the attempt by a ranger at the National Park Service to deter theft of petrified wood using a sign that reads "Your heritage is being vandalized every day by theft losses of petrified wood of 14 tons a year, mostly a small piece at a time" may in fact be causing visitors to steal more and his colleagues conducted an experiment comparing two signs designed to deter this theft (Cialdini 2003). Both signs urged people not to steal. One, though, showed three thieves and had the message "Many past visitors have removed petrified wood from the Park, changing the natural state of the Petrified Forest," and the other showed a single thief and simply said "Please don't remove the petrified wood from the Park, in order to preserve the natural state of the Petrified Forest." Visitors were four times more likely to steal after seeing the sign with three thieves than the sign with one.

These results suggest that in a community like eBay, where the descriptive norm is one of honesty, revealing a dishonest seller should increase members' honesty, not undermine it. However, highlighting bad sellers could backfire if the background prevalence of such sellers were higher. Similarly, if there are many people in a hobbyist community who, against the stated rules of the community, post advertisements for their businesses, highlighting these norm violations may serve only to embolden other members to advertise their businesses as well.

Thus, community managers face a difficult decision regarding what traces to leave behind about those actions when they consider taking administrative action to remove content or move it to a more appropriate place. On one hand, seeing a trace and being able to follow a link to find details about what was moved or removed and why may help people to learn the administrator's norms of behavior. On the other hand, seeing many such traces will suggest that the administrators' expectations do not represent a consensus of the community. The best decision often depends on the prevalence of the nonnormative behavior; perhaps counterintuitively, the more of it there is, the less trace of its existence should be left visible.

Design claim 15   Publicly displaying many examples of inappropriate behavior on the site leads members to believe such behavior is common and expected.

Although observing common online behavior illustrates the descriptive norm (i.e., behaviors that are common), observing responses to those behaviors teaches the injunctive norms (i.e., what behaviors are approved or disapproved). Observers need to see the consequences of behavior—for instance, the feedback that others provide regarding it—to understand its appropriateness. Do others say "thank you" for behavior x and not for behavior y? Do they rate person x higher than person y? Does one person seem to have a better reputation than others? Seeing behavior along with its consequences makes norms more learnable (Fehr, Fischbacher, and Gächter 2003).

The feedback can be informal, formal, or both. The informal feedback that one member of a health support group provided others who answered her questions clearly highlights valued behavior: "I want to thank all of you who responded to my posting. I don't know what my future will be with regards to diabetes, but knowing that there are people out there who care about each other is wonderful. I especially want to thank . . . ."[2] eBay's feedback mechanism combines informal comments (e.g., "Great honest eBayer! I would purchase from again tomorrow!") with formal, symbolic feedback (positive, neutral, or negative ratings).

Research suggests that formal feedback is more effective than informal feedback in helping people learn the norms of appropriate behavior. Moon and Sproull (2008) compared technical support groups for software problems that allowed only ad hoc member feedback about the quality of contributions in the text of replies to support groups that allowed more formal feedback (e.g., awarding points or stars). Consistent with a reinforcement model, in which quality answerers who get systematic feedback contribute more and lower quality answerers who get systematic feedback improve or drop out, they found that the formal approach was more effective than informal feedback, that technical problem resolution was more effective, and that people who had higher-quality contributions had longer participation duration.

Design claim 16   Displaying feedback of members to others increases members' knowledge of community norms and compliance with them; formal feedback is more effective than informal feedback.

Inferring a norm from a sample of behavior in a community can be difficult when there are many examples to observe and they vary in the extent to which people adhere to the norm. In large and active communities, there may simply be too much to look at to get a sense of what is appropriate in the community simply by looking at samples of behavior. To convey a descriptive norm, one alternative is to display easily interpreted statistics tallying certain types of behavior. For example, just as some workplaces prominently display a sign showing the number of days since the last workplace injury, a community could display the number of messages since the last reported abuse or the (low) percentage of messages flagged for violating the community's official policies.

Design claim 17   In large communities, displaying statistics that highlight the prevalence of normative behavior increases members' adherence to normative behavior.

When observers need to infer the norms by integrating over many and varying examples of behavior, it is often helpful to crystallize the generalization process by providing community members with explicitly stated guidelines or rules. These statements may be descriptive (e.g., "Generally, we are nice to each other even as we critique each other's photos") or injunctive (e.g., "Be nice even as you critique someone's photo"). They may describe either normative behavior or nonnormative behavior.

```
**** ETIQUETTE****

A note about etiquette. Keep in mind when responding
to a topic or entering a new one that the other users
also have feelings. Please avoid trampling on them.
Also, remember that comments entered in hasty
reaction to someone else's posting will be available to
be read long after you have entered them. So it is wise
to exercise some moderation and good judgment.
```

Figure 4.7
Early behavioral guidelines from The WELL (http://www.well.com), 1985.

They may be set at the origination of the community or articulated as a response to critical events in a community's history. Often, a rule is made in order to settle an argument about whether someone's behavior violates a norm or not. For example, LambdaMOO's norms about violence against others' avatars were codified only after the cyberrape incident described earlier.

The WELL's Host Manual (figure 4.7) was an early attempt to create community guidelines for The WELL (Whole Earth 'Lectronic Link), one of the first online communities, founded in 1985 (Hoag 1996; Williams 1997). Community designer Nancy White has a webpage that provides sample codes of conduct and rules for community businesses and associations at http://www.fullcirc.com/community/sampleguidelines .htm.

Research evidence indicates that when norms are clearly stated, people are more likely to act consistently with the norms and to do so over a wide variety of situations. Norms that can reasonably be inferred but are not directly stated may not be noticed, understood, or obeyed. For example, motorists returning to their cars were less likely to toss on the ground a handbill stuffed under their windshield wiper when the handbill explicitly reminded them not to litter ("April Is Keep Arizona Beautiful Month. Please Do Not Litter") than when it urged a related action ("April Is Preserve Arizona's Natural Resources Month. Please Recycle"), as shown in figure 4.8 (Cialdini, Kallgren, and Reno 1991, study 5).

The effects of making a social norm explicit are stronger when the norm itself is less clear. For example, Zitek and Hebl found that participants were far less likely to condone prejudice against others when they heard another person also condemn it and more likely to condone it when they heard others condone it, compared to conditions when they heard nothing (2007). These effects of hearing the norm made explicit

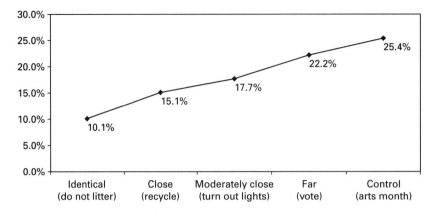

Figure 4.8
Effects of norm explicitness on compliance.
Source: Adapted from Cialdini, Kallgren, and Reno 1991.

were stronger when the preexisting social norms were more ambiguous (discrimination against ex-convicts and racists) compared to groups in which the preexisting norms were clear-cut (discrimination against blacks and gays).

Norms are often less clear in the early stages of a new community or any time there is fast growth. When reflecting on the current state of Wikipedia and lessons he learned as one of its founders, Larry Sanger expressed regret that the current Wikipedia community does not sufficiently defer to experts and specialists when they write in their areas of expertise, even though the community did so during the encyclopedia's early days:

"This is just common sense," as I wrote, "but sometimes common sense needs to be spelled out." What I now think is that that point of common sense needed to be spelled out quite a bit sooner and more forcefully, because in the long run, it was *not* adopted as official policy, as it could have been. (Sanger 2005, 318).

Design claim 18   Explicit rules and guidelines increase the ability for community members to know the norms, especially when it is less clear what others think is acceptable.

Another important design decision is how prominently to display guidelines and rules. Some communities require newcomers to read particular rules before they join or post, or post them prominently where everyone will see them frequently. Others do not.

Social news aggregation sites such as Reddit (http://www.reddit.com) face a special challenge in making norms and rules salient because the entire content of these sites revolves around voting and commenting on web links. Although Reddit has an area where rules are articulated (known collectively as "reddiquette"; http://www.reddit.com/help/reddiquette), this area has low salience for most users.

The Reddit community's solution is to post dummy "articles" in the main news area whose titles describe the norm or rule. Those "articles" that have widespread support and relevance in the community are voted up, often reaching the front page and thus becoming highly salient. An example of this is a post advocating using comments for conducting polls instead of articles. From reddiquette, "Please don't conduct polls using posts. If you feel you must use Reddit to conduct a poll, do it using a comment. Create a self-referencing post and then add a comment for readers to mod up or down based on their answer to your poll question. Also, be sure to indicate in the title of your post that the poll is being conducted using comments. Including something like '(use comments to vote)' in the title would probably be sufficient." This new rule was developed in response to a slew of polls taking over the front page of Reddit, as each poll "vote" had the side effect of increasing the poll's popularity and visibility. The new "article" garnered widespread support and high salience (it was voted up more than a thousand times), at one point reaching the number-one article spot.

Unfortunately, prominently displayed rules and guidelines can convey a negative impression. Potential members may fear that they will not be able to do what they want to or that they will accidentally fall afoul of one of the rules that they didn't understand. Newcomers to Wikipedia may inadvertently violate one of its many policies and guidelines designed to regulate behavior in "the encyclopedia that anyone can edit." As a result, their contributions are frequently reverted, and they become discouraged or driven away (Halfaker, Kittur, Kraut, and Riedl 2009, figure 5). When we have assigned students to edit a page of their choice on Wikipedia and tell them to read Wikipedia's guidelines first, many report feeling very intimidated about making an edit.

Paradoxically, prominently displayed or excessively detailed rules may also convey the wrong descriptive norm. A natural inference is that the rules were created in response to problematic behavior. It is also natural to infer that such behavior must occur fairly frequently; otherwise, it would not be necessary to prominently display the rules.

Design claim 19   Prominently displayed guidelines may convey a descriptive norm that the guidelines are not always followed.

Many sites have compromised by creating explicit rules and guidelines but burying them deep in the site where they are visible only to people who go looking for them.

Gaia (http://hubs.gaia.com) is a community site for teens age thirteen and up. It is a very challenging regulatory environment, due to the concern of many parents and many laws to protect children. The Gaia site has developed an extensive list of rules, safety tips, and information for parents. Yet teens have a strong dislike of rules and probably would run in the other direction if the rules were thrown in their face. So, the rules are there if you look for them, but they are not prominent. Although most members are probably unaware of these explicit rules, as we shall discuss shortly, even rules that are not noticed until people are pointed to them may have some value in creating legitimacy for assertions of norms or sanctions for violating them.

Another option is to make rules and guidelines prominent, but only at the point where people may be about to violate them. For example, eBay has a guideline that buyers should try to resolve conflicts with sellers before leaving negative feedback for them. This guideline is brought to the attention of buyers when they are about to leave negative feedback.

In a community with a strong norm of polite, supportive responses, automatic text analysis of posts that are submitted could be used to alert people that they might be about to violate that norm without forcing everyone to read about the guidelines. Similar features have been built into some email programs. For example, Eudora's MoodWatch software, invented by David Kaufer, automatically cautions users who are about to send an email containing "flame" words (Shankland 2000).

Design claim 20   Offering people reminders at the point of an action that may violate norms reduces the number of offenses.

Enhancing Compliance

To this point, we have argued that people must know the norms of a community before they can follow them and have suggested a number of design choices that should increase this knowledge. Even when they are aware of the norms, however, people may not always comply. Four things increase compliance: commitment to the community, legitimacy of the norms, the ability to save face, and expectations about rewards for compliance or sanctions for noncompliance.

Scholars since at least the time of Durkheim have argued that group cohesion contributes to the social order (Durkheim 1903). To the extent that community members care about the welfare of the community and see the norms as linked to that welfare, members are more likely to comply with and enforce the norms the more they identify with the community. Chapter 3 examined ways of promoting cohesion. As described in more detail in that chapter, designers can promote cohesion by emphasizing group identity though providing distinctive group names and missions, emphasizing group interdependence, and competing against outgroups. Alternatively, one can increase group commitment and cohesion by emphasizing the interpersonal relationships between individual group members, for example, by keeping group sizes small, by creating opportunities for members to repeatedly see and find out about each other, and by encouraging interpersonal communication and mutual self-disclosure.

Design claim 21   In more cohesive groups to which members are more committed, members are more likely to spontaneously comply with the norms.

Externally imposed rules and monitoring tend to be viewed as unfair and to lead to conflict. In Ostrom's studies of successful institutions for governing common pool resources, the third design principle was that "most of the individuals affected . . . can participate in making and modifying their rules" (Ostrom 2000, 150). Ostrom argues that collective choice leads to rules that are better tailored to specific situations, but also that it builds legitimacy and thus compliance with the rules. Even if the group spends more time initially in discussion and comes to the same decision in the end as that made by an elite core, involving everyone in the decision-making process should result in long-term benefits.

In May 2007, a member of the news aggregation site Digg (http://www.digg.com) posted a news story consisting of an HD-DVD cracking key—a set of hexadecimal numbers that provided people a way to circumvent DVD copyright protection. In a rare display of censorship, Digg's administrators removed the post. However, instead of accepting this enforcement of rules from above, community members reposted the key over and over until the Digg home page was little else than posts about the key and stories about how the Digg leadership had "betrayed" the members of the site. The disruption to the site was accompanied by an exodus of disgruntled members. Reddit—a competitor to Digg—included a top story welcoming the Digg exiles.

The management of the multiplayer game Everquest imposed rules when it perceived bad behavior was driving away subscribers. (Multiple-player gaming environments have experienced many hacker attacks, destruction of property, flame wars, and spirals of retaliation and cross-retaliation; see Kolbert 2001. In Yee's 2001 survey, 20 percent of the respondents answered "yes" to the question "Would you hack the game if you could?"). Rules were necessary, but only 12.5 percent of Everquest members thought that management's top-down "Play-Nice" rules helped the environment.

Social norms and rules generated by the community might have worked as well as external rules and would have had more staying power.

On the other hand, LambdaMOO, one of the first true online communities, used community rule making with good results:

We started having disagreements about what was and was not proper conduct here. Eventually, I was approached by a number of players and asked to draft a set of rules for proper MOO behavior. . . . I showed the draft to a bunch of people and asked for their comments on its style, completeness, and correspondence with their impressions of the "right" way of things. After incorporating suggested changes, the first version of "help manners" was publicized in the newspaper; I had, I think, done as good a job as I could of trying to capture the public consensus of that (admittedly early) time. Perhaps surprisingly, "help manners" worked quite well in reducing the number of incidents of people annoying each other. That society had a charter that reflected the general opinion and social pressure worked to keep the MOO society growing fairly smoothly. (Haakon 1992)

Design claim 22   Community influence on rule making increases compliance with the rules.

When people violate community norms and the violation is brought to their attention, they are much more willing to discontinue the bad behavior and correct previous errors if they can do so without having to admit that they deliberately violated the community's norms. If they can plausibly claim ignorance, or that their actions were misunderstood, or that the action was not theirs, they can save face.

For example, in the mid-1990s, MIT adopted procedures that they called "stopit" for dealing with harassment that occurred through computers on campus. A key element was a procedure for notifying norm violators that gave them a face-saving way out. As Gregory Jackson, then Director of Academic Computing, wrote:

The third stopit mechanism is a carefully structured standard note to alleged perpetrators of harassment, improper use, or other uncivil behavior. "Someone using your account," the note begins, "did [whatever the offense is]." The u.y.a. note (as this mechanism is known, for its introductory words) then explains why this behavior or action is offensive, or violates MIT harassment policy, or Rules of Use, or whatever. "Account holders are responsible for the use of their accounts. If you were unaware that your account was being used in this way," the note continues, "it may have been compromised. User Accounts can help you change your password and re-secure your account." Detailed directions to User Accounts follow. The note concludes with a short sentence: "If you were aware that your account was being used to [whatever it was], then please make sure that this does not happen again."

Two interesting outcomes ensue. First, many recipients of u.y.a. notes go to User Accounts, say their accounts have been compromised, and change their passwords—even when we know, from eyewitnesses or other evidence, that they personally were the offenders. Second, and most important, u.y.a. recipients virtually never repeat the offending behavior. This is important: even though recipients concede no guilt, and receive no punishment, they stop. If we had to choose one lesson from our experience with misbehavior on the MIT network, it is how effective and efficient u.y.a. letters are. They have drastically reduced the number of confrontational debates between us and perpetrators, while at the same time reducing the recurrence of misbehavior. When we accuse perpetrators directly, they often assert that their misbehavior was within their rights (which may well be true). They then repeat the misbehavior to make their point and challenge our authority. When we let them save face by pretending (if only to themselves) that they did not do what they did, they tend to become more responsible citizens with their pride intact. (Jackson 1994)

There are other face-saving mechanisms besides the "someone using your account" phrasing. Another possible phrasing for a notification message is something like, "You may not have been aware of this guideline, but we have a stated policy of [fill in here]. Please see [link to policy]. No big deal, but please stick to this in the future." Rather than allowing people to claim that it was someone else, it allows them to plead ignorance.

Giving people the option of undoing their offending action without leaving a trace of it also helps people save face. For example, suppose that someone makes a post that violates a community norm, and someone else posts a response chiding the original author. If the original author has the opportunity to remove both the original post and all replies to it, leaving no ongoing source of embarrassment, he or she may do so willingly. Without that option, he or she may feel the obligation to defend the action and even to repeat it to demonstrate that he or she thinks it acceptable.

Design claim 23   Face-saving ways to correct norm violations increases compliance.

Rewards and Sanctions

Both classic and contemporary theories of deterrence in criminology can help designers think through the best way of preventing misbehavior (Gibbs 1985; Pratt et al. 2006). These theories hold that the decision to commit a crime or more generally to violate a norm is in part a rational decision. Although people vary in their predisposition to commit crimes (e.g., by class, geographic area, and race), deterrence theory argues that those with criminal disposition will violate the rules only when it "pays." That is, based on an informal cost-benefit analysis, they perceive that benefits outweigh the costs. Thus, the argument is that actual punishment for offenders and the threat of punishment for future offenders deters misbehavior. Researchers have studied how various factors associated with the threat of punishment—such as the use of warnings and the certainty of punishment, and its swiftness or its severity—deter violations of norms and rules.

Sanctions may be delivered by community members but outside the online community. For example, students who send inappropriate messages to a school-wide email list may be shunned when they encounter fellow students in classrooms or hallways. More typically, external sanctions are not possible and sanctions are delivered within the community. For example, members may be publicly scolded, or their posts may get low ratings. Their contributions may be reverted or their messages deleted or moved. They may lose privileges such as posting in particular areas or committing code in open source projects. They may be shunned within the community: in a gaming community, being shunned detracts from the fun; in a commerce community like eBay, it subtracts from the profits. The offender may even be banned from particular activities or the community as a whole, temporarily or permanently.

For spammers, manipulators, and trolls, simply limiting the effectiveness of their actions reduces the incentive to participate. Thus, all the techniques described as ways to limit the damage they do—if effective—will also help reduce their incentives to try. For example, following a norm of not feeding the trolls not only limits the collateral damage their behavior can cause, but also makes it less appealing for trolls to participate in the community.

For spammers, reducing the chances that their posts will be seen has a similar effect. In the particular case of link spam, bots post links in online forums and blog comments to commercial sites (often porn). The spammers' real audience is not the readers of the forums or blogs but search engines that crawl the forums and blogs specifically looking for links. Most search engines give higher rankings to sites that have more incoming links (see, for example, the PageRank algorithm that was the initial inspiration for Google's search engine (Page et al. 1998)). Many blog platforms, including Blogger and WordPress, though allowing newcomers to post comments subject to the blog owner's preferences, also automatically include the `rel=nofollow` attribute in links embedded in comments. This mechanism directs search engines not to trust these links, preventing spam links from receiving PageRank and thus discouraging spammers from disguising links to their products within blog comments. Slashdot also uses the `nofollow` attribute in comments from potentially misbehaving users using heuristics based on the age of the user's account and the user's karma (Wikipedia 2010b).

Design claim 24   Telling search engines not to follow links discourages spammers from posting links.

For people, the simplest form of sanction is social approbation from others. People are very sensitive to the public impression they present to others (Goffman 1959). Their concern about "looking good" and how others evaluate them often causes them to underreport lying, stealing, drug use, and illicit sexual relations in in-person interviews compared with anonymous surveys (Kiesler, Weisband, and Drasgow 1999), to comply with experimenters' expectations in psychology experiments (Rosenberg 2009), to give more money to charities when the identities of contributors are revealed (Alpizar, Carlsson, and Johansson-Stenman 2008; Soetevent 2005), and to work harder in group settings when others know the identities of the contributors (Karau and Williams 1993). These effects all depend upon people believing that others can see their behavior and identify them with it.

Festinger, Pepitone, and Newcomb (1952) defined *deindividuation* in a group as being submerged in it. The individuals are not seen or paid attention to as individuals and do not feel that they stand out as individuals. Zimbardo's experiments on deindividuation suggest that people are more likely to violate established behavioral norms when they can conceal their identities under white robes (Zimbardo 1969). A systematic review of sixty separate experiments indicates that deindividuation encourages antinormative behavior, although the effect is not a strong one (Postmes and Spears 1998). Anonymity (at least to outsiders) and larger group sizes both lead to more antinormative behavior.

For the reasons we have just described, identifiable individuals may be more likely to adhere to group norms than anonymous individuals, especially when they face social sanctions for misbehavior (Sassenberg and Postmes 2002). Research suggests that the relative anonymity of online communication compared with phone and face-to-face communication is partially responsible for reduced normative pressure online (Bordia 1997) as revealed, for example, by more flaming and other incivilities online (Kiesler et al. 1985). For example, online, people are more willing to lie about themselves to potential romantic partners (Cornwell and Lundgren 2001). The observation that 97 percent of vandalism to Wikipedia articles is done by anonymous editors is also consistent with this rationale (Wikipedia 2010d).

Therefore, one way to increase people's willingness to comply with the norms of a community is to prevent anonymous participation. For example, Wikipedia requires editors to register before they can edit some especially contentious pages. Sites where misrepresentation is a problem often require verified or third-party authentication of identity for anyone who could potentially harm others. Many dating sites let anyone peruse the site but require driver license photos in exchange for the email addresses of other members. In 2009, Twitter began verifying the identities of well-known users, giving them a badge on their pages that serves to confirm that they are who they say they are. These communities use authentication of identities to discourage potential harm by community members.

Design claim 25   Verified identities and pictures reduce the incidence of norm violations.

Identifiability—the ability of others to see and judge actions and associate them with the actor—encourages good behavior and discourages bad behavior in the moment. That is, people are concerned about how others will judge them even in single-shot encounters, where they do not expect to interact with the same people in the future. But concern about future interactions can enhance the power of these social judgments. For example, in one experiment, people conformed more to group opinions when they anticipated future interaction with members of the group (Lewis, Langan, and Hollander 1972). A person's actions affect his or her reputation and thus how people will interact with him or her later. The "shadow of the future," as Axelrod and Keohane call it (1985, 232), creates an incentive for good behavior in the present.

Informal tracking of reputations sometimes yields only a small shadow, however, for two reasons. First, some actions are not publicly observable. For example, on eBay, a seller may misrepresent the goods he or she is selling. The buyer will recognize this and refuse to buy from the seller again, but the seller's ability to sell to other buyers will be unhindered unless the unhappy buyer has a way to communicate with other potential future buyers. Second, there may be so many actions that it is hard for people to judge someone's overall reputation.

In online communities, explicit reputation systems can help solve these problems (Resnick et al. 2000). For example, eBay provides an opportunity for buyers and sellers to leave comments about each other after their transactions. These comments are visible to others in the future, providing a public window onto the previously private transaction. Second, eBay provides summary statistics so that people do not have to read all of the individual comments and ratings. A potential buyer can quickly read that one seller has 99.5 percent positive feedback and another has only 94 percent, a difference that would take much longer to assess by looking at many pages of individual feedback report.

Empirical evidence suggests that explicit reputations can be an effective sanctioning mechanism. For example, in cross-sectional comparisons of naturally occurring transactions on eBay, more positive feedback led to higher prices and probability of sale, and the opposite was true for negative feedback (Bajari and Hortacsu 2004; Cabral and Hortacsu 2010; Dewally and Ederington 2006). In other communities, the deferred reward or sanction created by reputations may not be economic in nature but instead affect future interactions in other ways. For example, in the Omidyar community described earlier, reputation scores had an impact on members' ability to create new workspaces and discussion threads. Perhaps more important for members who were psychologically invested in the community was that each person's reputation score was displayed next to each post they made, and high scores became a valued status marker.[3]

Design claim 26   Reputation systems, which summarize the history of someone's online behavior, encourage good behavior and deter norm violations.

Rather than depending on reputation consequences to affect someone's future interactions in the community, rewards and sanctions can be charged directly to someone's account. Rarely, money might change hands. More commonly, accounts might be denominated in some internal currency that is earned through actions taken within the community, such as the one used in the Omidyar community. If prices are higher for undesirable actions than for desirable actions, people will do fewer undesirable actions. The problem is assigning prices when actions of the same form (e.g., posting a message) may be desirable or undesirable, depending on their contents. One solution is to assign the prices after the fact, based on feedback from other users.[4]

For example, Van Alstyne proposes that email senders should post a small "attention bond" (Van Alstyne 2007). Recipients who were unhappy to have received a message would have the right to collect that small fee. Those who thought the message was reasonable to send would return the fee. People sending direct messages to individuals would face little risk, but senders of commercial spam to thousands or millions of people might end up paying quite a bit to do so.

The Influence Limiter for recommender systems, described previously, works analogously (Resnick and Sami 2007). Each rating that changes the predictions that are made for other people is treated as a bet that other people will or won't like various items. When the other people enter their ratings for those items, the bets are resolved and people either gain or lose currency. Bad ratings—those that move predictions in the wrong direction—are costly, and good ratings actually earn currency. The amount of influence a person's rating has on a prediction determines the amount of the bet made, and bet sizes are limited by the currency holdings of the bettor. People whose ratings have been very helpful in the past get more influence on predictions for other people.

Design claim 27   Prices, bonds, or bets that make undesirable actions more costly than desirable actions reduce misbehavior.

Although identifiability creates opportunities for both informal and formal reputation sanctions, many communities allow either completely anonymous participation or participation under a long-lasting pseudonym that is not linked to an identity outside the community. For communities where members might not want to reveal their participation publicly, such as an HIV/AIDS discussion group or an activist political group fearing government repression, it is clear why members would prefer anonymous or pseudonymous participation. But even in many other, somewhat less sensitive, arenas people often prefer not to reveal their true identities in order to preserve some separation of context between different aspects of their lives. For example, one of the authors goes by the name "informationist" on eBay.[5]

Pseudonyms are popular in online communities. However, the impact of any kind of sanctions, including reputation consequences, for bad behavior is muted if someone can simply create a new account and start over. This problem is often referred to as *cheap pseudonyms*.

Cheap pseudonyms are especially problematic for sanctions such as bans: as mentioned previously, when bans were discussed as a means of limiting bad behavior, people who are banned from an online community can come back with a new account name and thus escape the consequences of their previous actions. If the community wants to be open to newcomers, the norm violator who returns under a new pseudonym will have the opportunity to violate norms again before being banned again. And again. And again. As Donath pointed out, eventually the community may become less open to newcomers, not giving them a chance to violate norms until they have proved themselves, but that may be a bad outcome for the community as well, as valuable newcomers may be turned away by the need to prove themselves (Donath 1997, 54; 1999).

The same problem can occur even if the sanction is not a complete ban. For example, consider a reputation-related consequence on eBay. Suppose buyers were very severe in their interpretations of seller feedback profiles. Suppose buyers were willing to spend $50 for an item from a seller with an unblemished record of only positive reviews from a hundred or more transactions, but only $40 to buy the same item from a seller with one negative review, and $45 to buy from a new seller. This approach would not be sustainable. After receiving a negative feedback, a seller would choose to start over and make $45 on his or her transactions rather than accepting the $40 he or she would receive from continuing to sell with an unfavorable feedback profile. If starting over is cost-free, then the worst possible seller feedback profile that anyone will continue to use will have to be treated by buyers no worse than they treat new sellers.

Friedman and Resnick (2001) created an analytic model that helps clarify the predicament created by cheap pseudonyms and some of the strategies for dealing with it. The fundamental constraint is that for someone who is sanctioned, the utility of continuing to participate under the current identity—accepting the sanction—must be higher than the utility of starting over with a new pseudonym. Even more so, the utility of participating with an established identity without sanctions must be higher than the utility of participating as a newcomer.

This formulation suggests three ways in which to maintain effective sanctions given the possibility of cheap pseudonyms. The first is to increase the benefits of maintaining a long-term pseudonym. Online role-playing games such as Everquest and World of Warcraft naturally include such a mechanism, as online characters need to be leveled up in order to gain access to new realms, equipment, or capabilities. When creating a new character, players lose these assets and can no longer play in the more interesting regions of the game. Other types of communities can use such mechanisms as well. These mechanisms may be explicit, such as requiring a threshold for certain capabilities (e.g., only allowing editors in Wikipedia with more than some number of posts to vote), or they may be implicit, such as providing more weight to old timers (e.g., Digg users with many friends and many front-page stories may be more likely to have their stories make it to the front page in the future).

Benefits need not be linked to functionality, either; other factors such as prestige may be effective as well. For example, Slashdot assigns user IDs sequentially, with the oldest users having the lowest numbers. Despite conferring no extra privileges, such a mechanism makes early accounts valuable: in 2007, Slashdot included a low user ID as one of the items in a charity auction. Someone possessing a low user ID might be more willing to accept sanctions to avoid having to start over with a new, high-numbered ID.

The benefits of using a long-term pseudonym can be financial as well. In a controlled experiment on eBay, the same seller earned about 8 percent more revenue selling matched items with an account having high reputation than with new accounts. That means that continuing with an established account is advantageous and thus the threat of sanctions can have a deterrent effect. But the maximum sanction will be equivalent to no more than 8 percent of the future sales revenue required to build up a new account's reputation (Resnick et al. 2006).

Some authors have suggested cross-community reputation systems (e.g., Pingel and Steinbrecher 2008) as a way to further increase the value of continued use of a single pseudonym, because people would have to abandon any benefits associated with the existing pseudonym in all the linked communities. But cross-community reputation systems are difficult to implement. Several companies and open source efforts have tried and failed to gain widespread adoption for "open" reputation systems.

Design claim 28   Increasing the benefits of participating with a long-term identifier increases the community's ability to sanction misbehavior.

A second way to maintain effective sanctions in the presence of cheap pseudonyms is to make the pseudonyms expensive. For example, if an invitation is necessary to create a new account, the effort involved in gaining an invitation may prevent members from creating an alternative persona and from misbehaving in their primary persona. Another possibility is to charge an entrance fee. Online multiplayer games such as World of Warcraft that limit the number of player characters enabled for a registered account use this approach. We have already discussed CAPTCHAs, which impose a small time-cost and thus deter the creation of thousands of accounts— though not the creation of a few.

At the extreme, it may be possible to completely prevent people from getting a second pseudonym once they have acquired one. A person wishing to obtain a pseudonym to participate in a community would have to provide a real-world identity credential to a registration authority, such as a credit card or driver's license. The registration authority would check to make sure that the real-world identity had not previously been issued a pseudonym. Although one community for doctors, Sermo (http://sermo.com), allows members to participate under pseudonyms, it requires them to register with a name that can be checked against national databases of physicians, which makes it very difficult to create a second account. Using a cryptographic technique called blind signatures, the registration authority could even be prevented from knowing the mapping from the user's real-world identifier to the user's pseudonym for the community, if that level of anonymity were important to users (Friedman and Resnick 2001).

Design claim 29   Imposing costs for or preventing pseudonym switching increases the community's ability to sanction misbehavior.

Rather than increasing the costs of creating a new pseudonym, another strategy is to require each new entrant to put something at stake that will be lost if the community decides to sanction the newcomer. One possibility is to require new members to post bonds that will be refunded if they build up good reputations in the community. A related strategy is to tie the reputation of existing members to new members whom they invite. Many studies have shown that recruiting new employees in organizations via referrals from existing employees is superior than more formal recruiting methods (e.g., Kirnan, Farley, and Geisinger 1989). This approach works in part because referrals lead to better fit, because sponsors know about both the candidate and organization and have an incentive to represent both accurately. The new member has an incentive to make his or her sponsor look good, and the sponsor has an incentive to help the new member learn the norms and regulations of the community so as to avoid violations. An additional explanation is that the sponsorship creates incentives for both the sponsor and newcomer to behave well. If the new members misbehave, sanctions may be visited on their sponsoring member.

Design claim 30   Forcing newcomers to post bonds that may be forfeited if the newcomers misbehave or forcing newcomers' sponsors to stake their own reputations increases the community's ability to sanction misbehavior.

Ostrom's fifth principle, culled from studies of successful institutions for managing common pool resources, is the need for graduated sanctions (Ostrom 1990). One reason is that sanctions disproportionate to the offense may be perceived as unfair and illegitimate. She writes, "A large monetary fine imposed on a person facing an unusual problem may produce resentment and unwillingness to conform to the rules in the future" (Ostrom 1990, 98). Minor sanctions, proportionate to the offense, are perceived as more legitimate, and errors in their application are also more tolerable. Because the decision about whether to categorize something as deliberate misbehavior versus an accidental or unknowing violation is noisy and subject to biases (e.g., newcomers are more likely to be considered deliberate violators than old-timers; Hollander

1958), lighter sanctions mitigate the ill effects from inevitable mistakes in categorization. Stronger sanctions are perceived as more legitimate when applied only after lighter sanctions have proven ineffective.

People tend to be happier and feel that they have been treated fairly and with more respect when they are persuaded to comply through expertise and judgment rather than commands and force (Koslowsky et al. 2001; Tyler 1997). Sometimes authorities use both nonforceful and forceful measures to gain compliance, and this strategy works as long as the forceful measures do not undercut the persuasiveness of nonforceful measures (Emans et al. 2003). Graduated sanctions that begin with persuasion based on expertise and judgment and proceed to more forceful measures can be especially effective.

In the online community setting, the lowest level of sanctions is a private message explaining the infraction, ideally accompanied by a link to an articulated guideline or rule and an invitation to discuss the matter further if desired. Unlike more public disapprobation, this method allows people to save face. Sanctions can escalate after repeated misbehavior to public rebuke, disemvoweling or other moderation of individual messages, or gags or bans.

For example, vandals in Wikipedia are initially greeted with an informational message assuming good faith (and allowing the vandal to save face while not continuing to vandalize), "Welcome to Wikipedia. Although everyone is welcome to make constructive contributions to Wikipedia, at least one of your recent edits did not appear to be constructive and has been reverted. Please use the sandbox for any test edits you would like to make, and read the welcome page to learn more about contributing constructively to this encyclopedia. Thank you" (Wikipedia 2010c).

Repeated misbehavior is dealt with through four levels of escalating sanctions and more strongly worded messages, culminating in the following brief message: "This is the *last warning* you will receive for your disruptive edits. If you vandalize Wikipedia again, you *will* be blocked from editing" (Wikipedia 2010c).

Design claim 31   Graduated sanctions increase the legitimacy and thus the effectiveness of sanctions.

Most research on crime prevention shows that perceived certainty of punishment has more deterrence value than factors such as the immediacy or severity of punishment (see Pratt et al. 2006 for a recent review). A mild but certain punishment is more effective in deterring misbehavior than a severe but uncertain punishment.

For instance, the most severe punishment in the United States is the death penalty, but this punishment is highly uncertain. The historical evidence is that the death penalty has not deterred murder or rape (see Bailey and Peterson 1997 for a review); in some cases, an increase in these crimes followed executions (Sakamoto et al. 2003). On the other hand, checking the blood alcohol level of every single motorist stopped at sobriety checkpoints is associated with dramatic reductions in drunk driving and alcohol related accidents. And across states, mild versus severe drunk driving penalties does not differentiate drunk driving rates, but certainty of punishment does. It is especially ineffective to ignore misbehavior that negatively affects a community. Rule breaking that goes without punishment encourages copycat offenses and undermines cooperation. Unpunished rule breaking causes even people predisposed to good behavior to cease doing so or exit (Fehr and Gächter 2000). This research has encouraged many real-world communities to fine people mildly but reliably for visible instances of rule breaking such as panhandling and littering.

One lesson for online communities is that there must be a high probability that norm violations will be detected. One option is that community members can be enlisted to flag violations. For example, YouTube has a safety center where users can report inappropriate users or content (see figure 4.9). Other online communities use software to increase the certainty of detection of inappropriate behavior. Some companies, for example, use software to flag photographs with large flesh-colored areas as potentially pornographic. Facebook uses software to detect when users or applications send requests to too many subscribers and then bans their accounts for a period. In many companies, the flagged material is then handed off to company employees or an outsourcing firm for further evaluation (Stone 2010).

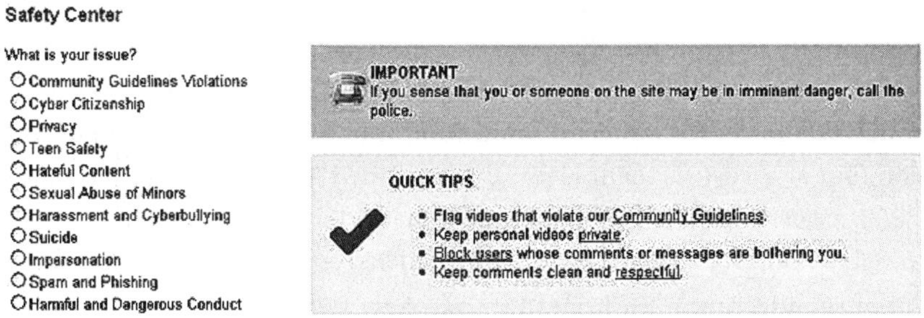

Safety Center

What is your issue?
- ○ Community Guidelines Violations
- ○ Cyber Citizenship
- ○ Privacy
- ○ Teen Safety
- ○ Hateful Content
- ○ Sexual Abuse of Minors
- ○ Harassment and Cyberbullying
- ○ Suicide
- ○ Impersonation
- ○ Spam and Phishing
- ○ Harmful and Dangerous Conduct

IMPORTANT
If you sense that you or someone on the site may be in imminent danger, call the police.

QUICK TIPS
- Flag videos that violate our Community Guidelines.
- Keep personal videos private.
- Block users whose comments or messages are bothering you.
- Keep comments clean and respectful.

Figure 4.9
YouTube's Safety Center for reporting inappropriate people or content (http://www.google.com/support/youtube/bin/request.py?contact_type=abuse).

Design claim 32 Peer reporting or automatic detection of violations increases the deterrent effect of sanctions.

To enhance certainty of sanctions for violations, there must also be a high probability that sanctions will be imposed after a violation is detected. In many online communities, many of the sanctions are decided and carried out by members, not by external administrators. But the members may not actually impose the sanctions, and for good reason: it is often costly for the person imposing the sanctions. The sanctions may lead to interpersonal drama and require a significant amount of time and emotional energy for the sanctioning party to defend a decision. Moreover, there may be retaliation against the sanctioning party. There have been instances in which offenders have harassed members who tried to sanction them. On eBay, leaving negative feedback often led to receiving negative feedback in return (Dellarocas and Wood 2008). One buyer explained, "I've had a few experiences where I didn't leave nonpositive feedback I felt was warranted only to avoid the retaliatory negative" (sqpantz 2008).

Ostrom and others refer to the delivery of sanctions as a second-order social dilemma or free-rider problem (Ostrom 1990). She quotes Jon Elster (1989), discussing the problem in the context of union members sanctioning (or not) workers who don't join the union: "Why, for instance, should a rational, selfish worker ostracize or otherwise punish those who don't join the union? What's in it for him? True, it may be better for all members if all punish nonmembers than if none do, but for each member it may be even better to remain passive. Punishment almost invariably is costly to the punisher, while the benefits from punishment are diffusely distributed over the members" (Ostrom 1990, p. 45).

Yet in many situations, people do voluntarily sanction others, even at some cost to themselves. One common laboratory experiment is called the *ultimatum game*. One party, the proposer, is given a sum of money. He or she chooses a division of the money between him- or herself and the decider. If the decider accepts, they each keep the proposed share. If not, neither gets any money. When proposers offer too small a share, many deciders reject the proposal, punishing the proposer for the unfair proposed division, but at a cost to themselves. In the United States, for example, when offers of a 70/30 percent split of the money were made, more than three-quarters of deciders rejected the offers. Somewhat fewer accepted bad splits in Slovenia and somewhat more in Japan and Israel. But even in Israel nearly one-third rejected the 70/30 split offers, and two-thirds rejected 90/10 offers (Roth et al. 1991).

What can designers do to increase the likelihood that members will impose sanctions when they are warranted? Some of the techniques described earlier also have the desirable side effect of increasing members' willingness to carry out sanctions. First, anything that increases community cohesion will help. Cohesive communities are more likely than noncohesive ones both to have well-defined norms and to enforce them by sanctioning misbehaviors. In particular, much scholarly research suggests that people sanction misbehaviors because in the long run, doing so improves the welfare of the groups of which they are a part. Consistent with this logic, Horne showed in a series of experiments that individuals in more cohesive groups (i.e., ones in which individuals are interdependent upon each other) were more likely to enforce norms through social sanctioning (Horne 2001 2007; Horne and Cutlip 2002). Second, graduated sanctions can help. The lowest level of lighter sanctions tend to be lower in cost to initiate than severe sanctions, which often require significant justification and debate. Third, explicit rules and guidelines that are referenced when applying sanctions can limit the amount of justification and debate that will occur afterward.

Finally, as experiments by Small and Loewenstein (2005) show, people are more punitive toward identified wrongdoers than toward equivalent unidentified wrongdoers. They propose that identifying an offender increases people's punitiveness because of the stronger feelings people have toward identified others. In support of this thesis, these researchers found that people's anger is much harsher toward identified offenders than unidentified offenders. Thus, when bringing instances of misbehavior to the attention of people deciding on sanctions, identifying the perpetrators by name or picture should increase willingness to impose sanctions.

There are also some additional measures, not discussed previously, that designers can take. First, the community can designate formal sanctioning roles so that those imposing sanctions have legitimacy. In message boards or blogs, these are typically *moderators*; in wikis, they are *administrators*. For example, a message with a gentle correction coming from someone who is a designated moderator is less likely to generate drama or retaliation than the same message coming from someone without a formal role.

Second, steps can be taken to prevent direct retaliation. For example, in 2008 eBay introduced a new rule under which sellers are not allowed to submit negative or neutral feedback any more—only positive. That change eliminated the possibility of sellers retaliating with negative feedback when they received it and should make buyers more willing to give negative feedback.

Design claim 33   Increased community cohesion, graduated sanctions, explicit rules, identifiable perpetrators, formal sanctioning roles, and antiretaliatory measures increase the likelihood that sanctions will be applied and thus increase the deterrent effect of sanctions.

5 Summary of Design Alternatives

This chapter has explored means for regulating behavior that violates behavioral norms, both limiting it and limiting the damage that it causes when it does occur. We conclude with a summary of the design alternatives considered throughout the chapter.

Several options are available that alter how information is used or displayed. Inappropriate posts can be moved to areas where they are less likely to be seen, scored so that they will be hidden from other users, or degraded through techniques like disemvoweling. Bad edits in wikis can be reverted, making them invisible except to people who examine a page's history. Ratings that are suspected to be from manipulators can be removed or discounted when making recommendations. Links can be annotated so that search engines will ignore them. These options can limit the damage that nonnormative behavior causes and/or can reduce incentives for doing such behavior in the first place.

Feedback and rewards can come in other forms as well. Feedback may be directly solicited and displayed along with messages or may be aggregated into reputation profiles. A good profile can lead to rewards in the form of better treatment from members in the future and the reverse for bad reputations. Instead of affecting reputation profiles, feedback about individual actions can lead to monetary payoffs (positive or negative) or payoffs in an internal currency that has value within the community. Rewards or sanctions can also be assigned to someone's cumulative behavior: a bond posted upon entry into the community can be forfeited if the person misbehaves.

Several technical features can be used to limit the actions available to people who may violate behavior norms. Throttles or activity quotas can limit repetitive behavior. Charging for actions using a currency accrued through normal participation can also limit repetitive behavior. For members who gain value from normal participation, such charges do not create a binding constraint but do serve as a disincentive for trolls and attackers because earning the currency may be costly for them. Gags and bans can silence bad actors altogether. To prevent people from sidestepping gags and bans, or any form of sanction, the account registration process can impose limits or costs on the creation of new accounts.

Roles, rules, policies, and procedures play a big part in regulating nonnormative behavior. Having clear rules and policies and fair procedures for applying any of the filters, sanctions, and participation limits decreases resistance to them. Legitimacy will also increase and resistance decrease if there is wide participation in setting of rules and policies and if the enforcement roles are widely distributed. Two particular features of the contents of rules and policies are also helpful. Sanctions should be graduated, both to increase their legitimacy and to increase the willingness of enforcers to apply them. And everyone should learn to ignore trolls.

Finally, as in other chapters, we find that there is considerable power in decisions about framing—ways of communicating what is happening in the community. Highlighting or leaving traces of bad behavior and prominently displaying behavior guidelines can help to clarify norms but runs the risk of conveying a descriptive norm that misbehavior is rampant. Showing names and pictures of those who took actions makes people think twice about misbehaving and increases people's willingness to enforce sanctions against those who do misbehave. Framing disciplinary actions in a way that allows people to save face ("Someone using your account . . . ," or "You may not have realized . . .") can make people more receptive and willing to change their behavior.

In the face of harmful behavior, it may feel natural to turn first to tangible remedies such as removing bad posts or banning or throttling the posters. An important theme of the chapter is that less tangible, softer, and more behavioral remedies may be desirable to try first. Guidelines can be clarified, and the community as a whole can be involved in that process, in order to build legitimacy. Individuals can be reminded and corrected in a way that allows them to save face. Off-topic communication can be gently encouraged to move to an interaction space where people don't mind the digressions. Trolls can be ignored. Responses can escalate if these mild approaches fail, with other behavioral remedies such as public rebuke. Behavioral responses, however, will not always be sufficient. Especially in the face of manipulators and spammers who create many accounts and act through bots, or in the face of trolls who gain rather than lose value from other members getting mad at them, communities need some more automated and tangible ways to limit damage.

Notes

1. Actually, CAPTCHAs do not eliminate the possibility of attackers creating many new accounts, but they do make it harder and a little more expensive. A *New York Times* article reports that sophisticated spammers are paying people in developing countries to answer CAPTCHAs, with the going rate at about $1 per 1,000 (Bajaj 2010). The solved CAPTCHAs are passed back to a computer program that automatically completes the rest of an account registration process.

2. Quoted from alt.support.diabetes. We don't provide a citation for this quote to protect the poster's privacy.

Table 4.1

Summary of design alternatives relevant to regulation of behavior, ordered by type

Type	Design alternative	Design claim
Selection, sorting, highlighting	Moderation systems that prescreen, degrade, label, move, or remove inappropriate messages	1
	Redirecting inappropriate posts to other places	2
	Reversion tools	5
	Filters or influence limits	6
	Telling search engines not to follow links	24
Community structure	Cohesive groups	21, 33
Feedback and rewards	Displaying feedback of members to others	16
	Reputation systems	26
	Prices, bonds, or bets that make undesirable actions more costly than desirable actions	27
	Increasing the benefits of participating with a long-term identifier	28
	Forcing newcomers to post bonds that may be forfeited if the newcomers misbehave or forcing newcomers' sponsors to stake their own reputations	30
Access controls	Activity quotas	8
	Gags and bans	9
	Paying to take actions in the community with currency accumulated through normal participation	11
	Limiting fake accounts with CAPTCHAs or identity checks	12
	Imposing costs for or preventing pseudonym switching	29

Table 4.1

(continued)

Type	Design alternative	Design claim
Roles, rules, policies, and procedures	Consistently applied criteria, a chance to argue one's case, and appeal procedures	3, 10
	Moderation decided upon by people who are members of the community, are impartial, and have limited or rotating power	4
	A widely followed norm of ignoring trolls	7
	Explicit rules and guidelines	18, 19, 33
	Community influence on rule making	22
	Graduated sanctions	31, 33
	Peer reporting or automatic detection of violations	32
	Formal sanctioning roles	33
	Anti-retaliatory measures	33
Presentation and framing	Publicly displaying examples of appropriate behavior	13
	Publicly contrasting examples of inappropriate behavior in the context of a descriptive norm of appropriate behavior	14
	Publicly displaying many examples of inappropriate behavior	15
	Publicly displaying statistics that highlight the prevalence of normative behavior	17
	Prominently displayed guidelines	19
	Reminders at the point of an action that may violate norms	20
	Face-saving ways to correct norm violations	23
	Verified identities and pictures	25, 33

3. The Omidyar Network is a charitable foundation set up by eBay founder Pierre Omidyar. It is probably not a coincidence that the Omidyar community thoroughly integrated a reputation system into its operations.

4. If we think of reputation scores as account values in some internal currency unit, then these currency charges are actually a form of reputation consequence. The difference is that currency units other than reputations may have consequences other than changing how other members perceive the currency holder.

5. Of course, revealing this information partially collapses the context separation between my professor persona and my trader persona. Interestingly, the collapse is largely one-way: readers of this book can look me up on eBay, but most eBay traders who encounter "informationist" will not know about my other life as an author and professor.

References

Akdeniz, Yaman. 2008. *Internet Child Pornography and the Law: National and International Responses.* Farnham, Surrey, UK: Ashgate Publishing, Ltd.

Alpizar, F., F. Carlsson, and O. Johansson-Stenman. 2008. Anonymity, Reciprocity, and Conformity: Evidence from Voluntary Contributions to a National Park in Costa Rica. *Journal of Public Economics* 92 (5–6): 1047–1060.

Apache Software Foundation. 2011. Public Forum Archive Policy. http://www.apache.org/foundation/public-archives.html.

Axelrod, R., and R. O. Keohane. 1985. Achieving Cooperation under Anarchy: Strategies and Institutions. *World Politics: A Quarterly Journal of International Relations* 38 (1): 226–254.

Bailey, W. C., and R. D. Peterson. 1997. Murder, Capital Punishment, and Deterrence: A Review of the Literature. In *The Death Penalty in America: Current Controversies*, ed. Hugo Adam Bedau, 135–161. New York: Oxford University Press.

Bajaj, Vikas. 2010. Spammers Pay Others to Answer Security Tests. *New York Times*, Apr. 26, 2010. http://www.nytimes.com/2010/04/26/technology/26captcha.html.

Bajari, P., and A. Hortacsu. 2004. Economic Insights from Internet Auctions. *Journal of Economic Literature* 42 (2): 457–486.

Bartle, Richard. 1996. Hearts, Clubs, Diamonds, Spades: Players Who Suit Mud. http://www.mud.co.uk/richard/hcds.htm.

Bordia, P. 1997. Face-to-Face versus Computer-Mediated Communication: A Synthesis of the Experimental Literature. *Journal of Business Communication* 34 (1): 99.

bunkerbuster1. What Is a Concern Troll? http://www.democraticunderground.com/discuss/duboard.php?az=view_all&address=364x1382185.

Burke, Moira, Robert E. Kraut, and Diane Williams. 2010. Social Use of Computer-Mediated Communication by Adults on the Autism Spectrum. In *CSCW 2010: Proceedings of the ACM Conference on Computer Supported Cooperative Work*, 425–434. New York: ACM Press.

Butler, Brian, L. Sproull, S. Kiesler, and R. Kraut. 2007. Community Effort in Online Groups: Who Does the Work and Why? In *Leadership at a Distance*, ed. S. Weisband. Hillsdale, NJ: Lawrence Erlbaum Associates.

Cabral, L., and A. Hortacsu. 2010. The Dynamics of Seller Reputation: Evidence from eBay. *Journal of Industrial Economics* 58 (1): 54–78.

Cialdini, R. B. 2003. Crafting Normative Messages to Protect the Environment. *Current Directions in Psychological Science* 12 (4): 105.

Cialdini, R. B., C. A. Kallgren, and R. R. Reno. 1991. A Focus Theory of Normative Conduct: A Theoretical Refinement and Reevaluation of the Role of Norms in Human Behavior. *Advances in Experimental Social Psychology* 24 (20): 201–243.

CmdrTaco. 2003. How Does Moderation Work? Slashdot. http://slashdot.org/faq/com-mod.shtml.

Colquitt, J. A., D. E. Conlon, M. J. Wesson, C. Porter, and K. Y. Ng. 2001. Justice at the Millennium: A Meta-Analytic Review of 25 Years of Organizational Justice Research. *Journal of Applied Psychology* 86 (3): 425–445.

Constant, D., L. Sproull, and S. Kiesler. 1996. The Kindness of Strangers: The Usefulness of Electronic Weak Ties for Technical Advice. *Organization Science* 7 (2): 119–135.

Cornwell, B., and D. C. Lundgren. 2001. Love on the Internet: Involvement and Misrepresentation in Romantic Relationships in Cyberspace versus Realspace. *Computers in Human Behavior* 17 (2): 197–211.

Crystal. 2009. The Twitter Rules. http://twitter.zendesk.com/forums/26257/entries/18311.

DeJong, W., S. K. Schneider, L. G. Towvim, M. J. Murphy, E. E. Doerr, N. R. Simonsen, K. E. Mason, et al. 2006. A Multisite Randomized Trial of Social Norms Marketing Campaigns to Reduce College Student Drinking. *Journal of Studies on Alcohol* 67 (6): 868.

Dellarocas, Chrysanthos, and Charles A. Wood. 2008. The Sound of Silence in Online Feedback: Estimating Trading Risks in the Presence of Reporting Bias. *Management Science* 54 (3): 460–476.

Dewally, M., and L. Ederington. 2006. A Comparison of Reputation, Certification, Warranties, and Disclosure as Remedies for Information Asymmetries: Lessons from the On-Line Comic Book Market. *Journal of Business* 79 (4): 693–729.

Dibbell, Juian. 1993. A Rape in Cyberspace: How an Evil Clown, a Haitian Trickster Spirit, Two Wizards, and a Cast of Dozens Turned a Database into a Society. *Village Voice* (December 23).

Donath, Judith S. 1997. Identity and Deception in the Virtual Community. In *Communities in Cyberspace*, ed. P. Kollock and M. Smith, 27–58. Berkeley: University of California Press.

Donath, J., K. Karahalios, and F. Viegas. 1999. Visualizing Conversation. *Journal of Computer Mediated Communication* 4 (4).

Ducheneaut, Nicolas. 2005. Socialization in an Open Source Software Community: A Socio-Technical Analysis. *Computer Supported Cooperative Work* 14 (4): 323–368.

Durkheim, Emile. 1903 [1953]. The Determination of Moral Facts. In *Sociology and Philosophy*, 35–63. London: Cohen and West.

Elster, Jon. 1989. *The Cement of Society: A Study of Social Order*. New York: Cambridge University Press.

Emans, B. J. M., L. Munduate, E. Klaver, and E. Van de Vliert. 2003. Constructive Consequences of Leaders' Forcing Influence Styles. *Applied Psychology* 52 (1): 36–54.

Facebook. 2010. Warnings. http://www.facebook.com/help/?page=421.

Fehr, E., and S. Gächter. 2000. Cooperation and Punishment in Public Goods Experiments. *American Economic Review* 90 (4): 980–994.

Fehr, E., U. Fischbacher, and S. Gächter. 2003. Strong Reciprocity, Human Cooperation, and the Enforcement of Social Norms. *Human Nature* 13 (1): 1–25.

Festinger, L., A. Pepitone, and T. Newcomb. 1952. Some Consequences of De-Individuation in a Group. *Journal of Abnormal and Social Psychology* 47 (2): 382–389.

4chan. 2011a. FAQ. http://www.4chan.org/faq.

4chan. 2011b. Rules. http://www.4chan.org/rules.

Friedman, E., and Paul Resnick. 2001. The Social Cost of Cheap Pseudonyms. *Journal of Economics and Management Strategy* 10 (2): 173–199.

Gibbs, Jack P. 1985. Deterrence Theory and Research. *Nebraska Symposium on Motivation. Nebraska Symposium on Motivation* 33:87–130.

Goffman, E. 1959. *The Presentation of Self in Everyday Life*. Garden City, NY: Doubleday.

Goffman, E. 1963. *Behavior in Public Places*. New York: The Free Press.

Haakon. 1992. LambdaMOO Takes a New Direction. In the LambdaMOO Help System.

Halfaker, A., A. Kittur, R. Kraut, and J. Riedl. 2009. A Jury of Your Peers: Quality, Experience and Ownership in Wikipedia. In *Wikisym 2009: Proceedings of the 5th International Symposium on Wikis and Open Collaboration*. New York: ACM Press.

Hardin, Garrett. 1968. The Tragedy of the Commons. *Science* 162:1243–1248.

Herring, S., K. Job-Sluder, R. Scheckler, and S. Barab. 2002. Searching for Safety Online: Managing "Trolling" in a Feminist Forum. *Information Society* 18 (5): 371–384.

Hoag, David. 1996. The WELL Host Manual. http://www.well.com/~confteam/hostmanual.

Hollander, E. P. 1958. Conformity, Status, and Idiosyncrasy Credit. *Psychological Review* 65 (2): 117.

Horne, Christine. 2001. The Enforcement of Norms: Group Cohesion and Meta-Norms. *Social Psychology Quarterly* 64 (3): 253–266.

Horne, Christine. 2007. Explaining Norm Enforcement. *Rationality and Society* 19 (2):139.

Horne, Christine, and Anna Cutlip. 2002. Sanctioning Costs and Norm Enforcement: An Experimental Test. *Rationality and Society* 14 (3): 285–307.

Jackson, Gregory A. 1994. Promoting Network Civility at MIT: Crime & Punishment, or the Golden Rule? http://www.mit.edu/activities/safe/data/mit-stopit.html.

JoBlo Movie Network. 2005. Basic Rules and Guidelines. http://www.joblo.com/forums/announcement.php?s=641f9cd5b47beab4ad423f0c861dba3c&forumid=21.

Karau, S. J., and K. D. Williams. 1993. Social Loafing: A Meta-Analytic Review and Theoretical Integration. *Journal of Personality and Social Psychology* 65 (4): 681–706.

Kiesler, S., S. Weisband, and F. Drasgow. 1999. A Meta-Analytic Study of Social Desirability Distortion in Computer-Administered Questionnaires, Traditional Questionnaires, and Interviews. *Journal of Applied Psychology* 84 (5): 754–775.

Kiesler, S., Zubrow, D., Moses, A., and Geller, V. 1985. Affect in Computer-Mediated Communication: An Experiment in Synchronous Terminal-to-Terminal Discussion. *Human-Computer Interaction* 1 (1): 77–104.

Kirnan, J. P., J. A. Farley, and K. F. Geisinger. 1989. The Relationship between Recruiting Source, Applicant Quality, and Hire Performance: An Analysis by Sex, Ethnicity, and Age. *Personnel Psychology* 42 (2): 293–308.

Kittur, A., B. Suh, B. A. Pendleton, and E. H. Chi. 2007. He Says, She Says: Conflict and Coordination in Wikipedia. In *CHI '07: Proceedings of the ACM Conference on Human Factors in Computing Systems*, 453–462. New York: ACM Press.

Kolbert, Elizabeth. 2001. Pimps and Dragons: How an Online World Survived a Social Breakdown. *The New Yorker* 77:13–88.

Kollock, P., and M. Smith. 1996. Managing the Virtual Commons: Cooperation and Conflict in Computer Communities. In *Computer-Mediated Communication: Linguistic, Social, and Cross-Cultural Perspectives*, ed. Susan Herring, 109–128. Amsterdam: John Benjamin.

Koslowsky, M., J. Schwarzwald, and S. Ashuri. 2001. On the Relationship between Subordinates' Compliance to Power Sources and Organisational Attitudes. *Applied Psychology* 50 (3): 455–476.

von Krogh, Georg, Sebastian Spaeth, Karim R. Lakhani, and Eric von Hippel. 2003. Community, Joining, and Specialization in Open Source Software Innovation: A Case Study. *Research Policy* 32 (7): 1217–1241.

Lessig, L. 1999. *Code and Other Laws of Cyberspace*. New York: Basic Books.

Leventhal, G. S. 1976. The Distribution of Rewards and Resources in Groups and Organizations. In *Advances in Experimental Social Psychology*, ed. L. Berkowitz and W. Walster, 91–131. New York: Academic Press.

Lewis, S. A., C. J. Langan, and E. P. Hollander. 1972. Expectation of Future Interaction and the Choice of Less Desirable Alternatives in Conformity. *Sociometry* 35 (3): 440–447.

Mobasher, B., R. Burke, R. Bhaumik, and C. Williams. 2007. Toward Trustworthy Recommender Systems: An Analysis of Attack Models and Algorithm Robustness. *ACM Transactions on Internet Technology* 7 (4): 23.

Moon, J. Y., and L. S. Sproull. 2008. The Role of Feedback in Managing the Internet-Based Volunteer Work Force. *Information Systems Research* 19 (4): 494–515.

Orion, Crystah. 2010. Godmodding and borderline goomodding. http://z3.invisionfree.com/NJORoleplayingSite/index.php?showtopic=1045&view=getnewpost.

Ostrom, E. 2000. Collective Action and the Evolution of Social Norms. *Journal of Economic Perspectives* 14 (3): 137–158.

Ostrom, E. 1990. *Governing the Commons: The Evolution of Institutions for Collective Action*. New York: Cambridge University Press.

Page, L., S. Brin, R. Motwani, and T. Winograd. 1998. *The Pagerank Citation Ranking: Bringing Order to the Web*. Stanford, CA: Stanford University.

Perkins, H. W., P. W. Meilman, J. S. Leichliter, J. R. Cashin, and C. A. Presley. 1999. Misperceptions of the Norms for the Frequency of Alcohol and Other Drug Use on College Campuses. *Journal of American College Health* 47 (6): 253–258.

Postmes, Tom, and Russell Spears. 1998. Deindividuation and Antinormative Behavior: A Meta-Analysis. *Psychological Bulletin* 123 (3): 238–259.

Powazek, Derek M. 2002. *Design for Community: The Art of Connecting Real People in Virtual Places*. Indianapolis, IN: New Riders.

Pratt, T. C., F. T. Cullen, K. R. Blevins, L. E. Daigle, and T. D. Madensen. 2006. The Empirical Status of Deterrence Theory: A Meta-Analysis. In *Taking Stock: The Status of Criminological Theory*, ed. F. T. Cullen, J. P. Wright, and K. R. Blevins, 367–396. New Brunswick, NJ: Transaction Publishers.

Pingel, F., and S. Steinbrecher. 2008. Multilateral Secure Cross-Community Reputation Systems for Internet Communities. In *Trust, Privacy and Security in Digital Business: 5th International Conference, TrustBus 2008, Turin, Italy*, 69–78.

Psych Central. 2008. Terms of Use. http://psychcentral.com/about/terms.htm.

Resnick, P., K. Kuwabara, R. Zeckhauser, and E. Friedman. 2000. Reputation Systems. *Communications of the ACM* 43 (12): 45–48.

Resnick, P., and R. Sami. 2007. The Influence Limiter: Provably Manipulation-Resistant Recommender Systems. In *Proceedings of the 2007 ACM Conference on Recommender Systems*, 25–32. New York: ACM.

Resnick, P., and R. Sami. 2008. The Information Cost of Manipulation-Resistance in Recommender Systems. In *Proceedings of the 2008 ACM Conference on Recommender Systems*, 147–154. New York: ACM.

Resnick, P., and R. Zeckhauser. 2002. Trust among Strangers in Internet Transactions: Empirical Analysis of eBay's Reputation System. *Advances in Applied Microeconomics: A Research Annual* 11:127–157.

Resnick, P., R. Zeckhauser, J. Swanson, and K. Lockwood. 2006. The Value of Reputation on eBay: A Controlled Experiment. *Experimental Economics* 9 (2): 79–101.

Rohrer, J. H., S. H. Baron, E. L. Hoffman, and D. V. Swander. 1954. The Stability of Autokinetic Judgments. *Journal of Abnormal and Social Psychology* 49 (4): 595–597.

Rosenberg, Milton J. 2009. The Conditions and Consequences of Evaluation Apprehension. In *Artifacts in Behavioral Research: Robert Rosenthal and Ralph L. Rosnow's Classic Books*, 211–263. New York: Oxford University Press.

Ross, W. H., and D. E. Conlon. 2000. Hybrid Forms of Third-Party Dispute Resolution: Theoretical Implications of Combining Mediation and Arbitration. *Academy of Management Review* 25 (2): 416–427.

Roth, A. E., V. Prasnikar, M. Okuno-Fujiwara, and S. Zamir. 1991. Bargaining and Market Behavior in Jerusalem, Ljubljana, Pittsburgh, and Tokyo: An Experimental Study. *American Economic Review* 81 (5): 1068–1095.

Sakamoto, A., K. Sekiguchi, A. Shinkyu, and Y. Okada. 2003. Does Media Coverage of Capital Punishment Have a Deterrent Effect on the Occurrence of Brutal Crimes?: An Analysis of Japanese Time-Series Data from 1959 to 1990. In *Progress in Asian Social Psychology: Conceptual and Empirical Contributions*, ed. K. Yang, K. Hwang, P. B. Pederson, and I. Daibo. Westport, CT: Praeger.

Seay, A. F., and R. E. Kraut. 2007. Project Massive: Self-Regulation and Problematic Use of Online Gaming. In *Proceedings of the SIGCHI Conference on Human Factors in Computing Systems*, 829–838. New York: ACM Press.

Sassenberg, Kai, and Tom Postmes. 2002. Cognitive and Strategic Processes in Small Groups: Effects of Anonymity of the Self and Anonymity of the Group on Social Influence. *British Journal of Social Psychology* 41 (3): 463–480.

Shankland, Stephen. 2000. New Email Software Can Help You Bite Your Tongue. *CNET News*. http://news.cnet.com/New-email-software-can-help-you-bite-your-tongue/2100-1040_3-245790.html.

Sherif, Muzafer. 1936. *The Psychology of Social Norms*. New York: Harper.

Small, D. A., and G. Loewenstein. 2005. The Devil You Know: The Effects of Identifiability on Punitiveness. *Journal of Behavioral Decision Making* 18 (5): 311–318.

Smith, J. H. 2007. Tragedies of the Ludic Commons: Understanding Cooperation in Multiplayer Games. *Game Studies* 7 (1). http://gamestudies.org/0701/articles/smith.

Soetevent, A. R. 2005. Anonymity in Giving in a Natural Context: A Field Experiment in 30 Churches. *Journal of Public Economics* 89 (11–12): 2301–2323.

sqpantz. 2008. Works for Me. http://www.techdirt.com/articles/20080205/160733184.shtml.

Stone, Brad. 2010, July 19. Policing the Web's Lurid Precincts. *New York Times* (July 19): B1.

Tyler, T. R., and R. J. Bies. 1990. Beyond Formal Procedures: The Interpersonal Context of Procedural Justice. *Applied Social Psychology and Organizational Settings* 77:98.

Tyler, T. R. 1997. Citizen Discontent with Legal Procedures: A Social Science Perspective on Civil Procedure Reform. *American Journal of Comparative Law* 45 (4): 871–904.

Van Alstyne, M. 2007. Curing Spam: Rights, Signals, and Screens. *Economists' Voice* 4 (2): article 4. http://www.bepress.com/ev/vol4/iss2/art4.

Vesperman, J., and V. Henson. 2004. Building and Maintaining an International Volunteer Linux Community. In *Proceedings of the Freenix Track: 2004 USENIX Annual Technical Conference*. Berkeley, CA: USENIX Association.

Viegas, Fernanda, Martin Wattenberg, and K. Dave. 2004. Studying Cooperation and Conflict between Authors with History Flow Visualizations. In *CHI 2004: ACM Conference on Human-Factors in Computing Systems*. New York: ACM Press.

Walker, J. M., R. Gardner, and E. Ostrom. 1990. Rent Dissipation in a Limited-Access Common-Pool Resource: Experimental Evidence. *Journal of Environmental Economics and Management* 19 (3): 203–211.

Wikipedia. 2010a. Blocking Policy. http://en.wikipedia.org/wiki/Wikipedia:Blocking_policy.

Wikipedia. 2010b. Spam in Blogs. http://en.wikipedia.org/wiki/Spam_in_blogs.

Wikipedia. 2010c. Vandalism. http://en.wikipedia.org/wiki/Wikipedia:Vandalism.

Wikipedia. 2010d. Wikiproject Vandalism Studies: Study 1. http://en.wikipedia.org/wiki/Wikipedia:WikiProject_Vandalism_studies/Study1.

Wikipedia. 2011a. Biographies of Living Persons. http://en.wikipedia.org/wiki/Wikipedia:Biographies_of_living_persons.

Wikipedia. 2011b. Neutral Point of View. http://en.wikipedia.org/wiki/Wikipedia:Neutral_point_of_view.

Wikipedia. 2011c. Sock Puppetry. http://en.wikipedia.org/wiki/Wikipedia:Sock_puppetry.

Wikipedia. 2011d. The Three-Revert Rule. http://en.wikipedia.org/wiki/Wikipedia:Edit_warring#The_three-revert_rule.

Williams, Gail Ann. 1997. Hosting: Online Moderator Guidelines and Community-Building Tips. The Well. http://www.well.com/confteam/hosting.html.

Wookieepedia. 2010. Wookieepedia: The Star Wars Encyclopedia That Anyone Can Edit. http://starwars.wikia.com/wiki/Main_Page.

Wysocki, M. D. 2003. Cracking the Hacker Code: An Analysis of the Computer Hacker Subculture from Multiple Perspectives. Communication Studies, Northwestern University, Evanston, IL.

Yee, Nick. 2001. The Daedalus Project. http://www.nickyee.com/daedalus.

Zimbardo, P. G. 1969. The Human Choice: Individuation, Reason, and Order versus Deindividuation, Impulse, and Chaos. In *1969 Nebraska Symposium on Motivation*, ed. W. J. Arnold and D. Levine, 237–307. Lincoln, NE: University of Nebraska Press.

Zitek, E. M., and M. R. Hebl. 2007. The Role of Social Norm Clarity in the Influenced Expression of Prejudice over Time. *Journal of Experimental Social Psychology* 43 (6): 867–876.

5 The Challenges of Dealing with Newcomers

Robert E. Kraut, Moira Burke, John Riedl, and Paul Resnick

In the face of inevitable turnover, every online community must incorporate successive generations of newcomers to survive. Without replacing members who leave, a community will eventually wither away. Newcomers can also be a source of innovation, new ideas, and work procedures or other resources that the group needs. However, attracting newcomers and incorporating them into an existing community can be a difficult endeavor. Newcomers have not yet developed the commitment to the group felt by old-timers. As a result, they are very sensitive to the public image of a community and to their own early experiences in it. They may not join or may leave in the face of even minor adversity. They have less motivation to be helpful to the group or to display good organizational citizenship characteristic of many old-timers (Organ and Ryan 1995). In addition, for reasons of ignorance or maliciousness, newcomers may behave in ways that can be harmful to the group. They do not yet know the norms guiding behavior in the group, and in their ignorance may act in ways that offend other group members or otherwise undercut the smooth functioning of the group. For example, when participating in Wikipedia, new editors may fail to follow the policy of writing with a neutral point of view, or they may add content that has already been determined by a consensus of more experienced editors to belong in another article.

Because they lack experience, when newcomers try to participate, they imperil the work that other community members have already performed. For example, they may introduce bugs in an open source development project, cause the (virtual) death of fellow group members in an online role-playing game, or ask redundant questions in discussion groups. Finally, their mere presence can increase diversity in the group—at least until they learn the group's norms—and may in itself be off-putting to more experienced members of the community who prefer the people and routines they were familiar with.

When dealing with newcomers, online communities must solve five basic problems:

1. *Recruitment* Communities need to advertise to recruit members and to ensure a supply of newcomers for replenishment and growth.

2. *Selection* The community should select only those potential members who fit well. This process may occur through self-selection, in which potential members who are a good fit find the community attractive and those who are not a good fit find it unattractive. Or it may occur through screening, in which the community screens out undesirable members, while encouraging or selecting the others.

3. *Retention* Both theory and experience suggest that newcomers' ties to the community are especially fragile. As a result, the community should engage in tactics that keep potentially valuable newcomers around until they can develop more robust ties to the community or learn how the group operates.

4. *Socialization* The group needs to socialize the newcomers, teaching them how to behave in ways appropriate to the group, as discussed in chapter 4. In the current chapter, we focus on socialization strategies that are of particular relevance to newcomers.

5. *Protection* Throughout its interactions with prospective members, visitors, and newcomers in their early interactions, the community needs to protect itself from the potentially damaging actions of those who either have little knowledge of appropriate group behavior or little motivation to follow community norms.

These problems vary in importance across different communities, although every community faces them to some degree. Some communities may have an abundant supply of people clamoring for membership, which makes them want to restrict growth; for these communities, word of mouth may be sufficient for recruiting. Communities like open source software (OSS) development projects may have strict standards for members, but other communities may want almost any warm body who shows up. But even these seemingly open communities would like to reject spammers, trolls, or others whose primary goal is to disrupt the community.

These problems reflect two perspectives—that of the newcomers and that of the online community and its existing members. The recruiting process, for example, consists of both the activities that potential members might perform in investigating different communities and weighting alternatives, and the activities that communities and their members might perform in soliciting new recruits and interacting with them. In this chapter, we consider the perspective of the newcomer only insofar as it has implications for how the online community needs to be designed to accommodate them. For example, as we discuss later, newcomers are happier in a community and contribute more effectively if they have a complete and accurate impression of the community before they join it. To collect the information they need to form this impression, they may lurk in the community, silently observing, or may try to participate and gauge the community's reaction to them. Even though prior research demonstrates that newcomers are happier, stay longer, and perform more effectively if they actively seek information about organizations before joining them (Bauer et al. 2007), this chapter does not address the proactive moves that newcomers should take in order to gain an accurate view of the community, which is not under the control of a site designer or manager. Instead, the chapter concentrates on how the community should be designed to provide the information newcomers need to make a decision about joining and how the community should respond to the common moves that newcomers use when forming impressions of the community. For example, prospective members are likely to gain a more accurate view of the community if communities publish FAQ pages to make policies visible and allow outsiders access to archives of conversation among members, enabling them to judge the nature of the interactions. However, some communities may decide not to make these resources available to outsiders. For example, the managers of cancer support groups hosted at ACOR (http://www.acor.org) believe that the privacy needs of current members outweigh the investigatory needs of prospective members. Therefore, outsiders must register to become a member of a support group before they can see any of the interactions that have occurred in that group. The catch, of course, is that most outsiders cannot determine whether they want to become a member unless they can sample the goods.

Researchers in both online and offline settings have identified an analogous set of stages that newcomers take on the path to becoming committed members of a group or community. Levine and Moreland (1994), in discussing offline groups, use the terms *investigation*, *socialization*, and *maintenance* to describe the set of activities that newcomers and groups engage in as they become increasingly committed to each other. Individuals and groups go through an investigatory phase in which newcomers gather information about the group to predict whether it will fit their needs; groups use recruiting and selection processes to identify prospective members who would fit well with the group. During the earliest stages of the socialization period—just after a person has joined the community—the central challenge for the community is to keep the newcomer around. The relationship between the newcomer and community during this early socialization phase is especially fragile, and even small problems may drive newcomers out. However, as the newcomer becomes more committed to the community, helping newcomers learn the norms of the community and how to behave becomes increasingly important. In describing the progressive commitment of newcomers to online communities, Preece and Shneiderman (2009) propose a *"reader-to-leader" funnel* in which some newcomers move from being readers to being contributors, then collaborators, and finally leaders. Their transition from reader to contributor—analogous to Levine and Moreland's (1994) description of the transition of potential members from outsiders to organizational members as they move through the investigatory phase to the socialization phase—is the focus of this chapter.

1   Problem 1: Recruiting Newcomers

In the face of turnover in their membership, online communities will inevitably die without a constant supply of newcomers. Recently leaders of Wikipedia have been bemoaning their dilemma that after years of exponential growth, the number of new contributors joining Wikipedia does not compensate for the number of experienced editors who drop out (http://strategy.wikimedia.org/wiki/Community_health). Thus, it is important to consider the processes by which online communities advertise their existence and recruit newcomers. These processes determine whether the community has enough members to accomplish its goals. In addition, the processes of recruitment may have direct consequences for later problems that the community must solve, such as selection, retention, and commitment. Although there are many differences between online communities and conventional organizations with employees, especially in terms of the formality of the recruiting and acceptance process, the research on employee recruiting is relevant and we use this material heavily in the following discussion. We follow the research tradition on employee recruiting and consider recruiting to be "those organizational activities that (1) influence the number and/or types of applicants who apply for a position [i.e., membership in an online community] and/or (2) affect whether a . . . [membership] offer is accepted" (Breaugh and Starke 2000, 4).

Many online communities do little active recruiting for new members. This lack of attention to recruiting characterizes most Usenet groups and the OSS development projects represented in SourceForge (http://sourceforge.net). One can ignore active recruiting if potential members' random browsing of the web and word-of-mouth endorsements from current members provide a sufficient supply of recruits to replace losses and meet the community's needs for growth. Active recruitment, however, will be necessary if laissez-faire approaches are insufficient. Online communities differ on both the degree and methods they use for recruiting, even among those that actively recruit new members. Blizzard uses a full gamut of TV, print, and online advertising to recruit new World of Warcraft players. In addition to impersonal advertising, Blizzard also uses interpersonal recruiting, such as its "recruit-a-friend" promotion, which provides perks to both the recruiter and the recruit when an existing subscriber invites a friend to activate a ten-day trial account (Blizzard Entertainment 2010). Within the game itself, some guilds seek new members by posting advertisements to sites like the guild-recruiting forums within the game or third-party sites like Looking for Guild (http://www.lookingforguild.net); many others recruit guild members from among friends and family (Williams et al. 2006).

Design Claim 1   Compared to laissez-faire approaches, in which prospective members seek out or stumble upon a community, active recruiting leads to the community having access to a larger pool of prospective members.

Recruiting messages, whether formal or informal, are a specific type of persuasive communication. Research on attitudes, attitude change, and the influence of both interpersonal and mass communication is voluminous. Although we consider persuasion at several points in this book, a complete review is beyond our scope. Instead, we sample some highlights in this book and refer the reader to relevant reviews for more detail on persuasion in general (e.g., Chaiken, Wood, and Eagly 1996; Cialdini and Goldstein 2004; McGuire, Lindzey, and Aronson 1985; Petty and Wegener 1998).

Interpersonal Recruiting

A long research tradition starting with Katz and Lazersfeld (Katz 1957; Katz 1955) and Coleman (Coleman, Katz, and Menzel 1957) indicates that interpersonal appeals—in which the persuasion attempt comes directly from other people, especially those whom the target knows—are more effective at influencing attitudes and adoption than are impersonal appeals through the mass media. It follows that interpersonal recruiting is more effective than mass communication. Latané's social impact model of social influence (1981) holds that social influence is proportional to the immediacy, strength, and number of influence sources that a target is exposed to. The immediacy of the source is inversely proportional to physical or psychological distance imposed by the communication modality. We are more influenced by people who are close by and by those who communicate with us in person than by those farther away or who communicate through some technology mediation. For example, in political get-out-the-vote campaigns, face-to-face contacts with potential voters are more cost effective than robo-calls and email solicitations, even though the in-person contacts can cost

$20US while the technology-mediated contacts cost pennies each (Green, Gerber, and Nickerson 2008); the persuasive power of the contact justifies its high cost. The strength of a source includes its status, its credibility, and the strength of the interpersonal tie between the source and target. We discuss the strength of a source later in our discussion of viral marketing.

The literature on the diffusion of innovation has long recognized the role of interpersonal communication as a primary mechanism by which earlier adopters of a new product or service induce those who have not yet used it to try it out and eventually to start using it regularly. The Bass model is one of the most widely used and accurate statistical models for predicting *product diffusion*, the rate with which new adopters start using new products and services and the numbers using it at any given time (Bass 1969; Mahajan, Muller, and Wind 2000; Mahajan, Muller, and Bass 1990). The Bass model holds that the number of new adopters at any time is based on four parameters: (1) the number of people who might potentially adopt, perhaps estimated from the adoption of competitive products or from surveys; (2) the number of people who have adopted to that point; (3) the parameter α, representing the constant proportion of potential adopters who convert because of advertising; and (4) the parameter β, representing the constant proportion of potential adopters who convert because of word-of-mouth information from people who have already adopted. Most empirical research using the Bass model shows that β, the impact of word of mouth, is substantially higher than α, the impact of advertising. For example, Montgomery used the Bass model to estimate the rate of increase in Hotmail subscribers from June 1996 to June 1997 (Montgomery 2001). As seen in figure 5.1, the model is quite accurate: the predicted values closely track the actual growth in subscribers. In this model, β is 6.7 times as powerful as α. One quantitative review of the literature estimated the word-of-mouth effect was ten times greater than the advertising one, across a wide range of durable goods and services (Sultan, Farley, and Lehmann 1990).

Design Claim 2   Word-of-mouth recruiting is substantially more powerful than impersonal advertising.

The Bass model shows that many people adopt new products and services because of word-of-mouth influences from existing users. Communities can strategically use word-of-mouth recruiting to gain new members. Viral marketing or personalized word of mouth are examples of targeting, in which existing community members reach out to potential members whom they identify as likely candidates. Churches, theaters,

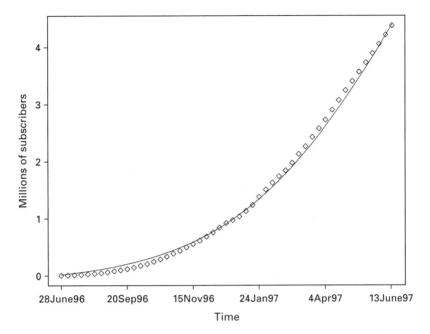

Figure 5.1

Comparing the cumulative number of Hotmail (http://www.hotmail.com) subscribers in millions (diamonds) at each weekly period with the predictions from the Bass diffusion model (solid line). *Source*: From Montgomery 2001.

doctors, and car mechanics all attempt to use word-of-mouth marketing from current patrons to recruit new ones. Recently, the car manufacturer Hyundai formalized this recruiting strategy by reframing their manufacturer's rebate to purchasers as a payment to mention their new purchases to family, friends, and neighbors.

Some of the best sources of new members for a community come from the social network links of people who are already members of the community. Many social networking sites, such as Facebook (http://www.facebook.com) and LinkedIn (http://www.linkedin.com), solicit new members by encouraging existing members to send invitations automatically to others in their email address books. (See figure 5.2.) Many smaller online groups, including guilds in World of Warcraft and projects in Wikipedia (http://en.wikipedia.org), recruit new members informally through their connections with existing members. However, it is possible for companies to go overboard with the technique of encouraging referrals from existing members. The social networking site Tagged (http://www.tagged.com) received thousands of complaints for "contact scraping" when—according to the company's founder—a software glitch accidentally

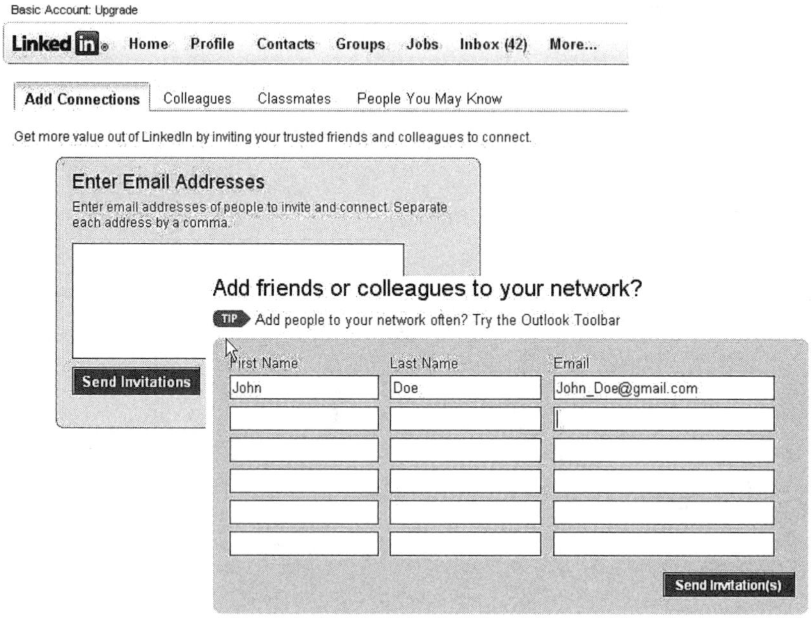

Figure 5.2
LinkedIn (http://www.linkedin.com) invitation screens.

sent invitations to people on members' email lists without the list owners' permission or knowledge (Tugend 2009).

One of the most successful examples of this sort of viral marketing is Facebook applications (apps), which often are designed so that with a single click, a user can invite friends to join him or her in using the app. B. J. Fogg of Stanford taught a class in which students were encouraged to build Facebook apps that used principles from psychology to draw in new members virally (Fogg and Eckles 2007). The result: in just ten weeks, the students had attracted an aggregate of sixteen million users to their apps. Fogg and Eckles (2007) explain that these approaches leverage users' credibility with their friends in a way that is more powerful than any message that appears to come directly from the community itself. This sort of recruiting is most effective in environments in which a user bringing in friends makes the community more valuable to him or her. For instance, one Facebook app lets a user see the places where friends have traveled, which is fun and engaging and valuable if the user wants advice on travel in the future.

Design Claim 3   Recruiting new members from the social networks of current members increases the number of new members more than impersonal methods.

Figure 5.3
Use of an "E-mail this" link to increase familiarity with a brand, here the *New York Times* (http://www.nytimes.com).

Even if it's difficult to talk users into recruiting their friends directly, one can make it easy for them to indirectly increase their friends' awareness of the community. For example, the *New York Times* (http://www.nytimes.org) makes it easy to share an article with friends via email. The *New York Times* benefits both by the increased visibility through a persuasive social network and by collecting the data: they list the "Top Emailed" articles of the day on their front page (see figure 5.3). Similarly, Costco Photo Center (http://www.costcophotocenter.com), a free photo sharing website, makes it easy for a user to share photos with friends and relatives. To use Costco Photo Center, the friends and relatives must create free accounts—after which it is easy for them to share their own photos (or to buy copies from Costco of the photos they see, but that's a different motivation). As with the *New York Times* and Costco, this sharing will be through channels outside of a community—such as email—but may bring members into the community over time.

Design Claim 4   Making it easy for users to share content from a community site with their friends (e.g., via easy email, Twitter, Facebook, and similar links) will increase the visibility of the community among the users' friends and thereby increase the likelihood of them joining.

Although using viral marketing, in which current members recruit future ones, can increase the numbers joining a site, some current members are more powerful conduits for new members than others. In his book *The Tipping Point*, Malcolm Gladwell (2002) described how marketers work to get key influencers to use their products because they know that many other consumers will follow their lead. Researchers have been studying ways to automatically discover these influencers by analyzing the graph structure of the social network with computer algorithms. For instance, Domingos and Richardson (2001) showed that by analyzing the way opinions appear to flow along a social network, one can choose users who would be the best people to market a product to. These users are the ones who would most influence other users in the social network to use the product. Kempe, Kleinberg, and Tardos (2003) showed that under more general models for disseminating information through a social network, a simple algorithm that maximized marginal gain at each step could do a very good job of choosing a good set of users to market to.

Design Claim 5   Identifying the most influential members of a community and encouraging them to recruit others in their social networks is more effective than soliciting referrals from members at random.

Conventional, Impersonal Advertising

Even though word-of-mouth recruitment is very effective, impersonal advertising also works (Assmus, Farley, and Lehmann 1984). These impersonal persuasion techniques can influence people's beliefs, affect, and behavior toward a stimulus object, such as a consumer product, health intervention, political candidate, or online community (Roberts and Maccoby 1985). However, the direct effects of impersonal advertising are weaker than many advertisers would like and Orwellian, critiques fear (see Klapper 1960). According to a recent review of almost five hundred field experiments of advertising effectiveness, for many mature brands the total amount of advertising a firm engages in (i.e., its "weight") is not critical in influencing sales: "More than half the time, increases in weight alone do not lead to an increase in sales. . . . [N]either do decreases in weight lead to sales decline, at least in the short term" (Tellis 2004, 79). There are two main reasons why impersonal advertising has weaker effects than its practitioners hope for: confirmatory biases, such as selective exposure, interpretation, and retention; and miscomprehension of advertising messages and competing advertising for other products (Nickerson 1998). Studies of selective exposure show that people are more likely to be exposed to beliefs that they already agree with. Thus, to some degree, advertisements are preaching to the choir and geared toward persuading those already convinced. People also differentially interpret persuasive messages based on their prior beliefs. For example, among viewers of presidential debates, people strongly believe that the candidate they initially supported won the debate (Munro et al. 2002). However, these debates can increase viewers' knowledge of the issues and the ones they consider important in a candidate and—despite viewers' biases—can influence vote preference, especially in elections in which voters have not yet formed strong political beliefs (Benoit, Hansen, and Verser 2003). Extrapolating from this literature, advertising may be a more effective recruiting technique for a new community, when information about the community and confidence in it is low, than it would be for an established one. For example, advertising can be more effective for the introduction of a new role-playing game than for a new release of the highly popular World of Warcraft (Tellis 2004, chapter 2).

Design Claim 6   Impersonal advertising can effectively increase the number of people joining an online community, especially among potential members with little prior knowledge of the community.

As discussed in more detail in chapter 2, the best way to construct a persuasive message depends on the degree of psychological engagement that potential recruits have in evaluating the messages. When the potential recruits are actively seeking a community to join, such as newly diagnosed cancer patients choosing an online support group, they are likely to use effortful "systematic processing" of the quality of the information they are exposed to, the consistency of the arguments, and the credibility of the sources. In many other cases, however, people are not actively seeking a group or are seeking one only casually. In such cases, people tend to form opinions based on what psychologists call *heuristic processing*. They don't think deeply and evaluate carefully the information they are exposed to. Instead, they use many cognitive shortcuts or heuristics to form their opinions. The difference in processing affects the kind of information that is most effective at attracting new members.

One common cognitive heuristic that people follow, the *halo effect* (Cooper 1981), is that if they perceive that a stimulus is good on one dimension, they assume that it will also be good on other, unrelated dimensions (Thorndike 1920). Thus, when evaluating information via heuristic processing such as the halo effect, people are likely to be influenced by superficial features. Researchers have indeed found that superficial features such as an attractive, professional site design enhance people's credibility evaluations of the sites (Fogg et al. 2003) and usage of them (Van der Heijden 2003).

On the other hand, with systematic processing, people are likely to be influenced by factual information, such as membership size, statistics about activity, or samples of activity. For example, because cancer patients are likely to be strongly motivated when evaluating alternative support communities to join, they are likely to carefully read messages posted to the group, see whether medical professionals are posting, and compare the advice they see in the group with the advice they are getting from their own physician. With systematic processing, people are also likely to assess the credibility of sites. For example, cancer patients may check to see whether the group is linked to a credible national organization like the American Cancer Society. Experiments by Stewart show that web links between one's site and credible other sites increases visitors' trust of the site and their willingness to purchase from it (2003).

These ideas about systematic versus heuristic processing also play out in the types of endorsements designers seek for their communities. As discussed further in chapter 2, the source of a persuasive attempt influences its success. People are more likely to be influenced by credible sources with relevant expertise, an effect that is deepened when people are engaged in systematic processing of the messages. Therefore, source credibility is especially important for serious sites, which potential members are likely to care about and be engaged in. For example, eminent biologist E. O. Wilson used his acceptance speech at the 2007 TED awards to pitch participation in the community creating the *Encyclopedia of Life* and endorses it on the encyclopedia's home page (see figure 5.4; Wilson 2007). Coming from a world-famous biologist like Wilson, an endorsement is likely to be more influential than an endorsement from a less reputable source.

For heuristic processing, celebrity endorsement can aid recruitment, even if the person's celebrity is unrelated to the community's topic or purpose. Many companies use celebrity endorsements as part of their advertising strategies, believing that the celebrities' attractiveness, likeability, and perceived trustworthiness will spill over to the product or cause they endorse. They are correct, in that celebrity endorsements result in more favorable product evaluations and can have a substantial positive impact on financial returns for the companies that use them (Agrawal and Kamakura 1995; Erdogan 1999). Game publisher Blizzard has used celebrities to pitch World of Warcraft, including actor William Shatner, who played Captain Kirk on the original *Star Trek* TV series, with the tagline "I'm William Shatner, and I'm a Shaman," and actor Mr. T with the tagline "I'm Mr. T, and this is my Night Elf Mohawk." (See figure 5.5.)

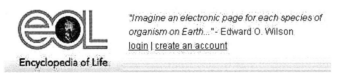

Figure 5.4
Credible endorsement for the Encyclopedia of Life (http://www.eol.org).

Figure 5.5
Blizzard advertisement with celebrity William Shatner pitching the game World of Warcraft.
Source: http://www.youtube.com/watch?v=ykb2A4FtyHQ.

Even serious communities can benefit from persuasive messages that appeal to heuristic processing, for two reasons. First, sometimes deep information is hard to convey. For example, it may be much easier for a cancer community to highlight the warm smiles of its members (see figure 5.6) than to convincingly demonstrate that people who participate feel that they get emotional support from others on the site. Second, when there are many alternatives for people to choose from, they may use heuristic processing to choose a smaller number that they will process more systematically.

Design Claim 7   Recruiting materials that present reasons to join and endorsements by credible sources and sites attract people who are actively searching for and evaluating communities.

Design Claim 8   Recruiting materials that present attractive surface features and endorsements by celebrities attract people who are casually assessing communities.

If people see signs that others are active on a site, then they are more likely to join than if they think the site is barren. In chapter 6, we explore how activity levels may be interpreted as signals of a community's future trajectory, enabling newcomers to make a rational cost-benefit analysis of whether it is worthwhile for them to join now.

Figure 5.6
Recruiting for the Macmillan Cancer Support Network (http://www.macmillan.org.uk).

However, seeing activity on the site may also simply invoke the *social proof heuristic* (Cialdini and Goldstein 2004) that it is a good idea to do what others are doing, without careful calculation of benefits and costs.

The social proof heuristic can be triggered by minor changes in wording in persuasive messages urging people to join a site. For example, an experiment by Goldstein and his colleagues showed that changing the wording of hotel notices asking guests to reuse their towels ("Help save the environment . . . by reusing your towels during your stay") to one emphasizing social proof ("Join your fellow guests in helping to save the environment") increased towel reuse by 44 percent (Goldstein, Griskevicius, and Cialdini 2007). Applying this logic to the domain of recruiting for an online community, invitations with a message that implies "Join the crowd" are likely to be much more effective than those that say "We need you." (See figure 5.7.)

Design Claim 9   Emphasizing the number of people already participating in a community motivates more people to join than does emphasizing the community need.

The familiarity heuristic is another powerful one. People tend to like people, things, and ideas they are familiar with (Zajonc 1968). It is for this reason, in part, that name recognition does wonders in both consumer products and politics. The familiarity heuristic, for example, helps incumbents to be overwhelmingly reelected in congressional and local elections (Mann and Wolfinger 1980), and movie stars with little experience and few qualifications to be regularly elected to public office. The implica-

Police Recruiting – Join the Team

To Protect With Courage, To Serve With Compassion

Explore the links below to learn about becoming a police officer with the Minneapolis Police Department.

Sworn Positions

- Recruit Police Officer
- Lateral Entry Police Officer

Non-Sworn Positions

- Community Service Officer
- Police Intern

[OTHER] We Need You! We're Recruiting!

HEY YOU?

WE NEED YOU?

picture inspired by this poster

Hello there **ADDICTEDS**! We really **need** extra people to help us out with G-BOM Facebook Fan page, and especially with this blog: **Géline**, **Yvonne** and **I(Toni)** are getting a lot busier, so we figured we might need one or two people who can help update our **facebook fan page and this blog**!

Figure 5.7

More (left) and less (right) effective recruiting pitches, based on social proof.

Source: From http://www.ci.minneapolis.mn.us/police/recruiting and http://gbomsince2006.blogspot.com/2010/07/other-we-need-you-were-recruiting.html.

Share

Figure 5.8
Widgets for sharing an object on the web.

tion is that managers of online communities should simply get the name of their community in front of the relevant population to increase their liking of the community and their likelihood of joining it. The placement of email and tagging links on many sites helps make the site familiar to others, increasing their liking for the brand and their willingness to become members. (See figure 5.8.)

Design Claim 10   Placing the name of a community in front of people will often activate the familiarity heuristic and their liking of the community and thus their willingness to try it.

2   Problem 2: Selecting the Right Newcomers

Ensuring a good fit between the newcomers and the community is a major challenge. A substantial amount of empirical research shows that good outcomes result when newcomers to a group or organization perceive themselves as having a good fit with it on dimensions such as interests, attitudes, and values that they and the group share or the knowledge, skill, and motivations they possess and that the organization desires (Chapman et al. 2005; Kristof-Brown, Zimmerman, and Johnson 2005; Kristof 1996). When potential recruits see that they share a good fit with a group or organization, they are more likely to be attracted to it, pursue membership in it, join it if given a chance, and be satisfied with their membership and remain in the group or organization longer if they do join.

   Although most research on the benefits of fit has been done in the context of job candidates and employees in conventional organizations, the same phenomena also occur in the context of voluntary organizations, which are similar in many ways to online communities. Volunteers to organizations like Big Brothers Big Sisters or the American Red Cross vary in their motivations (Clary et al. 1998), just as do participants in online communities (e.g., Ridings and Gefen 2004; Roberts et al. 2006). Some participate out of altruism or because they share the organization's goals. Others participate for the social experiences they get when working with similar others, to learn new skills, to exercise skills and abilities that might otherwise go unpracticed, to obtain credentials or experiences relevant to a new career, or to make themselves feel good. Fit is important for volunteers. When they participate in volunteer activities that match their motivations, they are more satisfied with their volunteerism and are more likely to volunteer again (Clary et al. 1998). In addition, volunteer organizations can take advantage of this variability in volunteers' motivation by varying the wording in their advertising to attract those with appropriate motives. For example, brochures that highlight the way in which volunteering helps one explore career options, develop a strong resume, and network to make career contacts were especially likely to appeal to recruits with career-related motivations (Clary et al. 1998).

The problem of selecting applicants for membership is common to all groups, but it may be especially problematic in online communities because of the relative anonymity of the interaction in them and the ease of creating new identities online. For example, one Wikipedia administrator who had presented himself as a professor with degrees in theology and canon law was forced to resign when a magazine revealed that he had no advanced degrees. He "used texts such as *Catholicism for Dummies* to help him correct articles on the penitential rite or transubstantiation" (Elsworth 2007).

Consider the two messages in figure 5.9 recruiting new members for guilds in World of Warcraft. The announcement on the left describes a testosterone-driven raiding guild seeking "hard-core" players. It demands both time and particular types of equipment from its members. In contrast, the guild on the right is more laid back and socially oriented. It describes itself as a group that "spends way too much time on ventrilo [the chat program that supports voice communication among guild members] and not nearly enough time raiding." It seems to be seeking players with cooperative personalities and good social skills (no drama, whining, or getting angry over loot distribution).

Imagine the problems that would flare if the raid-oriented Premonition guild, on the left, ended up with a laid-back chatterer, or if the socially oriented Damage Networks, on the right, recruited a hard-core warrior. Our own research shows that new recruits to World of Warcraft guilds who prefer the style of play that the guild values remain in their guilds substantially longer than players for whom there is a style-of-play mismatch (Choi, Kraut, and Fichman 2011).

A better fit between new members and a community also promises benefits for the community. For example, in World of Warcraft, players may apply to become members of a guild with the intention of staying only a short time, merely to "level up" their

Raid-oriented

<Premonition> WotLK Cleared! Recruiting hardcore players!!

We are Premonition --- a mature Alliance PvE raiding guild ... We are recruiting hard core, geared players for WotLK. ... We have completed Malygos 25 man/10 man, Sartharion 25 man/10 man, and Naxxramas 25 man/10 man. ...

Here's some key information about the guild and our expectations.

1. Raiding schedule is Sunday-Thursday 8:00pm -11:30pm PST (server time). You are REQUIRED to attend 4/5 raids each week.
2. We have vent and EPGP.
3. *Most* gear will be EPGP based, but there will be some pieces that will go to the class/spec it will suit the most to help progression of the guild. Very few pieces will be decided in this manner but the best interests of the guild and its progression will be considered first and always.
...
4. We're very serious about having the most optimal raid composition and most potential while raiding. To maintain that we'll require you to have:

   a. PvE spec when you come to raids.
   b. You will show up on time and ready and you will have consumables to last the entire raid.
   ...
   g. You will know encounters having read strategies, watched videos, read forums before we engage those encounters.

Socially-oriented

<Damage Networks> - LF Warlock, SPriest, HPriest, Ele Shaman, Paladin

... Damage Networks is currently looking to add a few more people to our family. We're a PvE/PvP guild that spends way too much time on ventrilo, and not nearly enough time raiding. As a guild, we've been around for a long time (completing MC and BWL in their primes, and landing a top 20 US Kel'Thuzad kill). We're not going anywhere. Damage Networks began as a porn site, then an NS team, and now it's a wow squad. So if you're interested in more than just a raiding guild, we're probably right for you.

What are we looking for? Players are expected to hold at least 75% raid attendance. Drama bombs, Loot %%#!*s, ego-maniacs, self-centered retards, incessant whiners, immature babies and idiots in general should not apply (we have plenty of those already, they give us "flavor"). ...

Figure 5.9

Sample World of Warcraft recruiting announcements.

Source: From http://www.lookingforguild.net.

character (i.e., gain experience points) before moving to a superior guild (Ducheneaut et al. 2007). However, it is not in the guild's interest to recruit players who have intentions to leave as soon as they have accumulated more experience, skills, or gear. Similarly, in an OSS development community, some newcomers may be highly skilled software developers with deep knowledge of the application domain, some may be novice developers or ignorant of the domain with little knowledge or skill to bring to the project, and others may have the malicious intent of introducing bugs or Trojan horses. In an online support group for abused women, valuable members are the survivors who have experience, wisdom, and support to offer to others or women who are themselves currently the victims of abuse, and spectators or stalking husbands are highly undesirable. Even seemingly open communities may want to discriminate between valuable and less valuable members. For example, the Democratic Underground (http://www.democraticunderground.com), a news and discussion site for the exchange of progressive political ideas, wants to enroll Democrats and "other progressives who will work with us to achieve our shared goals" and wants to reject Republicans and right-wing trolls who join to bait legitimate members. In eBay, legitimate sellers would like to weed out scammers who sell used goods as new, or copies as originals, or those who collude to inflate bids (Kinch 2003; Postmedia 2010).

Overall, ensuring that new recruits match the style and values of an online community will lead them to stay longer and be more satisfied with their membership, and it will lead to more benefits for the group as a whole and for existing members. Different recruiting and selection methods lead to different degrees of player-community fit. It's relatively easy to identity hard-core players valued by the hard-core Premonition guild in figure 5.9 by examining players' online resume (e.g., the weapons they have accumulated) and by playing with them a little while. In contrast, guilds may need to get referrals from existing members and play with the new recruits for longer probationary periods to identity the personality configurations valued by the laid back Damage Networks. The general lesson is that the amount and type of information and interaction between a community and newcomers needed for selecting people who fit well depends upon the ease of revealing or assessing attributes of both the recruits and the community.

In the following section, we consider two general approaches to selecting new recruits who fit with the style, values, and needs of the community. The first is self-selection, or making sure that only potential recruits who are a good fit choose to join. The second is screening, or making sure that only potential recruits who are a good fit are allowed to join.

Self-Selection

When conventional organizations provide recruits accurate and complete information about the organization, prospective members can form accurate expectations about it, which influences their decisions to seek employment, to join if employment is offered, and to have realistic expectations about the organization and their role within it once they join. In the context of conventional organizations, this accurate information often is conveyed in the form of realistic job previews, in which recruiters and other members of the organization present both favorable and unfavorable job-related information to job candidates (Rynes 1991). Realistic job previews are associated with lower expectations that recruits have about the nature of the job, lower levels of attrition from the recruitment process, and lower turnover if recruits are offered a job. Although the effects are small, they are reliably larger if the realistic preview is delivered verbally than via a written document or video (Phillips 1998). Realistic job previews seem to have beneficial effects on recruiting success through two separable routes. First, they selectively attract people who have certain characteristics, including motives, skills, and attitudes that better fit the existing community. Second, they lower the expectations that newcomers have when they actually join the community, reducing the chances that the reality that newcomers experience once they join will clash with unrealistic idealizations.

Online communities can use the methods typical of conventional organizations to give off realistic information about the community—websites, online recruiting brochures and other documents, videos, direct contact with recruiters or other formal representatives of the community, and informal contact with community members. For example, when soliciting new members, World of Warcraft guilds often post recruiting statements, with information about their mission and style of play, at forums such as Looking for Guild or similar recruiting sites. Others post videos of their exploits on YouTube (http://www.youtube.com), WarcraftMovies (http://www.warcraftmovies.com), and other media-sharing sites. One famous clip is the animated saga of the Onyxia Wipe—with more than four million views on YouTube and other sites—in which a guild leader shouts at, commands, and curses his guild as they try to kill the Onyxia monster and are all killed by it (Alachas1985 2007).

Although these realistic previews can be effective, they are rare compared to the use of FAQs in many online communities; in these FAQs, the community posts a mission statement or goals but not realistic previews of life inside (see http://www.faqs.org for an index to many FAQs for Usenet newsgroups and websites). For example, the FAQ for a support group for people who are trying to quit smoking lists a policy of bans on commercial posts but provides little information about the frequency of this practice (Internet FAQ Archives 2010). Comparatively few online communities explicitly create realistic membership previews for recruiting purposes.

Even though online communities could use the same recruiting mechanisms as conventional organizations, they have a potentially unique advantage: much of the communication and production work in the community is archived automatically. In a conventional organization, new recruits must rely on the organization's explicit descriptions via brochure and similar sources or upon word of mouth from current and former organizational members, but with an online community, they can see the interactions on which these impressions are based. The archival nature of the Internet means that complete records of prior interactions among community members are available for newcomers to examine and to get an unedited, realistic view of life in the community. Investigation is a major reason that newcomers silently read posts (*lurk*) before posting (Preece, Nonnecke, and Andrews 2004); they are trying to get sufficient information about the group to decide whether they should join. They can see, for instance, how members treat each other on various online forums and how team members work together in creating Wikipedia articles by examining the histories and talk pages associated with each article.

However, not all communities provide public archives. In the online cancer support group for ACOR, readers cannot search or browse archived messages without a subscription. Though subscribing is free, prospective subscribers are vetted by the list owners, which delays the newcomer's opportunity to evaluate the group and his or her expected fit. Furthermore, the archives are hidden from search engines. Though this protects the privacy of existing members, it also reduces the likelihood that desirable members will find the group.

Compared to lurking, newcomers' direct interaction with the group provides more useful and personally relevant information to allow them to estimate the benefits that they will receive if they join. The investigatory phase in the socialization process is an especially fragile one for newcomers. During this early period when they first encounter a group, they have little commitment to it and often little data to make judgments about whether to invest effort in finding out more or to explore alternatives. As a result, small amounts of either positive or negative evidence about how the group behaves and how it treats members may have an especially large impact on whether they leave for good or return again (Arguello et al. 2006).

Design Claim 11   Providing potential new members with an accurate and complete picture of what the members' experience will be once they join increases the fit of those who join.

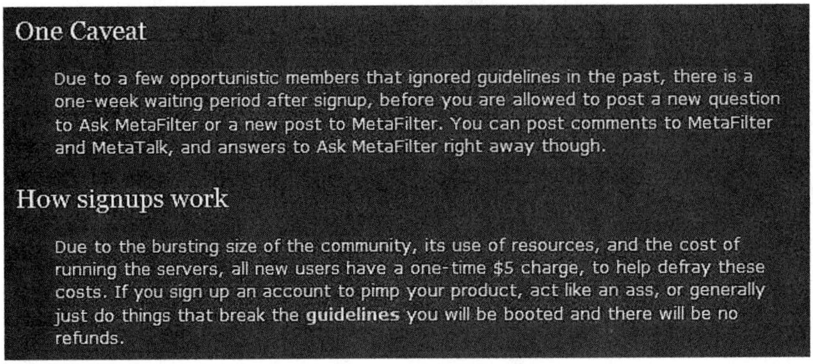

One Caveat

Due to a few opportunistic members that ignored guidelines in the past, there is a one-week waiting period after signup, before you are allowed to post a new question to Ask MetaFilter or a new post to MetaFilter. You can post comments to MetaFilter and MetaTalk, and answers to Ask MetaFilter right away though.

How signups work

Due to the bursting size of the community, its use of resources, and the cost of running the servers, all new users have a one-time $5 charge, to help defray these costs. If you sign up an account to pimp your product, act like an ass, or generally just do things that break the guidelines you will be booted and there will be no refunds.

Figure 5.10
MetaFilter's delay and payment entry fee policies (http://www.metafilter.com/newuser.mefi), which encourage useful self-selection.

Another way in which community designers can encourage self-selection of potential members who fit the community well is to require an action that those who are a better fit are more willing to undertake. This action could simply be an entry fee. For example, MetaFilter charges $5 for new members (see figure 5.10). If normal members get more than $5 of benefit from joining and trolls, spammers, and other disrupters get less than $5 of benefit, the entry fee can cause the undesirables to self-select out of participation. MetaFilter also imposes a waiting period before new users can post questions to Ask MetaFilter or make new posts to MetaFilter, although they can reply to others immediately. Presumably, those users who are willing to wait and remember to come back will create content that is more valuable to other members.

Design Claim 12   Forcing potential new members to pay or wait makes people who value the community more likely to join and weeds out undesirables.

Alternatively, the required action could be to undertake some task. If the task is inherently interesting to people who are a good fit for the community but not for others, then it will lead to the desired self-selection. Tasks that are more interesting or less onerous for people who are a good fit for the community are *separating tasks*. In many communities, reading and rating or editing material written by other members might be effective separating tasks.

Design Claim 13   Forcing potential new members to undertake separating tasks will encourage those who are a good fit to the community to join while weeding out undesirables.

One other interesting point about tasks that induce self-selection is that for those who do undertake the tasks, the tasks may lead to enhanced commitment to the community. Chapter 3 explores cognitive dissonance theory and other theories that predict impacts of entry barriers that cause newcomers to suffer a little before joining.

Screening

We now consider ways in which the community can act to screen out those who are not a good fit. Screening requires both accurate signals about who is a good fit and mechanisms for exclusion. The latter is relatively straightforward in communities that require membership for access. Only those passing the screening are allowed to read the group's contents or are given some other level of access privilege.

We discussed previously how lurking may provide newcomers with information about their fit to the group. However, because the group is also evaluating whether the newcomer would be a good fit, it needs the newcomer to do more than simply lurk. Encouraging interaction between newcomers and old-timers can provide some information that the group can then use to evaluate newcomers.

Acquiring accurate signals about who is a good fit can be problematic. First, it may be cumbersome for the potential members to emit relevant signals. Second, if the signals will be used for screening, recruits who would not pass the screen may be motivated to lie. They may try to mimic the signals of those who are a good fit, and it can be hard for the community to tell which signals are truthful. For example, some new recruits to a World of Warcraft guild may honestly describe themselves as extroverted and friendly and seeking a relaxed style of play. However, guild masters or recruiters have little way to distinguish recruits who will be difficult to get along with from those who are easy to get along with. Economists often refer to these cases as *signaling problems* (Spence 1973).

The challenge for designers, then, is to create signals that are hard to mimic. The first approach is to assign diagnostic tasks. The most basic diagnostic task is the CAPTCHA, as described in chapter 4, which is intended to provide a signal that the visitor is human. These tests are difficult for machines to accomplish but easy for humans, and they are often used to separate people who sign up for services, such as free email accounts or server space, from scripts automatically creating hundreds of accounts. A CAPTCHA is an automated test, such as the challenge to recognize a distorted word presented against a cluttered background. Craigslist requires posters of classified ads to enter their email address and then respond to an invitation sent to that address before the ad goes public. The goal is similar to the goal for CAPT-CHAs: to prevent bots and other software agents from gaining membership in the community. At some cost, motivated attackers can pass either of these tests. For example, computer programs can automatically respond to emails, and attackers have been able to circumvent CAPTCHAs by employing people at low wages to solve them (Bajaj 2010) or motivating them with promises of pornography (see http://www.captcha.net).

To distinguish among humans, a diagnostic task may come after initial entry but before full privileges are granted. In many communities, the people who eventually go on to become leaders are distinguishable from peripheral participants in their first interactions (Panciera, Halfaker, and Terveen 2009; Panciera et al. 2010). OSS development projects often rely upon candidates' participation in technical discussions and contributions of bug patches and software enhancements to make such assessments. Potential members must first demonstrate their competence and commitment to the group by offering bug fixes or small enhancements before they are given "committer" status, permission to commit (save) their own changes to the software database (Ducheneaut 2005; Krogh, Spaeth, Lakhani, and Hippel 2003). In the Freenet Project (http://freenetproject.org), only 8.4 percent of individuals who participated in the technical discussions were ever given committer status and considered developers in the project. Without committer status, programmers must pass their modifications to more trusted members of the group, who then vet the software and decide whether to merge it with the existing code base. Mere talk without code—such as describing one's offline technical accomplishments, asking for tasks to work on, or proposing modifications—did not lead to committer status; potential members had to pass substantive contribution barriers to become full members.

In World of Warcraft, the diagnostic task may be to accumulate experience points, weapons, or steeds used for transportation. Guild masters and others recruiting players for guilds can screen based on these visible acquisitions. They are signals of past performance as well as tools that the candidates can use to carry out quests, if they become members.

In one depression forum online, the diagnostic task was to write knowledgeably about one's symptoms and treatment. To weed out spectators, established members of one such forum had an unspoken practice of engaging newcomers in discussion about their symptoms and treatments (Susan Fussell, personal communication). Producing these medical terms is likely to be easier for people who are clinically depressed than for those who aren't.

Design Claim 14   Requiring potential members to complete a diagnostic task screens out some undesirable members.

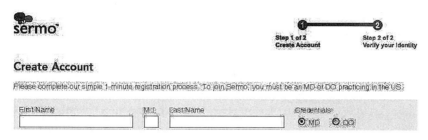

Figure 5.11
Account creation for Sermo (http://www.sermo.com).

Another type of signal-based screening is the *credential check*: Sermo (http://www
.sermo.com), a discussion forum for physicians to discuss medical decisions, asks
potential members for their names and the zip code of their primary practice and then
cross-checks that against a national physician database to ensure that its membership
includes only physicians (see figure 5.11). Pornographic websites that ask prospective
members to provide a credit card number or license do so to try to differentiate adults
from minors (or to at least give the illusion of doing so) because adults are more likely
to have a credit car or driver's license than are minors.

Design Claim 15   Requiring potential members to provide external credentials screens
out some undesirable members.

Some communities judge new members by depending upon referrals from existing
members. Many exclusive BitTorrent tracker sites (groups that provide private BitTorrent seeds) require existing members to vouch for new members. Bad behavior on the
part of a new member (such as downloading much more than they upload) can result
in sanctions to both the new member and the sponsor. This approach to selecting
new members is effective because referees have detailed and long-term information
about both the newcomers and the group to which they are being invited and
are motivated to present the information accurately to both parties. For example,
when friends have played World of Warcraft together, they can provide detailed information about each others' skills and strategy of play when making a referral to a guild.
The usefulness of references from group members depends, however, upon the type
of information to which the referrer has access. By interacting with the candidate
in nongroup settings, the referee might know about a candidate's sociability and
conscientiousness, for example, but not whether the candidate has specific skills the
group needs. Our own research shows that referrals are especially helpful in selecting

newcomers to World of Warcraft guilds when the group is a low-key social guild but not when it is a high-powered, goal-oriented raiding guild. In addition, referees have their own reputations to protect, which generally deters them from bringing inappropriate members into a group of which they are part (Fernandez and Weinberg 1997).

Some online groups institutionalize referrals by accepting new members only through invitations from existing ones and limiting the number of invitations that each existing member gets. Invitations to Google's exclusive Gmail Beta were so highly coveted that some users put them up for bid on eBay, and Google's Wave roll-out used a similar invitation procedure (Kawamoto 2004). A number of Flickr (http://www .flickr.com) photo groups have requirements that users' photos have awards or have been marked as favorites by some number of other users.

Design Claim 16   Requiring potential members to provide referrals from existing ones screens out some undesirable members.

As with CAPTCHAs, these signals are rarely perfect separators of desirable and undesirable new members. At some cost, an undesirable member can usually mimic the signal. To gain commit privileges in an open source community or experience points in a gaming environment, a rich dilettante could hire someone else to do the work that the community assesses. To pass the diagnostic test in the depression forum online, pretenders could conduct an online search to discover the names of antidepressants. Even credentials and referrals could be faked with a sufficient investment of time and money.

Conversely, even those who are desirable members may find it costly to provide signals that will pass a screening test. For example, people who are not yet connected with existing members, but who are a good fit to the community, will be excluded by a referral screen. If a health support community for a rare disease required referrals from existing members, it would negate one of the most valuable features of online support groups: the ability to connect people across distance who would not otherwise be able to meet. In those communities, it would make more sense to rely on an outside credential such as a referral from a participating hospital or treatment organization, or a diagnostic interview or task.

To the extent that people can invest in acquiring signals, a screening mechanism based on signals also becomes a self-selection mechanism. For example, programmers who want to influence the direction of an OSS project will contribute repairs and new code because they know that the community uses these as signals of quality. The designer's challenge is to find signals that are much less costly for the desirable members to emit than for the undesirable members. As with self-selection mechanisms, most screening systems are likely to be imperfect, letting in some undesirable members and excluding some desirable ones.

3   Problem 3: Keeping Newcomers Around

For newcomers to gain benefits from an online group and eventually become committed members who will take on core responsibilities, they must stick around long enough to learn the ropes, form relationships with other group members, and begin to identify with the group as a whole. However, the research on online communities also shows that these groups experience a substantial amount of turnover and that this turnover is especially high among newcomers. For example, 68 percent of newcomers to Usenet groups are never seen after their first post; in contrast, those who have participated even once in the past are much more likely to return (Arguello et al. 2006). Fifty-four percent of developers who registered to participate in the Perl open-source development project never returned after posting a single message (Ducheneaut 2005). Sixty percent of registered editors in Wikipedia never make another edit after their first twenty-four hours participating (Panciera, Halfaker, and Terveen 2009). Forty-six percent of the members of guilds in World of Warcraft leave their group within one month, generally migrating to other groups rather than abandoning the game itself (Williams et al. 2006).

Entry Barriers and Initiation Rituals

In general, barriers and initiation rituals that cause newcomers to suffer a little before joining a group should increase their eventual commitment. As discussed in chapter 3, the theory of cognitive dissonance holds that if people have two ideas that are psychologically inconsistent, they experience the negative drive state of cognitive dissonance and try to find a way to reconcile the ideas, generally by changing one or both to make them consonant (Festinger 1957). This theory explains why people like groups more if they have to endure a severe initiation process to join them than if they undergo a milder initiation (Aronson and Mills 1959; Gerard and Mathewson 1966). According to Aronson, people come to like things for which they suffered because this is the only way they can reconcile their views of themselves as intelligent people with the actions they have performed (Aronson 1997).

Initiation rituals imposed by online communication can range from nonexistent to quite severe. At one extreme, Usenet discussion groups impose no initiation at all.

Newcomers can read and post without any formal barrier. Wikipedia explicitly encourages gentle treatment of new editors, with its "Don't bite the newcomer" policy (Wikipedia 2010c). At the other extreme are communities like Fark (http://www.fark.com), a website for posting and commenting on weird news headlines and stories. Newcomers who make mistakes that violate the norms of the community can be publicly criticized or humiliated. Their FAQ states that "message boards on sites like Fark are forever plagued with morons posting 'First Post' anytime a link is posted. Fark automatically turns the words 'first post' into the word 'boobies' and resets the timestamp on the message to some time in the future" so that the post actually appears to be a late one. Newcomers trying to introduce themselves occasionally fall victim to this and post a message that ends up saying something like, "This is my boobies on Fark" (Fark 2010).

Game-playing groups like World of Warcraft and OSS projects require newcomers to go through a long period of initiation before they can become members. Some guilds, for example, require the newcomer to play with the group for a month or longer before the newcomer is allowed to become a regular member. In OSS projects, it is common practice for newcomers to offer "gifts" of code before they are granted membership (Krogh, Spaeth, Lakhani, and Hippel 2003). Although these activities provide data by which existing group members can evaluate the newcomers and may weed out the least motivated, the activities are also effortful actions that probably increase the newcomers' loyalty to the group.

Severe initiation rituals are common in fraternities and the military. However, given the ease with which people can leave an online community (as opposed to a military academy or training), a severe initiation process or entry barrier is likely to drive away potentially valuable contributors at the same time that it increases the commitment of those who endure the initiation or overcome the barrier. Therefore, online community designers should not instigate these types of initiations unless there is a surplus of prospective members or the increased quality in membership is important. However, the newcomers who survive the initiation should have stronger loyalties than those who were invited in without initiation. As we discuss in more detail in chapter 3, Drenner, Sen, and Terveen (2008) demonstrated that forcing new members to work hard for their membership had both of these effects—driving away some potential members while increasing the commitment of those who expended this effort.

Design Claim 17   Entry barriers for newcomers may cause those who join to be more committed to the group and contribute more to it.

Initial positive interactions help retain new members. Newcomers to Usenet groups are more likely to come back for subsequent visits if others reply to them (Arguello et al. 2006). These effects are stronger if the people conversing with the newcomer are themselves old-timers who have been visible in the discussion in the recent past. The effects are also stronger if the responses use more welcoming and inclusive language, such as emoticons and first-person plural ("we") pronouns, often used to indicate solidarity between a speaker and audience, rather than second-person ("you") pronouns, which often indicate a divide between a speaker and the people being addressed. In an analogous study, songwriters in the February Album Writing Month community were heavily influenced by their early experiences (http://www.fawm.org). Here, each year, writers attempt to complete an entire album (fourteen songs) in the twenty-eight days of February. Compared to new songwriters who were not contacted by other group members, new songwriters who received comments during their first week went on to write about two more songs in their first month and were 20 percent more likely to return the following year. Comments containing in-group jargon and "we" words—indicating the newcomer has been accepted as a member of the community—boosted these effects (Burke and Settles 2011). Similarly, Facebook members were likely to post more photographs if others commented on the initial ones they added (Burke, Marlowe, and Lento 2009).

Lampe and Johnston (2005) found that at Slashdot (http://slashdot.org), new members whose first comment received a rating from other members posted a second comment more quickly than new members whose comments weren't rated. They also found that even newcomers who received negative ratings on their first comments came back faster; they hypothesized that these newcomers returned quickly to improve their records or intentionally wrote inflammatory content that they posted more often.

Our analysis of initial interactions between newcomers and old-timers in Wikipedia projects shows a similar pattern. WikiProjects are groups of editors who work together on articles within a domain, like military history, sports, or medicine. New members to a project who receive more communication from existing editors during the month that they join subsequently edit more on project pages (and in Wikipedia in general) and stay active in the project for a longer period. Again, the effects vary with the nature of the communication they receive. Personalized messages, such as comments about the newcomers' background or requests to work on a particular task, led to more powerful effects than generic ones in which the newcomer received a standardized message such as a welcome-to-the-project template.

Wikipedia explicitly encourages gentle treatment of new editors, with its "Don't bite the newcomer" policy (Wikipedia 2010c). Newcomers whose first edits were reverted (rejected and the article restored to its earlier form) are especially likely to leave the community (Halfaker, Kittur, and Riedl 2011; Zhang and Zhu 2006). Edits by newcomers are disproportionately reverted (Panciera, Halfaker, and Terveen 2009); to lessen the negative impact, Wikipedia editors are encouraged to "assume good faith" by the editor they are reverting and to carefully explain their rationale for the reversion so as not to deter a potential contributor. There are many pages documenting the social framework that accompanies the reversion tools—including guidelines to "reword rather than revert" and to "revert only when necessary" (Wikipedia 2010c).

Design Claim 18   When newcomers have friendly interactions with existing community members soon after joining a community, they are more likely to stay longer and contribute more.

Discussion forums often include a prominent introduction thread where newcomers are encouraged (or required) to post brief biographies. Newcomers to PGHDance (http://www.pghdance.com), a forum for Pittsburgh swing dancers, go to the "Hi, I'm . . ." thread to describe their level of dance experience, day job, and other cities where they've danced. The forum is a hybrid community in which many members socialize in person at local dances; however, that socialization is often hindered by loud music and a norm of silence while dancing. Thus, PGHDance allows members to get to know each other off the dance floor and, compared to the dance floor, provides a less evaluative platform where skill is less salient. Veteran forum members greet the newcomers and offer to dance with them at local events. Similarly, WrongPlanet (http://www.wrongplanet.com), a community for individuals with autism and other developmental disabilities, hosts a "Getting to know you" section where newcomers describe their hobbies and diagnoses. These introduction threads serve two purposes: first, they allow the newcomers to move beyond the lurking stage and provide enough information to invite interaction with other members, and second, the threads allow newcomers a safe space to practice using the posting tools. As much research in social psychology shows, when people self-disclose, others reciprocate and reveal information in exchange. This mutual self-disclosure often leads to the strengthening of the relationship between the pair. People like others who self-disclose to them more. In addition, they like the people to whom they self-disclose (Collins and Miller 1994).

Facebook uses a highly distributed welcoming mechanism. It has a feature that encourages long-time members to send membership invitations to people in

Figure 5.12
Feature encouraging friends to welcome newcomers to Facebook (http://www.facebook.com).

their friends list and to reach out to newcomers by adding them as friends (see figure 5.12).

Design Claim 19   Encouraging newcomers to reveal themselves publicly in profiles or introduction threads gives existing group members a basis for conversation and reciprocation with them and increases interaction between old-timers and newcomers.

One technique to encourage initial positive interaction between newcomers and old-timers is to assign welcoming responsibilities to designated old-timers. The host guide for one of the earliest online communities, The WELL, explains that hosts are responsible for welcoming newcomers:

Nobody likes to go into a conference for the first time, post a response, then have it sit there without ever being acknowledged. Learning to welcome, inspire and incorporate new visitors into the conversation is perhaps the most important talent a host can acquire. At the very least, as host, you will want to keep an eye out for postings by folks who have never responded in your conference before, and acknowledge their participation. (Hoag 1996)

Wikipedia has a "Welcoming Committee" whose main activity is to greet new editors, known as *red users* because they have not yet made a personal page for themselves and thus their usernames appear in red. Welcoming committee members skim Wikipedia's account creation log and lists of contributions by newcomers, select friendly text from a set of welcoming templates, and post the text to the user's talk page, creating the page if necessary. Welcoming committee members encourage anonymous contributors, identified by their IP addresses, to register, post links to tutorials, and offer to answer questions (Wikipedia 2010d).

Design Claim 20   Assigning the responsibilities of having friendly interactions with newcomers to particular community members increases the frequency of these interactions.

The previous examples from Wikipedia and The WELL are prescriptive in a positive way, assigning some people the responsibilities for welcoming newcomers and giving the welcomers tools to make the task easier. Another way to encourage newcomers is to discourage the hostility that is often the result of the interactions between long-time members of a group and newcomers. As the FAQ for the Mozilla project notes, "Be kind to newcomers. Newcomers may be annoying. They ask the wrong questions, including ones that seem obvious (or whose answers seem easy to find). But lots of valued contributors started out this way, and treating newcomers kindly makes them more likely to turn into the valuable community members we all know and love (and cut some slack when they mess up)" (Mozilla 2010). Similarly, policies for experienced users answering questions in the forum for Ubuntu, a graphical user interface for the Linux operating system, discourage experienced users from being rude to newcomers:

Be considerate to the person asking the question. We were all a green user at one point. . . . If you wish to remind a user to use search tools or other resources when they have asked a question you feel is basic or common, please be very polite. Any replies for help that contain language disrespectful towards the user asking the question, i.e. "STFU" [Shut the fuck up] or "RTFM" [Read the fucking manual] are unacceptable and will not be tolerated. (Ubuntu Forums 2010)

Wikipedia's Don't Bite the Newcomer policy cautions old-timers that "New contributors are prospective 'members' and are therefore our most valuable resource. We must treat newcomers with kindness and patience—nothing scares potentially valuable contributors away faster than hostility or elitism" (Wikipedia. 2010c; see figure 5.13).

Design Claim 21   Explicitly discouraging hostility toward newcomers who make mistakes can promote friendly initial interactions between newcomers and old-timers.

Figure 5.13
Wikipedia's "Do not bite the newcomers" policy (http://en.wikipedia.org/wiki/Wikipedia :Please_do_not_bite_the_newcomers).

4 Problem 4: Teaching Newcomers the Ropes

Different communities have standards and norms that shape and constrain the behavior of their members. Some of these norms are broad and open to different interpretations. In Wikipedia, for example, a series of guidelines and policies remind members to adopt a neutral point of view in the articles that they write (Wikipedia 2010d) and that they should not use their personal talk pages to discuss personal topics and promote relationships with other Wikipedians (Wikipedia 2010e). Others are more narrowly targeted, such as the Wikipedia copyright policy (Wikipedia 2010a) or formatting guidelines (Wikipedia 2010b). Although many of the norms and behavioral standards are explicitly described in Wikipedia, in many other online communities the norms that prescribe how members should behave are implicit and must be learned by observation.

As described in more detail in chapter 4, violation of the behavioral norms can be harmful to existing groups for a variety of reasons. Although we treat the general topic of norms in online communities in more detail chapter 4, the current chapter deals with issues that especially concern newcomers.

Organizational socialization theory identifies six dimensions that differentiate the techniques that organizations use to help newcomers get adjusted to the organization and learn their place in it (Van Maanen and Schein 1979). This research distinguishes institutionalized socialization practices, with formal training being its hallmark, from more individualized socialization, based on on-the-job training. Table 5.1 provides an overview of these socialization tactics. Jones (1986) created a self-report scale measuring these tactics, which has been extensively used in empirical research examining antecedents and consequences of socialization of newcomers in organizations. At the institutionalized end of these continua, newcomers are segregated from contact with old-timers, are all given the same experiences together as a cohort, are told the sequence of stages they will go through as they progress though the organization and the amount of time they will spend at each stage, and get training from experienced role models. In addition, the organization gives them positive feedback, encouraging them to build on their distinctive personal characteristics in the process of trying to fit into the organization. Students going though their PhD training, who are given strong mentorship and clear expectations about requirements, are at the institutionalized end of these

Table 5.1
Six dimension of organizational socialization tactics[1]

Institutionalized	Individualized
Collective: Newcomers go through a common set of experiences designed to produce standardized responses to situations.	Individual: Each newcomer receives unique training in isolation from others.
Formal: Newcomers are segregated from other organizational members and put through experiences tailored to newcomers.	Informal: Newcomers receive on-the-job training to learn their roles.
Sequential: Newcomers are given a clear sequence of experiences or stages they will go through.	Random: The sequence of stages isn't communicated in advance.
Fixed: Newcomers are given a fixed timetable regarding when they will move through stages.	Variable: The timing of role transitions is variable.
Serial: Newcomers observe and get training from experienced role models, who give newcomers a clear view of the experiences they will encounter in the organization.	Disjunctive: Newcomers must develop their own definition of the situation and do not have more senior people to observe.
Investiture: Newcomers receive positive feedback confirming their prior identity.	Divestiture: Newcomers receive negative feedback expressing organizational disapproval of their prior identity.

Jones (1986) and later authors group divestiture with the right column's other "individualized" tactics because they have all been found to have similar effects (Bauer et al. 2007).
Source: Adopted from Van Maanen and Schein 1979; Jones 1986.
1. Jones (1986) and many of the researchers who followed him reversed the conventional meaning of divestiture and investiture when they put investiture in the "institutionalized" column in this table and divestiture in the "individualized" one. Conventional English would label hazing and other divestiture tactics as depersonalizing, and they are often practiced by "total institutions" such as mental institutions, militaries, prisons, and religious orders (Goffman 1961).

dimensions. In contrast, newcomers who join the organization one at a time are at the more personalized end of these continua and are immediately surrounded by more experienced organizational members, receive personalized, on-the-job training, and are not given clear guidelines about their progress through the organization.

The original theory hypothesized that these tactics would be used in very different contexts (e.g., that collective tactics would be used for jobs in which newcomers needed to learn technical skills, and individual socialization would be used for jobs in which already existing organizational members were being prepared for promotions) and would have different consequences (e.g., collective socialization would lead to newcomers adopting existing social roles and individualistic socialization would encourage role innovation) (van Maanen and Schein 1979). However, subsequent research has developed a simpler picture of the effects of using these socialization tactics. The meta-analysis of Bauer and colleagues (2007) summarized seventy separate studies of newcomer socialization to organizations; in most cases, measures of organizations' use of these socialization tactics shortly after newcomers joined were correlated with newcomers' subsequent adjustment, commitment, and performance in the organizations (see also Saks, Uggerslev, and Fassina 2007).

The main results are summarized in figure 5.14. Both active information-seeking by newcomers and the use of a more institutional style of socialization by the organization is associated with more successful outcomes: newcomers do their jobs better, are more satisfied with their jobs, become more committed to the organization, and are less likely to leave it. The research suggests these effects of the organizations' use of institutionalized socialization tactics as well as newcomers' active information seeking have their effects by increasing newcomers understanding of how they should behave in the organization (role clarity), their beliefs that they could do what is asked of them (self-efficacy), and their beliefs that others in the organization accept them (social acceptance).

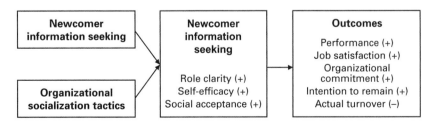

Figure 5.14
Antecedents and outcomes of newcomer adjustment during organizational socialization.
Source: From Bauer et al. (2007).

Although the evidence is strong that institutionalized socialization tactics are effective in developing commitment and appropriate behavior in conventional organizations, they are not commonly used in online communities. Socialization processes in most online communities are informal and individualistic. For example, in Usenet groups, lurking newcomers have no opportunities for formal mentorship because their presence is unknown to old-timers. WikiProjects rarely uses institutional socialization tactics to socialize new members who join these task-oriented groups (Choi et al. 2010). For example, they do not have newcomers join the project in a group and rarely assign new members mentors or provide clear guidance about how to behave in the project.

Ducheneaut's description of the socialization of newcomers to the Python OSS development community also illustrates the lack of institutionalized socialization practices in online organizations where they would probably be helpful (2005). Even in this production-oriented environment, with defined workflows and sharp distinctions among the social roles of those participating in the project, socialization is still informal, with new members learning the ropes primarily via trial and error. For example, although there is a progression of participation in this community, with newcomers first participating in technical discussion and then submitting bug fixes before obtaining committer status, this progression of roles is not documented. When one new developer who was slowly making his way toward the core of the community attempted to introduce a new module to the standard library used in this project, he did not know the organizational routines he needed to engage in to make his contribution. A core member of the community eventually stepped in to offer advice (i.e., provided mentorship), but mentoring was not a regular socialization practice in this community.

Rarely do online communities socialize and train newcomers as a group in isolation from other members, provide mentors to give guidance, or give newcomers a clear timetable about how to progress in the community. Consider the community that develops the popular Firefox web browsers. Although the Mozilla foundation maintains an extensive set of forums for communication among developers, except for FAQ-style documents we were unable to find forums or other resources for training newcomers or socializing them to the project. Newcomers who want to join this project must struggle to make sense of how to contribute on their own.

Online communities generally adopt individualized socialization tactics or none at all. The primary exception to this generalization is that many communities provide standardized FAQs and help documents to familiarize newcomers with how the community operates, which can be thought of as a variant of collective socialization. For example, the Distributed Proofreaders project (http://www.pgdp.net), a community of volunteers proofreading digitized public-domain books, has an extensive set of frequently asked questions with answers for newcomers on the project mission, ways to get involved, and ways to handle common problems in proofing and formatting documents (Rowe 2004).

The more institutionalized socialization tactics used in conventional organizations can be applied online, and some online communities do indeed provide elements of institutionalized socialization, although this is rare. For example, World of Warcraft offers formal and sequential socialization. When new players start the game, they are placed in an area that is isolated from more experienced players. Although they have the opportunity to interact with other new players, they also can interact with non-playing characters (NPCs, or scripts) that give newcomers tasks through which they gain both knowledge of basic methods for acting in the world (e.g., navigating, attacking monsters, and collecting loot) and experience points. The rules of the game lay out clear progressions and role transitions (e.g., players gain new powers at specified levels, for example acquiring a mount or gaining special weapons). World of Warcraft does not, however, encourage new players to become socialized in groups, as socialization theory suggests would be helpful, even though groups are central to World of Warcraft. Indeed, as of mid-2011, players using the ten-day free trial to sample the game are prevented from participating in groups.

Hattrick, a multiplayer game for managing fantasy European football teams (http://www.hattrick.org), is another informative exception, providing both formal and collective socialization tactics. Each player in this game is the manager of a soccer team and competes against other managers. The players must make decisions in areas such as acquiring, training, and trading players; game tactics; building stadiums; and handling finances. To encourage newcomers to read the full manual, new managers participate in the Hattrick Manager License Challenge (also known as Hattrick University), where they earn in-game money for studying the rules and answering challenge questions during their first weeks in the community. If they successfully answer all twenty-four questions, they graduate and receive a manager's license (see figure 5.15). To encourage the development of cohorts of players, new players initially play in leagues composed of other new players; if players win their division, they are promoted to the next level division the following season.

Design Claim 22   By using formal, sequential, and collective socialization tactics, new members are likely to become more committed to the community, learn how to behave in it, and contribute more.

Figure 5.15
Hattrick's manager's license (http://wiki.hattrick.org/wiki/Hattrick_Manager_License
_Challenge).

Some communities have successfully deployed mentorship practices, both formal and informal. Everything2 (http://everything2.com) is an online community whose members submit written material about any topic they want. The Everything2 Mentor System matches new users with experienced mentors who share interests and a time zone, who agree to log into the site at least once a day, and who are willing to answer the new members' questions and critique their work. New sellers at eBay benefit from Trading Assistants, experienced and active eBay sellers with feedback that is at least 97 percent positive. Trading Assistants help new sellers assess whether an item is sale-able, plan starting prices and shipping methods for items, and communicate directly with bidders. Newcomers benefit from the Trading Assistants' high reputation scores, proficiency with seller tools, and familiarity with listing policies and best practices. Newcomers search a directory for assistants who are geographically close and have expertise in their particular areas, such as estate liquidation or motor vehicles. Trading Assistants themselves have training tutorials, guides to best practices and promotion, and a discussion board. Help from Trading Assistants is not limited to newcomers; any busy seller can outsource items to others in this way. However, unlike voluntary mentorship in other communities, eBay's Trading Assistants negotiate fees with new sellers for their services (eBay 2010).

Similarly, one of the benefits to being a member of a World of Warcraft guild is explicit help from higher-level guild members. Higher-level guild members are expected to help their junior colleagues overcome difficult quests or kill monsters more rapidly. The higher-level players coach the lower-level players, explaining which quests are most valuable, and demonstrating the way to defeat the more difficult challenges. Of course, sometimes the mentoring backfires: once the lower-level player becomes more powerful, he or she sometimes leaves to join a more powerful guild.

Design Claim 23   When old-timers provide newcomers formal mentorship, the newcomers become more committed to the community, learn how to behave in it, and contribute more.

5   Problem 5: Protecting the Group from Newcomers

Although newcomers are essential to the survival of online communities, they also pose real threats. Because newcomers have no history in the community, existing group members do not know how much to trust them. There is risk involved if one allows a new member of a guild in World of Warcraft to participate in a high-stakes raid, a new seller on eBay to sell an expensive item, or a new member of the Apache project to commit code.

Because newcomers have not yet developed commitment to the group and have not yet learned how the group operates, it is rational for established group members to distrust them. Because new members don't yet identify with the group, they are less likely to have the best interests of the group at heart in deciding how to behave. In addition, because they are relatively unsophisticated in how the group operates, they may not have the skill or knowledge to operate in the group's best interest, even if they cared to. For example, in Wikipedia, newcomers (including those who have not registered and those who have registered but not yet edited extensively) are more likely to vandalize pages or offer changes that other, more experienced Wikipedians will later delete (Adler and Alfaro 2007). As a result of this lack of history and potential lack of goodwill or relevant skills, groups need to protect themselves against the damage that newcomers can cause. Empirical evidence suggests that established members do indeed distrust newcomers. For example, Resnick et al. (2006) showed experimentally that buyers pay less for comparable items on eBay when purchasing from newcomers (i.e., those with no prior transactions), distrusting them because of their lack of sales history in eBay.

Even if newcomers are not actively behaving inappropriately, the mere fact that they are different from the old-timers may change the environment in such a way to make the community less desirable for old-timers. Indeed, the simple classification of some group members as old-timers and others as newcomers can lead to strong ingroup-outgroup biases (Moreland 1985). An influx of new members to social networking sites may change the culture for old-timers. This degrading of the culture for old-timers happened when Myspace (http://www.myspace.com) transitioned from a promotion platform for small bands to a crowded venue for teenagers to post MP3s and hang out with friends (Boyd and Ellison 2008). Similarly, as new members joined Systers, an email list for women in computer science mentioned in chapter 3, both the increase in message volume and the very different concerns held by old-timers and newcomers caused hundreds of senior members to leave (Spertus, Jeffries, and Sie 2001).

So far, we have suggested that newcomers be socialized through friendly initial interactions with old-timers and that old-timers be explicitly discouraged from being hostile to newcomers who make mistakes. Yet this is not to say that newcomers should receive carte blanche access to the group and its resources. Resources include both people—other members' attention and support—and any artifacts the group produces, such as wikis, collective movie ratings, or software. Should newcomers be isolated to prevent annoying other members and damaging community artifacts, or should they be allowed to ask questions, write on others' walls, delete code, or join raiding parties right away? It depends on the kind of community and its goals.

The question of whether to quickly attempt to integrate newcomers with the existing community depends on several factors, including whether the community produces a group artifact with interdependent parts and the consequences of newcomers' mistakes on themselves and other members. The more likely it is that that the presence of newcomers and their inappropriate behavior can damage the current community or its products and the harder it is to repair this damage, the more the community should isolate newcomers until they become more committed and knowledgeable about the community. Many common protection mechanisms serve multiple purposes, not only to prevent damage but also to discourage newcomers who would be a bad fit and to socialize those who are a good fit.

Chapter 4 discusses ways to protect a community from misbehaving participants, not just newcomers. Here we focus on two methods, sandboxes and progressive access controls, which are especially relevant to the socialization process for newcomers.

Sandboxes are safe, isolated areas for exploration and skill development. They achieve dual goals of protection and training. Sandboxes take many forms, from text

Figure 5.16
Sandbox in Second Life (http://wiki.secondlife.com/wiki/Sandbox).

boxes for practicing wiki syntax to virtual land parcels for practicing construction or simple scripting, as in the virtual world Second Life (http://secondlife.com; see figure 5.16). Content created in the sandbox is removed regularly, protecting the community from clutter. For example, consider how Wikipedia uses sandboxes. All Wikipedia editors have a personal sandbox by default, as well as access to communal sandboxes (see figure 5.17). Typical policies, such as formatting guidelines or notifying other users before making large changes, do not apply to the sandbox, although civility and copyright policies still apply. Content in the communal Wikipedia sandboxes is automatically cleaned every twelve hours, although other users tend to overwrite content much faster.

Design Claim 24   Sandboxes both speed up the learning process for newcomers and reduce the harm to the community that newcomers might otherwise cause.

Another common protection mechanism is *progressive access control*, or allowing newcomers to participate in less-critical tasks initially and then gradually increasing their access to more central and important tasks. This progression may simply be a suggestion in the training documents or FAQs, or it may be enforced by technical constraints that prevent newcomers from performing risky actions until they have demonstrated competence with simpler ones. Many OSS development projects use some version of

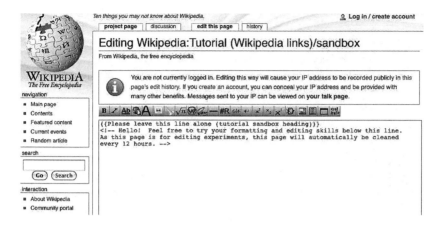

Figure 5.17
Wikipedia Sandbox for practicing wiki formatting (http://en.wikipedia.org/wiki/Wikipedia :Sandbox).

progressive access control, for example allowing newcomers to comment in technical discussion forums or to send senior contributors patches for bug fixes for their review, but preventing them from directly making changes in the project's code base until they have earned the community's trust (Krogh, Spaeth, Lakhani, and Hippel 2003; Ducheneaut 2005).

Progressive access control prevents newcomers from causing damage while at the same time giving them a legitimate but peripheral position in the community to learn skills and the community's norms. Lave and Wenger (1991) proposed the theory of legitimate peripheral participation, by which newcomers become more experienced members through small but productive actions in the community. Their research describes apprenticeships for midwives, tailors, and butchers, in which the new members of the occupation not only acquire occupational knowledge but also take part in social practices and learn to understand the community's activities, artifacts, and language. By technically constraining newcomers so they learn through small and peripheral but helpful tasks, progressive access control serves as both a protection mechanism and socialization tool.

Similar techniques are occasionally used successfully in online communities. For example, Distributed Proofreaders restricts unregistered users, allowing them only to proof "Smooth Reading" pages, which are nearly error-free. These pages have been reviewed in previous rounds and need light checks by people reading for pleasure, rather than readers trained in the formal procedures used by experienced checkers. A missed typo in one of these pages will have little consequence for the community and will likely be caught by another smooth reader. Newly registered users are also restricted to editing "Beginners Only" pages and cannot move to more advanced material until they have demonstrated mastery of community editing standards. "Beginners Only" edits also trigger special reviews by second-level mentors, who email friendly feedback that is sensitive to the tenuous relationship a novice editor may have to the community. One such review reads, "I have reviewed page 294 that you proofed for this project. It looks like you've made a good start! For example, you joined the hyphenated words, and you 'closed' the em-dash at the end of a line. Nice job!"

Design Claim 25   Progressive access controls reduce the harm a newcomer can do to a community while learning the ropes.

6   Summary of Design Alternatives

As in other chapters, we conclude with a table of the design alternatives considered in this chapter and an index to the design claims that discuss their implications. In this chapter, we examined the challenges of renewing online communities with newcomers. We identified five separate subchallenges: recruitment, selection, retention, and socialization of newcomers, and protecting the community from newcomers while they are learning the ropes. We conclude by inverting that focus. We reflect on the design space of alternatives and the ways in which alternative designs affect the ability to meet those challenges.

Some design alternatives involve communication about the community outside the community. This communication is especially important to the recruitment of potential new members. Active rather than passive recruiting, and targeting communication to those who are a good fit to the community, brings in more recruits. Relying on word of mouth and recruiting from social networks—in part by enabling sharing of content with friends outside the community—both can attract people to consider the community and generate leads who are a good fit for the community.

The content and activities of the community have an impact on potential newcomers once they have been recruited to consider it. Newcomers who have friendly interactions with old-timers and who reveal information about themselves will be more likely to stick around. On the other hand, newcomers whose contributions are ignored or rejected without explanation are less likely to be retained. Collective socialization tactics, in which newcomers form a cohort and learn about the community together, can also contribute to retaining newcomers. Sandboxes can give newcomers a safe way to explore and try out the software features without fear of damaging the community.

There is a large scope for design choices that assign special roles to people who interact with newcomers and policies for how they will be treated. Specified roles for a welcomer and a mentor, with associated privileges that help in accomplishing those roles, can help with retention and socialization. Explicit policies that discourage hostility toward newcomers can both reduce the amount of that hostility and make newcomers who do experience it feel that it is unrepresentative of the community, thus aiding retention.

Access control mechanisms can be used to balance newcomers' needs for information when exploring a community with the community's need to prevent damage from people without commitment or skill. Allowing nonmembers to see archives of communication within the community can help them evaluate whether they want to be members. A variety of barriers can prevent progression to the next stage of privileges. For example, people may have to wait, pay, complete a diagnostic task, or provide external credentials or referrals in order to enter the community. These entry barriers are effective at selecting the right people to the extent that it is easy for those who are a good fit for the community to surmount the barriers and difficult for those who are not a good fit. A sequence of stages for entry—each involving specified socialization activities—can also help build commitment in the early phases of joining a community. Access restrictions, and the progressive removal of them, can also help with protection.

As in other chapters, we find that there are a variety of ways in which designers can meet the socialization challenges, by changing the contextual information that provides a frame through which members and potential members understand what they are doing without making large changes to the structure or technological features of a community. Endorsements of the community by a celebrity or a credible source can help recruit potential members. Visibly presenting attractive features of the site, such as the physical attractiveness of members, can also help. Highlighting that many other people have joined can serve as social proof that the community is valuable. Providing an accurate picture of the community's purpose and activities can help the right people self-select for membership. These framing actions are often the least costly to implement and should thus be the first to be considered. Sometimes they will be enough. When they are not, designers must consider more structural options.

Table 5.2

Summary of design alternatives relevant to newcomers, ordered by type

Type	Design alternative	Design claim
External communication	Active recruiting	1
	Word of mouth versus impersonal recruiting	2, 6
	Recruiting from social networks of existing members	3
	Making it easy for users to share content from a community site with their friends	4
	Disseminating information through well-connected members	5
Content, tasks, and activities	Providing newcomers friendly interactions with existing community members soon after joining a community	18
	Encouraging newcomers to reveal themselves publicly in profiles or "introduction threads"	19
	Socializing newcomers in groups, with collective tactics	22
	Providing sandboxes for newcomers	24
Roles, rules, policies, and procedures	Assigning the responsibilities of having friendly interactions with newcomers to particular community members	20
	Explicitly discouraging hostility toward newcomers who make mistakes	21
	Encouraging old-timers to mentor newcomers	23
Access controls	Forcing potential new members to pay or wait	12
	Forcing potential new members to undertake "separating" tasks	13
	Requiring potential members to complete a diagnostic task	14
	Requiring potential members to provide external diagnostic credentials	15
	Requiring potential members to provide referrals	16
	Erecting entry barriers for newcomers	17
	Socializing newcomers with formal and sequential tactics	22
	Instituting progressive access controls	25
Framing	Presenting reasons to join and endorsements by credible sources and sites	7
	Presenting attractive surface features and endorsements by celebrities	8
	Emphasizing the number of people already participating in a community	9
	Placing the name of a community in front of people often	10
	Providing potential new members with an accurate and complete picture of what the members' experience will be once they join	11

References

Adler, B. Thomas, and Luca de Alfaro. 2007. A Content-Driven Reputation System for Wikipedia. In *Proceedings of the 16th International Conference on World Wide Web*, 261–270. New York: ACM Press

Agrawal, J., and W. A. Kamakura. 1995. The Economic Worth of Celebrity Endorsers: An Event Study Analysis. *Journal of Marketing* 59 (3): 56–62.

Alachas1985. 2007. Onyxia Wipe Animation. YouTube. http://www.youtube.com/watch?v=HtvIYRrgZ04.

Arguello, Jaime, Brian S. Butler, Lisa Joyce, Robert E. Kraut, Kimberly S. Ling, Carolyn Rosé, and Xiaoqing Wang. 2006. Talk to Me: Foundations for Successful Individual-Group Interactions in Online Communities. In *CHI 2006: Proceedings of the ACM Conference on Human Factors in Computing Systems*, 959–968. New York: ACM Press.

Aronson, E. 1997. Back to the Future: Retrospective Review of Leon Festinger's "A Theory of Cognitive Dissonance." *American Journal of Psychology* 110 (1): 127–137.

Aronson, Elliot, and Judson Mills. 1959. The Effect of Severity of Initiation on Liking for a Group. *Journal of Abnormal and Social Psychology* 59:177–181.

Assmus, G., J. U. Farley, and D. R. Lehmann. 1984. How Advertising Affects Sales: Meta-Analysis of Econometric Results. *Journal of Marketing Research* 21 (1): 65–74.

Bajaj, Vikas. 2010. Spammers Pay Others to Answer Security Tests. *New York Times*, April 25, B6.

Bass, F. M. 1969. A New Product Growth Model for Consumer Durables. *Management Science* 15 (5): 215–227.

Bauer, Talya N., Todd Bodner, Berrin Erdogan, Donald M. Truxillo, and Jennifer S. Tucker. 2007. Newcomer Adjustment During Organizational Socialization: A Meta-Analytic Review of Antecedents, Outcomes, and Methods. *Journal of Applied Psychology* 92 (3): 707–721.

Benoit, W. L., G. J. Hansen, and R. M. Verser. 2003. A Meta-Analysis of the Effects of Viewing U.S. Presidential Debates. *Communication Monographs* 70 (4): 335–350.

Blizzard Entertainment. 2010. Recruit-a-Friend FAQ. http://us.blizzard.com/support/article.xml?locale=en_US&articleId=20588.

Boyd, D. M., and N. B. Ellison. 2008. Social Network Sites: Definition, History, and Scholarship. *Journal of Computer-Mediated Communication* 13 (1): 210–230.

Breaugh, J. A., and M. Starke. 2000. Research on Employee Recruitment: So Many Studies, So Many Remaining Questions. *Journal of Management* 26 (3): 405.

Burke, M., C. Marlow, and T. Lento. 2009. Feed Me: Motivating Newcomer Contribution in Social Network Sites. In *CHI 2009: Proceedings of the ACM Conference on Human Factors in Computing Systems*, 945–954. New York: ACM Press.

Burke, M., and B. Settles. 2011. Plugged in to the Community: Social Motivators in Online Goal-Setting Groups. In *Proceedings of C&T 2011: Fifth International Conference on Communities and Technologies*. New York: Springer Publishing.

Chaiken, Sehlly, Wendy Wood, and Alice H. Eagly. 1996. Principles of Persuasion. In Social Psychology: Handbook of Basic Principles, ed. E. Tory Higgins and Arie W. Kruglanski, 702–742. New York: Guildford Press.

Chapman, D. S., K. L. Uggerslev, S. A. Carroll, K. A. Piasentin, and D. A. Jones. 2005. Applicant Attraction to Organizations and Job Choice: A Meta-Analytic Review of the Correlates of Recruiting Outcomes. *Journal of Applied Psychology* 90 (5): 928–944.

Choi, Bo Reum, Kira Alexander, Robert E. Kraut, and John M. Levine. 2010. Socialization Tactics in Wikipedia and Their Effects. In *CSCW '10: Proceedings of the ACM Conference on Computer-Supported Cooperative Work*, 107–116. New York: ACM Press.

Choi, Bo Reum, Robert E. Kraut, and Mark Fichman. 2011. Matching People and Groups: An Exploratory Study of Recruitment and Selection in Online Games. Unpublished manuscript.

Cialdini, R. B., and N. J. Goldstein. 2004. Social Influence: Compliance and Conformity. *Annual Review of Psychology* 55 (1): 591–621.

Clary, E. G., M. Snyder, R. D. Ridge, J. Copeland, A. A. Stukas, J. Haugen, and P. Miene. 1998. Understanding and Assessing the Motivations of Volunteers: A Functional Approach. *Journal of Personality and Social Psychology* 74:1516–1530.

Coleman, James, Elihu Katz, and Herbert Menzel. 1957. The Diffusion of an Innovation among Physicians. *Sociometry* 20 (4): 253–270.

Collins, N., and L. Miller. 1994. Self-Disclosure and Liking: A Meta-Analytic Review. *Psychological Bulletin* 116 (3): 457–475.

Cooper, W. H. 1981. Ubiquitous Halo. *Psychological Bulletin* 90 (2):218–244.

Domingos, P., and M. Richardson. 2001. Mining the Network Value of Customers. In *Proceedings of the Seventh ACM SIGKDD International Conference on Knowledge Discovery and Data Mining*, 57–66. New York: ACM.

Drenner, S., S. Sen, and L. Terveen. 2008. Crafting the Initial User Experience to Achieve Community Goals. In *Proceedings of the 2008 ACM Conference on Recommender Systems*, 187–194. New York: ACM Press.

Ducheneaut, Nicolas. 2005. Socialization in an Open Source Software Community: A Socio-Technical Analysis. *Computer Supported Cooperative Work* 14 (4): 323–368.

Ducheneaut, Nicolas, Nicholas Yee, Eric Nickell, and Robert J. Moore. 2007. The Life and Death of Online Gaming Communities: A Look at Guilds in World of Warcraft. In *Proceedings of the SIGCHI Conference on Human Factors in Computing Systems*, 839–848. New York: ACM Press.

eBay. 2010. eBay Trading Assistant Program. http://pages.ebay.com/tahub/index.html.

Elsworth, Catherine. 2007. Wikipedia's Image Is Tarnished as an Editor Is Exposed as Fraud. *Daily Telegraph*, Mar. 7, 2007.

Erdogan, Z. B. 1999. Celebrity Endorsement: A Literature Review. *Journal of Marketing Management* 15 (4): 291–314.

Fark. 2010. FAQ. http://www.fark.com/farq.

Fernandez, R. M., and N. Weinberg. 1997. Sifting and Sorting: Personal Contacts and Hiring in a Retail Bank. *American Sociological Review* 62 (6): 883–902.

Festinger, Leon. 1957 [1962]. *A Theory of Cognitive Dissonance*. Reprint edition. Stanford, CA: Stanford University Press.

Fogg, B. J., Cathy Soohoo, David R. Danielson, Leslie Marable, Julianne Stanford, and Ellen R. Tauber. 2003. How Do Users Evaluate the Credibility of Web Sites? A Study with over 2,500 Participants. In *Proceedings of the 2003 ACM Conference on Designing for User Experiences*, 1–15. San Francisco: ACM Press.

Fogg, B. J., and D. Eckles. 2007. The Behavior Chain for Online Participation: How Successful Web Services Structure Persuasion. *Lecture Notes in Computer Science* 4744:199.

Gerard, Harold B., and Grover C. Mathewson. 1966. The Effect of Severity of Initiation on Liking for a Group: A Replication. *Journal of Experimental Social Psychology* 2 (3): 278–287.

Gladwell, M. 2002. *The Tipping Point: How Little Things Can Make a Big Difference*. New York: Little Brown.

Goldstein, N. J., V. Griskevicius, and R. B. Cialdini. 2007. Invoking Social Norms: A Social Psychology Perspective on Improving Hotels' Linen-Reuse Programs. *Cornell Hotel and Restaurant Administration Quarterly* 48 (2): 145.

Goffman, E. 1961. *Asylums: Essays on the Social Situation of Mental Patients and Other Inmates*. Garden City, NJ: Anchor Books.

Green, D. P., A. S. Gerber, and D. W. Nickerson. 2008. Getting Out the Vote in Local Elections: Results from Six Door-to-Door Canvassing Experiments. *Journal of Politics* 65 (4): 1083–1096.

Halfaker, Aaron, Aniket Kittur, and John Riedl. 2011. Don't Bite the Newbies: How Reverts Affect the Quantity and Quality of Wikipedia Work. In *Proceedings of WikiSym 2011*.

Hoag, David. 1996. The WELL Host Manual. Version 4.4. http://www.well.com/~confteam/hostmanual.

Internet FAQ Archives. 2010. Alt.Support.Stop-Smoking Compost. Internet FAQ Archives. http://www.faqs.org/faqs/support/stop-smoking/compost/part1.

Jones, G. R. 1986. Socialization Tactics, Self-Efficacy, and Newcomers' Adjustments to Organizations. *Academy of Management Journal* 29 (2): 262–279.

Katz, E. 1957. The Two-Step Flow of Communication: An Up-to-Date Report on an Hypothesis. *Public Opinion Quarterly* 12 (1): 61–78.

Katz, E., P. Lazersfeld. 1955. *Personal Influence: The Part Played by People in the Flow of Mass Communication.* New York: The Free Press.

Kawamoto, Dawn. 2004. Gmail Accounts Go up for Bid. CNET News. http://news.cnet.com/2100 -1023_3-5203162.html.

Kempe, D., J. Kleinberg, and É. Tardos. 2003. Maximizing the Spread of Influence through a Social Network. KDD '03: Proceedings of the Ninth ACM SIGKDD International Conference on Knowledge Discovery and Data Mining, 137–146. New York: ACM.

Kinch, Richard J. 2003. A Case of Fraud on eBay. TrueTeX. http://www.truetex.com/ebayfraud.htm.

Klapper, J. T. 1960. *The Effects of Mass Communication.* Glencoe, IL: Free Press.

Kristof-Brown, A. L., R. D. Zimmerman, and E. C. Johnson. 2005. Consequences of Individuals' Fit at Work: A Meta-Analysis of Person-Job, Person-Organization, Person-Group, and Person-Supervisor Fit. *Personnel Psychology* 58 (2): 281–320.

Kristof, A. L. 1996. Person-Organization Fit: An Integrative Review of Its Conceptualizations, Measurement, and Implications. *Personnel Psychology* 49 (1): 1–49.

Krogh, Georg von, Sebastian Spaeth, Karim R. Lakhani, and Eric von Hippel. 2003. Community, Joining, and Specialization in Open Source Software Innovation: A Case Study. *Research Policy* 32 (7): 1217–1241.

Lampe, Cliff, and Erik Johnston. 2005. Follow the (Slash) Dot: Effects of Feedback on New Members in an Online Community. In *Group '05: Proceedings of the 2005 International ACM SIGGROUP Conference on Supporting Group Work*, 11–20. New York: ACM Press.

Latané, B. 1981. The Psychology of Social Impact. *American Psychologist* 36:343–356.

Lave, Jean, and Etienne Wenger. 1991. *Situated Learning: Legitimate Peripheral Participation.* New York: Cambridge University Press.

Levine, John M., and Richard L. Moreland. 1994. Group Socialization: Theory and Research. In European Review of Social Psychology vol. 5, ed. Wolfgan Strocher and Miles Hewstone, 305–336. New York: John Wiley & Sons.

Mahajan, V., E. Muller, and Y. Wind. 2000. New-Product Diffusion Models: From Theory to Practice. In New-Product Diffusion Models, ed. V. Mahajan, E. Muller, and Y. Wind, 4–24. Boston: Kluwer Academic Publishers.

Mahajan, V., E. Muller, and F. Bass. 1990. New Product Diffusion Models in Marketing: A Review and Directions for Research. *Journal of Marketing* 54:1–26.

Mann, T. E., and R. E. Wolfinger. 1980. Candidates and Parties in Congressional Elections. *American Political Science Review* 74 (3): 617–632.

McGuire, W. J. 1985. Attitudes and Attitude Change. In Handbook of Social Psychology, ed. Gardner Lindzey and Elliot Aronson, 233–346. New York: Random House.

Montgomery, A. L. 2001. Applying Quantitative Marketing Techniques to the Internet. *Interfaces* 3 (2): 90–108.

Moreland, R. L. 1985. "Social Categorization and the Assimilation of "New" Group Members. *Journal of Personality and Social Psychology* 48 (5): 1173–1190.

Mozilla. 2010 Mozilla Forum Etiquette. Mozilla.org. http://www.mozilla.org/about/forums/etiquette.html.

Munro, G. D., P. H. Ditto, L. K. Lockhart, A. Fagerlin, M. Gready, and E. Peterson. 2002. Biased Assimilation of Sociopolitical Arguments: Evaluating the 1996 U.S. Presidential Debate. *Basic and Applied Social Psychology* 24 (1): 15–26.

Nickerson, R. S. 1998. Confirmation Bias: A Ubiquitous Phenomenon in Many Guises. *Review of General Psychology* 2:175–220.

Organ, D. W., and K. Ryan. 1995. A Meta-Analytic Review of Attitudinal and Dispositional Predictors of Organizational Citizenship Behavior. *Personnel Psychology* 48 (4): 775–802.

Panciera, K., A. Halfaker, and L. Terveen. 2009. Wikipedians Are Born, Not Made: A Study of Power Editors on Wikipedia. In *Proceedings of the ACM 2009 International Conference on Supporting Group Work Table of Contents*, 51–60. New York: ACM Press.

Panciera, Katherine, Reid Priedhorsky, Thomas Erickson, and Loren Terveen. 2010. Lurking? Cyclopaths?: A Quantitative Lifecycle Analysis of User Behavior in a Geowiki. In *CHI '10: Proceedings of the ACM Conference on Human Factors in Computing Systems*, 1917–1926. New York: ACM Press.

Petty, R. E., and D. T. Wegener. 1998. Attitude Change: Multiple Roles for Persuasion Variables. *The Handbook of Social Psychology* 1:323–390.

Phillips, J. M. 1998. Effects of Realistic Job Previews on Multiple Organizational Outcomes: A Meta-Analysis. *Academy of Management Journal* 41 (6): 673–690.

Postmedia. 2010. Scam Watch: The Most Popular Scams on eBay. eBay. http://reviews.ebay.com/Scam-Watch-The-Most-Popular-Scams-on-Ebay_W0QQugidZ10000000000025238.

Preece, Jenny, Blair Nonnecke, and Dorine Andrews. 2004. The Top Five Reasons for Lurking: Improving Community Experiences for Everyone. *Computers in Human Behavior* 20 (1): 201–223.

Preece, J., and B. Shneiderman. 2009. The Reader-to-Leader Framework: Motivating Technology-Mediated Social Participation. *AIS Transactions on Human-Computer Interaction* 1 (1): 13–32.

Resnick, P., R. Zeckhauser, J. Swanson, and K. Lockwood. 2006. The Value of Reputation on eBay: A Controlled Experiment. *Experimental Economics* 9 (2): 79–101.

Ridings, Catherine M., and David Gefen. 2004. Virtual Community Attraction: Why People Hang out Online. *Journal of Computer-Mediated Communication* 10 (1).

Roberts, D. F., and N. Maccoby. 1985. Effects of Mass Communication. In Handbook of Social Psychology, ed. Gardner Lindzey and Elliot Aronson, 539–598. New York: Random House.

Roberts, Jeffrey, Il-Horn Hann, and Sandra Slaughter. 2006. Understanding the Motivations, Participation and Performance of Open Source Software Developers: A Longitudinal Study of the Apache Projects. *Management Science* 52 (7): 984–999.

Rowe, Robert. 2004. Beginning Proofreaders' Frequently Asked Questions (FAQ). Distributed Proofreaders. May 27, 2004 version. http://www.pgdp.net/c/faq/ProoferFAQ.php.

Rynes, S. 1991. Recruitment, Job Choice, and Post-Hire Consequences: A Call for New Research Directions. In Handbook of Industrial and Organizational Psychology, ed. M. D. Dunnette, 399–444. Palo Alto, CA: Consulting Psychologists Press.

Saks, Alan M., Krista L. Uggerslev, and Neil E. Fassina. 2007. Socialization Tactics and Newcomer Adjustment: A Meta-Analytic Review and Test of a Model. *Journal of Vocational Behavior* 70:413–446.

Spence, Michael. 1973. Job Market Signaling. *Quarterly Journal of Economics* 87 (3): 355–374.

Spertus, E., R. Jeffries, and K. Sie. 2001. Scaling Online Communities with Javamlm. Paper presented at the Fifteenth Systems Administration Conference (LISA), USENIX, San Diego.

Stewart, K. J. 2003. Trust Transfer on the World Wide Web. *Organization Science* 14 (1): 5–17.

Sultan, F., J. U. Farley, and D. R. Lehmann. 1990. A Meta-Analysis of Applications of Diffusion Models. *Journal of Marketing Research* 27 (1): 70–77.

Tellis, G. J. 2004. *Effective Advertising: Understanding When, How, and Why Advertising Works.* Thousand Oaks, CA: Sage.

Thorndike, E. L. 1920. A Constant Error in Psychological Ratings. *Journal of Applied Psychology* 4 (1): 25–29.

Tugend, Alina. 2009. Typing in an E-Mail Address, and Giving up Your Friends' as Well. *New York Times*, June 20, 2009.

Ubuntu Forums. 2010. Ubuntu Forums Code of Conduct 2010. http://ubuntuforums.org/index.php?page=policy.

Van der Heijden, H. 2003. Factors Influencing the Usage of Websites: The Case of a Generic Portal in the Netherlands. *Information & Management* 40 (6): 541–549.

Van Maanen, J., and E. H. Schein. 1979. Toward a Theory of Organizational Socialization. *Research in Organizational Behavior* 1:209–264.

Wikipedia. 2010a. Copyrights. http://en.wikipedia.org/wiki/Wikipedia:Copyrights.

Wikipedia. 2010b. Manual of Style. http://en.wikipedia.org/wiki/Wikipedia:Manual_of_Style.

Wikipedia. 2010c. Please Do Not Bite the Newcomers. http://en.wikipedia.org/wiki/Wikipedia:Please_do_not_bite_the_newcomers.

Wikipedia. 2010d. Welcoming Committee. http://en.wikipedia.org/wiki/Wikipedia:Welcoming_committee.

Wikipedia. 2010e. What Wikipedia Is Not. http://en.wikipedia.org/wiki/Wikipedia:What_Wikipedia_is_not.

Wikipedia. 2010f. Wikipedia:Neutral Point of View. Wikipedia, http://en.wikipedia.org/wiki/Wikipedia:Neutral_point_of_view.

Williams, Dmitri, Nicholas Ducheneaut, Li Xiong, Yuanyuan Zhang, Nick Yee, and Eric Nickell. 2006. From Tree House to Barracks: The Social Life of Guilds in World of Warcraft. *Games and Culture* 1 (4): 338–361.

Wilson, E. O. 2007. E.O. Wilson on Saving Life on Earth. TED Conference. http://www.ted.com/talks/e_o_wilson_on_saving_life_on_earth.html.

Zajonc, Robert B. 1968. Attitudinal Effects of Mere Exposure. *Journal of Personality and Social Psychology* 9 (2): 1–27.

Zhang, Xiaoquan (Michael), and Feng Zhu. 2006. Intrinsic Motivation of Open Content Contributions: The Case of Wikipedia. Paper presented at the Workshop on Information Systems and Economics (WISE), Chicago.

6 Starting New Online Communities

Paul Resnick, Joseph Konstan, Yan Chen, and Robert E. Kraut

"Build it and they will come." If only it were that simple.

In reality, most online communities never really get off the ground. On SourceForge (http://sourceforge.net), for example, which offers free tools to open source projects, thousands of projects have been created, but only 10.3 percent have more than three members.[1] In an effort to test the effects of an online community for helping people to quit smoking, researchers gave 684 people access to an online community in addition to the informational website Smokefree.gov (http://smokefree.gov), but so few people used the online community features that they were not able to report on its effectiveness (Stoddard, Augustson, and Moser 2008).

Online communities fail to take off for many reasons. For some, it's just not clear whether the community offers services or experiences that potential members want. In these cases, why would anyone want to join? In other cases, the people who would want to join never find out about it. Some lose in a competition for members with another community. Some attract a stream of potential members, one at a time, but fail to hold them because there never seems to be anyone else around.

There are three major challenges in starting a new community. The first is to carve out a useful niche. The second is to defend that niche in the ecology of competing communities and alternative ways that potential members can spend their time. Meeting these two challenges requires making strategic choices about the scope of the community and about its compatibility and integration with other communities. The third challenge is to get to critical mass. A new community must recruit members before it has become the kind of community that they will value. There are a number of design approaches to meeting this challenge, including substituting professionally generated content for user-generated content in the early stages, leveraging early participants to attract later ones, and setting expectations about the likely future evolution of the community.

Because so little empirical research has studied how new communities start, support for most of the design claims in this chapter come not from empirical evidence but from anecdotes and from theoretical arguments. Many of the theoretical arguments are based on simple cost-benefit assessments. Participating in a community involves opportunity costs of time and effort that could be spent elsewhere. Some of the costs, such as learning the community's software and getting integrated socially, are incurred only on entry. Others are incurred on an ongoing basis. Participating also can bring benefits, such as information, social connection, or a sense of identity and purpose.

Within this cost-benefit framework, the first challenge can be reframed as ensuring that net utility, benefits minus costs, is positive for all members in steady state. The second is to make net utility be higher than that of competing communities. The third challenge—getting to critical mass—can be reframed as assuring net-positive utility for each of the members as they join, even though the community has not yet reached steady state.

1 Carving Out a Niche

There are three major design decisions to make when carving out a niche. One is the scope of the community, in terms of the breadth of topics to cover, the kinds of people to try to attract as members, the activities to support, and the purpose of the community. Sometimes the community is defined by a topic and activities and attracts a set of people who coalesce around the topic. For example, a Minnesota Twins fan community is defined by the topic of the baseball team and the activity of discussion about the team. The purpose is to inform and entertain the members. A diabetes support group for teens includes teens with diabetes, and perhaps their caregivers, with the purpose of providing information and emotional support. Sometimes a community is defined around a preexisting set of people, such as an alumni group, with a purpose of staying connected and the topics and activities emerging from the actions of the members.

The second major design decision is the extent of compatibility and integration with other sites, including the borrowing of features and user interface elements, the sharing of user identifiers, and the import and export of content and people. Many new communities are integrated in some way with existing communities or platforms. For example, Facebook applications (http://www.facebook.com) often define new communities. Individuals can also create new groups on platforms like Google groups (http://groups.google.com), Yahoo! Groups (http://groups.yahoo.com), Ning (http://www.ning.com), and Meetup (http://www.meetup.com), as well as Facebook. Each platform offers a slightly different bundle of features such as email lists, forums, chat, event calendars, and photo sharing. Building on an existing platform typically means that the new community shares user interface elements with other communities using the same platform, that members use the same user ID across communities on that platform, and sometimes that content is shared between communities. Stand-alone communities can also have some degree of compatibility and integration with other communities. For example, if they use common software packages like MediaWiki, Drupal, or Microsoft SharePoint, then user interface elements will be shared. User identities can be shared using technologies like OpenID. Content can be imported. It can also be exported to other communities, using technologies like RSS feeds or Facebook Connect.

The third design decision is the internal organization of content, people, and activities within the community. All but the smallest online communities let people do more than one thing. Forum-based communities offer multiple forums covering related topics and frequented by different, overlapping subsets of the membership. Open source software projects subdivide into work on different modules. Chat communities offer multiple rooms. Some communities, like Facebook, depend on a *pull model*, in which members regularly visit the community to see any new activity. Others, like Meetup, make use of *push alerts*, whereby members are notified when there is something potentially worth seeing.

We first assess the impact of those design alternatives on the marginal costs and benefits of participating and then add considerations of fixed initiation and switching costs to and from competing communities. Chapter 3 discussed some of the fixed benefits, the psychic value people get from membership in a community that is only loosely tied to their level of participation. Wenger, White, and Smith (2009) offer an alternative, useful framework for defining a community's internal organization by analyzing its activity orientations.

Opportunities Model

Online communities are complex constellations of activities; we begin with analysis of the basic building block—a single interaction space. We model each space as a collection of interaction opportunities. For example, upon visiting Facebook, a user might look at the newsfeed, which has a list of status updates or other activities from the user's friends or groups—each update an opportunity to be amused, bored, or annoyed. In a forums-based site, each forum is a collection of individual messages. In a chat community, a single chat room at any one time offers the opportunity to interact with each of the other people present at that time.

To analyze the costs and benefits of visiting a space, think of each opportunity as having an expected *match_value*, the expected utility of examining the opportunity and possibly engaging with it. Note that the expected match_value may be negative: for example, spam messages or messages about a topic that does not interest the user. We define *collection_size* as the number of new opportunities since the last visit, such as the number of messages in a forum or the number of status updates on a page of a Facebook newsfeed. In the typical pull design, in which a user visits a web page (or an email folder or an RSS feed) to get a collection, there is a per-collection *navigation_cost*, the cost of getting to the space and waiting for its contents to display. Clearly, when a space is nearly empty (i.e., collection_size is low), the navigation cost may outweigh the total value, and the net benefits may be negative. The following expression gives the expected net benefit from accessing a space:[2]

(match_value × collection_size) – navigation_cost   **[pull model]**

When there are few interaction opportunities, an alternative push model may be appropriate, in which users are notified each time a new interaction opportunity becomes available. For example, in forums with few posts, new posts may be forwarded by email to subscribing members. In synchronous interaction communities like multiplayer games or Second Life, users may receive alerts when their friends log on or enter particular spaces. The problem with the push model is that users are interrupted once for each new interaction opportunity, whereas in the pull model users expend time once to navigate to the whole collection. The following expresses the net benefit of push notifications for a collection of interaction opportunities:

(match_value × collection_size) – (interruption_cost × collection_size)   **[push model]**

The lower the per-item interruption cost is, the more attractive push notifications are. For example, many people—depending on their email reading habits—find email notifications to be a relatively small interruption cost. Pop-up alerts, on the other hand, may have somewhat higher interruption costs because they may interrupt an activity that is more time-sensitive than email reading (Horvitz and Apacible 2003).

The other consideration in assessing push notifications is the time sensitivity of the opportunities. For example, when a collection offers synchronous interactions (e.g., a chat room), the match value of an interaction opportunity exists only while the other person is present. Thus, for example, push notifications about favorite chat partners coming online or favorite chat rooms having people in them may be especially useful. On the other hand, notifications about new messages in a forum would be less useful if the messages are not time-sensitive (e.g., a site like

Lightbulbjokes.com (http://lightbulbjokes.com) dedicated to collecting old lightbulb jokes).

Design Claim 1 Lower volume and higher time sensitivity of interaction opportunities and lower interruption costs increase the benefits of push notification.

In the remainder of the analysis, we focus on the predominant pull model, in which users visit a collection. Because there is a per-visit navigation cost that is independent of the number of opportunities actually present, the challenge is to increase the collection size while still maintaining the expected match value for each opportunity. One way to increase the volume of activity is to expand the scope, adding more topics and people with more diverse interests. As a thought experiment, imagine simply merging spaces with different topics. As an extreme example, consider a forum with posts about the Minnesota Twins baseball team, Pablo Picasso's paintings, and U.S. Civil War reenactments. Mixing the three topics may triple the number of messages, but each visitor will discover that two-thirds of the content is uninteresting, and the community will likely shrink or fail. We refer to lumping several independent topics together as a *mixed-topic scope.*

Design Claim 2 A mixed-topic scope reduces expected match value.

Even when the scope for an interaction space is not deliberately mixed, ambiguity about its scope may make it mixed anyway. Different people, thinking that the "true" scope is different, will use it differently. Match values are lower when people interact with others who have a different interpretation of what the community is about.

Design Claim 3 An ambiguous scope for an interaction space reduces expected match value.

In some cases, mixing different topics need not reduce match value. Consider assembling the various Major League Baseball fan communities into a larger MLB forum. Will doing so help? If people are simply there to talk about their own teams, then probably not. The best we can hope for in that case is a set of separate communities sharing infrastructure. But if fans of different teams get some value from interacting with each other, then the situation changes. There are two ways this might occur: bridging activities and transcendent identities (explained shortly).

Bridging activities occur when there is an intersection of interests between two topical scopes. For example, fans of two teams that are about to play each other may enjoy talking with each other. Detroit Tigers fans may be interested in interacting with New York Yankees fans to discuss the performance of a player who switched from one team to the other or upcoming games between the two teams. Or fans of other teams may join into discussion with Minnesota Twins fans about their new stadium. When a space has a mixed-topic scope, designers would do well to identify potential bridging activities and seed the community with them.

Design Claim 4   Activities that bridge interests in different topics increase match value in spaces with mixed-topic scope.

Members may also have an interest in or identify with a broader topic. To continue with the baseball fan analogy, some people are fans of Major League Baseball as a whole, instead of or in addition to any particular team. They may be happy to discuss the use of instant replay in baseball, the use of the All-Star Game results to determine the World Series home field advantage, or the differences between professional baseball in the United States and Japan.

Over time, names arise for those topics and identities that transcend component topics and identities. Over the years, most major sports leagues and events have expended significant marketing resources to create widely recognized names like the NBA, the World Cup, or Wimbledon to encourage fans to identify with the league or event as a whole rather than just individual competitors or teams. One useful rule of thumb for designers is to look for topical scopes that do not require compound names to describe. If the simplest description for a community is that it covers topics A, B, and C, it is a sign that there is not yet a transcendent identity.

Sometimes the connections between specific identities or topics can itself become a new topic around which identities and a community can form. Wenger refers to these as bridging communities of practice (Wenger 1999). For example, a forum devoted to reconciliation (or just argument) between Israelis and Palestinians may have a high match value for people who want to make connections between the groups. In the case of bridging communities, it may be fine if the only descriptive name is a compound one that describes the component topics and the fact that connections between them are the purpose of the community. Contrast that with a forum devoted to two separate topics, Israeli politics and Palestinian politics. If it attracted two groups of people, each interested in discussing only one of the two topics, but their discussions were mixed together, there would be a low match value.

Design Claim 5   A transcendent or bridging topical identity increases match value in communities with mixed-topic scope.

Communities with Multiple Spaces

Combining multiple spaces in a single online community offers several advantages. First, it amortizes the fixed costs of development and branding over more users and uses. For example, Craigslist has a unified software infrastructure, but interaction spaces are partitioned geographically and by category within each locale. Second, it reduces search costs for members: once someone finds a useful community or a space within it, they are likely to be interested in several of the spaces. Third, because there is participant overlap in the different parts of a community, synergies are created—that is, a personal connection that two people make through interacting in one space also increases the value they get from interacting in another space within the community. We refer to the second and third advantages, reduced search costs and benefits of overlapping memberships, as *synergies among spaces* within a community.

The first question facing designers when a community has multiple subspaces is whether these should be globally defined, looking the same to all members, or whether there should be personalized views of the community's activity. Facebook provides groups and pages, which look the same to all users who visit them, but also provides a personalized newsfeed containing content posted by the user's friends. Because those friends may not be friends with each other, they may not see the same content in their news feeds that the user sees.

As another example, UpMyStreet (http://www.upmystreet.com) is a site in Britain that provides information about local businesses and real estate. It also provides a message board for conversations with one's neighbors. This feature may be more popular in some regions than in others. Rather than defining a separate forum for each city or region, all conversation goes into a single container with messages indexed by the location of the person posting. In figure 6.1, messages from the previous two weeks that were posted by people near the city of Cambridge are displayed. In a city with more participants, such as London, it automatically selects conversations within a smaller geographic radius. When people in a city such as Cambridge with no recent conversations explore the site, they are more likely to view the site favorably if presented with activity in nearby towns than if they are shown no activity at all.

The same idea could be applied to other distance metrics. For example, sites could determine what to display for a particular user through text-processing algorithms that

Figure 6.1
Personalized views in UpMyStreet (http://www.upmystreet.com).

select the most relevant content or people profiles or recommender algorithms that select content or people most likely to be liked by a particular person. Again, this method would have the effect of always showing the closest content or people, so that something would be displayed even when a perfect match does not exist. By contrast, dividing the people and content up into spaces creates hard boundaries, so that when a space is empty, it looks truly empty. Computer simulations suggest that these personalized displays of information provide more benefit to participants than do nonpersonalized displays, which show all content or show the same subset of content for everyone (Ren and Kraut Under review).

What is lost with personalized spaces is a shared context. In a forum whose boundaries are the same for everyone, it is reasonable to write a comment that alludes to other recent threads in the same forum. Most readers will also have seen those threads. In UpMyStreet, responding to a post at a distance of 4 miles with an allusion to another post would risk confusing readers who may live on the other side of town and not have seen the other post. Similarly, when commenting on a Facebook status message, it is unreasonable to assume that other commenters, or even the poster of the status message, will have seen the same other posts in their newsfeeds (though this doesn't seem to stop some people from posting comments that assume such a shared context).

Design Claim 6 Personalized collections of "most related content" enhance match value but reduce shared context.

Assuming that designers do create rooms, groups, forums, or other globally shared contexts, the next question is which ones and how many. A search-cost perspective suggests that it is important for people to be able to easily identify those spaces that will have high utility for them, meaning a high match value for the contents and a high level of activity, so that there are many interaction opportunities.

A common mistake that online community designers make is to imagine all the topics that their hoped-for members might want to discuss, and to create separate forums or chat rooms for each topic. Initially, at least, most of these spaces will be empty. People who choose a space to visit based solely on the topic name will find an empty space. Because there is a cost to each such visit, the net benefit of spaces with few items will be negative.

An alternative is to provide initially just one space for interaction. Although the interaction in that space may cover a broader range of topics and thus not completely match a visitor's interests, it will at least limit the number of separate access costs that need to be paid to examine the community's content. As a space gets enough activity, it can be split into multiple spaces that are all active. A secondary benefit is that the community designers or decision makers will have the opportunity to observe the naturally occurring topics of conversation and create spaces based on the topics actually of interest to the membership rather than on a priori assumptions about the hot topics. On Usenet, there is a long history of broader groups forking into more specialized groups: for example, the denizens of the rec.humor newsgroup eventually split it into subspaces, rec.humor.funny for actually funny posts and rec.humor.d for discussion of humor. Similarly, Slashdot (http://slashdot.org) started with a single collection of news items, under the tagline "news for nerds." After Slashdot grew in popularity, it subdivided into specialized sections including topics such as hardware, games, science, and rights online, each of which attracted enough commenters to maintain a lively feel.

Design Claim 7   Subdividing spaces after they become active creates more net benefits for participants than having lots of inactive spaces.

One way to mitigate the negative effects of empty spaces is to decrease the chances that visitors will stumble on them, which can be done through navigation aids that filter or sort based on activity or at least provide activity indicators. For example, the online support community for the Drupal software package (http://drupal.org) lists the time of the most recent message for each forum topic (see figure 6.2). In this case, all of the support forums are relatively active. In startup communities, however, sorting the forums by most recent activity could help newcomers find the most active forums.

Forum	Topics	Posts	Last post
★ Support			
Try searching the site or a specific project's bug reports first. Remember all support on this site is on a volunteer basis, so please visit the forum tips for posting hints.			
● Post installation Drupal is up and running but how do I ...?	134727	482163	1 min 38 sec ago by riccardogalli
● Before you start Is Drupal a viable solution for my website? Please see the documentation Getting Started before posting.	6098	25670	1 hour 24 min ago by anshuljain2k8
● Installing Drupal Installing Drupal? Please see the documentation in the handbook and the video resources for Drupal 5 and Drupal 6 for additional installation resources.	13519	57387	10 min 1 sec ago by TWD
● Upgrading Drupal Questions regarding upgrading an existing Drupal site. Don't forget to read the UPGRADE.txt that comes with evey Drupal download.	5112	20148	5 hours 2 min ago by ziepe
● Converting to Drupal Need help migrating your site to Drupal?	2524	9661	36 min 7 sec ago by AlonGoldberg

Figure 6.2
Drupal (http://drupal.org) support forums with indicators of recent activity.

In the group chat community Paltalk (http://www.paltalk.com), most of the open chat rooms at any one time have very few participants in them—people who are regulars in those rooms may be satisfied with the small number of participants and the occasional interactions that occur in them. New users, however, who are exploring and evaluating the service, are less likely to find such rooms attractive. The user interface to select chat rooms encourages users to select a room to visit from a display of the rooms that are currently most active, sorted in descending order by number of people in them (see figure 6.3).

Design Claim 8   In communities with lots of interaction spaces, navigation aids that highlight more active spaces increase the net benefits members experience.

In communities with synchronous interaction spaces such as chat rooms or islands in Second Life (http://secondlife.com), if they are not always active, it may be helpful to schedule times when they are expected to be active. That way, people can avoid visiting only to find the space empty and, if the space is compelling enough, can plan to visit when it will be open and active. The times may be announced when the space

Figure 6.3
The Paltalk (http://www.paltalk.com) chat rooms in the category "Government and Politics," sorted by number of people currently logged in to them.

is created, based on intuitions about when people will want to participate or just the availability of the moderator or creator of the space. For example, the Wellness Community (http://www.thewellnesscommunity.org) organizes small online support groups for cancer patients. Each group has a scheduled ninety-minute weekly synchronous session in addition to a private asynchronous discussion forum. Similarly, on PalTalk, someone who stumbles on the room titled "Bobby Likis Car Clinic Show" and finds it empty will be informed that it is "Live every Saturday from 10a to 12n ET." In the absence of fixed schedules, information may be provided based on historical data about when a space has been active, with the "expected popular hours" posted.

Design Claim 9 In synchronous spaces that are not always active, a schedule of "expected active times" coordinates visitors and can become a self-fulfilling expectation.

Navigation aids can reduce search costs not only by identifying active spaces but also by identifying spaces that are likely to have a high match value. A visitor who finds one space he or she likes can be directed to other spaces that are "similar" in some way, where similarity may be defined by text matching (content-based filtering) or based on the participants in them (collaborative filtering). For example, in a chat community where there are hundreds or thousands of separate rooms, someone might be informed of other rooms frequented by the people he or she has interacted with previously.

Design Claim 10   In communities with many interaction spaces, recommender systems that help people navigate to spaces that best suit them increase the net benefits people experience.

Although ambiguity about the scope of individual spaces is largely harmful, some ambiguity about the scope of the community as a whole is natural and sometimes beneficial. Organization theorists point out that uncertainty and disagreement about the purpose is a natural and unavoidable part of the startup phase of any new community of practice, including new online communities (Wenger, McDermott, and Snyder 2002). It can be more or less painful, and cause more or fewer problems in the retention of members, depending on design choices that are made. But the negotiation of a shared purpose cannot be eliminated entirely. Even if the founder of a community announces a purpose, the members may not accept it as their purpose—it becomes a shared purpose only through the actions of members that serve to reinforce or challenge it. One example: Amy Jo Kim (2000, 19) described how the L'eggs pantyhose website discussion area—against the wishes of its owner—became a site whose main purpose, shared by its active participants, was to provide an anonymous forum for men to discuss the joys of wearing pantyhose.

Some ambiguity about the eventual scope of the community has some advantages. First, it allows the community designers to learn from the members what the members want. A topic may attract an unexpected audience or the audience may be interested in different topics or activities than the designer first intended. Fighting against what the members want, by trying to stick to the original vision, can alienate them. For example, the founder of Friendster (http://www.friendster.com), the first widely popular social networking site, alienated many of its members when he refused to allow them to engage in playful uses of the site with fake profiles that did not accurately describe themselves. According to boyd and others, the active deletion of these "Fakester" accounts ruptured trust between the company and its users, causing many to leave (Anderson 2003; boyd 2006; Ellison 2007). Second, the activity of negotiating the scope—especially through explicit meta-discussion about it—can itself be a rewarding activity for some members and can lead them to feel "ownership" of the community and thus commitment to it, as discussed in chapters 3 and 4.

Design Claim 11   Ambiguity of scope for the community creates opportunities for adjustment and member ownership.

Even when everyone is interested in a narrow topic, communities with too many people may have a reduced match value. As described in more detail in chapter 3, in so-called *bond-based communities* the primary source of commitment to the group derives from interpersonal bonds with other individual members. Those interpersonal bonds depend on repeated exposure to the same people. Consider, for example, a cancer support community. A person who reads thirty messages per day will likely get more emotional support if the same people write those messages each day. Indeed, the match value might be enough higher that it would be worth restricting the community size (or subdividing it so that it effectively creates several smaller communities). For this reason, the Wellness Community, mentioned previously, deliberately launches small subcommunities of just twelve people, in addition to offering a set of forums for the community as a whole.

Design Claim 12   A larger community leads to lower match value in bond-based communities.

2   Competing for a Niche

Some new communities enter a crowded landscape. If a company introduces enterprise social networking software, it needs to be cognizant of the other social networking sites its employees may already be participating in, such as Facebook and LinkedIn (http://www.linkedin.com), because the internal site will be competing with those other sites for employees' time and attention. If a new site for cooking enthusiasts starts up, its potential members will have many other options for places to interact online with other cooking enthusiasts. Even when a new community does not have any obvious competition, it will be useful for designers to conduct a competitive analysis for two reasons. First, potential members always have the option of muddling through with their existing communication patterns. For example, a newly diagnosed diabetic, instead of joining a diabetes support group, has the option to just communicate with his or her existing email, IM, or Facebook networks, even if the people in those networks are not very interested in or knowledgeable about diabetes. Second, even if there is not currently a crowded landscape, there may be competitors in the future. For example, if you start a fan club for an obscure band, there are likely to be competing clubs in the future if the band becomes popular. By conducting a competitive analysis, the designer can carve out a niche that can be defended against future competitors. Shapiro and Varian analyze competitive strategies for information products more generally (1999, chapters 5–8). Drawing on that analysis, we pull out implications for online communities.

Our initial interaction opportunities model for analyzing costs and benefits considered only the marginal costs of continued participation once someone had already joined. For competitive analysis, we need to consider also a new member's switching costs of leaving a community and getting started with a new one. Startup and switching costs come from a number of sources. First, new users have to learn to operate the community's software. Second, new users have to learn their way around, finding the areas of the community that have high match value for them. Third, new users have to learn the social norms of appropriate behavior. Finally, to achieve maximum benefits from participation, new users have to build up social connections and gain status in the community. We will model the sum of all these as a single quantity, the *switching_cost*.

These switching costs must be amortized in some way if we are to compare them against the benefits from participating over a period of time. We simplify this comparison by assuming there is some expected duration of participation. We roll up the expected net participation benefits (i.e., benefits minus costs) from the opportunities model of the previous section over the expected duration of participation into a single number: the *participation_benefits*.[3]

In a competition between an incumbent community that someone is already a member of and a competitor that the person could join, the competitor must offer participation benefits that are enough better than the incumbent to compensate for the switching cost. Incumbents gain strategic advantage when switching costs are higher: the costs serve to lock in members. In the startup stage, a community is in the role of competitor and will generally want the switching costs to be low, making it easy for people to join. Once people have joined, however, the community is in an incumbent role, and a community designer will want the costs of those same members switching out to be high.

Choices about compatibility will affect switching costs. For example, if the new community uses the same interface elements as other communities, it reduces the costs of learning to use the software, thereby reducing switching costs. One way to do that is to use a popular software platform for online communities, like phpBB (http://

www.phpbb.com), Drupal, Ning, or Yahoo! Groups. Employing innovative user interface elements makes sense in a community's startup stage only if they create significant additional participation benefits—enough to outweigh the additional switching costs. Moreover, innovative interface elements that are truly valuable may not convey a long-term edge against future competitors, as other communities can copy them.

Another compatibility decision that affects switching costs is sharing user IDs or profiles. A competitor that allows members to register and login using OpenID credentials issued by an incumbent (or by some other popular site such as Facebook) can reduce potential members' switching costs. If a user can import his or her profile and friend links from the incumbent site as well, switching costs are further reduced. Of course, the incumbent may not allow the sharing of IDs and profiles, in order to keep switching costs high (e.g., eBay does not allow its members' feedback profiles to be imported to other sites). When sharing IDs and profiles is an option, designers must judge which is more important: the initial strategic value when recruiting members or the later strategic value when trying to retain them. In addition, in some cases differentiated IDs may be critical to the participation benefits in the community, preserving the ability for members to separate their different online social contexts rather than collapsing them as happens when people from different parts of one's life access the same online persona (boyd 2008). For example, a health support community might advertise itself as a safe environment for sharing personal experiences, which inherently requires that the user ID not be shared between the health support community and other communities. In interviews with people who participated in a stand-alone health community as well as Facebook, a recurring theme was that people were willing to share some things in the stand-alone community, like weight loss setbacks or even just weight loss goals, that they did not want to share with all their Facebook friends (Newman et al. 2011).

Design Claim 13   Differentiated user interface elements in the competitor community create startup costs and thus favor the incumbent community in any competition over members.

Design Claim 14   Nonshared user IDs and profiles between incumbent and competitor communities create startup costs and thus favor the incumbent community in any competition over members.

Design choices about import and export of content from competing communities affect the relative benefits of the communities. Importing content from an incumbent competitor incorporates some of the benefits of the other community into the new community. That is, participation benefits increase in the importing community. In the next section, we explain how temporarily importing data can be an effective tool to get through the initial stages before there is sufficient participation in the community.

The opposite analysis holds for exporting data: if the new community exports content, then its competitors are able to increase their net participation benefits and thus compete more effectively. Why, then, would any community export its data? One possibility is that it does not think it is in competition with the communities to which it exports its content. A second reason is that it increases visibility for the community that is the source of the content, allowing it to compete for members who would not otherwise have been aware of it. This is especially true if the exported content is read-only, in which case it may serve as a lure to those who wish to respond or join a discussion. A third possibility is that some content contributors may be motivated to reach as wide an audience as possible: exporting the content may increase their benefits of participation in the community where they post. For example, someone who has many friends on Facebook but few followers (so far) on Twitter might post on Facebook only, if that person had to choose one or the other. An application that automatically reposts his or her tweets as Facebook status messages might tip the balance so that the user would post on Twitter.

As with many design choices, trade-offs are involved. A community that is not yet well established may benefit from importing content (to enhance the value of reading there) and from exporting content (to enhance the value of writing, and to enhance awareness of the community). Sharing with less well established competitors, however, may help the competitor more than the incumbent.

Design Claim 15   Content sharing between competing communities raises awareness of the exporting community and the value of posting there, but raises the value of consuming content in the importing community.

In competitive situations, it is especially important to clearly convey the benefits of a community. Many people will not carefully investigate the community, but will instead assess the community based on short descriptions or reviews from others who do investigate. Given limited attention from evaluators, it is difficult to convey the value of a large set of small improvements. Instead, it is far more effective to identify one or two key elements. In television advertising, Rosser Reeves argued for conveying a "unique selling proposition," a benefit to the user that the competing product doesn't offer (Reeves 1961). In the online community setting, the unique selling proposition or core selling proposition may be a topic not covered elsewhere (e.g., "the Wikipedia of news translation"), a different set of participants (e.g., "the dating site for artists and lawyers"), a different set of activities and interaction tools (e.g., "an easier way to connect with your friends") or a different set of social norms ("a truly *supportive* community to help you lose weight").

Design Claim 16   Conveying a succinct unique selling proposition attracts members.

Economists describe some competitions as "winner-take-all." For example, if there are two communities competing for exactly the same niche, if either community attracts most of the available members, their membership will make that community more attractive than its competitor for the remaining people as well. In a winner-take-all situation, it is more important to convince people that your community will succeed than to convince them that your community is inherently better. If everyone thinks that others will join community C2, they will join it, but if they all think others will join C1, they will join that one. If either C1 or C2 becomes what is called a *focal point* (Schelling 1958), widely shared expectations of success will be self-fulfilling.

As Shapiro and Varian argue, "The aura of inevitability is a powerful weapon" (1999, 181). Cultivating public awareness is one way to create that aura. If the public is much more aware of C1 than C2, then even people who are aware of both know that many people are familiar only with C1. Therefore, they will expect C1 to win and will prefer to join it. Consider, for example, Angie's List (http://www.angieslist.com), a site that provides reviews of local contractors and businesses that serve household needs, which has spent much more visibly than other sites in this arena. It has advertised extensively on NPR and even television spots (Adweek 2006). In a city where there are competing online communities providing this service, many more people will be aware of Angie's List than its competitors. Even people who are aware of competitors may participate in Angie's List simply because they expect others to join it.

Celebrity endorsements can also help to create a focal point. For example, online poker sites have emerged and grown rapidly in the past several years as poker itself has grown and become a major televised activity. The sites themselves are organized into poker tables based on the game played and the betting limits. Because play is against other members, a site without enough traffic to have members populating nearly every type of table is likely to lose out to its competitors. PokerStars (http://www.pokerstars.net) heavily advertises its team of celebrity poker professionals. Its home page prominently features three recognizable "world champions," and its television advertisements (which run during televised poker tournaments) highlight the professionals associated with the site. Indeed, all of the major online poker sites build their image around a set of nationally visible poker stars (and with mottos like "play where the pros play"). Even though amateurs will probably never play with the pros (unless they are willing to play for high monetary stakes and lose a lot of money to them), the endorsements from stars help to create a focal point that amateurs will visit when they want to play poker online.

Design Claim 17   Advertising and celebrity endorsements help create awareness of a community and thus make it a focal point in a competition between communities.

3   Getting to Critical Mass

The third major challenge is to get past the initial growing pains to a critical mass of participation. There are two ways in which a community in the startup stage may provide less value initially than it will after it reaches steady state. First, it may not have enough members to provide the content and interaction opportunities that some prospective members want. Second, the members may not yet have a shared purpose, including rough agreement about the scope of activity and membership, along with the norms and governance needed to achieve that purpose, so that less valuable content and interactions may crowd out the valuable activity. Social science theory can help us understand the challenges and point us in the direction of strategies to help online communities succeed through the initial growing pains.

The economic theory of network externalities or network effects explains situations in which one person's value from using a product or system increases with the number of participants in the system (Katz and Shapiro 1985; Farrell and Saloner 1985). A good example is the fax machine. Being the only person in the world who owns a fax machine does not generate much utility. A user's value for a fax machine increases with the number of other people who use the fax machines. The term "Metcalfe's Law", invented by George Gilder, is often used to describe situations in which the benefits of increasing the network size dwarf the costs of doing so.

There are two problems, however, when individuals decide sequentially whether to join a network. First, below the critical mass size, adding a member may not create enough benefits to outweigh the costs. In the extreme case, people may decide sequentially, one at a time, not to join, even if they could all benefit from a coordinated decision to join. Second, joining creates an externality—a benefit for all the other members. Thus, even when the total benefits to the community outweigh the new member's costs, the benefits to the new member may not outweigh the costs, and the member may not join.

The same concepts can easily be applied to online communities. A social networking site such as LinkedIn or Facebook has little or no value if nobody else is using it and much greater value if many of the friends or colleagues of a prospective user are already signed up. Communities built more around content rather than connections not only face the public goods underprovision problem addressed in Chapter 2 but may also have a notion of critical mass—a level of usage at which it becomes clear that one's efforts are worthwhile. There must be both enough people editing and reading and enough high-quality articles at a site such Wikipedia for new users to perceive it as a venue worthy of their own participation.

Given these problems, there are two useful approaches. One is to make the community more attractive to early joiners. The other is to make more effective use of the early members, leveraging them to attract additional members. An understanding of how to leverage early joiners has implications for the types of people that are most valuable as early members. Thus, we first analyze how to leverage early joiners. Then, in our discussion of how to attract them to join early, we are able to suggest design alternatives that are tailored to attracting the most valuable types.

Bootstrapping: Leveraging Early Members to Get More Members
A community may go through a series of states, each of which is attractive enough to engage a new subset of members who improve the quality of the community for the next wave of membership. When the presence or actions of early members lead other people to join the community, we describe it as *bootstrapping*. One approach is to organize activity so that it creates content that will be attractive to future users. A second approach is to include viral elements so that current members bring in their friends and acquaintances, who increase the value of the community to others.

The natural use of a site by early members may not always be sufficient to generate content that attracts others. But they may be more inclined if they are paid to do so. For example, Epinions initially paid contributors for providing reviews. Chapter 2 examined ways to motivate contributions more generally. Here we note some special considerations about tangible rewards for early content contributions. The fact that other members are paid to perform certain activities may demotivate volunteers from performing those same actions for free. Once offered, it is also demotivating to take away rewards for actions. When Epinions reduced the payments to reviewers and changed its terms, it lost many contributors and had to put a lot of customer service energy into quelling dissatisfaction. Discounts or free service may be a less problematic way to encourage early members to contribute. It is easier to discontinue these motivations once the community reaches a critical mass. They may also be continued for the early members without offering them to those who join later, creating a form of early-adopter benefit that we will discuss shortly. Discounts and free service may avoid creating the kind of envy that direct cash payments would generate.

Design Claim 18 Incentives for early members to generate content can increase bootstrapping.

In order to leverage early members, it is most useful to encourage them to create primary content. In online communities, the primary content consists of blog entries, forum posts and responses, audio, video, and text documents, items for sale, and the like. Metadata consists of tags, ratings, commentary about primary content, and behavioral clickstream data regarding which primary content items were accessed. Metadata adds a lot more value once it is needed to help navigate through a large quantity of primary content. For example, imagine a new, specialized photo sharing site. Suppose that it had only three photos posted, but hundreds of tags for those photos and votes from users about which of the three they liked best. It would be less likely to attract new members than one with hundreds of photos and only a few tags and votes.

Design Claim 19 User-generated primary content does more to bootstrap additional membership than does user-generated metadata in the community startup stage.

In addition to generating attractive content, members can directly attract other members. Because people are members of multiple groups and communities, awareness of one community can spread to other communities. Indeed, a viral spread of membership is a natural phenomenon that may occur organically, without special intervention from designers. For example, Backstrom and colleagues examined patterns of joining communities within the blogging site LiveJournal and of joining (participating in) academic conferences that occur annually. They found that people are more likely to join groups the more of their existing friends are members and the more those friends are friends with each other (Backstrom et al. 2006).

One trick for designers who want to supercharge the normal viral dissemination process is to get some marker of membership to display on web pages or in .sig (signature) lines of messages that are viewed by people who are not members. For example, within the overall Facebook site, there are lots of specific communities.

When a person joins one of those communities, that membership can be displayed on the user's profile, visible to any of his or her acquaintances who view the profile. The action of joining the group may also be propagated to the feeds of other people on Facebook who are official "friends" but who may not yet be a member of the group.

Design Claim 20   Services that enable displays of membership that are visible to non-members lead to bootstrapping.

An even more effective way to leverage the fact that early members are also members of other communities is to make actions within the community visible to acquaintances outside the community. For example, presidential candidate Barack Obama's website allowed members to create blogs on the site and take various actions. It gave members the option of linking with their existing Facebook accounts, so that some of their actions on the Obama site generated entries in Facebook and thus were visible in the feeds of the Facebook "friends." Numerous Facebook apps work similarly. For example, many people have been introduced to the FarmVille and Foursquare apps by seeing status messages in their main Facebook newsfeeds that describe their friends' notable—or not so notable—events within those apps (see figure 6.4).

RECENT ACTIVITY

in Tempe, Arizona:
unlocked the '**Barista**' badge.

in San Francisco, CA:
unlocked the '**Swarm**' badge.

in bangkok, thailand:
became the mayor of หมู่บ้านกลางเมือง **Rama IX**.

in São Paulo, SP:
wrote a tip @ **Andiamo Morumbi Shopping**: Absurdo, precisava de uma nota fiscal e nao incluem o valor do servico. Reclamei e disseram para nao pagar o servico. Preferem prejudicar os garcons que nao tem nada a ver com isso.

Figure 6.4
Foursquare (http://foursquare.com) newsfeeds.

Design Claim 21 Services that make members' actions in the community visible to their acquaintances outside the community lead early participants to attract later participants.

News and content sites often provide a feature that lets readers notify friends about content that they found interesting. For example, the *New York Times* website offers buttons that allow readers to forward content by email or to recommend the article on news aggregator services like Digg. Because the site facilitates the forwarding, the notification about the interesting content can also highlight the existence of the site as a whole. The same mechanism can be provided in online communities for forwarding interesting content. For example, the Food Network (http://www.foodnetwork.com) has an Email button that allows a user to email a recipe to a friend with an embedded sentence, "Checkout this awesome recipe on FoodNetwork.com!"

Design Claim 22 Services that allow members to forward content from the community to their acquaintances outside the community lead early participants to attract later participants.

The viral marketing approach is even more evident in some of the explicit social networking sites. When signing up for the professional social network site LinkedIn, members are invited to let the software scan their instant messenger contacts and their email contacts both to help them connect with those already in the site (increasing value) and to invite those who are not there (bootstrapping). Thus, each new member potentially brings in other acquaintances, and the site provides tools that reduce the effort needed for such invitations.

Design Claim 23 Services that allow members to invite acquaintances outside the community to join lead early participants to attract later participants.

As with content generation, explicit incentives may be provided for referring new members. Physician community Sermo has offered cash and prizes to members who refer their friends. Cloudmark's SpamNet offered a free month of service for each customer referred. One challenge with pay-for-referral schemes—and the reason that most free sites don't use them—is ensuring that members refer actual people who are likely participants rather than their own six other email accounts. Sermo handles this with an elaborate signup process; even though the site is free to members, those members have to demonstrate that they are licensed physicians. Cloudmark's model is similar to many pay services; you get the credit only after the referred member has been a paying subscriber for two months. Other commercial sites offer members the chance to give discounts with their referral (10 percent off the items you recommend) or give a percentage back to the referrer, in a form of multilevel marketing.

Design Claim 24 Pay-for-referral methods and revenue sharing from referrals increase bootstrapping.

Attracting Early Members

We adapt the previous cost-benefit analysis framework to consider the problem of attracting early members, who decide whether to join before the community has reached a critical mass of participation from other people. There are many possible futures for a community in its early stages, with each providing a different level of possible benefits for members. The key idea for understanding the impacts of different design choices is that they affect the likelihood of those future states or the value that members will get from them. To present that idea in its simplest form, imagine that after an initial time period in its current state (the first stage), there are only two possible future states: one in which the community fails completely and one in which it succeeds completely. A potential member will have a belief about the *success_probability*, the likelihood that the community will achieve the success state.

We model the expected utility of a decision to join early and compare it to the expected utility of waiting and joining later.[4] Joining early, in the first stage, requires paying the *startup_cost*, as in the model from the previous section. It also yields an expected total net benefit from the first stage, prior to either achieving critical mass or failing, which we represent as *participation_benefit*$_{stage1}$. If the community goes to the failure state, assume that no one will continue to use it, so there are no additional costs or benefits for anyone. If the community succeeds, participation in the second stage will yield additional benefits, *participation_benefit*$_{stage2}$. In addition, as we shall describe, in the success state, there may be additional benefits for the early members, such as status in the community, which we model with the variable *early_adopter_benefit*.

In summary, we have expected utility of joining the community in the first stage:

util(join now) = *participation_benefit*$_{stage1}$ - *startup_cost* +

success_probability × (*participation_benefit*$_{stage2}$ + *early_adopter_benefit*)

Instead of joining in the first stage, a member has the option of waiting until stage 2. If the community succeeds, the new member can join then. The member gets no benefits in stage 1, but has the advantage of not paying the startup costs in those cases in which the community is not going to succeed. The expected utility of that option is:

util(wait) = *success_probability* × (*participation_benefit*$_{stage2}$ - *startup_cost*)

For someone to prefer joining now rather than waiting, the expected utility must be higher:

util(join now) - util(wait) > 0

Expanding the two quantities and simplifying, people prefer joining now only if:

participation_benefit$_{stage1}$ − *startup_cost*(1 − *success_probability*) + *early_adopter_benefit* × *success_probability* > 0

From this inequality, it is easy to list approaches that make it more attractive to join now rather than waiting. The following subsections examine the approaches in more detail.

1. *Increase stage 1 value of the community*   Ideally, the net benefits of early stage participation can be made positive, despite the lack of other members. We describe ways to provide nonsocial value that is independent of other members' participation, in the form of access to content or services that are exogenously generated rather than provided by community members.

2. *Reduce startup costs of joining the community*   Reducing startup costs makes early joining more attractive relative to waiting because these costs are paid by early joiners even when the community fails. The effects of design choices such as user interface compatibility that affect these joining costs were already explored in the previous section and are not repeated here.

3. *Early adopter benefits*   We present three approaches for creating early adopter benefits. One focuses on the benefits of having skills and familiarity when the community becomes popular. A second focuses on the benefits of establishing a reputation as a leader early in a community's life. A third, in communities expected to generate revenues, is to promise a share of future monetary revenues to early contributors, analogous to startup companies' offers of stock to early employees.

4. *Expectation setting*   Increasing expectations about the probability of the community's success reduces the chances that an early joiner's entry costs will be wasted. It also increases the probability of receiving any early adopter benefits that will be available if the community succeeds. Expectations can be shaped through signaling about commitments to future resource expenditure. Other expectation-setting approaches include conveying a trajectory of growth, conveying images of what the community

is expected to be like at some future time, drawing analogies to other successful communities, and communicating contingent participation commitments that other potential members have made.

All of these approaches can be targeted toward specific subpopulations. One possibility is to target the natural "lead adopters," those who need the least extra encouragement to join early. The lead adopters for many innovations are people with special needs for the good or service being offered. For example, men seeking sexually oriented entertainment were early adopters of the French Minitel system in 1982 and 1983, an early information service widely deployed in homes. Shortly after Minitel offered text-based communication, sexually oriented chats known as *messagerie rose* (*pink messaging*) became "one of the main forces behind Minitel's success, especially between about 1983 and 1987, by which year 'pink sites' were clocking up staggeringly high usage figures" (Jacobs 2003, 81). Doctors, factory managers, and isolated farm women—all social categories with strong needs for communication—became early adopters of the telephone system in the United States (Fischer 1992). Translated to the online community domain, early adopters would be the people who are most interested in the topic to be discussed or who most want to use the products (e.g., open source software) that the community will create. One study found that the people most likely to make use of the online community features of a pedometer-based walking program were those who had the least offline social support for their efforts to become more physically active (Richardson et al. 2010).

Those who need the community most may not always be the best targets for early adoption. Rogers (1995, chapter 7) notes other characteristics of early adopters of innovations, some of which are relatively easy to discern among potential members of a new community, and some of which are less so. In terms of their demographic characteristics, early adopters tend to be richer, of higher social status, and better educated than later adopters. In terms of personality and cognitive and attitudinal individual differences, early adopters tend to be more intelligent, rational, better able to deal with abstractions, and have more favorable attitudes toward change and toward science than later adopters. In addition, they are better able to cope with risk and uncertainty. Taken together, these characteristics fall along two dimensions: (1) the education, intelligence, rationality, and ability to deal with abstractions, which allows them to understand better the potential future benefits they may receive from adopting the innovation; and (2) the wealth, status, and ability to deal with uncertainty that allows them to cope with the risks associated with adopting an innovation. These characteristics can also partly explain what Rogers calls the "innovation-need paradox" (Rogers 1995, 275)—the observation that in many cases those who most need the benefits of a new idea (e.g., the poorer or less educated) are among the last to adopt it. In the United States, the poor, the less educated, and the elderly are among the last to use online resources, including health support groups, to deal with illness (Fox and Jones 2009). They may not have the financial resources to absorb the risks associated with innovations or the information or education to understand sufficiently the potential advantages. In starting an online health support group, then, it may be better to focus first on attracting younger, more connected people, even though they may have less need than people at a more advanced illness stage who are homebound and more socially isolated.

Another useful population to target is the people who provide the greatest leverage in attracting other members. We have already argued that content production is more valuable than metadata production for attracting additional members. In many communities, there are some people who are natural content producers and others who are more naturally content consumers or producers of metadata. For example, on a blogging site like LiveJournal, which has many groups, there are some people who primarily benefit from having an audience for what they write and others who primarily benefit from being the audience. In the early stages of starting a blogging community, it is more important to attract those who want to write than those who want to read.

More generally, economists describe two-sided networks (Armstrong 2006; Caillaud and Jullien 2003; Rochet and Tirole 2003; Parker and Van Alstyne 2005). These are situations in which there are complementary types of participants, each of which produces value for the other type. For example, in a LiveJournal group, the presence of a lot of readers makes the site more attractive for writers, and vice versa. The presence of other writers may not be so attractive for writers, as they create competition for reader attention, though their presence may be tolerated if it is the reason that there are many readers. Dating sites for heterosexuals are another type of online community with two-sided externalities. eHarmony (http://www.eharmony.com) is more attractive for women if there are more men participating, and vice versa. Thus, a useful strategy in the startup phase may be to provide incentives for one gender to participate in order to attract the other, much as bars and nightclubs sometimes offer free entry to women on "ladies night" in order to make the venue more attractive for men.

When there is a choice about which type to try to attract first, there are a couple of considerations to keep in mind. First, it may be that only a few of one type are needed to attract the other type, yet many of the other type are required to attract the first type. For example, attracting a few blog writers may be sufficient to subsequently attract many readers. By contrast, attracting a few readers is rarely sufficient to subsequently attract many writers. Second, one type or the other may be more patient about waiting for the second type to arrive or more willing to endure the first stage before the other arrives. If either type will attract the other, it may be useful to target the early recruitment to the more patient type.

Increase Stage 1 Value of the Community

Many online sites with successful social content started by providing services of value to their customers in the absence of critical mass for an online community. Delicious (http://www.delicious.com, formerly Del.icio.us) pioneered online bookmarking. It has offered the personal productivity tool of keeping and organizing one's personal tags for web content on a server on the Internet. That service allows people who use multiple computers to access their tags regardless of which computer they are using. This personal productivity aid provided sufficient value to some users that they would use the service even in the absence of any other users, and thus helped attract users even before the service reached a critical mass of social usage.

Instead of offering a service that is individually valuable to one person, it is sometimes possible to offer a group service that is valuable to a small enough group that the group can collectively decide to join. For example, to many of the users of Yahoo! Groups, the value lies entirely within the groups they (or their friends) create. Presumably, however, some people who were first invited by an acquaintance to join a particular group subsequently became involved in the larger constellation of Yahoo! Groups, helping to build the critical mass for the overall service.

Shopping opportunities may provide another nonsocial source of benefits. Shutterfly (http://www.shutterfly.com) is an online photo printing/storage/sharing site. Unlike some photo sharing sites (such as Flickr, http://www.flickr.com), Shutterfly started primarily as a site at which digital photos could be uploaded and printed, both as traditional prints and as enhanced products such as calendars, mugs, prints with fancy borders, and so forth. People uploaded their pictures to Shutterfly for the nonsocial purpose of ordering prints. Social interaction, however, was a natural side effect. From the start, Shutterfly allowed photographers to share their photos with friends and family (and to thereby allow those friends and family to order prints). Today, the site has grown to build its theme around the tag line "tell your story" and to have a gallery of community-created photo books, complete with personal profiles of the photographers and scrapbookers. What was initially single-user commerce activity of photo printing attracted users to what eventually became a social site for many.

Amazon (http://www.amazon.com) is another example of a site that attracted initial users for shopping. It has a large collection of successful social content options within its site. It uses collaborative recommender technologies (both contextual "customers who bought this item also bought" and overall recommendations for products of interest to an individual). It has an extensive set of product reviews. Many people have posted gift or wish lists that others can browse (and shop from). Each of these "social applications" would have had trouble launching without critical mass, however, and indeed most did not exist when Amazon was launched. Instead, Amazon amassed a critical mass of people and data by offering a distinctly nonsocial application—book buying.

Design Claim 25   Single-user and small-group productivity, entertainment, or commerce tools can attract people to an online space before the community features are successful.

The *New York Times* is a content site that hosts both the newspaper's print articles and a substantial number of online-only columns and blogs. Although it did not start out as a social site, it has clearly become one. A quick review of this morning's articles finds that many of them have reader discussion postings from ten or more different readers and that many of those discussions are truly interactive (with messages, responses, and responses to the responses). Launching a stand-alone news discussion site from scratch has a serious critical mass problem: many have tried, but only a few (notably Slashdot, Digg, and Reddit) have been successful. Instead, by using their content to attract people for nonsocial purposes—reading news articles and columns— the *New York Times* easily created a community of readers who then generated comments and discussion.

Design Claim 26   Providing access to professionally generated content can help attract people to an online space before the community features are successful.

Another way to compensate for an initially small community is to import user-generated content from elsewhere. In section 2, we pointed out that importing content can create some of the same positive externalities that other members would provide because some of the benefit their presence would provide is through the content they would provide. This may be especially useful in the startup stage, when there are few members generating content locally. Consider, for example, MovieLens. Users rate movies and the system uses the ratings of other people to predict how well individuals will like particular movies. When MovieLens started, it imported a database of ratings that had been gathered by another movie rating site, EachMovie, which was no longer operational. With the EachMovie data available, even the first MovieLens subscriber received useful predictions (after entering a few ratings so that the site could calibrate the user's tastes). Subsequent MovieLens subscribers benefited from both the preexisting EachMovie data and from the ratings that other MovieLens subscribers had entered. The imported data compensated for a small membership. Once MovieLens was well established, the marginal value of the imported data was reduced.

A number of product review sites appear to follow the syndicated data strategy. For example, Epinions generated a large number of product reviews as a stand-alone site. It then sold its content to other sites that wanted to include product reviews but did not have enough users to generate their own. There are a large number of travel review sites; on occasion they seem to share content. For example, we found the same review for a hotel in Florence on several different sites.[5]

As described in section 2, one danger with using syndicated data as a strategy for jump-starting an online community is that users may discover the original source and choose to join the already active community instead. Syndicated data provide value to individuals, but don't create the stickiness or competitive advantage that having a large community would create. In combination with other useful content or services, however, or with a novel presentation, syndicated data can increase the value of a community before it becomes self-sustaining.

Design Claim 27 Providing access to syndicated data can help attract people to an online space before the community features are successful, if the syndicated data is not otherwise easily accessible or if it is presented in a novel way that adds value.

Another way to compensate for an initially small community is for paid staff to participate and provide the benefits that will eventually be provided by members. For a community in which the externalities come from a large number of participants, such as a movie recommendation site, this approach would be prohibitively expensive. For smaller niches, however, such as technical support for products, this may be a viable option. For example, when launching discussion boards for a group of patients enrolled in a research study on how to motivate increased exercise, staff members pre-populated the forums with introductions and questions before inviting the study participants and made sure to respond to all the study participants' posts (Resnick et al. 2010). This approach made it more attractive to post and to check the boards for new messages and thus helped build participation by patients.

As another example, in January 2007, Microsoft embarked on an effort to grow the peer technical support that occurred in the online forums of MSDN, the Microsoft

Developer Network. Managers hypothesized that a low answer rate for posted questions (about 35 percent) was discouraging people from posting questions, so they hired staff to answer some of the questions. The answer rate went up to about 80 percent. Not surprisingly, the volume of posts tripled in a year.[6]

Design Claim 28 Participation by professional staff can help attract people to an online space before the community features are successful.

The need for staff involvement in the early stages suggests that it may be helpful to start a community with an original scope narrower than its eventual aspirations. For example, a book site that is hoping to eventually have reviews for all books might start with a subset (current bestsellers or book club selections) as a way of building more content in a narrower area (rather than fewer reviews per item across a broad area). In addition to the need for staff attention to seed the contents, staff attention may be needed for marketing.

Communities based on geographic locality, with little synergy between activity in different locations, offer the strongest case for starting with a small scope and expanding gradually. A wide range of sites from Angie's List to Citysearch (http://www.citysearch) to Craigslist launched over time in different cities. A smaller site—Localfiles (http://localfiles.com), a directory for the Indian expatriate community in the United States—followed the same approach, launching a site in Minneapolis before expanding to other cities.

Other communities may have more synergy between activities in different parts of the eventual community scope. A restricted scope in the startup stage involves a trade-off between the focusing of staff resources for marketing and content creation and the lost synergies. For example, in a community for baseball fans, many people might be interested in discussing a particular favorite team and also discussing the state of the sport as a whole. If the community starts with just a single team's fans, it may not have enough people to generate good discussion of baseball as a whole and may thus also lose some people who would have joined if there were lively discussion of baseball as a whole in addition to their favorite team. On the other hand, trying to simultaneously seed discussion spaces for all of the teams might overtax the available staff resources.

Design Claim 29 Starting with a limited scope and expanding later allows focusing of staff resources toward getting to critical mass in the limited scope.

One problem with paying staff to participate is that it may be difficult to get volunteers to assume the roles initially filled by staff. People are less motivated to contribute when they think that someone else will carry the load if they don't, as explored in detail in chapter 2. Worse yet, people may also be less motivated to contribute on a voluntary basis when they know that someone else is getting paid for similar work.[7] Perhaps most critically, staff may notice tasks and complete them even before volunteers notice them and volunteers may thus never develop the habit of taking on tasks that they could do. There is thus a real danger that the roles for professional staff will become permanent, with a need for continued payments.

One possible solution to a community becoming dependent on staff contributors is for them to wait for volunteers to perform tasks and take on only those tasks that volunteers do not. This method not only gives volunteers enough time to find tasks, but also degrades the quality of service provided by the professionals (because of the delay) and thus encourages members to take on the tasks so that they will be completed sooner. For example, when Microsoft hired staff to answer questions on MSDN forums, as a way to encourage more posting of questions, the staff answered only questions that had gone unanswered for twenty-four hours, which was the approximate time it took for items to scroll off the front page, at which point they were unlikely to be noticed by volunteer members. Over time, the percentage of questions answered by members increased and the need for staff went down.

Design Claim 30   If professionals act as contributors of last resort, they will be needed less as the community achieves critical mass.

In some cases, software bots can offer a partial substitute for the value that would be provided by other participants. For example, the now-defunct jsettlers.com was a website for playing an online version of the popular German board game Settlers of Catan. Three or four players are needed for a game session. Visitors to the site who tired of waiting for other opponents to join their games could invite software bots to play instead. The software bots may not be quite as fun to play against, but sometimes they're better than waiting for real opponents.

Similarly, the online ESP Game, mentioned earlier, pairs two people for a coordination game in which each tries to assign the same tag the partner does, without communicating with each other. Part of the fun is the sense of connection one experiences with an unknown partner, especially when a partnership selects matching tags that are unusual or quirky. The game has become popular; often, one can be matched with a partner with little waiting. When there are few participants, however, the game pairs a live player with a replay of a previously recorded game session (von Ahn and Dabbish 2004). Knowing that one can always find a partner makes it more attractive to visit the site, even if the partner is sometimes not live.

Design Claim 31 Bots that simulate other participants can help attract people to an online space before the community features are successful.

Early Adopter Benefits

We now turn to early adopter benefits as a way of convincing potential members to join early. Early adopter benefits are common outside of online communities. For example, early employees in a company receive larger numbers of stock shares than later employees receive. As another example, early employees in a presidential political campaign—even those with little prior experience—can expect White House jobs, should their candidate win. Joining the campaign after the Iowa caucuses, when it's easier to pick the winner and there are more people involved, leads to less personal benefit, should one's candidate win.

We describe three approaches to providing early adopter benefits in online communities. One focuses on continuing monetary advantages for the early adopters, in terms of either payments or discounts. The other two focus on benefits within the community, either the benefits of having skills before others do or the status and privileges that stick with early adopters even after the community becomes sustainable.

First, consider promises of future discounts. One example comes from the previously mentioned antispam service SpamNet by Cloudmark. An important ingredient in the service was reports, from customers, of particular emails that were spam. These reports enabled Cloudmark to flag and filter similar messages sent to other customers. Clearly, this service exhibits significant network externalities because it will be useful to join only if there are many other members reporting on spam. In its early stages, Cloudmark offered the service for free and—more important—promised a special lifetime subscription rate to its early users when it went commercial. Although intended primarily as a retention strategy, this type of offer can be an additional incentive for early users by increasing the expected future value of the service, should it achieve critical mass (i.e., many people will find it worth paying full price for, but I won't have to).

Design Claim 32 Promising permanent discounts to early adopters can attract early adopters to the community.

There are many less tangible benefits that early joiners of an online community can expect. For example, early members are likely to be better known and have higher status once the community gets large. This change may occur through informal processes of preferential attachment. For example, in a blogging network such as LiveJournal, new members will be more likely to link to blogs of people who are already prominent, thus making them even more prominent for people who come even later.

Joining early can lead to higher status or positions of leadership after a community succeeds. The reputation and status benefits of being an early adopter may emerge naturally in an online community, or they may be more explicit. A conversation-based community may need to do little more than make a poster's identity visible for such benefits to emerge because people will recognize the identifier and treat the long-time members with extra respect. When a group of old-timers reminisced about Usenet news, it occurred to us that we all remembered a large number of the early active Usenet posters, moderators, and administrators—even though nearly twenty-five years had passed since encountering them and many of them were no longer active. In communities with clear leadership roles having differential privileges, such as Wikipedia and open source projects, many people understand intuitively that there are more opportunities to assume the high status roles if one "gets in on the ground floor." For example, the process for gaining editor privileges at Wikipedia has becomes more codified and presumably more stringent over time (Burke and Kraut 2008). Empirically, longevity was found to matter in promotion decisions: each additional month as editor led to a 2.9 percent increase in the probability of approval for administrator status.

Early joining benefits may also occur through explicit status markers not tied to explicit leadership roles. For example, just as American Express prints "Member since" dates on credit cards (and advertises this fact), eBay shows a "Member since" date on its user feedback profiles. Many online forums display the date a user first entered the community alongside each post. Some communities, such as Slashdot, assign user IDs sequentially, and display these ids with posts; people with very low IDs have status in the community, much as people with low "badge numbers" have high status in large high-tech companies.

One of the challenges of participating in communities is the time and investment needed to "get up to speed" building skills and a social network. This challenge can be reframed as a benefit of early adoption. One of the benefits of early adoption germane to online communities is the ability to build skills ahead of other members. In online gaming communities such as World of Warcraft there is a tremendous surge of activity as new levels are introduced, in part so that those achieving them can do so before their friends. In a virtual world, an early adopter may show off his or her skills at moving around, knowledge of the world, and even the special features of his or her avatar that early adoption provided before his or her peers joined.

Turning these potential benefits of early adoption into early adoption decisions requires careful communication so that potential members are aware of the advantages of learning the ropes early. Potential members need to be informed about benefits available only to early adopters. One common technique is to fix either an expiration time ("this week only") or the number of people who can claim the benefit ("the first 100 members get . . .").

Design Claim 33   Promoting the status or readiness benefits of being early to an online community can attract early adopters to the community.

It may be possible to market an online community as "undiscovered" with the implication that those who adopt early will be recognized by their peers as trend-setters. In social networking communities, early adopters may see a benefit in being the one to invite all their friends (rather than being the last one to the party). Exclusivity, or the appearance thereof, is one way to promote a site as cool. Google did this particularly well with Gmail, which had a limited beta release in which you could only get an account by being invited by someone who already had one—this approach linked social word of mouth with scarcity. The goals are to reach potential early adopters and to reframe the message from one in which "new" might imply uncertain and risky to one in which "new" implies the chance to get in while it's still cool and undiscovered.

Design Claim 34   Promoting a site as cool but undiscovered can attract early adopters.

The default assumption in most online communities is that supply is infinite and that hence there is no chance of a resource running out. If the supply can be limited or differentiated in such a way so as to create a limited amount of "preferred" membership, then individuals can be enticed to join early. The namespace of usernames within a community is a naturally scarce resource. On eBay, memorable usernames like "coinguy" and "informationist" are available on a first-come, first-served basis. The hundredth member had more options than the millionth. Similarly, nearly all of the free email services and many virtual world communities allow you to select your name, as long as it is not already in use. Interestingly, many online community sites have specifically chosen different paths (e.g., many social networking sites use your email address, which is already unique, and Second Life limits character names to those chosen from a template, which are unlikely to be particularly meaningful in the real world). Nonetheless, we've observed a rush of users to new email sites when announced (to claim their names). Making this opportunity salient in marketing is a way to encourage earlier membership. Namespace isn't the only resource that can be made scarce. In online games, limited quantities of special objects may be made available to early users.

Design Claim 35 Creating scarce, claimable resources can induce prospective members to join earlier.

One challenge when creating scarcity is that members may "squat" on their names or other resources without contributing to the community. That is, they may join but not participate. A common technique for preventing squatting is to require a certain level of sustaining activity to maintain the claimed resource. In the early days of the Internet, people who claimed domain names understood that they had to pay a regular fee to keep them, but they were never required to use them. Many of today's email addresses and site addresses expire if they are not used at least every three to six months. Indeed, greater demands can likely be made; the endowment effect (Kahneman and Thaler 1990) suggests that people will do more to keep such "property" than they would have done to acquire it.

Design Claim 36 Contribution minima for maintaining scarce status can lead to greater contribution by status-holding members.

An extra beneficial side effect for the community designer is that members who join early in order to get in on the ground floor will be especially motivated to help make the community thrive. There is nothing valuable about knowing one's way around before others do if no one else joins. There is no value in a permanent discount if the community doesn't survive. There's nothing cool about being first to a community that failed. And it is meaningful to have high status only if there are other people who join the community who have lower status.

The investments that people make through early adoption are sunk costs that in principle should not affect a rational decision maker's future choices. People do, however, often take into account sunk costs, in part out of a desire to make the earlier decisions seem like good ones. Thus, people who join because of early adopter benefits will therefore be more likely to help the community succeed through recruitment, content creation, or other actions. The effects of sunk costs on commitment more generally is explored in chapter 3.

Setting Expectations for Success

Whether a community is likely to succeed is not always obvious to potential members. Expectations of success make it more attractive to join early, which in fact fuels success, so that the expectations become self-fulfilling. A number of design choices can affect expectations of success. Some convey signals of the community convener's skill and commitment. Some convey signals that potential members are reacting favorably or are committed. Some convey external expectations. We consider each in turn next.

Signals of Convener Quality and Commitment   In the early days of the Internet, users had low expectations for usability, design, and interaction. With few choices, even venues with poor appearances might hold promise as the source for valuable content. As professionalism increased, ordinary web users learned a set of heuristics to distinguish legitimate high-quality sites from low-quality or fraudulent ones. Fogg et al. (2003) studied how users determine the credibility of websites, finding that the two influences on credibility cited most often were the design look of the site (e.g., professional look, pleasing graphics) and the information design/structure of the site (e.g., organization). Other oft-cited influences include tone of the writing (e.g., slang, poor language), functionality of the site (e.g., error messages, poor search), clarity of information, and readability of text.

Today, the importance of credibility and professionalism is even greater. Internet users are regularly inundated with unprofessional-looking spam and phishing attacks (unwanted messages that attempt to elicit personal information). Indeed, the prevalence of poor writing, spelling, and layout in such scam attacks is one of the reasons people generally don't fall for them (a test of various phishing attacks found that ones without such errors caught a high percentage of even skilled users (Egelman, Cranor, and Hong 2008).

Design Claim 37   Professional site design increases expectations about the probability of success.

In addition signaling a convener's capabilities through professional site design, it may also be useful to demonstrate the convener's ongoing commitment. If potential members believe that the individuals or organization who started the community are committed to additional investment even if the community does not immediately take off, these expected future investments will factor into a judgment about whether the community will take off—there will be less risk that one's own early efforts will be stranded. It is not, however, simple for the conveners of a community to credibly convey such a commitment. After all, they might be expected to "cut their losses" if there is no immediate success.

The theory of credible signaling (Spence 1973), as discussed in the context of screening and self-selection mechanisms in chapter 5, begins with one key insight: in order to distinguish between high-quality and low-quality actors, it must be easier or less costly for the high-quality actors to provide the signal. In our situation, a "high-quality" actor is a community convener that is committed to future resource expenditures on a community, even if it does not immediately achieve critical mass. A "low-quality" actor is one that needs to see more immediate indicators of success in order for it to continue making investments. It is more costly for the low-quality community convener to make an immediate expenditure because it has a lower assessment about the probability of eventual success (in part because it knows about its own lack of future commitment). Thus, we should expect the high-quality community convener to be more willing to undertake early expenditures. And when we observe such resource expenditures, it is a credible signal of greater commitment to future expenditures.

Sermo started an online community for doctors. It is relatively easy to create such a community using generic technologies such as Yahoo! Groups or an email list or a forum site using phpBB. Indeed, there were existing competitors. One way in which Sermo signaled a commitment to continued investment in its community was through expenditure on a custom software platform that it developed. It also had paid staff whose presence was very visible in the community early on, and did one-on-one demos for physicians at medical conferences. In the early days of Sermo, when it did not have more members than some of its noncommercial competitors, the visible expenditures and claims of its venture capital backing contributed to a sense that Sermo would eventually be a bigger, better community than its competitors—even though that was not yet the case.

When a number of new features are available, we speculate that deliberately holding some new features back so that they can be released on a more even time interval might be a better strategy than releasing all of them at once. There are three reasons for this speculation. First, user utility for new features might exhibit decreasing returns; that is, their marginal utility for the first new feature of the day might be higher than subsequent new features. Therefore, sequential releases might increase overall user utility. Furthermore, from a usability perspective, the sequential release approach also helps the site isolate and evaluate the effects of the new feature. Finally, from a signaling perspective, frequent releases of new features convey a trajectory of growth and continued commitment. This approach is especially applicable to the initial public announcement of a new community. If some features that are implemented are deliberately held back, it may make it easier for people to get started. The held-back features can then be released a week or two later, conveying an image of continuing investment from the site's founders.

Design Claim 38   Visible expenditures can be a credible signal of commitment to future investment in a community and thus help to increase expectations about the probability that the community will eventually succeed.

Signals of Positive Member Response   When the quality of a public good is uncertain, announcing early contributions provides a credible signal that the public good is valuable and thus helps to attract later contributors (Vesterlund 2003), which is why major fundraising campaigns begin publicly only after "quiet periods" in which major donors make commitments. Similarly, indicators that other potential members are responding favorably to a new community are a form of social proof, enhancing expectations that the community will succeed. This impression can be accomplished by making membership and activity visible and by showing a trajectory of growth.

One way to convey membership is to prominently post photos of members. Simply adding photos of random people to a move ratings site did not have a noticeable effect on user behavior (experiment with MovieLens; Regina Tassone and Sara Kiesler, personal communication). We speculate, however, that posting photos of members alongside their user-contributed content, or posting photos of the most recent new members, may convey a signal that others like the community and are joining it.

Design Claim 39   Images of members convey the presence of other people and thus expectations of future success.

One way to convey activity in the community is through examples. Recent user contributed content can be made prominent—perhaps even on the front entry page. Of course, making user-contributed content visible on the entry page risks conveying an image of amateurism if that content is not good, which is a negative signal of quality. One solution is to include user-contributed content but to confine it to a small sidebar

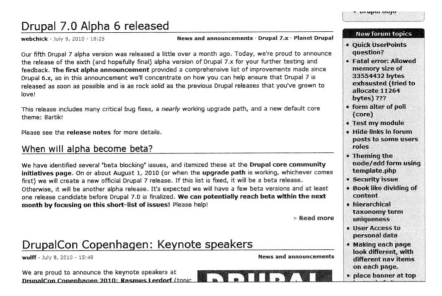

Figure 6.5
Making recent user contributions visible in a sidebar in Drupal (http://drupal.org).

so that new visitors will first notice the professional-looking presentation of the community. Another solution is to allow only a limited number of members—those who can be trusted to produce professional-looking content—to post messages that go on the front page. For example, the online community for developers and users of the Drupal content management system software includes a top area with static information, a wide blog-style left column with official announcements that are added by only certain people, and a narrow block on the right with the titles of the most recent forum topics, which can be added by anyone (see figure 6.5).

Design Claim 40   Prominent display of user-contributed content conveys activity, and thus expectations of future success, as long as there is new user-contributed content.

Another way to convey activity without actually showing the contents—which may be amateurish—is to show indicators. For example, rather than showing the actual comments on blog entries, the number of comments can be shown and users can click through to see the actual comments, or the number of new forum topics can be shown without showing the actual posts. As another example, many sites show an indicator of how many people are currently logged in to the site. Even if there is no synchronous interaction, many others currently using the community is an indicator that it is well

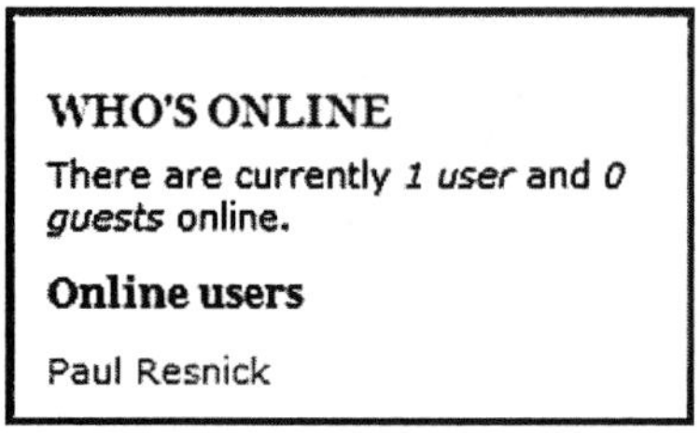

WHO'S ONLINE
There are currently *1 user* and *0 guests* online.

Online users

Paul Resnick

Figure 6.6
Activity indicators can highlight activity, or lack of it.

liked. Of course, such an indicator is more effective at showing activity if—at most times when visitors would arrive—many other people are actually logged in. The indicator in figure 6.6, conveying that there is only one current user of a site, would discourage rather than encourage visitors. In sites that are intermittently active, it may be helpful at inactive times to show indicators about times when a lot of people were active.

Design Claim 41   Indicators of participation levels convey activity, and thus expectations of future success, as long as there actually is activity.

Conveying a trajectory of growth in membership and activity is especially helpful in raising expectations. There are several ways to display indicators of growth. One possibility is to publicly acknowledge each new member or each new content entry. Another possibility is to show a running tally of the current membership size or amount of content. A third possibility is to show the percentage growth. Depending on the size and growth rate of the community, one or another of these options may paint a more favorable picture of the community's current quality and long-term prospects.

For example, in the earliest days of Wikipedia, the most effective signal of growth on the front page would probably have been a list of new pages that had reached an acceptable quality level and a list of new first-time contributors. When it started to take off, the most effective signal would have been to show the percentage change in content and contributors from month to month. Now that it is wildly successful, the site creates a signal that it has already succeeded by showing the absolute number of articles in each language (3.6 million in English as of April 6, 2011).

Design Claim 42   Indicators of membership and content growth signal a higher probability that the community will eventually reach critical mass, provided that there really is growth.

Design Claim 43   When a community is small and growing slowly, acknowledging each new member or contribution creates a more favorable signal of growth than showing total numbers or percentage change.

Design Claim 44   When a community is small and growing quickly, displaying percentage growth creates a more favorable signal of growth than displaying absolute numbers.

Design Claim 45   When a community has reached critical mass, displaying absolute numbers conveys a signal that the community is already successful.

Designers can also allow for conditional commitments of membership and activity, which allow the community to convey an expectation of success. Under this approach, potential members can commit to joining (or to taking certain actions), but only if enough other people also commit to membership or actions that will cause the community to succeed. Conditional commitments can reduce the risk of an early membership decision being a wasted cost when the community fails to catch on. RSVPs for meetings or parties are good examples of commitment mechanisms: if not enough people indicate a willingness to attend, an event can be canceled without anyone suffering the cost of attending an empty event.

Meetup makes extensive use of conditional commitments. In the first couple of years of Meetup's operation, there were no long-standing groups. Instead, each hobby or other interest group had a standard day of the month to meet at a local café, restaurant, or other venue. If you RSVP'd for the next meeting of a group, you were notified if not enough others had RSVP'd to hold the event. More recently, Meetup has also reified the notion of a group and provided a conditional quasicommitment mechanism for memberships. If you are interested in a topic, you can register that interest with the site. Meetup then notifies you when other people also register an interest in the topic. When enough people have indicated an interest, and someone has sufficient energy to lead the formation of a group, Meetup provides a mechanism to contact all the people who have registered an interest in the group. Because there is relatively little cost involved with signaling an interest in a topic, people are willing to signal interest in topics that do not yet have a critical mass of other interested participants.

Another example in a slightly different setting is Groupon (http://www.groupon .com). Each day there is an offer for one item, typically a gift certificate or coupon to a restaurant or entertainment venue (see figure 6.7). People commit to buy an offer, knowing that the offer is on only if enough people buy it to meet the maker's threshold

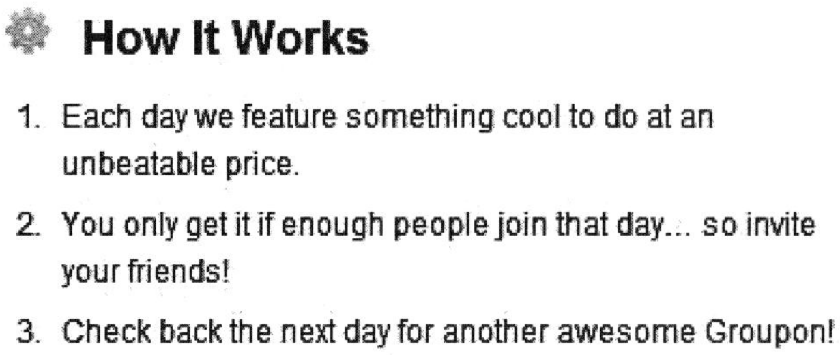

⚙ How It Works

1. Each day we feature something cool to do at an unbeatable price.

2. You only get it if enough people join that day... so invite your friends!

3. Check back the next day for another awesome Groupon!

Figure 6.7
Commitment contingent on others' participation at Groupon (http://www.groupon.com).

(e.g., we'll give out $40-off dinner coupons, but only if 250 people buy them for $20 each). In principle, the conditional commitment here has two sides. On the seller side, it ensures enough participants to make it worthwhile to produce the items. On the buyer side, it is a safety measure—a buyer may not want to commit to an unknown restaurant, even at a good price, unless hundreds of other people (who may know more about it) also do.[8]

The idea of conditional commitments can be applied to forming a new purely online community or to starting up a new forum within an existing online community. Rather than simply launching, which may lead to a problem of a sequence of visitors each seeing an empty forum and giving up, people can preregister an interest in a topic, or even tag their content as being applicable to the potential new forum. When enough people have registered an interest, or enough relevant content has been accumulated, the new forum can be launched and people who registered an interest can be notified.

Design Claim 46 Conditional participation commitments can draw people to join communities that they would not join if they had to do so without knowledge that others were also joining.

External Signals External signals can also fuel expectations of success. One way is to draw analogies to other communities that are successful. We previously described the value of analogies in conveying the intended scope of a community. But describing something as the "Wikipedia of Numbers" or the "Wikipedia of Music" not only conveys an intended scope but also subtly suggests that because Wikipedia was successful at attracting many editors and readers, so will these other sites. Mommasource. com, an online community for mothers, rebranded itself as mamapedia (http://www.mamapedia.com) with the tagline "The wisdom of moms."

Design Claim 47   Drawing analogies to successful communities can raise expectations that a new community will be similarly successful.

External publicity in mainstream media and the blogosphere can also fuel expectations of success. Online communities that are fortunate enough to get such external publicity can post links to it on their sites for members and potential members who might have missed it (see mamapedia's press page in figure 6.8).

Design Claim 48   Drawing attention to external publicity and endorsements can raise expectations about future success.

4   Summary of Design Alternatives

This chapter has explored two critical challenges for communities that are just getting started. The first is to carve out a useful and defendable niche in the ecology of competing communities. The second is to get to a self-sustaining critical mass of users. We

Figure 6.8
Highlighting external publicity in Mamapedia (http://www.mamapedia.com).

conclude with a summary of the design alternatives considered throughout the chapter.

The first category of design alternatives are ones that structure the set of interaction opportunities: selecting, sorting, and highlighting them; grouping them into interaction spaces; and notifying people about them. The various alternatives are most useful in carving out a useful niche where people will gain benefits from participating. Techniques such as subdividing spaces after they become active also help in conveying a sense of activity, which can affect expectations about the community's likely future success and thus help the community get through its initial stage prior to achieving critical mass.

A related category of design alternatives involve the structure of the community: its size and the breadth of topics covered. Larger communities have more activity, but that may not be so desirable in niches where the value of participating comes from interpersonal bonds with a few people. Starting with a limited scope and expanding later can also focus staff and marketing attention on getting to a critical mass of participation in a more limited scope.

A number of design alternatives involve the content, tasks, and activities in the community. Topics and activities that bridge separate interests can make mixed-topic spaces work well—and these spaces can be subdivided into single-topic spaces later. Offering valuable activities or content that is not generated by other members can make the community attractive in its early stages before it achieves critical mass.

Because new communities often share people and content with other communities, the chapter also analyzed several design alternatives that involve external communication and integration. Decisions about the sharing of user IDs and profiles and the import and export of content are critical elements of a competitive strategy. In addition, making people's membership and participation in a community visible to their friends outside the community and enabling members to invite friends are valuable ways to leverage a community's early adopters and get to critical mass.

There are several ways to create rewards that help a community reach critical mass. Promises of future discounts or status for joining early or the presence of scarce, claimable resources can make it more attractive for people to join early. And those early members can be given incentives for creating content that will attract other members or for directly recruiting other members.

Finally, we find that there is remarkable power in framing things in the right way. Articulating a clear rather than an ambiguous topical scope for interaction spaces makes them more useful for most participants. Conveying a unique selling proposition makes it easy for people to see why they should join. Advertising and celebrity endorsements can make one community a focal point when there is fierce competition among communities. Presenting the community as cool but not yet discovered can make early joining attractive. Drawing analogies to successful communities, highlighting external publicity, and a variety of ways of highlighting good things happening in the community can all convey an expectation that the community is well on its way to success, even if it has not yet achieved critical mass.

There is a lot to think about, and dream about, in the startup stage of an online community. Don't just build it and hope for the best. Build it, provide content and activities that people want, structure them in a way that provides maximal benefit, give people some reason to be early members, leverage their early participation to recruit others, and frame things in a way that conveys expectations of success. Then they'll come.

Table 6.1

Summary of design alternatives relevant to community startup, ordered by type

Type	Design alternative	Design claim
Selection, sorting, highlighting	Push notification	1
	Mixed-topic scope for an interaction space	2
	Personalized collections of "most related content"	6
	Subdividing spaces after they become active	7
	Navigation aids that highlight more active spaces	8
	A schedule of "expected active times"	9
	Recommender systems that help people navigate to spaces that best suit them	10
Community structure	Larger community	12
	Starting with a limited scope and expanding later	29
Content, tasks, and activities	Activities that bridge interests in different topics	4
	Differentiated user interface elements	13
	User-generated primary content versus user-generated metadata	19
	Productivity, entertainment, or commerce tools	25
	Access to professionally generated content	26
	Access to syndicated data	27
	Participation by professional staff	28, 30
	Bots that simulate other participants	31

Table 6.1
(continued)

Type	Design alternative	Design claim
External communication	Nonshared user IDs and profiles between competing communities	14
	Content sharing between competing communities	15
	Displays of membership that are visible to nonmembers	20
	Members' actions in the community visible to their acquaintances outside the community	21
	Allow members to forward content from the community to their acquaintances outside the community	22
	Allow members to invite acquaintances outside the community to join	23
Feedback and rewards	Incentives for early members to generate content	18
	Pay-for-referral and revenue sharing from referrals	24
	Promising permanent discounts to early adopters	32
	Promoting the status or readiness benefits of being early	33
	Creating scarce, claimable resources	35, 36
Presentation and framing	Ambiguous scope for an interaction space	3
	Transcendent or bridging topical identity	5
	Ambiguity of scope for the community	11
	Conveying a succinct unique selling proposition	16
	Advertising and celebrity endorsements	17
	Promoting a site as cool but undiscovered	34
	Professional site design	37
	Visible expenditures	38
	Images of members	39
	Prominent display of user-contributed content	40
	Indicators of participation levels	41
	Indicators of membership and content growth	42, 43, 44, 45
	Conditional participation commitments	46
	Drawing analogies to successful communities	47
	Drawing attention to external publicity and endorsements	48

Notes

1. January 2008 data pulled by Nate Oostendorp.

2. Of course, interaction design options can have a big impact on the expected value of each opportunity, even for identical content. For example, consider a dating site. If the potential matches are presented as a list of names, each one has to be clicked on, and there is a ten-second delay before the page for a person loads, then the average match value may be low. By contrast, the same set of potential dates may have higher average value if there is a page that shows photos and a few key attributes and it thus takes very little time to weed out those who are incompatible. Interaction design alternatives are largely beyond the scope of this book. For the purposes of the model, assume that the interaction design has been optimized to yield the best possible match value and navigation cost.

3. Readers familiar with economic models may think of a discount-rate delta for benefits or a per-period probability of exit delta. The participation_benefits quantity would then be the expected discounted net benefits, integrated over all time periods.

4. The decision is taken against a backdrop of some other ways in which the person could spend their time. All utilities in the model should be thought of as net utilities relative to the outside option—the best other way the user could spend their time. That is, we have normalized the value of the outside option to 0, allowing us to omit it from the models for simplicity.

5. For example, the comment, "Was disappointed in Villa de Vedetta . . . thought was quite stuffy" was found at one point on http://en.venere.com, http://bookingclick.com, http://www.alibabuy.com, and http://www.tvtrip.es.

6. Sean O'Driscoll, personal communication, April 2008.

7. This is not always a showstopper, as there is a countervailing effect in which people are more likely to participate in more successful communities. Wagstrom, Herbsleb, Kraut, and Mockus (2010) found that getting more "community-focused" professional developers involved in open source projects within the GNOME community actually drew in more unpaid labor, rather than alienating the volunteer participants. More "product-focused" professional developers had no net impact on volunteer participation in a project.

8. In practice, the items tend to be services in which there is no minimum production level required to keep costs down, and the threshold always seems to be met early in the morning, so the signaling value of others buying may be limited.

References

Anderson, Lessley. 2003. Attack of the Smartasses. *SF Weekly News*, August 13. http://www.sfweekly.com/2003-08-13/news/attack-of-the-smartasses.

Armstrong, Mark. 2006. Competition in Two-Sided Markets. *Rand Journal of Economics* 37 (3): 668–691.

Backstrom, L., D. Huttenlocher, J. Kleinberg, and X. Lan. 2006. Group Formation in Large Social Networks: Membership, Growth, and Evolution. *Proceedings of the 12th ACM SIGKDD International Conference on Knowledge Discovery and Data Mining*, 44–54. Philadelphia, PA: ACM.

boyd, dana. 2006. Friendster Lost Steam. Is Myspace Just a Fad? *Apophenia Blog.* http://www.danah.org/papers/FriendsterMySpaceEssay.html.

boyd, dana. 2008. *Taken Out of Context: American Teen Sociality in Networked Publics.* PhD diss., Berkeley: University of California.

Burke, Moira, and Robert E. Kraut. 2008. Mopping Up: Modeling Wikipedia Promotion Processes. In *CSCW 2008: Proceedings of the ACM Conference on Computer-Supported Cooperative Work.* New York: ACM Press.

Caillaud, Bernard, and Bruno Jullien. 2003. Chicken & Egg: Competition among Intermediation Service Providers. *Rand Journal of Economics* 34 (2): 309–328.

Egelman, S., L. F. Cranor, and J. Hong. 2008. You've Been Warned: An Empirical Study of the Effectiveness of Web Browser Phishing Warnings. In *CHI 2008: Proceeding of the ACM SIGCHI Conference on Human Factors in Computing Systems*, 1065–1074. New York: ACM Press.

Ellison, N. B. 2007. Social Network Sites: Definition, History, and Scholarship. *Journal of Computer-Mediated Communication* 13:210–230.

Farrell, Joseph, and Garth Saloner. 1985. Standardization, Compatibility, and Innovation. *Rand Journal of Economics* 16 (1): 70–83.

Fischer, C. S. 1992. *America Calling: A Social History of the Telephone to 1940.* Berkeley: University of California Press.

Fogg, B. J. Cathy Soohoo, David R. Danielson, Leslie Marable, Julianne Stanford, and Ellen R. Tauber. 2003. How Do Users Evaluate the Credibility of Web Sites?: A Study with over 2,500 Participants. In *Proceedings of the 2003 Conference on Designing for User Experiences*, 1–15. San Francisco, CA: ACM.

Fox, Susannah, and Sydney Jones. 2009. *The Social Life of Health Information.* Washington, DC: Pew Internet & American Life Project.

Gilder, George. 1993. Metcalfe's Law and Legacy. *Forbes ASAP*, Sept. 13, 1993.

Horvitz, Eric, and Johnson Apacible. 2003. Learning and Reasoning About Interruption. In *Proceedings of the 5th International Conference on Multimodal Interface*, 20–27. New York: ACM Press.

Jacobs, Gabriel. 2003. Cyberculture. In *French Popular Culture: An Introduction*, ed. Hugh Dauncey, 77–87. London: Hodder Headline Group.

Kahneman, Daniel, Jack L. Knetsch, and Richard H. Thaler. 1990. Experimental Tests of the Endowment Effect and the Coase Theorem. *Journal of Political Economy* 98 (6): 1325–1348.

Katz, Michael L., and Carl Shapiro. 1985. Network Externalities, Competition, and Compatibilty. *American Economic Review* 75 (3): 424–440.

Kim, Amy Jo. 2000. *Community Building on the Web: Secret Strategies for Successful Online Communities*. Berkeley, CA: Peachpit Press.

Newman, Mark, Debra Lauterbach, Sean Munson, Paul Resnick, and Margaret Morris. 2011. "It's not that I don't have problems, I'm just not putting them on Facebook": Challenges and Opportunities in Using Online Social Networks for Health. In *Proceedings of CSCW 2011*. Hangzhou: ACM Press.

Parker, Geoffrey G., and Marshall W. Van Alstyne. 2005. Two-Sided Network Effects: A Theory of Information Product Design. *Management Science* 51 (10): 1494–1504.

Reeves, R. 1961. *Reality in Advertising*. New York: Alfred A. Knopf,

Ren, Yuqing, and Robert E. Kraut. Under review. A Simulation for Designing Online Community: Member Motivation, Contribution, and Discussion Moderation. *Information Systems Research*.

Resnick, Paul J., Adrienne W. Janney, Lorraine R. Buis, and Caroline R. Richardson. 2010. Adding an Online Community to an Internet-Mediated Walking Program. Part 2: Strategies for Encouraging Community Participation. *Journal of Medical Internet Research* 12 (4): e72.

Richardson, Caroline R., Lorraine R. Buis, Adrienne W. Janney, David E. Goodrich, Ananda Sen, Michael L. Hess, Laurie A. Fortlage, et al. 2010. An Online Community Improves Adherence in an Internet-Mediated Walking Program. Part 1: Results of a Randomized Controlled Trial. *Journal of Medical Internet Research* 12 (4): e71.

Rochet, Jean-Charles, and Jean Tirole. 2003. Platform Competition in Two-Sided Markets. *Journal of the European Economic Association* 1 (4): 990–1029.

Rogers, E. 1995. *The Diffusion of Innovations*. 4th ed. New York: Free Press.

Schelling, T. C. 1958. The Strategy of Conflict. Prospectus for a Reorientation of Game Theory. *Journal of Conflict Resolution* 2 (3): 203.

Shapiro, Carl, and Hal Varian. 1999. *Information Rules: A Strategic Guide to the Network Economy*. Boston: Harvard Business School Press.

Spence, Michael. 1973. Job Market Signaling. *Quarterly Journal of Economics* 87 (3):355–374.

Stoddard, J. L., E. M. Augustson, and R. P. Moser. 2008. Effect of Adding a Virtual Community (Bulletin Board) to Smokefree.gov: Randomized Controlled Trial. *Journal of Medical Internet Research* 10 (5): e53.

von Ahn, Luis, and Laura Dabbish. 2004. Labeling Images with a Computer Game. In *Proceedings of the SIGCHI conference on Human factors in computing systems*, 319–326. Vienna, Austria: ACM.

Vesterlund, Lise. 2003. The Informational Value of Sequential Fundraising. *Journal of Public Economics* 87 (3–4): 627–657.

Wagstrom, Patrick, James Herbsleb, Robert Kraut, and Audris Mockus. 2010. The Impact of Commercial Organization on Volunteer Participation in an Online Community. Academy of Management Annual Meeting, Montreal, Canada, August 2010.

Wenger, Etienne. 1999. *Communities of Practice: Learning, Meaning, and Identity*. New York: Cambridge University Press.

Wenger, Etienne, Richard McDermott, and William Snyder. 2002. *Cultivating Communities of Practice*. Boston: Harvard Business School Publishing.

Wenger, Etienne, Nancy White, and John D. Smith. 2009. *Digital Habitats: Stewarding Technology for Communities*. Portland, OR: CPSquare.

Y&L Brings Angie's List to Life. *Adweek*. March 22, 2006. http://www.allbusiness.com/marketing -advertising/4163708-1.html.

Contributors

Moira Burke   HCI Institute, Carnegie Mellon University, moira@cmu.edu

Yan Chen   School of Information, University of Michigan, yanchen@umich.edu

Sara Kiesler   HCI Institute, Carnegie Mellon University, kiesler@cs.cmu.edu

Aniket Kittur   HCI Institute, Carnegie Mellon University, nkittur@cs.cmu.edu

Joseph Konstan   Department of Computer Science and Engineering, University of Minnesota, konstan@cs.umn.edu

Robert E. Kraut   HCI Institute, Carnegie Mellon University, robert.kraut@cmu.edu

Yuqing Ren   Carlson School of Management, University of Minnesota, chingren@umn.edu

Paul Resnick   School of Information, University of Michigan, presnick@umich.edu

John Riedl, University of Minnesota   Department of Computer Science and Engineering, University of Minnesota, riedl@cs.umn.edu

Index

Page numbers with a *t* indicate a table and with an *n* a note.

Access controls, 6–8, 168t, 218–222, 223t

ACOR, 181, 199

Administrators, 6
 authority figures and, 32
 commitment and, 102, 125, 134, 138, 145, 151, 164–165
 contribution and, 25–27, 32, 57, 61
 newcomers and, 195
 new online communities and, 263

Adoption
 behavior regulation and, 141, 148, 152, 160
 early adopter benefits and, 250, 253–256, 262–266, 274, 276t
 goals and, 36
 neutrality and, 125–126, 211
 nontransparency and, 57–58
 norms and, 141
 open reputation systems and, 160
 participation benefits and, 244–246, 253–254, 277n3
 pattern language approach and, 14
 permanent discounts and, 262–265, 276t
 product diffusion and, 184
 recruitment and, 183–184
 reward systems and, 57
 socialization and, 213–214

Advanced Breast Cancer Community, 108

Advertising
 behavior and, 142, 145
 celebrity endorsements and, 190–192, 222, 247–248, 274–275, 276t
 contribution and, 30, 33, 38
 conveying deep information and, 191
 effectiveness of, 188–189
 familiarity principle and, 192–194
 halo effect and, 189
 heuristic processing and, 189–194
 interpersonal, 188–194
 prior beliefs and, 188–189
 recruiting newcomers and, 180, 182–184, 188–195
 starting new online communities and, 245–248, 263, 274–275, 276t
 systematic processing and, 189–190

Advocacy, 85, 102, 149

Affective commitment
 anonymity and, 87
 balance theory and, 88
 bond-based, 79–81, 87–102
 common fate and, 84–85
 content feeds and, 93
 diversity of members' interest and, 99–100
 external threats and, 87
 familiarity principle and, 90–91, 99
 frequency of interaction and, 91–92
 friends of friends and, 89–91

Affective commitment (cont.)
  going off-topic together and, 101–102
  group cohesiveness theory and, 79, 85, 88
  group size and, 97–102
  identity-based, 79–87, 90, 95, 99–102
  ingroups and, 86, 97
  interchangeable members and, 81
  interdependent tasks and, 85–86
  interpersonal similarity and, 97
  joint tasks and, 85
  labels and, 82
  names and, 82–85
  off-topic conversations and, 99–102
  online neighborhoods and, 92–93
  outgroups and, 86–87
  personal conversation and, 92–94
  personal information and, 94–95, 100
  photos and, 91–92
  psychology and, 79, 89–90, 95, 99
  recruitment and, 81, 88–89, 99
  repelling forces that undercut, 97–102
  resistance to disruptive forces and, 88
  self-disclosure and, 90, 94–97, 100
  social identity theory and, 79–82, 99
  software monitoring and, 93–94
  subgroups and, 81–85
Alexander, C., 14
Alliance, 86
Altruism, 106, 195
Amazon, 52–54, 109–110, 257–258
American Cancer Society, 190
American Express, 263
American Red Cross, 194
Angie's List, 247, 260
Anonymity
  accountability and, 5
  commitment and, 87, 114–115
  newcomers and, 195
  pseudonyms and, 95, 112t, 158–161, 168t
  regulation and, 155, 161
AOL, 100
Apache, 21, 26, 86, 126, 217
Archives, 5, 80, 181, 199, 222
Aristotle, 24

Arkes, H. R., 110–111
Aronson, E., 111
Asperger's syndrome, 128
Association of Cancer Online Resources
  (ACOR), 81–82
Authority figures, 31–32
Autokinetic effect, 141
Axelrod, R., 156

Back, M. D., 79
Backstrom, L., 88, 250
Balance theory, 88
Bandura, A., 36
Bans
  commercial posts and, 198
  newcomers and, 198
  regulation and, 137–139, 158, 162–163, 166,
    168t–169t
Barker, Roger, 78
Bass model, 184
Bauer, Talya N., 213
Beenen, Gerard, 36, 82–83
Behavior, 16
  acceptable, 125–126, 135, 141–142, 148, 153
  advertising and, 142, 145
  altruistic, 106, 195
  anonymity and, 5, 87, 114–115, 155,
    161, 195
  authority figures and, 31–32
  coerced compliance and, 136–140
  commitment and, 77
  common pool resource and, 129–130,
    151, 161
  competition and, 5, 231, 236, 243–248, 256,
    259, 267, 274–275
  contact scraping and, 185–186
  contrast and, 144–145
  cost of undesirable, 158–160
  cyberrape and, 125, 147
  decision frame and, 17n1
  deindividuation and, 155
  design claims for, 132–165, 168t–169t
  displayed statistics and, 146–148
  displaying examples of preferred, 143–144

Don't Bite the Newcomer policy and,
  206–208, 210
door-to-door canvassing and, 29
email and, 126, 131–132, 139, 150, 154,
  156–157
examples and, 145–146
expectancies and, 23–25, 55–56, 62–66
explicit rules and, 146–149
fairness and, 133
fake profiles and, 242–243
fear campaigns and, 31–32
filters and, 131, 135, 167, 168t
flame wars and, 126–127, 132, 150–151
framing and, 167, 169t
free riders and, 164
friendship and, 5, 129, 137, 159
games and, 127–130, 151, 159–160, 164
gaming the system and, 13, 53–58
hackers and, 103, 127–128, 151
high-status people and, 31–33, 35
identifiability and, 155–157
inappropriate, 5, 144–145, 163, 217–218
influence limiters and, 135, 138–139, 157
initiation rituals and, 205–210
interpersonal relationships and, 151, 164
laws and, 130–131, 150
limiting effects of bad, 131–140
lurking, 181, 199, 201, 208, 214
manipulators and, 128, 135, 139, 154,
  166–167
moderation systems and, 131–134, 168t
MoodWatch and, 150
morality of design and, 9–10
motivation and, 23–24 (*see also* Motivation)
music download experiment and, 35
newcomers and, 127–128, 134, 136–139,
  148–149, 154, 158–161, 168t, 179–182,
  188, 199, 203, 211–218
non-normative, 128, 130, 140, 143–146,
  166
normative, 125–127, 142–143, 146, 155,
  169t (*see also* Norms)
off-topic conversations and, 5, 132, 167
organizational, 23

peer pressure and, 35–37, 146–148
peer reporting and, 164–165, 169t
persuasion and, 12, 24, 27–33, 68, 70, 162
power of liking and, 32–33
preferential attachment and, 35, 263
protection from newcomers and, 217–221
pseudonyms and, 158–161, 168t
psychology and, 129, 131, 141, 155, 157
  (*see also* Psychology)
public bad problem and, 129
reciprocity and, 8, 31, 102–104, 113t, 115
recruitment and, 161
regulation of, 125–170 (*see also* Regulation)
reputation systems and, 131, 156–158, 160,
  168t, 170n3
rewards and, 153–166
sanctions and, 153–166
shills and, 68, 128, 135
Slashdot and, 131, 133–134, 154, 159
social contact and, 43–47, 106
social dilemma and, 129–130, 164
socially desirable characteristics and,
  33, 35
social proof and, 35
social science and, 1, 10–13, 248
spammers and, 5, 84, 136–137, 139,
  154–155, 157, 167, 180, 200, 234,
  252, 262, 266
status and, 7, 24, 41, 52–58, 60, 68, 109,
  138, 157, 202, 214, 244, 253, 255, 262–265,
  274, 276t
summary of design alternatives for, 166–167,
  168t–169t
trolls and, 5, 9, 127–128, 135–136, 139, 154,
  166–167
utility and, 128–129, 159
value and, 129, 145, 150, 157, 160, 162,
  166, 170n4
voluntary compliance and, 140–166
Bejeweled, 90
Big Brothers Big Sisters, 194
BitTorrent, 203
Blizzard, 86, 110, 183, 190
Blogger, 58, 154

Blogs
  commitment and, 81, 88, 93, 95
  new online communities and, 250–251, 256,
    258, 263, 269, 273
  promise of, 1
  regulation and, 125, 154, 165
Bond-based communities, 243
Bonds-based commitment, 79–81, 87
  balance theory and, 88
  building, 88–89
  content feeds and, 93
  familiarity principle and, 90–91, 99
  frequency of interaction and, 91–92
  friends of friends and, 89–91
  going off-topic together and, 101–102
  group size and, 97–102
  interpersonal similarity and, 97
  off-topic conversations and, 99–102
  online neighborhoods and, 92–93
  personal conversation and, 92–94
  personal information and, 94–95, 100
  photos and, 91–92
  recruitment and, 88–89, 99
  repelling forces that undercut, 97–102
  resistance to disruptive forces and, 88
  self-disclosure and, 90, 94–97, 100
  software monitoring and, 93–94
Bookmarking, 257
Boot, Das (film), 64
Bootstrapping, 249–253
boyd, danah, 242
Breastcancer.org, 95
Bridging activities, 236
Bruckman, Amy, 85
Bryant, Susan L., 85
Bugs
  GNOME and, 22t, 25–26
  goals and, 36
  open source software (OSS) and, 15, 22t, 23,
    25–26, 126, 179, 197
Bugzilla, 26
Bulletin boards, 126–127
Burke, Moira, 128

Cameron, J., 59
CancerCare, 108
Cancer Support Community, 82
Cancer Support Group, 108
CAPTCHA (Completely Automated Public
  Turing Test to tell Computers and Humans
  Apart), 8, 139–140, 160, 167n1, 168t,
  201–202, 204
Carnegie, Dale, 32
Catholicism for Dummies, 195
Celebrity endorsements
  recruiting newcomers and, 190–192, 222
  starting new online communities and,
    247–248, 274–275, 276t
CET theory, 59
Chat rooms, 28, 136–137, 233–234, 239–241
Chen, P. Y., 109–110
Cialdini, R. B., 31, 141, 143
Cisco, 2, 52
Citysearch, 260
Clark, Caleb, 132
Clickworker, 21
Cloudmark, 252–253, 262
Clustering, 81–82, 92, 99
CNET, 101
Code base, 15, 202, 220
Coleman, James, 183
Collection size, 234–235
Collective effort model
  commitment and, 87
  contribution and, 11, 25, 62–64
  motivation and, 62–64
Colquitt, J. A., 133
Commitment, 16
  administrators and, 102, 125, 134, 138, 145,
    151, 164–165
  advocacy and, 85, 102, 149
  affective, 78–102
  alternative groups and, 4
  anonymity and, 87, 114–115
  behavior and, 77
  blogs and, 81, 88, 93, 95
  bonds-based, 79–81, 87–102

as building block, 77
clustering and, 81–82, 92, 99
collective effort model and, 87
common fate and, 84–85
competition and, 83, 86, 107–108, 115
compliance and, 150–151
content feeds and, 93
contribution and, 77
convener quality and, 266–268
design claims for, 81–112, 113t, 115
difficulty of achieving, 77
discussion groups and, 81, 100, 105–106
diversity of members' interest and, 99–100
effortful barriers and, 110–112
email and, 26, 29–30, 32, 36, 80, 89, 94, 98
entry barriers and, 206–208
external threats and, 87
Facebook and, 79, 84–85, 89–97, 109
familiarity principle and, 90–91, 99
feedback and, 104
field theory and, 78
filters and, 101–102, 113t, 114
flight and, 77–78
formation of, 79
framing and, 113t
friendship and, 79–80, 88–97, 100, 105–106, 109, 113t, 114–115
friends of friends and, 89–91, 113t, 114
games and, 84–86, 90–92, 96, 105, 109–110
GNOME and, 106–107
goals and, 83–85, 97, 105, 114
going off-topic together and, 101–102
group cohesiveness theory and, 79, 85, 88
group dynamics and, 78
group norms and, 77, 81–82, 87, 103–104, 113t
group size and, 97–102
guilds and, 84–86, 93
identity-based, 79–87, 90, 95, 99–102
ingroups and, 86, 97
initiation and, 78–79, 111–112
interdependent tasks and, 85–86, 113t, 114

interpersonal-based, 79–80, 90, 92–97, 100, 107, 113t, 114
joint tasks and, 85
lock-in and, 109–110
loyalty and, 78–79, 102
moderators and, 96, 105
names and, 82–85
needs-based, 78, 105–112
newcomers and, 89, 99–100, 102, 112, 179, 182, 199, 201–202, 205–206, 208–209, 213–214, 217, 222
new online communities and, 77
normative, 78, 102–105
obligation and, 102–105
off-topic conversations and, 99–102, 113t, 114–115
online neighborhoods and, 92–93
outgroups and, 86–87, 113t, 114–115, 151
performance and, 86
personal information and, 94–95, 100, 109, 114
posters and, 86, 98
presentation and, 95, 113t, 155–156, 169t
principle of proximity and, 4, 78, 92
pseudonyms and, 95, 112t
psychology and, 78–79, 89–90, 95, 99, 104, 108–109
reciprocity and, 102–104, 113t, 115
recruiting and, 81, 88–89, 99, 106, 114–115
regulation and, 77
repelling forces that undercut, 97–102
rewards and, 84, 105, 109
sanctions and, 5
screening and, 112
self-disclosure and, 90, 94–97, 100, 113t
skills and, 110
Slashdot and, 108, 110
social contact and, 106
social identity theory and, 79–82, 99
social networks and, 88–90, 94, 97
social science and, 11–12
software monitoring and, 93–94
spam and, 84

Commitment (cont.)
  starting new online communities and, 243,
    254–255, 266–268, 271–272
  subgroups and, 81–85, 114
  summary of design alternatives for, 112–115
  support groups and, 77, 80, 82, 95, 103, 108
  taglines and, 83, 113t, 114
  testimonials and, 103–104
  turnover and, 80–81, 99, 109–110
  value and, 77, 82–83, 97, 102–105, 109–110
  volunteers and, 106
  Wikipedia and, 77, 83, 85–86, 88, 104, 107
Common fate, 84
Common pool resource, 129–130, 151, 161
Community structure, 6, 7t, 79t, 112t, 168t,
  275t
Competition, 2, 5, 15, 151
  commitment and, 83, 86, 107–108, 115
  content sharing and, 245–247
  contribution and, 41–42, 46t, 49–50, 67–68
  newcomers and, 184
  for a niche, 243–248
  starting new online communities and, 231,
    236, 243–248, 256, 259, 267, 274–275
  unique selling proposition and, 247–248
Compliance
  access ladders and, 138
  anonymity and, 155, 161
  clear/salient norms and, 141–150
  coerced, 136–140
  cohesion and, 150–152, 165–166
  commitment and, 150–151
  community influence on rulemaking and,
    152–153
  compromising displays and, 149–150
  consistent criteria and, 138–139
  contrast and, 144–145
  currency and, 138–139, 157–158, 166, 168t,
    170n4
  deindividuation and, 155
  displayed statistics and, 146–148
  enhancing, 150–153
  examples and, 143–146

explicit rules and, 146–149, 165–166
feedback and, 138, 141–146, 150, 156–159,
  164–166
gags and, 137–138, 162, 166, 168t–169t
identifiability and, 155–157
influence limiters and, 135, 138–139,
  157–158
long-term identities and, 160–161
newcomer bonds and, 161–162
peer pressure and, 146–148
peer reporting and, 164–165, 169t
pseudonyms and, 158–161, 168t
quota mechanisms and, 136–137
reputation systems and, 156–158, 160
rewards and, 153–166
sanctions and, 153–166
saving face and, 153
search engine algorithms and, 155–156
stopit procedures and, 152–153
throttles and, 136–137, 166
voluntary, 140–166
Contact scraping, 185–186
Content feeds, 93
Contest design, 66–68
Continuance commitment. *See* Needs-based
  commitment
Contribution, 16, 130
  administrators and, 25–27, 32, 57, 61
  advertising and, 30, 33, 38
  authority figures and, 31–32
  basic drives and, 41
  CET theory and, 59
  collective effort model and, 11, 25, 62–64
  commitment and, 77
  competition and, 41–42, 46t, 49–50, 67–68
  contests and, 66–68
  deadlines and, 40
  design alternatives and, 63, 68–70
  design claims for, 26–66, 69t
  discussion groups and, 64
  door-to-door canvassing, 29
  do your best (DYB) and, 36–37
  early adopter motivations and, 265–266

economics and, 23, 30, 66
enthusiasm for, 22–23
expectancy and, 23–25, 55–56, 62–66
extrinsic motivation and, 24, 51–62
Facebook and, 26–27, 63
fairness and, 65
false praise and, 48–49
familiarity principle and, 33, 69t
fear campaigns and, 31–32
feedback and, 24, 26, 40, 44, 46t, 47–50,
   56–57, 59, 67–68, 69t
formatting improvement and, 26
framing and, 60t
friendship and, 24, 27, 32, 42
games and, 24, 35, 39–47, 50–54, 57–58, 67
gaming the system and, 13, 53–58
GNOME and, 22, 25, 39, 42–43
goals and, 24–25, 35–40, 44, 46t, 47, 61, 65,
   67–68
group context and, 35
group size and, 62–64
high-challenge goals and, 35–40
high-status people and, 31–33, 35
initiation and, 23
intrinsic motivation and, 24, 41–50, 58–62
lists of needed, 25–27
lost causes and, 65
motivation and, 28–70 (see also Motivation)
newcomers and, 30, 52, 63, 181–182,
   202–210, 214–217, 220–222
norms and, 58, 65–66
peer pressure and, 35–37
performance and, 23–25, 36, 40, 47–50,
   53–63, 67–68
persuasion and, 24, 27–29, 31–33, 68, 70
posters and, 32, 52
power-law distribution of, 4–5, 64
power of liking and, 32–33
presentation and, 68, 70
problems of, 21–25
psychology and, 23–24, 32, 36, 58, 61, 66
recruiting and, 27
requests for, 22, 24–40

rewards and, 12, 24–25, 40–41, 47, 49–62,
   66–70
self-determination theory (SDT) and, 59
self-efficacy and, 36, 40, 68
simple requests and, 30–31
skill and, 25–27, 39–40, 44–47, 64
Slashdot and, 47, 49, 52, 54–57, 61
social contact and, 41–47
socially desirable characteristics and, 33, 35
social networks and, 26, 32, 35, 63
social proof and, 35
social science and, 10–12
starting new online communities and, 246,
   249–250, 254, 261, 265–271
stressing benefits of, 31
stubs and, 5, 21–22, 26
support groups and, 4–5, 21, 41
task interest and, 27
tracking tools and, 27
uniqueness principle and, 11, 14, 63–68
useful tasks and, 22
user support and, 23
utility and, 23–24, 56, 64, 66
volunteers and, 21–23, 26–27, 61
watchlists and, 26
Wikipedia and, 21–27, 30–32, 35, 38–39, 49,
   60–64
Coordination work, 21
Copyright, 151, 211, 219
Cosley, Dan, 27
Costco Photo Center, 187
Craigslist, 139, 201, 237, 260
Credentials, 8, 195, 203–204, 222,
   223t, 245
Critical mass of participation
   attracting early members and, 253–257
   bootstrapping and, 249–253
   convener quality/commitment and, 266–268
   cost-benefit analysis of new members and,
      248–249
   early adopter benefits and, 250, 253–255,
      262–266, 274, 276t
   external signals and, 272–273

Critical mass of participation (cont.)
  increasing value of community and,
    257–262
  innovation-need paradox and, 255–256
  Metcalfe's Law and, 248
  network externalities and, 248
  participation benefits and, 253–254, 277n3
  permanent discounts and, 262–265, 276t
  pink sites and, 255
  positive member response and, 268–272
  scope of the community and, 260–261
  startup cost and, 245, 253–254
  success indicators and, 253–254, 266–273
  syndicated data and, 259–260
  theory of credible signaling and, 267–268
  two-sided networks and, 256
Crossword puzzles, 44
Crowdfunding, 108
Csikszentmihalyi, Mihaly, 43–44
Cutlip, Anna, 165
Cyberrape, 125, 147

Dabbish, Laura, 44
Damage Networks, 195
Dave, K., 127
Deadlines, 40
Defense Advanced Research Projects Agency
    (DARPA), 66
Deindividuation, 155
Del.icio.us, 257
Dellarocas, Chrysanthos, 142
Democratic Underground, 127, 197
Design
  access controls and, 6–8, 168t, 218–222,
    223t
  community structure and, 6, 7t, 79t, 112t,
    168t, 275t
  content and, 6–7
  contests and, 66–68
  external communication and, 7, 233t, 274,
    276t
  goals for, 12–16
  morality of, 9–10

positivists and, 12
social science and, 1, 10–13, 248
sociotechnical systems and, 6–8
Design claims
  affective commitment and, 81–102
  behavior regulation and, 132–165, 168t–169t
  carving out a niche and, 232–243
  commitment and, 81–112, 113t, 115
  competing for a niche and, 243–248
  compliance and, 136–166
  contribution and, 26–66, 69t
  critical mass of participation and, 248–273
  deadlines and, 40
  expectancy enhancement and, 62–66
  extrinsic motivation and, 53–62
  fear campaigns and, 31–32
  feedback and, 40 (see also Feedback)
  high-challenge goals and, 35–40
  high-status people and, 31–33, 35
  intrinsic motivation and, 43–50
  needs-based commitment and, 107–112
  newcomers and, 183–194, 199–210,
    215–221, 223t
  new online communities and, 232, 235, 253,
    275t–276t
  normative commitment and, 103–105
  pattern languages and, 13–14
  peer pressure and, 35–37
  power of liking and, 32–33
  preferential attachment and, 35
  prescriptive rules and, 14–15
  recruitment and, 183–194
  regulation and, 132–133 (see also Regulation)
  retaining newcomers and, 206–210
  screening and, 201–205
  simple requests and, 30–31
  socialization and, 215–217
  socially desirable characteristics and, 33, 35
  social proof and, 35
  specific requests and, 29–30
  task interest and, 27
  teaching newcomers and, 215–217
  tracking tools and, 27

Diagnostic tasks, 201–203
Dibbell, Julian, 125
Digg, 151, 159, 252, 258
Discussion groups
  commitment and, 81, 100, 105–106
  contribution and, 64
  newcomers and, 179, 205
  regulation and, 5, 158
Disemvoweling, 131, 143, 162, 166
Distributed Proofreaders, 220–221
DNFTT (Do Not Feed the Troll), 135
Doctors Without Borders, 101
Dodds, P. S., 35
Dogster, 83
Domingos, P., 188
Donath, Judith S., 158
Don't Bite the Newcomer policy, 206–208, 210
Door-to-door canvassing, 29
Drenner, S., 111
Drupal, 104–105, 134, 233, 245
Ducheneaut, Nicolas, 39
Dunbar, Robin, 97
Durkheim, Emile, 150

EachMovie, 258–259
Early adopter benefits, 250, 253–255, 262–266, 274, 276t
Eating clubs, 80
eBay, 5, 11
  behavior regulation and, 142, 145–146, 150, 154, 156–159, 164–165, 170nn3,5
  commitment and, 109–110
  feedback and, 216, 263
  Gmail Beta auctions and, 204
  newcomers and, 197, 204, 216–217
  sharing profiles and, 245
  Trading Assistants and, 216
  usernames and, 264
Economics
  behavioral, 17n1, 129 (see also Behavior)
  contribution and, 23, 66

crowdfunding and, 108
decision frame and, 17n1
face-to-face recruitment and, 183–184
motivation and, 1, 10, 17n1
permanent discounts and, 262–265, 276t
shopping and, 109, 257–258
tragedy of the commons and, 129
Effortful barriers, 110–112
eHarmony, 256
Elster, Jon, 164
Email, 1, 3, 14
  behavior and, 126, 131–132, 139, 150, 154, 156–157
  commitment and, 80, 89, 94, 98
  contact scraping and, 185–186
  contribution and, 26, 29–30, 32, 36
  LISTSERV communities and, 98–99
  motivation and, 183–184
  newcomers and, 183–187, 194, 201–202, 218, 221
  recruitment and, 183–187
  regulation and, 126, 131–132, 139, 150, 154, 156–157
  starting new online communities and, 233–234, 243, 252, 262, 264–267
Encyclopedia Brittanica, 86
Encyclopedia of Life, 190
Entry barriers
  newcomers and, 201, 205–211, 222, 223t
  normative commitment and, 111–112
Entry fees, 200
Epinions, 54–55, 88, 108, 249, 259
ESP Game, 44, 261–262
Ethnicity, 81
Eudora, 150
Everquest, 151
Everything2, 54, 216
Expectancy
  contribution and, 23–25, 55–56, 62–66
  enhancing, 62–66
  motivation and, 23–25, 55–56, 62–66
Expertise, 32
Explorers' group experiment, 83

External communication, 7, 223t,
  274, 276t
External signals, 272–273

Facebook, 2–3, 11
  carving out a niche and, 232–233
  commitment and, 79, 84–85, 89–97, 109
  Connect, 233
  contribution and, 26–27, 63
  friending and, 89, 93, 137
  newcomers and, 185–187, 207–209
  new online communities and, 232–234,
    237–238, 243, 245–246, 249–251
  pull model and, 233
  recruitment and, 185–186
  regulation and, 129, 137, 142, 163
  viral marketing and, 186
  welcoming mechanism of, 208–209
Face-to-face interaction, 5, 141,
  183–184
Fairness, 65, 133
Fake profiles, 242–243
False praise, 48–49
Familiarity principle
  advertising and, 192–194
  commitment and, 90–91, 99
  contribution and, 33, 69t
  newcomers and, 179, 192–194, 214, 216
  recruitment and, 192–194
  starting new online communities and,
    247, 254
Familiar stranger, 90
FAQs, 15, 86, 181, 198–199, 206, 210, 214,
  219
Fark, 206
Fear campaigns, 31–32
February Album Writing Month, 207
Feedback. See also Rewards; Sanctions
  attackers and, 57
  commitment and, 104
  comparative, 49–50, 68
  compliance and, 138, 141–146, 150,
    156–159, 164–166
  contribution and, 24, 26, 40, 44, 46t, 47–50,
    56–57, 59, 67–68, 69t
  eBay and, 216, 263
  editors and, 26
  encouraging contribution and, 24, 26, 40,
    44, 47–50, 56–57, 59, 67–68
  formal vs. informal, 7, 145–146
  games and, 44
  goals and, 44, 47
  motivation and, 40, 44, 46t, 47–50, 56–57,
    59, 67–68, 69t
  negative, 146, 150, 157, 159, 164–165, 212
  neutral, 146, 165
  newcomers and, 212, 216, 221
  new online communities and, 245, 263
  nonverbal, 47
  performance, 40, 47–50, 59, 67–68
  persuasive techniques and, 24
  positive, 47, 59, 142, 146, 156–157, 164, 212
  praise and, 47–49
  profile of, 5, 158–159, 245, 263
  on progress, 40
  quantitative, 47–49
  regulation and, 138, 141–146, 150, 156–159,
    164–166
  sellers and, 142, 158
  sincere, 49–50
  solicited, 166
  trustworthiness and, 11
  verbal, 47–49, 56
Festinger, Leon, 78–79, 155
Field theory, 78
FilterMyRSS, 27
Filters
  behavior regulation and, 131, 135, 167, 168t
  commitment and, 101–102, 113t, 114
  contribution and, 26–27, 68
  starting new online communities and, 239,
    242, 262
Flame wars, 126–127, 132, 150–151
Flickr, 93, 204, 257
Focal point, 247–248, 275
Fogg, B. J., 186, 266

Food Network, 252
Forte, Andrea, 85
43Things, 47
4Chan, 126, 131
Framing, 8
  behavior regulation and, 167, 169t
  commitment and, 113t
  contribution and, 60
  newcomers and, 185, 222, 223t
  starting new online communities and,
    274–275, 276t
Fraternities, 80, 206
Freenet Project, 4, 202
Free-rider problem, 164
Friedman, E., 159
Friend feeds, 7, 94, 113t, 251
Friending, 89, 93, 137
Friends, 7
  behavior regulation and, 5, 129, 137, 159
  commitment and, 79–80, 88–97, 100,
    105–106, 109, 113t, 114–115
  contribution and, 24, 27, 32, 42
  eating clubs and, 80
  familiar stranger and, 90
  fraternities and, 80, 206
  of friends, 89–91, 113t, 114
  newcomers and, 183–187, 201, 203,
    208–210, 218, 221, 223t
  recruitment and, 183, 186–188
  starting new online communities and,
    233–234, 237, 242, 245–252, 257, 263–264,
    274
Friendster, 2, 242

Gags, 137–138, 162, 166, 168t–169t
Gaia, 150
Game levels, 39–40
Games, 11
  behavior and, 127–130, 151, 159–160, 164
  challenging, 44, 47
  clear goals for, 44–45, 46t
  commitment and, 84–86, 90–92, 96, 105,
    109–110

  contribution and, 24, 35, 39–47, 50–54,
    57–58, 67
  designing enjoyable, 44–47
  feedback and, 44
  God-modding and, 130
  motivation and, 35, 39–47, 50–54,
    57–58, 67
  MUDs, 92–93
  newcomers and, 179, 183, 189–191,
    205–206, 215
  non-playing characters (NPCs) and, 215
  online neighborhoods and, 92–93
  role-playing, 84, 92–93, 159, 179, 189
  socialization and, 215
  starting new online communities and, 234,
    236, 239, 247, 261–262, 265
  ultimatum experiment and, 164
Games with a Purpose, 44
Gaming the system, 13, 53–58
Gardner, R., 129
Gender, 12
  commitment and, 79, 82
  contribution and, 62
  starting new online communities and,
    256
Gilder, George, 248
Git, 134
Gladwell, Malcolm, 187–188
Gmail Beta, 204
Gneezy, 62
GNOME
  commitment and, 106–107
  contribution and, 22, 25, 39, 42–43
  starting new online communities and,
    277t
Gnutella, 21
Goals
  behavior regulation and, 126
  clarity of, 44, 46t, 47
  commitment and, 83–85, 97, 105, 114
  common fate and, 84–85
  contribution and, 24–25, 35–40, 44, 46t, 47,
    61, 65, 67–68

Goals (cont.)
  deadlines and, 35–40
  high-challenge, 35–40
  motivation and, 24–25, 35–40, 44, 46t, 47,
    61, 65, 67–68
  newcomers and, 180, 182, 195, 197–198,
    201, 204, 218
  online communities and, 6, 9–16
  starting new online communities and,
    245, 264
God-modding, 130
Goffman, Erving, 141–142
Going off-topic together, 101–102
Goldstein, N. J., 31, 192
Good faith, 162, 208
Google, 3, 53, 57–58, 154, 204, 232, 264
Griefers, 127
Gross, N., 88
Group cohesiveness theory, 79, 85, 88
Group context, 35
Group dynamics, 78
Groupon, 271–272
Guest books, 96
Guilds
  commitment and, 84–86, 93
  joint tasks and, 85
  newcomers and, 183, 185, 195–198,
    201–206, 217

Hackers
  alt.hackers newsgroup and, 127–128
  behaving like, 103
  regulation and, 127–128, 151
  thinking time of, 103
Hardin, Garrett, 129
Hattrick, 83, 215
Hebl, M. R., 147–148
Henderlong, J., 48
Heuristic processing, 189–194
High-challenge goals, 35–40
High-status people, 31–33, 35
Hitt, L. M., 109–110
Hollander, E. P., 161–162

Horde, 86
Horne, Christine, 165
How to Win Friends and Influence People
  (Carnegie), 32
Huffington Post, 125
Hutzel, L., 110–111

IBM, 23
Idealism, 42
Identifiability
  behavior and, 155–161, 168t
  long-term, 160–161
  pseudonyms and, 95, 112t, 158–161, 168t
Identity-based commitment, 90, 95
  anonymity and, 87
  common fate and, 84–85
  diversity of members' interest and,
    99–100
  encouraging, 80–87
  external threats and, 87
  going off-topic together and, 101–102
  group cohesiveness theory and, 79, 85
  ingroups and, 86
  interchangeable members and, 81
  interdependent tasks and, 85–86
  joint tasks and, 85
  labels and, 82
  names and, 82–85
  outgroups and, 86–87
Influence limiters, 135, 138–139,
  157–158
Ingroups, 86, 97, 218
Initiation
  commitment and, 78–79, 111–112
  contribution and, 23
  mild, 111
  newcomers and, 205–211
  new online communities and, 233
  recruitment and, 16 (see also Recruitment)
  regulation and, 165
  rites of, 111–112, 205–211
  severe, 111
  volunteer, 23

InnoCentive, 66–67
Innovation, 17
  newcomers and, 179, 184, 213
  new online communities and, 255–256
  online bookmarking and, 257
Instant messaging (IM), 94, 252
Interdependent tasks, 85–86, 113t, 114
Internet Movie Database (IMDB), 98
Internet Relay Chat (IRC), 98
Interpersonal relationships, 5
  advertising and, 188–194
  behavior regulation and, 151, 164
  bond formation and, 10–12
  commitment and, 79–80, 90, 92–97, 100,
    107, 113t, 114
  newcomers and, 183–194
  recruitment and, 183–189
  starting new online communities and,
    243, 274
Investigation, 100, 181, 199
Israel, 62, 164, 236

Japan, 164, 236
JoBlo Movie Network, 100, 126
John McCain Facebook Challenge,
  84–85
Johnston, Erik, 207
Joint tasks, 85
Jones, G. R., 212

Karau, S., 25
Karma points, 54–55, 57, 61, 154
Katz, Elihu, 183
Kaufer, David, 150
Kempe, D., 188
Kennedy, John F., 36
Keohane, R. O., 156
Kiesler, Sara, 268
Kim, Amy Jo, 84, 242
Kittur, Aniket, 83
Kleinberg, J., 188
Knitters Without Borders, 101
Kolbert, Elizabeth, 151

LambdaMOO, 125, 147, 152
Lampe, Cliff, 207
Latané, B., 183
Lave, Jean, 220
Laws, 130–131, 150
Lazersfeld, P., 183
Lea, Martin, 81
Lepper, M. R., 48
Leskovec, J., 88
Lessig, L., 130
Levine, John M., 181–182
Lewin, Kurt, 78
Liking, 7
  commitment and, 79, 91–97
  contribution and, 25, 31–33, 63
  newcomers and, 194
  photos and, 91–92
LinkedIn, 63, 89, 94, 185, 243, 249, 252
Linksys, 2
Linux, 106, 126, 210
LinuxChix, 126–127
LISTSERV, 98–99
LiveJournal group, 88, 256
Localfiles, 260
Lock-in, 109–110
Loewenstein, G., 165
Lost causes, 65
Lott, Bernice, 78
Loyalty
  commitment and, 78–79, 102
  newcomers and, 206
Ludford, Pamela J., 64
Lurking, 181, 199, 201, 208, 214

Maintenance, 181
Mamapedia, 272
Manipulators, 128, 135, 139, 154, 166–167
Markey, P. M., 63
Martin, W. E., 88
Massachusetts Institute of Technology (MIT),
  152–153
Matching algorithms, 5–6
Match value, 234–239, 241, 243–244, 277n2

MathWorks, 66
McCain, John, 84–85
Mechanical Turk, 52–54
MediaWiki, 134, 233
Meetup, 232, 233, 271
Mentors
  newcomers and, 212–217, 221–223
  Trading Assistants and, 216
Meridian 59, 84
Metadata, 250
MetaFilter, 200
Microsoft, 233, 259–261
Milgram, S., 31, 90
Minitel system, 255
Mixed-topic scope, 235–237
Moderation systems, 131–134, 168t
Moderators
  commitment and, 96, 105
  member self-disclosure and, 96
  new online communities and, 241, 263
  regulation and, 131–134, 137, 143,
  165
Mommasoure.com, 272
MoodWatch, 150
Moreland, Richard L., 181–182
Motivation
  Aristotle and, 24
  authority figures and, 31–32
  basic drives and, 41
  CET theory and, 59
  collective effort model and, 62–64
  contests and, 66–68
  contribution and, 28–70
  deadlines and, 40
  door-to-door canvassing and, 29
  do your best (DYB) and, 36–37
  economics and, 1, 10, 17n1
  email and, 183–184
  expectancy and, 23–25, 55–56, 62–66
  extrinsic, 24, 51–62
  false praise and, 48–49
  family and, 42
  fear campaigns and, 31–32

  feedback and, 40, 44, 46t, 47–50, 56–57, 59,
    67–68, 69t
  flow and, 43–44
  games and, 35, 39–47, 50–54, 57–58, 67
  gaming the system and, 53–58
  "get out the vote" campaigns and, 28–29
  goals and, 24–25, 35–40, 44, 46t, 47, 61, 65,
    67–68
  group context and, 35
  group size and, 62–64
  high-challenge goals and, 35–40
  high-status people and, 31–33, 35
  idealism and, 42
  intrinsic, 24, 41–50, 58–62
  music download experiment and, 35
  peer pressure and, 35–37
  performance and, 23–25, 36, 40, 47–50,
    53–63, 67–68
  personal, 28–29
  persuasion and, 24, 27–29, 31–33, 68, 70
  power of liking and, 32–33
  preferential attachment and, 35, 263
  psychology and, 1, 23–24, 32, 36, 58, 61, 66
  Reiss's sixteen types of, 41–44
  request structuring and, 28–40
  rewards and, 47, 49–62, 66, 67–70
  romance and, 42
  self-determination theory (SDT) and, 59
  self-efficacy and, 36, 40, 68
  skill and, 25–27, 39–40, 44–47, 64
  social contact and, 41–47
  socially desirable characteristics and, 33, 35
  social proof and, 35
  specific questions and, 28
  trade-offs in, 58–62
  uniqueness principle and, 11, 14, 63–66, 68
  value and, 23, 25, 29, 31, 35, 42, 49, 52, 57,
    62–66
  Wikipedia and, 24–25
MovieLens, 135, 268
  commitment and, 97, 104, 109, 111
  comparative performance feedback and,
    49–50

contributions and, 30, 36–37, 49–50, 64
member uniqueness and, 64
power of goals and, 36–37
professionally-generated content and, 258–259
Mozilla, 210, 214
Mr. T., 190
MUDs (Multi–User Dungeon) games, 92–93
Myspace, 218

Names, 82–85
NASA, 21, 36
National Park Service, 144–145
National Rifle Association, 81
Navigation cost, 234–235, 240–241, 277n2
Needs-based commitment
  benefits and, 105–110
  cohesion and, 105
  defined, 105
  open source software (OSS) and, 106
Netflix, 66–67, 109
Network externalities, 10, 248, 256, 258–259, 262
Neutrality
  moral, 9, 17n2
  newcomers and, 179, 211
  regulation and, 125–126, 128
Newcomb, T., 97, 155
Newcomers, 1, 3–5, 12, 16
  administrators and, 195
  anonymity and, 195
  bans and, 198
  behavior and, 127–128, 134, 136–139, 148–149, 154, 158–161, 168t, 179–182, 188, 199, 203, 211–218
  bug introduction by, 179
  commitment and, 89, 99–100, 102, 112, 179, 182, 199, 201–202, 205–206, 213–214, 217, 222
  contribution and, 30, 52, 63, 181–182, 202–210, 214–217, 220–222
  design claims for, 183–194, 199–210, 215–221, 223t

diagnostic tasks and, 201–203
discussion forums and, 179, 205, 208–210
diversity and, 179
Don't Bite the Newcomer policy and, 206–208, 210
early adopter benefits and, 250, 253–255, 262–266, 274, 276t
email and, 183–187, 194, 201–202, 218, 221
entry barriers and, 201, 205–211, 222, 223t
entry fees and, 200
external credentials and, 203–204
Facebook and, 185–187, 207–209
familiarity principle and, 179, 192–194, 214, 216
feedback and, 212, 216, 221
framing and, 185, 222, 223t
friendship and, 183–187, 201, 203, 208–210, 218, 221, 223t
games and, 179, 183, 189–191, 205–206, 215
goals and, 180, 182, 195, 197–198, 201, 204, 218
group values and, 197
guilds and, 183, 185, 195–198, 201–206, 217
information collections and, 180–181
initiation rituals and, 205–210
innovation and, 179, 184, 213
interpersonal relationships and, 183–194
investigation and, 181, 199
loyalty and, 206
lurking and, 181, 199, 201, 208, 214
maintenance and, 181
mentors and, 212–217, 221–223
neutrality and, 179, 211
norms and, 179–180, 206, 211, 220
old-timers and, 179, 201, 207, 209–214, 217–218, 221, 223t
performance and, 202, 213
persuasion and, 183–184, 187–192
posters and, 201
posting bonds and, 161–162

Newcomers (cont.)
  product diffusion and, 184
  progressive access control and, 219–221
  protection and, 180, 218–222
  psychology and, 183, 186, 189, 205, 208
  public profiles and, 209–210
  reader-to-leader funnel and, 182
  recruitment of, 180–202, 221–223
  referrals and, 185, 188, 197, 203–205, 222,
    223t
  retention of, 180, 182, 188, 205–210,
    221–222
  sanctions and, 203
  sandboxes and, 218–222
  screening and, 180, 197, 200–205
  selection of, 180–182, 194–201, 204–205,
    221
  self-efficacy and, 213
  separating tasks and, 200–201
  skills and, 194–198, 203, 208, 213, 217–222
  Slashdot and, 207
  socialization and, 128, 180–182, 199, 208,
    211–222, 223t
  social networks and, 218
  spam and, 180, 200
  starting new online communities and, 240
  support groups and, 181, 189, 197–199,
    204
  switching cost and, 233, 244–245
  Trading Assistants and, 216
  transparency for, 199–200
  trolls and, 180, 197, 200
  turnover and, 179, 182, 198, 205
  Usenet groups and, 182, 205–207, 214
  value and, 194, 195, 197, 200, 210
  volunteers and, 194–195, 215
  welcomers and, 6, 8, 210, 222
  Wikipedia and, 179, 182, 185, 195, 199,
    205–211, 217, 219–220
New Israeli Shekels (NIS), 62
Newsfeeds, 142, 237, 238, 251
Newsgroups, 1, 98, 102, 127, 198, 239
New York Times, 187, 258

Niches
  bridging activities and, 236
  carving out, 232–243
  collection size and, 234–235
  compatibility/integration with other sites
    and, 232–233, 244–245
  competing for, 231, 243–248
  distance metrics and, 237–238
  expected active times and, 241–242
  fake profiles and, 242–243
  focal point and, 247–248, 275
  import/export of content and, 245–247
  internal organization of content and, 233,
    243
  match value and, 234–239, 241, 243–244,
    277n2
  multiple-space communities and,
    237–243
  navigation cost and, 234–235, 240–241,
    277n2
  opportunities model and, 233–237
  participation benefits and, 244–246,
    253–254, 277n3
  personalized collections of related content
    and, 238–239
  pull model and, 233–235
  push alerts and, 233
  recommender systems and, 242–243
  scope of the community and, 232, 235–237,
    242–243
  subdividing spaces and, 239–240
  switching cost and, 233, 244–245
  synergies among spaces and, 237, 260
  time sensitivity of opportunities and,
    234–235
  unique selling proposition and, 247–248
Ning, 232, 245
Nokia, 23
Non-playing characters (NPCs), 215
Normative commitment
  defined, 102
  effortful barriers and, 110–112
  experience provision and, 107–108

exporting assets and, 110–112
lock-in and, 109–110
moral obligation and, 103
niche information and, 108–110
obligation and, 102–105
open source software (OSS) and, 102–103
reciprocity and, 102–104
testimonials and, 103–104
Norms
  behavior regulation and, 127–133, 137,
    139–155, 158, 161, 165–167, 169t
  clear, 141–150
  commitment and, 77, 81–82, 87, 103–104,
    113t
  compliance with, 81–82
  contrast and, 144–145
  contribution and, 58, 65–66
  descriptive, 141–146, 149, 167, 169t
  examples and, 143–144
  explicit, 146–149
  injunctive, 141, 145
  newcomers and, 179–180, 206, 211, 220
  reciprocity and, 8, 31, 102–104, 113t, 115
  salient, 141–150
  starting new online communities and, 244,
    247–248

Obama, Barack, 85
ObHack, 127–128
Off-topic conversations
  behavior regulation and, 5, 132, 167
  commitment and, 99–102, 113t,
    114–115
Old-timers, 263
  behavior regulation and, 161
  commitment and, 99
  mentoring and, 212–217, 221–223
  newcomers and, 5, 179, 201, 207, 209–214,
    217–218, 221, 223t
Omidyar Network, 138, 157, 170n3
"One Million Strong for Barack"
  campaign, 85
Online bookmarking, 257

Online communities
  access controls and, 6–8, 168t, 218–222,
    223t
  attracting members and, 3–4 (see also
    Recruitment)
  benefits of joining early, 250, 253–255,
    262–266, 274, 276t
  bootstrapping and, 249–253
  commitment and, 77–115
  content and, 6–7
  contribution and, 21–70 (see also
    Contribution)
  critical design challenges and, 2–6
  defined, 1
  design claims and, 12–15
  fake profiles and, 242–243
  goals and, 6, 9–16
  increasing value of community and,
    257–262
  morality and, 9–10
  multiple-space, 237–243
  navigation cost and, 234–235, 277n2
  network externalities and, 10, 248, 256,
    258–259, 262
  newcomers and, 179–223 (see also
    Newcomers)
  newsgroups and, 1, 98, 102, 127, 198, 239
  pattern languages and, 13–14
  platforms for, 1, 154, 208, 218, 232–233,
    244, 267
  promise of, 1–2
  purpose of, 2
  regulating behavior and, 125–170 (see also
    Regulation)
  setting expectations for success and,
    266–273
  social science and, 10–12
  sociotechnical systems design and, 6–8
  starting new, 3, 231–277 (see also Starting
    new online communities)
  subdividing spaces and, 239–240
  success probability and, 253–254
  switching cost and, 233, 244–245

Onyxia Wipe, 198
OpenID, 233, 245
Open reputation systems, 110, 160
Open source software (OSS), 2–4
  access ladders and, 138
  bugs and, 15, 22t, 23, 25–26, 126, 179, 197
  commitment and, 77, 85, 102–107, 112
  common purpose and, 85
  contribution and, 21–26, 41–42, 65
  diagnostic tasks and, 202
  Drupal and, 104–105
  initiation rituals and, 206
  internal organization of content and, 233
  Linux and, 106, 126, 210
  needs-based commitment and, 106
  newcomers and, 179–180, 182, 197, 202, 204–206, 214, 219
  normative commitment and, 102–103
  paying employees for, 23
  Perl, 205
  progressive access control and, 219–220
  public forums and, 126
  Python, 214
  referrals and, 204–205
  regulation and, 126, 134, 138, 154, 160
  salient purpose and, 102–103
  social contact and, 42–43
  SourceForge and, 231
  starting new online communities and, 231, 233, 255, 263, 277n7
  Ubuntu and, 210
  version-control tools and, 134
Opportunities model, 233–237
Ostrom, E., 129–130, 151, 161, 164
Outgroups, 86–87, 113t, 114–115, 151, 218

PageRank, 58, 154
PalTalk, 137, 240, 241
Participation benefits, 244–246, 253–254, 277n3
Passive disclosure, 96–97
Patriotism, 87

Pattern Language, A: Towns, Buildings, and Construction (Alexander), 14
Pattern languages, 13–14
Peer pressure, 35
Peer reporting, 164–165, 169t
Pepitone, A., 155
Performance
  Aristotle and, 24
  behavior and, 133 (see also Behavior)
  commitment and, 86
  contribution and, 23–25, 36, 40, 47–50, 53–63, 67–68
  enhancing expectancy value and, 62–66
  feedback and, 104 (see also Feedback)
  high-challenge goals and, 35–37
  motivation and, 23–25, 36, 40, 47–50, 53–63, 67–68
  newcomers and, 202, 213
  regulation and, 133
  starting new online communities and, 236
Perl, 205
Permanent discounts, 262–265, 276t
Personal conversation, 92–94
Personal information
  commitment and, 94–95, 100, 109, 114
  starting new online communities and, 266
Persuasion, 12
  behavior regulation and, 162
  contribution and, 24, 27–29, 31–33, 68, 70
  motivation and, 24, 27–29, 31–33, 68, 70
  newcomers and, 183–184, 187–192
PGHDance, 208
phpBB, 244–245, 267
Pink messaging, 255
Platforms, 1, 154, 208, 218, 232–233, 244, 267
PokerStars, 247–248
Posters, 2
  commitment and, 86, 98
  contribution and, 32, 52
  newcomers and, 201
  new online communities and, 238, 263
  regulation and, 127–128, 142, 167

Postmes, Tom, 81
Powazek, Derek, 132
Power-law distribution, 4–5, 64
Preece, Jenny, 10, 182
Presentation
  commitment and, 95, 113t, 155–156, 169t
  contribution and, 68, 70
  framing and, 274–275 (*see also* Framing)
  misrepresentation and, 155–156
  starting new online communities and, 259, 269, 276t
Principle of proximity, 4, 78, 92
Product diffusion, 184
Progressive access control, 219–221
Protection
  copyright, 151, 211, 219
  newcomers and, 180, 218–222
Pseudonyms
  behavior regulation and, 158–161, 168t
  cheap, 158–160
  commitment and, 95, 112t
Psych Central, 125–126
Psychology, 10
  authority figures and, 31–32
  basic drives and, 41
  Carnegie and, 32
  CET theory and, 59
  commitment and, 78–79, 89–90, 95, 99, 104, 108–109
  competition and, 231, 236, 243–248, 256, 259, 267, 274–275
  contribution and, 23–24, 32, 36, 58, 61, 66
  door-to-door canvassing and, 29
  do your best (DYB) and, 36–37
  expectancies and, 23–25, 55–56, 62–66
  extrinsic motivation and, 51–62
  false praise and, 48–49
  familiar stranger and, 90
  fear campaigns and, 31–32
  field theory and, 78
  group cohesiveness theory and, 79, 85, 88
  halo effect and, 189
  heuristic processing and, 189–194
  high-challenge goals and, 35–40
  high-status people and, 31–33, 35
  interpersonal relationships and, 79–80
    (*see also* Interpersonal relationships)
  intrinsic motivation and, 41–50
  Milgram experiment and, 31
  motivation and, 1, 23–24, 32, 36, 58, 61, 66
  music download experiment and, 35
  names and, 82–85
  newcomers and, 183, 186, 189, 205–206, 208
  patriotism and, 87
  peer pressure and, 35–37
  persuasion and, 12, 24, 27–29, 31–33, 68, 70
  power of liking and, 32–33
  preferential attachment and, 35, 263
  recruitment and, 183–194
  regulating behavior and, 129, 131, 141, 155, 157
  Reiss and, 41–44
  self-determination theory (SDT) and, 59
  self-efficacy and, 36, 40, 68, 213
  social contact and, 43–47, 106
  socially desirable characteristics and, 33, 35
  social proof and, 35
  status rewards and, 7, 24, 41, 52–58, 60, 68, 109, 138, 157, 202, 214, 244, 253, 255, 262–265, 274, 276t
  systematic processing and, 189–190
  ultimatum experiment and, 164
  uniqueness principle and, 11, 14, 63–66, 68
Public bad problem, 129
Public forums, 126
Pull model, 233–235
Push alerts, 233
Python, 214

Question-answering sites, 42
Quota mechanisms, 136–137

Rape, 125, 147, 163
Rape in Cyberspace, A (Dibbell), 125
Rathunde, Kevin, 44

Ravelry, 1–2
Raymond, Eric S., 103
Reader-to-leader funnel, 182
Reciprocity, 8
  commitment and, 102–104, 113t, 115
  contribution and, 31
  normative commitment and, 102–104
Recruitment, 3–4, 6, 11, 16
  active, 182–183
  advertising and, 180, 182–184, 188–195
  attracting early members and, 253–257
  Bass model and, 184
  bootstrapping and, 249–253
  celebrity endorsements and, 190–192, 222,
    247–248, 274–275, 276t
  commitment and, 81, 88–89, 99, 106,
    114–115, 266–268
  contact scraping and, 185–186
  content sharing and, 187–188
  contribution and, 27
  convener quality and, 266–268
  conveying deep information and, 1
  diagnostic tasks and, 201–203
  early adopter benefits and, 250, 253–255,
    262–266, 274, 276t
  email solicitation and, 183–187
  entry barriers and, 205–210
  entry fees and, 200
  external credentials and, 203–204
  external signals and, 272–273
  face-to-face, 183–184
  familiarity principle and, 192–194
  free trial accounts and, 183
  friends and, 183, 186–188
  halo effect and, 189
  heuristic processing and, 189–194
  increasing community visibility and,
    187–188
  increasing value of community and,
    257–262
  influential members and, 188
  interpersonal, 183–194
  laissez-faire approaches to, 182–183
  newcomers and, 180–202, 221–223
  participation benefits and, 253–254, 277n3
  passive, 182–183, 221
  permanent discounts and, 262–264
  positive member response and, 268–272
  product diffusion and, 184
  psychology of, 183–194
  referrals and, 161, 185, 188, 197, 203–205,
    222, 223t, 252–253, 276t
  regulating behavior and, 161
  robo-calls and, 183
  screening and, 200–205
  selection and, 180–182, 194–201, 204–205,
    221
  separating tasks and, 200–201
  setting expectations for success and,
    266–273
  social networks and, 185–188, 221, 223t
  starting new online communities and, 231,
    245, 247–248, 257, 265, 274–275, 276t
  success probability and, 253–254
  systematic processing and, 189–190
  targeting and, 184, 221
  unique selling proposition and, 247–248
  viral marketing and, 184–187, 252
  word of mouth, 180, 182, 184–186, 188,
    199, 221, 223t
Reddit, 148–149, 151, 258
Red Hat, 23
Red users, 209–210
Referrals
  benefits of, 161
  newcomers and, 185, 188, 197, 203–204,
    222, 223t
  starting new online communities and,
    252–253, 276t
Regulation, 16
  access ladders and, 138
  advertising and, 142, 145
  anonymity and, 155, 161
  appeal procedures and, 133–134
  bans and, 137–139, 158, 162–163, 166,
    168t–169t

blogs and, 125, 154, 165

clear/salient norms and, 141–150

coerced compliance and, 136–140

commitment and, 77

community influence on rulemaking and, 152–153

compromising displays and, 149–150

consistent criteria and, 138–139

contact scraping and, 185–186

contrast and, 144–145

currency and, 138–139, 157–158, 166, 168t, 170n4

cyberrape and, 125, 147

deindividuation and, 155

discussion groups and, 5, 158

disemvoweling and, 131, 143, 162, 166

displayed statistics and, 146–148

email and, 126, 131–132, 139, 150, 154, 156–157

examples and, 143–146

explicit rules and, 146–149, 165–166

Facebook and, 129, 137, 142, 163

fairness and, 133

fake profiles and, 242–243

feedback and, 138, 141–146, 150, 156–159, 164–166

filters and, 131, 135, 167, 168t

flame wars and, 126–127, 132, 150–151

framing and, 167, 169t

free riders and, 164

friendship and, 5, 129, 137, 159

gags and, 137–138, 162, 166, 168t–169t

goals and, 126

identifiability and, 155–157

import/export of content and, 245–247

influence limiters and, 135, 138–139, 157–158

initiation and, 165

interpersonal relationships and, 151, 164

labeled posts and, 131

laws and, 130–131, 150

legitimacy and, 132–134, 137–138, 150–151, 161–162, 165, 167

long-term identities and, 160–161

markets and, 129–130

moderators and, 131–134, 137, 143, 165

neutrality and, 125–126, 128

newcomers and, 127–128, 134, 136–139, 148–149, 154, 158–161, 168t, 217–221

norms and, 127–133, 137, 139–155, 158, 161, 165–167, 169t

off-topic conversations and, 5, 132, 167

peer reporting and, 164–165, 169t

performance and, 133

persuasion and, 162

posters and, 127–128, 142, 167

progressive access control and, 219–221

pseudonyms and, 158–161, 168t

psychology and, 129, 131, 141, 155, 157

publication of research and, 126

public forums and, 126

quota mechanisms and, 136–137

rated posts and, 131

recruitment and, 161

redirecting inappropriate posts and, 132–133

reputation systems and, 131, 156–157, 160, 168t, 170n3

reversion tools and, 134–135

rewards and, 150, 153–166

sanctions and, 5, 7, 128, 130–132, 137, 150, 153–167

sandboxes and, 162, 218–222

Slashdot and, 131, 133–134, 154, 159

spam and, 5, 136–137, 139, 154–155, 157, 167

summary of design alternatives for, 166–167, 168t–169t

support groups and, 145–146

technology and, 127, 130–131

three-revert rule and, 127

throttles and, 136–137, 166

trolls and, 5, 9, 127–128, 135–136, 139, 154, 166–167

utility and, 128–129, 159

value and, 129, 145, 150, 157, 160, 162, 166, 170n4

Regulation (cont.)
  voluntary compliance and, 140–166
  wikis and, 125–128, 138, 143, 148–149,
    154–155, 159, 162, 165–166
  work safe environment and, 126
Reiss, S., 41–44
Religion, 82
Republicans, 197
Reputation systems, 110, 131, 156–158, 160,
    168t, 170n3
Retention
  newcomers and, 180, 182, 188, 221–222
  starting new online communities and, 242,
    262
Rewards
  bootstrapping and, 249–250
  CET theory and, 59
  commitment and, 84, 105, 109
  compliance and, 153–166
  contribution and, 12, 24–25, 40–41, 47,
    49–62, 66, 67–70
  expectancies and, 23–25, 55–56, 62–66
  gaming the system and, 13, 53–58
  intrinsic/extrinsic trade-offs and, 58–62
  labels and, 52
  monetary, 52, 59–60, 62
  motivation and, 40–41, 47, 49–62, 66, 67–70
  new online communities and, 242–243, 249,
    274
  performance-contingent, 53, 56
  permanent discounts and, 262–265, 276t
  predictable, 13
  privileges and, 52–53, 57–58
  regulation and, 7, 150, 153–166
  self-determination theory (SDT) and, 59
  small tangible, 12, 14–15
  status and, 7, 24, 41, 52–58, 60, 68, 109,
    138, 157, 202, 214, 244, 253, 255, 262–265,
    274, 276t
  task-contingent, 53, 55–56, 60–62
  Turkers and, 52–54
Richardson, M., 188
Robo-calls, 183

Rogers, E., 255
Role-playing games, 84, 92–93, 159,
    179, 189
Romance, 42
Rotten Tomatoes, 101
RSS feeds, 26–27, 93, 233–234
Rustichini, A., 62

Salganik, M. J., 35
Sanctions. *See also* Rewards
  commitment and, 5
  compliance and, 153–166
  enhancing certainty of, 164–165
  graduated, 130, 161–166, 169t
  increasing deterrent effect of, 164–165
  newcomers and, 203
  regulation and, 5, 7, 128, 130–132, 137, 150,
    153–167
Sandboxes
  defined, 218–219
  newcomers and, 218–222
  Wikipedia and, 162, 219
Sanger, Larry, 148
Sassenberg, K., 81
Schachter, S., 79
Scrabulous, 11
Screening
  acquiring accurate signals for, 201–202
  commitment and, 112
  design claims for, 201–205
  diagnostic tasks and, 201–203
  external credentials and, 203–204
  newcomers and, 180, 197, 200–205
  new online communities and, 267
  referrals and, 203–205
  separating tasks and, 200–201
  signaling problems and, 201
Search engine optimization (SEO), 58
Seekers, 66–67
Selection
  entry fees and, 200
  external credentials and, 203–204
  FAQs and, 198–199

newcomers and, 180–182, 194–201,
  204–205, 221
screening and, 200–205
self, 180, 198–201, 204–205, 267
separating tasks and, 200–201
signaling problems and, 201
Self-determination theory (SDT), 59
Self-disclosure, 6
  behavior regulation and, 151
  commitment and, 90, 94–97, 100, 113t
  moderators and, 96
  newcomers and, 208
  pseudonyms and, 95–97
Self-efficacy, 36, 40, 68, 213
Self-selection, 180, 198–201, 204–205, 267
Sen, S., 111
Separating tasks, 200–201
September 11 attacks, 87
Sermo, 54, 252, 267
Shapiro, Carl, 244, 247
Shatner, William, 190–191
Sherif, Muzafer, 141
Shills, 68, 128, 135
Shneiderman, B., 182
Shopping, 109, 257–258
Shutterfly, 257
Sierra Club, 81
Skills, 3
  commitment and, 110
  contribution and, 25–27, 39–40, 44–47, 64
  motivation and, 25–27, 39–40, 44–47, 64
  newcomers and, 194–198, 203, 208, 213,
    217–222
  starting new online communities and, 254,
    262–264, 266
Slashdot
  behavior regulation and, 131, 133–134, 154,
    159
  commitment and, 108, 110
  contribution and, 47, 49, 52, 54–57, 61
  newcomers and, 207
  starting new online communities and, 239,
    258, 263

Small, D. A., 165
Smith, John D., 233
Smokefree.gov, 2–3
Smooth Reading pages, 220–221
Social contact, 41–47, 106
Social dilemma, 129–130, 164
Social identity theory, 79–82, 99
Socialization
  collective tactics and, 215–217
  FAQs and, 214–215
  formal, 215–217
  games and, 215
  mentoring and, 212–217, 221–222,
    223t
  newcomers and, 128, 180–182, 199, 208,
    211–222, 223t
  organizational theory and, 211–217
  reader-to-leader funnel and, 182
  sequential, 215–217
  six dimensions of tactics for, 212–213
  stages of, 181–182
  Trading Assistants and, 216
Social networks, 2
  commitment and, 88–90, 94, 97
  encouraging contribution and, 26, 32,
    35, 63
  newcomers and, 218
  recruitment and, 185–188, 221, 223t
  starting new online communities and,
    242–243, 249, 252, 263–264
Social proof, 35
Social science, 1, 10–13, 248
Sociotechnical systems design, 6–8
Sock puppets, 128
Solvers, 66–67
Source code, 21, 57
SourceForge, 231
Spam
  commitment and, 84
  newcomers and, 180, 200
  new online communities and, 234, 252,
    262, 266
  quota mechanisms and, 136–137

Spam (cont.)
  regulation and, 5, 84, 136–137, 139,
    154–155, 157, 167, 180, 200, 234, 252, 262,
    266
  search engine algorithms and, 155–156
  throttles and, 136–137, 166
SpamNet, 252–253, 262
SparkPeople, 95
Speakeasy, 101
Spears, Russell, 81
Specialized groups, 239, 250
Starting new online communities, 16
  administrators and, 263
  advertising and, 245–248, 263, 274–275,
    276t
  benefits of early adoption and, 250,
    253–256, 262–266, 274, 276t
  blogs and, 250–251, 256, 258, 263, 269, 273
  bridging activities and, 236
  carving out a niche and, 231–243
  celebrity endorsements and, 247–248,
    274–275, 276t
  collection size and, 234–235
  commitment and, 77, 243, 254–255,
    266–268, 271–272
  competition and, 231, 236, 243–248, 256,
    259, 267, 274–275
  contribution and, 246, 249–250, 254, 261,
    265–271
  convener quality and, 266–268
  critical mass of participation and, 248–273
  design claims for, 232, 235, 253–273,
    275t-276t
  distance metrics and, 237–238
  early adopter benefits and, 250, 253–255,
    262–266, 274, 276t
  email and, 233–234, 243, 252, 262, 264–267
  expected active times and, 241–242
  external signals and, 272–273
  Facebook and, 232–234, 237–238, 243,
    245–246, 249–251
  failure of, 231
  fake profiles and, 242–243

familiarity principle and, 247, 254
filters and, 239, 242, 262
focal point and, 247–248, 275
framing and, 274–275, 276t
friendship and, 233–234, 237, 242, 245–252,
  257, 263–264, 274
games and, 234, 236, 239, 247, 261–262,
  265
getting to critical mass and, 248–273
GNOME and, 277t
goals and, 245, 264
import/export of content and, 245–247
incumbent communities and, 244–246
initiation and, 233
innovation-need paradox and, 255–256
interpersonal relationships and, 243, 274
match value and, 234–239, 241, 243–244,
  277n2
Metcalfe's Law and, 248
moderators and, 241, 263
navigation cost and, 234, 240–241
newcomers and, 240
norms and, 244, 247–248
opportunities model and, 233–237
participation benefits and, 244–246,
  253–254, 277n3
performance and, 236
permanent discounts and, 262–265, 276t
personal information and, 266
personalized collections of related content
  and, 238–239
positive member response and, 268–272
posters and, 238, 263
presentation and, 259, 269, 276t
professionally-generated content and, 231,
  258–262, 266–268, 275t
pull model and, 233–235
push alerts and, 233
recommender systems and, 242–243
recruitment and, 231, 245, 247–248, 257,
  265, 274–275, 276t
retention and, 242, 262
rewards and, 242–243, 249, 274

scope of the community and, 232, 235–237, 242–243, 260–261

screening and, 267

skills and, 254, 262–264, 266

Slashdot and, 239, 258, 263

social networks and, 242–243, 249, 252, 263–264

spam and, 234, 252, 262, 266

startup cost and, 245, 253–254

success indicators and, 266–273

support groups and, 3, 232, 241, 243, 256

syndicated data and, 259–260

synergies among spaces and, 237, 260

targeting and, 255–257

theory of credible signaling and, 267–268

time sensitivity of opportunities and, 234–235

two-sided networks and, 256

unique selling proposition and, 247–248

user-generated content and, 231, 250–251, 275t

utility and, 232, 234, 239, 248, 253–254, 267–268

value and, 231, 233–235, 272, 274, 277nn2,8

volunteers and, 249, 261–262, 277n7

Wikipedia and, 247, 249, 263, 270, 272

word of mouth approach and, 264

Startup cost, 245, 253–254

Star Wars (film), 143–144

Stewart, K. J., 190

Stopit procedures, 152–153

Stubs, 5, 21–22, 26

Subgroups, 6, 11, 81–85, 114

Subversion, 134

Success indicators

displaying absolute numbers and, 271–272

displaying user-contributed content and, 269–270

external signals and, 272–273

member images and, 268–269

participation-level indicators and, 270

positive member response and, 268–273

signals of convener quality and, 266–268

starting new online communities and, 266–273

Success probability, 253–254

SuggestBot, 27

Sun, 23

Sunstein, Cass R., 17n2

Support groups

commitment and, 77, 80, 82, 95, 103, 108

contribution and, 4–5, 21, 41

health, 2–3, 21, 77, 81–82, 95, 108, 126, 145, 181, 199, 204, 245, 256

newcomers and, 181, 189, 197–199, 204

new online communities and, 3, 232, 241, 243, 256

regulation and, 145–146

technical, 4, 14, 21, 42, 77, 146, 259

Switching costs, 233, 244–245

Synergy, 237, 260

Systematic processing, 189–190

Systers, 79, 99

Tagged, 185–186

Taglines, 8, 15, 83, 113t, 114, 190, 239, 272

Tajfel, H., 82

Tardos, É., 188

Targeting, 184, 221, 255–257

Tassone, 268

TED awards, 190

Terrorism, 87

Terveen, L., 111

Testimonials, 103–104

Thaler, Richard, 17n2

Theory of credible signaling

convener quality and, 266–268

external signals and, 272–273

newcomers and, 191, 201–205

positive member response and, 268–273

Threadless, 33, 61, 62

Threats, 87

Throttles, 136–137, 166

Tipping Point, The (Gladwell), 187–188

Titanic (film), 64

Trading Assistants, 216

"Tragedy of the Commons" (Hardin), 129

Transparency, 49, 57–58, 126, 199–200

TripAdvisor, 128, 135

Trojan horses, 197

Trolls
  griefers and, 127
  ignoring, 135–136
  newcomers and, 180, 197, 200
  regulation and, 5, 9, 127–128, 135–136, 139, 154, 166–167
  Usenet and, 127–128

Turing tests, 8, 139–140, 160, 167n1, 168t, 201–202, 204

Turkers, 52–54

Turnover
  commitment and, 80–81, 99, 109–110
  contribution and, 47
  newcomers and, 179, 182, 198, 205

Twitter, 93, 137, 156, 187, 246

Ubuntu, 210

Ultimatum game, 164

Uniqueness principle, 11, 14, 63–66, 68

UpMyStreet, 237

Usenet, 85
  benefits of joining early, 263
  defection and, 107–108
  needs-based commitment and, 107
  newcomers and, 182, 205–207, 214
  newsgroups and, 1, 98, 102, 127, 198, 239
  recruitment and, 182
  specialization and, 239
  support groups and, 2, 5
  trolls and, 127–128

User profiles, 6, 40, 94–96, 113t

User support, 23

Utility, 11–12
  behavior regulation and, 128–129, 159
  contribution and, 23–24, 56, 64, 66
  new online communities and, 232, 234, 239, 248, 253–254, 267–268

Value
  affiliation and, 83
  behavior and, 129, 145, 150, 157, 160, 162, 166, 170n4
  commitment and, 77, 82–83, 97, 102–105, 109–110
  contribution and, 23, 25, 29, 31, 35, 42, 49, 52, 57, 62–66
  expectancy and, 23–25, 55–56, 62–66
  motivation and, 23, 25, 29, 31, 35, 42, 49, 52, 57, 62–66
  newcomers and, 194, 195, 197, 200, 210
  political, 82
  regulation and, 129, 145, 150, 157, 160, 162, 166, 170n4
  starting new online communities and, 231, 233–235, 272, 274, 277nn2,8

Van Alstyne, M., 157

Vanguard, 109

Varian, Hal, 244, 247

Viegas, F., 127

Viral marketing, 184–187, 252

Volunteers
  appealing to, 22–23
  commitment and, 106
  contribution and, 21–23, 26–27, 61
  newcomers and, 194–195, 215
  new online communities and, 249, 261–262, 277n7
  political, 61–62
  user support and, 23

Von Ahn, Luis, 44

Walker, J. M., 129

Wang, Xiaoqing, 108

WarcraftMovies, 198

Watchlists, 26

Wattenberg, Martin, 127

Watts, D. J., 35

Welcomers, 6, 8, 210, 222

WELL (Whole Earth 'Lectronic Link), 147, 209, 210

Wellness Community, 241

Wenger, Etienne, 220, 233, 236
White, Nancy, 147, 233
White, Robert W., 41
Wikifying, 26
Wikimedia, 2–3, 104, 182
Wikipedia, 2
  commitment and, 77, 83, 85–86, 88, 104,
    107
  contribution and, 21–27, 30–32, 35, 38–39,
    49, 60–64
  Don't Bite the Newcomer policy and,
    206–208, 210
  English-language version of, 3, 5
  Featured Article status and, 38
  growth challenges of, 182
  meaningful content and, 21–22
  motivation and, 24–25
  named subprojects and, 83
  newcomers and, 179, 182, 185, 195, 199,
    205–211, 217, 219–220
  new online communities and, 247, 249, 263,
    270, 272
  red users and, 209–210
  regulation and, 125–128, 138, 148–149,
    154–155, 159, 162
  relevancy and, 21–22
  reversions and, 127
  sandboxes and, 162, 219
  stubs and, 5, 21–22, 26
  SuggestBot and, 27
  three-revert rule and, 127
  Welcoming Committee of, 209–210
WikiProjects, 25, 38–39, 85, 207, 214
Wikis
  Apache Software Foundation (ASF) and, 126
  information-sharing, 3
  newcomers and, 218
  promise of, 1
  regulation and, 126, 143, 165–166
Williams, K., 25
Wilson, E. O., 190
Wood, Charles A., 142
Wookieepedia, 143–144

Word of mouth
  recruitment and, 180, 182, 184–186, 188,
    199, 221, 223t
  starting new online communities and, 264
WordPress, 58, 154
Work safe environment, 126
World of Warcraft, 263
  behavior regulation and, 127, 159–160
  commitment and, 84, 86, 92, 105, 109–110
  contribution and, 24, 29, 49
  corpse camping and, 127
  guilds and, 195, 197
  newcomers and, 183, 185, 189–191, 195,
    198, 201–206, 215, 217
  Shatner and, 190–191
  socialization and, 217
World Trade Center, 87
WrongPlanet, 208

X–Fileaholics, 100

Yahoo!, 1, 3, 42, 100, 232, 245, 257, 267
Yarn Harlot, 100–101
Yelp, 128
YouTube, 3, 21, 163, 198

Zeckhauser, R., 142
Zimbardo, P. G., 155
Zitek, E. M., 147–148